IRISH
LITERARY
MAGAZINES

IRISH
LITERARY
MAGAZINES

An Outline History
and Descriptive Bibliography

TOM CLYDE

IRISH ACADEMIC PRESS
DUBLIN • PORTLAND, OR

First published in 2003 by
IRISH ACADEMIC PRESS
44 Northumberland Road, Dublin 4, Ireland

and in the United States of America by
IRISH ACADEMIC PRESS
c/o ISBS, 5824 N.E. Hassalo Street, Portland
Oregon 97213-3644

Website: www.iap.ie

British Library Cataloguing in Publication Data

A catalogue record of this book is available from the British Library.

ISBN 0-7165-2751-0

Library of Congress Cataloging-in-Publication Data

A catalogue record of this book is available from the Library of Congress.

Typeset by FiSH Books, London WC1
Printed by Bookcraft (Bath) Ltd

Contents

List of illustrations

Preface

During my earlier researches, it became clear that much valuable material was locked up in journals, and that greater use could be made of this exciting primary material if some sort of practical guide was available. This book is designed to meet that need. An important pointer to the sort of work which I wanted to produce was Rudi Holzapfel's 1964 M Litt thesis 'A Survey of Irish Literary Magazines from 1900 to the present day', and I would like to acknowledge this debt. Sincere thanks are, of course, due to Professor Edna Longley, who not only guided me through my MA at Queen's University Belfast, but volunteered to repeat the task with this work; and also to Dr Gillian McIntosh, of the Institute of Irish Studies, QUB, for her sustained support and sound advice, without whom this work would not have been completed. Any mistakes or omissions are, of course, all my own work.

Introduction

From the quality of their paper and print to the virtue of what is printed, little mags [*sic*] indicate a country's imaginative resource.
                    Gerald Dawe, 'Preface', *Criterion 1953–1983, An Anthology* (1983), pp. 9–10

... for I know that magazines can alter the shape of a literary landscape ...
                    James Liddy (ed.), 'Introduction', *This Was Arena* (Naas, 1982)

This book is a work of reference and a guide; it provides a high-level overview of the history and development of Irish literary magazines (ILMs), charting the most significant features in terms, for instance, of format, linkages, and distribution. It provides the most comprehensive, most accurate and most up-to-date descriptive bibliography of the field.

Important work has already contributed to this area: from listings such as those of the Wellesley and Sader indexes,[1] through essentially bibliographical works by Wolfgang Görtschacher[2] or Hoffman, Allen and Ulrich,[3] and Alvin Sullivan's four-volume study of British literary magazines.[4] Additionally, broader works of cultural criticism have relied in key chapters on an analysis of Irish literary magazines, for example Gerry Smyth's *Decolonisation and Criticism*[5] and Brian Fallon's *An Age of Innocence*.[6] One of the most influential, unpublished, predecessors of this work is Rudi Holzapfel's *Survey*.[7] The focus and intent of this study is different from any of these, however, and will address some deficiencies and omissions in the works listed above. Most of the few previous studies, for example Görtschacher's, have tended to concentrate on Little Magazines. In this respect I have been more inclusive, for three reasons: first because the Little Magazines alone present too narrow a field; secondly, much important work has appeared in other types of publication, such as the *Irish Homestead*; and, finally, because these categories are necessarily arbitrary, many magazines do not fall neatly into any of these 'boxes'. Additionally, the listings are plagued with inaccuracies (Sullivan, in the 'Preface' to his first volume, describes previous indexes (including Wellesley) as 'frequently unreliable').[8] Sullivan's own study is an impressive production, four large volumes covering three centuries, the entries not only detailed and accurate, but also contextualised; however, his focus is primarily on England, and he covers less than a dozen Irish titles. Gerry Smyth's chapter is undermined by his obsession with his decolonisation theme, which clouds his judgement; for example, he clearly regards *Kavanagh's Weekly* as being both more important and more successful than the *Bell*, simply because it fits better with his thesis. In a revealing phrase, he talks about *Poetry Ireland* as being '*narrowly* literary' [my emphasis].[9] Brian Fallon is too conservative in his outlook: he laments the passing of the *Dublin Magazine* and 'a society which was speeding towards the raucousness and self-advertisement of the Sixties';[10] and he says (of the *Bell*, *Irish Writing*, *Envoy* and the *Dublin Magazine*): 'There has been little to compare with this quartet since, even allowing for the obvious eclipse of the literary magazine as a genre'[11] (they are virtually the only magazines he uses from his period). The latter part of this statement is breathtakingly wrong-headed. He ignores the crucial importance of the successive flurries of short-lived little magazines, their *collective* relevance and impact, their roles as test-beds and breeding-grounds. Even allowing this to pass, he also ignores the big names (for example, *Poetry Ireland*, in all its guises; *HU*; the *Crane Bag*). Finally, he refuses to see that the magazines must embody, in an organic way, the culture which produces them – the detached, decorous élitism of O'Sullivan's *Dublin Magazine* simply could not have reflected vital aspects of Irish culture and society in the 1960s and 1970s. A number of other works have made limited use of the potential of ILMs as a resource. For example, Seamus Deane,[12] Dillon Johnston[13] or, more recently, Declan Kiberd in his monumental *Inventing Ireland*;[14] in none of these is substantive use made of literary magazines (and it is revealing how many of these references cover a page or less), and none strays far from the central canon of *DUM*, *Nation*, *Bell* or *Honest Ulsterman*. Norman Vance avoids that charge, although the focus of his work is elsewhere (indeed, Vance's case is the more frustrating since, given the titles he selects – *Belfast Monthly Magazine*, *Irish Penny Journal*, the *Northman* – it is clear that he is more familiar with this material than most).[15] In a similarly positive vein, Edna Longley has recently taken an (almost unique) look at the strengths and deficiencies of criticism in Ireland, threading together her own string of magazines to illustrate her points.[16]

The forerunner of this study is Holzapfel's thesis; it is most unfortunate that, although he later brought out the author indexes from this himself, the main thesis was never published. However, this work also has important limitations. Failing to address anything pre-twentieth century, Holzapfel refers the reader to the seriously outdated Madden.[17] This is rather cavalier: Madden was writing to the scholarly standards of an earlier age, and his work is quirky, engaging, incomplete and frustrating; he is likely to devote dozens of pages to digressions on Dublin printers, or dozens more to simply reproducing much of one issue of a magazine he liked. Holzapfel is equally dismissive of the difficulties of definition, although he then concedes that there are important titles like the *Dublin Penny Journal* (1832) which would have escaped his rather tightly drawn net.[18] There are, in addition, some flaws in his main principles. He argues that 'the great discrepancy between the Twentieth Century Irish literary periodical and its predecessors is not one of form... but rather one of *feeling*'.[19] This is patently untrue, as it ignores the emergence of the Little Magazine at the turn of the century, an important new form which would dominate the twentieth century. (Of course, events after his publication were to go further against him, as the technical experiments of titles like *Id* or *Crab Grass* were as much formal as ideological.)

This book reveals the wealth of ILMs as an important resource. As the opening editorial to the first number of *Atlantis* (March 1970) states: '... In any culture, discussion, informed commentary, a climate of literate interest, are a necessary hypothesis. It is one to which

Ireland pays lip service ... We propose ... to provide a focus for all that buzz ...'; this is a little pompous, but a good definition of why any literary magazine is important. Maurice Harmon, one commentator who has made use of this material,[20] puts it thus:

> ... they are important scholarly outlets and contain critical articles, bibliographies and creative writing... To make a complete bibliography of almost any Irish writer or to get a proper understanding of contemporary issues at any particular period it is necessary to examine the relevant periodicals... [since] it is virtually impossible to be fully accurate in factual data about dates of publication, number of issues, changing editors, frequency of contribution by particular writers, the list is provided with many reservations, but in the belief that it may nevertheless be useful in pointing towards a rich source of information that is frequently ignored ... [21]

These magazines are of great value to almost any kind of researcher, including political, social and cultural historians, biographers and economists; in particular (since they have '... usually been the sponsors of innovation, the gathering places for the "irreconcilables" of our literary tradition. They have been broadly and amply tolerant of literary experiment ... ') to those researching in the field of Irish literature.[22] An essential quality of the journals is their *currency*, they are simultaneously the training ground for new writers, a forum in which established writers have licence to experiment, a sounding-board for whatever issues – political, ethical, artistic – agitated sensibilities at the time, and of course a vital source of data in their poems, sketches, advertisements, letters, reviews, obituaries and satires.[23]

On a deeper level, ILMs constitute an important medium by which intellectual élites have carried on the discourses from which have emerged key concepts of nationality.[24] Central to this is the idea of the nation as an 'imagined' community, '... *imagined* because the members of even the smallest nation will never know most of their fellow-members, meet them, or even hear of them, yet in the minds of each lives the image of their communion ... all communities larger than primordial villages of face-to-face contact ... are imagined'.[25] This leads to the conclusion that '... nationality ... as well as nationalism, are cultural artefacts of a peculiar kind ...'.[26] One can suggest a variety of mechanisms by which this imagining may take place, for example the formation of a political movement. ILMs represent another such mechanism, and one which is crucial to the development of the various cultural nationalisms (Young Ireland, Ulster Regionalism) of this island.

Anderson discusses the move from kinship and clientship groupings to nations which took place in Europe in the eighteenth century; this occurring at the same time as developments in literacy, media, communications and transportation is not merely coincidental (interestingly, in the light of the imposition of a Protestant Ascendancy over this period, Anderson also posits a 'coalition between Protestantism and print-capitalism').[27] The emergence and development of the ILM over the last two and a half centuries is not simply concurrent with the evolution in this country from Colony, to the Siamese twins of Protestant Nation and Catholic Nation, and latterly to the more fluid and permeable definitions of Irishness which were being developed at the end of the last century. Rather, if a nation is an 'imagined community', then these publications are not just an accidental by-product of that imagining, but a key mechanism by which it takes place, at the same time a forum *for* and an embodiment *of* it. From *Anthologia Hibernica*, through *The Nation* and the *Irish Review*, to the *Crane Bag*, the exact same process of imagining is evident, avant-garde élites discussing, and embodying, their hoped-for New Irelands.

Joep Leerssen has discussed the concept of 'Print Culture', and argued that in the Print Age people across the country may hear new ideas discussed, or stories read aloud from newspapers, coining the phrase 'to hear is to participate'.[28] In the context of ILMs, this can be extended thus: 'to *read* is to participate', and even (with regard to the élite of opinion-formers), 'to *write* is to participate', participate that is in the imagining of new forms of Irishness. For example, when we look at the personalities involved in the tortuous development of these imaginings (say, Wolfe Tone, Thomas Davis and Patrick Pearse, in different centuries) it is important to know not simply *what* they thought, but also the context, where they chose to express these thoughts, the intellectual company they kept.[29] As Eisenstein has concluded: 'Printed materials encourage silent adherence to causes whose advocates could not be located in any one parish and who addressed an invisible public from afar.'[30]

Referring to newspapers, Anderson celebrates:

> ... this extraordinary mass ceremony: the almost precisely simultaneous consumption ('imagining') of the newspaper ... each communicant is well aware that the ceremony he performs is being replicated simultaneously by thousands (or millions) of others of whose existence he is confident, yet of whose identity he has not the slightest notion. Furthermore, this ceremony is ... repeated at ... intervals throughout the calendar. What more vivid figure for the secular, historically-clocked, imagined community can be envisioned?[31]

The scale of the ceremony is much more limited with small-circulation literary magazines, but the quality of the experience is essentially the same. Periodicals produce a sense of cohesion amongst 'virtual groups' of individuals, they position their readers in a particular way which allows them to label themselves, as 'Tories', or 'women', or 'interested in literature and culture'. This offers the readers a sense of identity which they can buy into, and which gives them a way of interpreting the world. However, the situation is more complex than that; as Beetham acknowledges, magazines are contradictory, for they are also: '... marked by a radical heterogeneity ... [they] refused, and still refuse, a single authorial voice ... [they] also mix media and genres... the more successful periodical forms ... are the least homogenous ...'.[32] These magazines are the cultural world's equivalent of newspapers, providing information hot from the front, unmediated by mature reflection and giving us a direct line to the formulation of concepts and the creation of art. As Smyth says: '... the essay, the editorial, the work-in-progress and the review are present-oriented discourses ... They are *discursive* in the sense that they are recognisable interventions in on-going debates.'[33]

Irish literary magazines are, by their very nature, protean; this gives them much of their vitality and interest, but inevitably leads to problems of definition – a rigid definition will be both arbitrary and subjective. All previous commentators have recognised this. For example Madden: 'To determine the true character of periodicals…is often no easy matter…[it is also difficult] to distinguish…literary periodicals…[from] early newspapers.'[34] Or Sullivan:

> As the operative term for classifying periodicals and deciding their suitability for this reference guide, *literary* might be defined so broadly as to include virtually all magazines or so rigorously as to permit only a handful. Many magazines that began self-consciously as literary endeavours published only mediocre work that today we relegate to belles-lettres, or they soon abandoned the literary calling to argue politics or current events. As editors or publishers changed or magazines merged, the foci shifted so that a magazine might be regarded as literary for only part of its career.[35]

It is clear then that the term 'Irish literary magazines' could mean magazines produced in Ireland, magazines produced by Irish people (in England, Scotland, Canada, the USA or Australia), or magazines concerned with Irish literature (from all those countries, plus others, from France to Japan); it could also mean those in all languages, including English, Irish or French. Taken to its logical extreme it could also (as with current projects on the history of the book in Scotland or Ireland) include literary magazines *read* by Irish people. This would not only hugely expand the numbers to the point where it became difficult to give any shape to the matter, but would also include such fundamental disparities of material that it would be impossible to pass any sustainable judgements upon it. It is helpful in this context to return to our idea of a nation as an 'imagined community', and these publications as a key mechanism by which that imagining takes place. This is an important reason why this study has excluded both Irish language literary magazines, and English language ILMs published abroad. The former have been so few in number, have rarely if ever coexisted to form a critical mass, and have for a variety of reasons never entered into sustained dialogue with the titles and personalities examined here.[36] The latter seem to be even further removed from the sort of 'imagining' under discussion, having much the same relation to the development of Ireland, Irishness and Irish literature as Yeats' Noh plays have to Japan.

In conclusion then, any attempt at a hard and fast definition is not only doomed to failure, but possibly counterproductive; while this means that my choice is, necessarily, to some extent arbitrary, I have been guided by how well an individual title sits with the essential function defined above of an effective mechanism by which literary and cultural élites in Ireland have carried on their imaginings of Irishness. The need for discrimination may be illustrated by the fact that, had I relaxed my own implicit definition even slightly, this would have added another fifty titles to the Descriptive Bibliography in Part 2 at a stroke. Nevertheless, it remains the case that this is the only study of ILMs which has attempted to view the entire range of publications from 1710 whole; it has none of the Dublin-centric limitations of previous surveys, and includes many more titles from 'peripheral' areas such as the North, or Cork; and it is, of course, more up-to-date.[37]

As with every survey, I have excluded titles which others might have covered. It would be tedious to attempt to list these, but it might be useful to give a couple of examples, and the reasons for their exclusion. Extending my cut-off date by just one year would have led to the inclusion of a number of important new titles, including Gerald Dawe's *Krino* (Galway, first issue Spring 1986), *Graph* (Dublin, started Autumn 1986), and the *Irish Review* (Cork and Belfast, first issue 1986). However, it seemed to me that these journals do not belong to the period 1953–1985, but rather to a new Ireland, that of historical revisionism, social liberalisation, the Celtic Tiger and a European identity, and so must wait for a future study of the post-1985 scene. *The Christian Examiner, and Church of Ireland Magazine* (Dublin, 1825–1869), on the other hand, clearly falls within my scope, and did publish early stories by William Carleton; however, I did not feel that this was, in itself, enough to justify inclusion, as no other literary material of importance appeared, and indeed the vast bulk of its pages are given over to castigating Catholicism for its 'errors and calumnies' and its 'superstition'.[38] A case could also be made for including the *Dublin Review* (1836–1969) on the basis of its Maynooth connections, but I have to agree with the major authorities on this period (including Barbara Hayley,[39] Nancy Cummings[40] and Alvin Sullivan[41]) that it should not appear in a survey such as this.[42]

The lack of a comprehensive and coherent guide to ILMs has led to their being ignored and under-used as a resource for research. For example, in Dorgan's *Irish Poetry Since Kavanagh*,[43] only sixteen ILMs are looked at; ten are simply mentioned in passing, three more get a sentence or two, and all of it amounts to a grand total of around 180 words. Two of the references to *HU* are factually inaccurate, while for the others the level of analysis rarely rises higher than 'X's poems first appeared in Y magazine'. In Welch's *Companion*[44] there are entries for around three dozen ILMs, but this means that many of even the well-known and important titles are missing. Of those covered, only a handful get more than a listing of title, dates, editors and main contributors. There are general articles on, for example, Irish-language publishing, but until now no similar survey of ILMs, nor anything which attempts to show how a magazine can provide a generation of writers with their village square, club and debating society rolled into one.

This study is structured as follows: Part 1 is a series of short chapters which together comprise a high-level, outline history of ILMs, tracing important innovations in form, in tone and subject-matter, and in the literatures they address. This section also highlights important groupings of titles, and attempts some provisional assessments of the *collective* contribution, achievement and importance of each era. The chronological divisions which these chapters reflect are not arbitrary, but arise rather from an objective statistical analysis of the start and end dates of all the titles; from this analysis it emerged that there are clear chronological periods, marked by a low level of activity which builds to a peak and then declines. The vast majority of magazines in each period live and die within this timeframe, and then the whole process starts over.[45] Part 2 is the Descriptive Bibliography, which provides the same set of core bibliographical data (for example, editors, dates, number of issues published) and a brief summary of its content, for each title.[46] Obviously, the length of this summary varies widely, with the most important journals (like the *Dublin University Magazine* or the *Bell*) getting most coverage. I have, however, operated a policy of positive discrimination toward lesser titles, and the space given is often not proportionate. This is because many minor publications have not been examined at all elsewhere; because it is impossible to do full justice to the most important magazines in a general survey (other, more detailed, material is available elsewhere on the major titles, and references are given for these); and because the minor items not only build up to give a cumulative picture of each period or genre, but also give vital context for the 'big guns'. The title entries are ordered chronologically. This arrangement is easy to use, but also adds an extra dimension to the data by implicitly demonstrating development. Finally, there are three Appendices containing: an alphabetical index, which gives a second route by which the information may be accessed; a series of maps illustrating the geographical distribution of titles in each of the periods covered by the chapters in Part 1; and finally, three chronological charts showing how many new titles were started up in each decade of the last three centuries.

NOTES

1 Walter Houghton (ed.), *The Wellesley Index to Victorian Periodicals 1824–1900*, 5 volumes (Toronto, 1966–1989); M. Sader (ed.), *Comprehensive Index to English-Language Little Magazines 1890–1970* (Millwood, 1976).

2 Wolfgang Görtschacher, *Little Magazine Profiles: The Little Magazines in Great Britain* (Salzburg, 1993).

3 Frederick J. Hoffman, Charles Allen and Carolyn F. Ulrich (eds), *The Little Magazine, A History and Bibliography* (Princeton, 1946).

4 Alvin Sullivan (ed.), *British Literary Magazines: The Augustan Age and the Age of Johnson, 1698–1788* (Westport, 1983); *British Literary Magazines: The Romantic Age, 1789–1836* (Westport, 1984); *British Literary Magazines: The Victorian and Edwardian Age, 1837–1913* (Westport, 1985); *British Literary Magazines: The Modern Age, 1914–1984* (Westport, 1986).

5 Gerry Smyth, *Decolonisation and Criticism: The Construction of Irish Literature* (London, 1998, Chapter 5, 'The Periodical'), pp. 101–142.

6 Brian Fallon, *An Age of Innocence: Irish Culture 1930–1960* (Dublin, 1998), Chapter 17, 'Press and Periodicals'.

7 Rudi Holzapfel, 'A Survey of Irish Literary Magazines from 1900 to the Present Day', M Litt thesis (Trinity College Dublin, 1964).

8 Sullivan, *British Literary Magazines* (1983), p. x.

9 However, Smyth's basic model – taking a horizontal slice of ten years at a turning point in history, and taking a comparative look at all the ILMs then in print – is a potentially useful one.

10 Fallon, *An Age of Innocence*, p. 232.

11 Fallon, *An Age of Innocence*, p. 13.

12 Seamus Deane, *Celtic Revivals* (London, 1985).

13 Dillon Johnston, *Irish Poetry After Joyce* (Notre Dame, 1985).

14 Declan Kiberd, *Inventing Ireland* (London, 1995).

15 Norman Vance, *Irish Literature: A Social History; Tradition, Identity and Difference* (Oxford, 1990).

16 Edna Longley, '"Between the Saxon Smile and Yankee Yawp": Problems and Contexts of Literary Reviewing in Ireland', Jeremy Treglown and Bridget Bennett (eds), *Grub Street and*

the Ivory Tower: Literary Journalism and Literary Scholarship from Fielding to the Internet (Oxford, 1998), pp. 200–223.

17 Robert Madden, *The History of Irish Periodical Literature* (London, 1869).

18 Holzapfel, 'A Survey', p. xv.

19 Holzapfel, 'A Survey', p. v.

20 And himself editor of an ILM, the *Irish University Review*.

21 Maurice Harmon, *Select Bibliography for the Study of Anglo-Irish Literature and Its Backgrounds* (Dublin, 1977).

22 Hoffman, Allen and Ulrich (eds), *The Little Magazine, A History and Bibliography*, pp. v–ix.

23 Sullivan (ed.), *British Literary Magazines: The Augustan Age and the Age of Johnson, 1698–1788*, p. xix.

24 I am heavily indebted for many of the concepts outlined in this section to Benedict Anderson's *Imagined Communities, Reflections on the Origin and Spread of Nationalism* (London, 1983).

25 Anderson, *Imagined Communities*, p. 15.

26 Anderson, *Imagined Communities*, p. 13.

27 Anderson, *Imagined Communities*, p. 44. The theory of 'print-capitalism' sees printed books as the first form of mass-reproducible capitalist enterprise.

28 Joep Leerssen, lecture to QUB Historical Society, 22 April 1999, my notes.

29 This is one reason why I have recorded the key contributors to, and participants in, these magazines in Part 2 of this work.

30 Elizabeth L. Eisenstein, 'Some Conjectures about the Impact of Printing on Western Society and Thought', *Journal of Modern History* 40, 1 (March 1968), p. 39.

31 Anderson, *Imagined Communities*, p. 39.

32 Margaret Beetham, *A Magazine of Her Own?: Domesticity and Desire in the Woman's Magazine 1800–1914* (London, 1996), p. 7.

33 Smyth, *Decolonisation and Criticism*, p. 101.

34 Madden, *The History*, p. 87.

35 Sullivan, *British Literary Magazines*, p. viii.

36 Perhaps their authors were imagining a rather different community from their Anglophone contemporaries? Another practical problem is that I have no Irish, and the political, cultural and literary hinterland from which literature in Irish emerges, and the problems it has to deal with, are so specialised, that it would be an insult to the material for them to be tackled other than in a dedicated study of their own.

37 The cut-off point of 1985 was not chosen arbitrarily, but rather seems to be the end of the most recent of the discrete historical periods of activity outlined below.

38 *Christian Examiner*, 5, 25 (July 1827).

39 'It was the leading Roman Catholic organ *in Britain*' [my emphasis]; 'It does not fall into the category of "Irish Periodicals"' – Hayley (1987), p. 37.

40 *Wellesley Index to Victorian Periodicals*, II, 'Introduction' to article on the *Dublin Review*, p. 19.

41 Sullivan (ed.), *British Literary Magazines: The Romantic Age, 1789–1836*: '[it] quickly became a major voice of the Catholic revival in England', p. 114; '...proprietorship...[lay] officially with the archbishops of Westminster', p. 115.

42 There were twelve publishers down the years, every one of them based in London; although figures such as Daniel O'Connell played an important part in setting it up, Wiseman was the dominant force; and it was primarily intended to counter the *Edinburgh Review*, not the *DUM*.

43 Theo Dorgan (ed.), *Irish Poetry Since Kavanagh* (Blackrock, 1996).

44 Robert Welch (ed.), *Oxford Companion to Irish Literature* (Oxford, 1996).

45 Each period also has a small number of titles (usually two or three) which survive beyond it, and then can continue for decades.

46 At the end of slightly more than half of the entries there are cross-references, where there is existing commentary on that magazine. It should be noted that this means that for almost half the magazines listed here, this is the first time they have been seriously examined.

Part 1
Outline History

Chapter 1

The prehistory of Irish literary magazines

It is important before beginning this study of Irish literary magazines to familiarise oneself with their 'prehistory', that is the development of printing and publishing up to the start of the eighteenth century, and to understand how this prehistory shaped their first hundred years. The Irish literary magazines of the eighteenth century, in particular, have been criticised for their provincial character and their lack of artistic attainment;[1] this broader context will reveal the underlying restrictions which handicapped them, as it is only by understanding this context that we can truly appreciate their achievement.

Although the technology of printing was revolutionary, the infrastructure on which it depended was already in place in most European societies by the start of the modern period. Stationers acted as 'proto publishers',[2] commissioning scribes to copy books, then selling them to the public; other associated trades such as illustrators and binders also existed already. For a variety of reasons, this was not true in Ireland – the non-urban, non-literate nature of much of Gaelic culture; the lack of a university; the crushing of the native aristocracy; and the abolition of the monasteries. The result was that printing was introduced into Ireland by its conquerors, onto a virtual 'clean sheet', and this contributed enormously to the path which future developments were to take.

Printing also came late to Ireland. Gutenberg was conducting his experiments in Strasbourg in the 1440s, after which the revolution spread with electrifying speed through the European heartland. It had reached Italy, the Netherlands, Switzerland and France by the 1460s; Hungary, Poland, Spain and England during the 1470s; and Denmark and Portugal in the 1480s.[3] The first printing press was not set up in Dublin until 1550, a decade after printing had arrived in Mexico, and only shortly before it reached Russia; this gives an accurate picture of Ireland's place on the edge of the emerging European culture of the modern era.

Another crucial determining factor whose influence was to be long felt in Ireland was the exact circumstance by which printing arrived here. In mainland European countries such as Germany and Italy, printing developed in a devolved, diverse way, with many monasteries, city states and universities having their own presses; in England, the path taken was the exact opposite, and under the direct control of the Crown. The English printing trade was centralised on London from the very beginning, with even Oxford taking many years to develop a viable press (the monasteries which, elsewhere in Europe, had been early centres of the new technology, were of course soon to be dissolved by Henry VIII). This seems to have been a consequence of the trade's having emerged just as the York and Tudor monarchs were building a strong, centralised state, with the bitter conflicts of the Reformation and Counter-Reformation ensuring that they would not allow this potent new propaganda weapon to develop outside their control.[4]

Humfrey Powell, an Englishman, was appointed King's Printer in Ireland in 1550.[5] The circumstances of this belated birth indicated that printing, publishing, and the rest of 'high' culture in Ireland would remain the servant of the Ascendancy, mostly centralised in Dublin, and subject to close state supervision;[6] the legacy of the Cromwellian and Williamite wars, and the ensuing Penal Laws, virtually guaranteed it. There was to be no significant change in this (despite the radical challenge at the end of the eighteenth century), until the emergence of a strong Catholic civic culture after the Napoleonic wars. Printing presses were set up in Cork, Waterford and Kilkenny during the struggles of the 1640s, but the output of the press in Cork for the rest of the century was negligible, and those in Waterford and Kilkenny fell silent until 1729 and 1759, respectively. The first printers, Patrick Neil and James Blow, did not arrive in Belfast until 1694.[7]

The first officially printed record of a public event in the British Isles was the pamphlet *The trewe encountre*, published after the battle of Flodden Field in 1513, and the next century saw the halting emergence of periodical newsbooks, confining themselves mostly to reports of wars overseas. The British newspaper industry was kick-started by the English Civil War, in three ways. First of all, both sides quickly produced their own propaganda sheets: the Royalist *Mercurius Aulicus* in 1643, the Parliamentarian *Mercurius Britannicus* the following year. Secondly, the King's expulsion from London led to the re-emergence of printing in centres such as Oxford. And thirdly, the tumult of these years led to the breakdown of central controls, and so to a brief period of unprecedented freedom.[8] In addition, of course, the ongoing struggle led to a thirst for news across a wide range of society. The desire for reports of the war in Ireland led to the establishment of the first Irish newspaper, the *Irish Monthly Mercury*, in 1649.[9]

The Restoration led to a determined attempt to re-establish the old system of control by the Crown, as the Printing Acts of 1662 and 1665, and the 1680 Royal Proclamation banning unofficial newspapers testify; the level of resistance can also be gauged from the fact that the Act had to be tightened up in 1685, and again in 1693.[10] In 1695 the Act was again presented to Parliament, but this time it was rejected, and the age of modern newspapers and periodicals in Britain began.

The era of continuous newspaper production in Ireland begins with the *Flying Post* (Dublin) in 1699. The first newspapers to be published outside Dublin were in Cork (the *Cork Idler*, 1715), Limerick (the *Limerick News Letter*, 1716), Waterford (another *Flying Post*, 1729) and Belfast (the *Newsletter*, 1737);[11] Belfast, Limerick and Cork would later become the only towns in Ireland outside Dublin to produce literary magazines during the eighteenth century.

The historical arrangement with the Crown had been a very cosy one for the authorised London printers and booksellers, who had benefited from a cartel arrangement – indeed, in some areas, absolute monopolies were granted to individuals by the authorities. So Parliament's action in 1695 was deeply unsettling for the trade, and, as a result of intense lobbying, they secured the passage in April 1710 of an *Act for the Encouragement of Learning*, more usually known as the first Copyright Act.[12] With the passage of this Act, the last of the defining circumstances of eighteenth-century Irish publishing was set in place, for the Act did not apply in Ireland, and so encouraged the development of piracy here. Although enforcement was always difficult, the English trade obtained the 1739 *Import of Books Act* to protect their home markets, but in Ireland itself the state of freedom from the law continued for almost another century, with unforeseen consequences.

NOTES

1 Inglis describes them as 'ephemeral, featureless, and dull', while conceding that 'they cannot be entirely ignored', Brian Inglis, *The Freedom of the Press in Ireland 1784–1841* (London, 1954), p. 244.
2 John Feather, *A History of British Publishing* (London, 1988), pp. 1–3.
3 Feather, *A History*, p. 8.
4 Feather, *A History*, pp. 16–18.
5 Robert Welch (ed.), *Oxford Companion to Irish Literature* (Oxford, 1996), p. 484.
6 Between 1604 and 1618, John Franckton was appointed 'Printer-general to his majesty within the realm of Ireland', giving him a complete monopoly over not just printing, but also binding and bookselling, for works in both English and Irish – Robert Munter, *The History of the Irish Newspaper, 1685–1760* (Cambridge, 1967), pp. 1–2.
7 J.R.R. Adams, *The Printed Word and the Common Man: Popular Culture in Ulster 1700–1900* (Belfast, 1987), pp. 23–24.
8 Feather, *A History*, pp. 45–48.
9 Munter, *The History*, p. 6.
10 Feather, *A History*, pp. 51–53, 62–63.
11 From the introduction to the Report of the NEWSPLAN project in Ireland (London/Dublin, 1992).
12 Feather, *A History*, pp. 70–76.

Chapter 2
Irish literary magazines of the eighteenth century

The emergence of modern English democracy at the end of the seventeenth century, and the start of an extended period of stability and rising prosperity, brought about the coming of age of the English newspaper and periodical. The introduction of the two-party system and triennial parliaments after the Restoration meant that any minister could suddenly find himself in opposition; this cooled politicians' ardour for permanent, suppressive legislation. At the same time, commercially successful daily newspapers (the first was the *Daily Courant*, 1702) began to establish themselves, swiftly becoming the pre-eminent medium of political debate. As a result, a new breed of politician appeared, exemplified by Robert Harley, first Earl of Oxford, with a much more sophisticated approach to the press than that which had obtained previously.[1]

Very soon after, a completely new form of publication began with the first *Tatler* in 1709. This first issue was virtually indistinguishable from other newspapers, but over the next six months the straight news quotient declined and eventually disappeared. A new format, the periodical essay accompanied by a little brief literary criticism, was enormously popular; Addison's advice to Pope 'not to be content with the applause of half the nation' (i.e. to steer clear of political faction), and Swift's accusation that Addison had 'fair sexed' the periodical (i.e., deliberately made it accessible to women) illustrate the new commercial drive, and the intention to attract as broad an audience as possible.[2]

As well as the developments in printing and publishing, to understand the nature of eighteenth-century Irish literary magazines and in particular their modest achievements, it is necessary to have some conception of the society which they served. It was essentially an extension of that of southern England, and comparable with that of the upper classes in the more far-flung English regions; as Beckett puts it, 'an English culture, modified by local circumstances, not an Irish culture that had been partly Anglicised'.[3] Although they were mostly resident in Ireland, either on their estates or in Dublin, and their wealth derived from those estates, this social and cultural attachment to England left them with a kind of schizophrenia: Irish lands, English culture; 'To the influence of this ambiguous position can be traced most of the special characteristics of Anglo-Irish writers.'[4] In fact, Beckett even objects to using the term Anglo-Irish to describe most of the writings of the period; he sees them as simply English. Certainly most of the Irish writers who appear in the eighteenth-century Irish literary magazines share no common style, no shared interest in form or technique, and above all no unifying cultural agenda which might mark them out as a distinct group: 'Taken out of their proper place in the mainstream of English literature, they are just so many individuals whose combined work does not form in any understandable sense a literature of its own.'[5] Some examples of this dependency are stark. As if it was not bad enough that a new publication trumpeted by a Dublin publisher early in the century was simply a reprint of the *Tatler*, he has to add the humiliating caveat, 'if packets come in'; no packet boats from England, no publication,[6] and during the winter, the service could be suspended for weeks at a time. Even in good weather, it took four to six days for news to travel from London to Dublin.[7] Although one might be tempted to point to an increasing coverage of Irish subject matter – ancient monuments, the older literature – in later publications like the *Hibernian Magazine* as evidence of the emergence of a distinct national culture, it would be difficult in the extreme to argue on the evidence in the literary magazines alone against Beckett's assertion that:

> England was the dominant source of ideas. Even when, in the later 18th century, some Anglo-Irish writers turned their attention to Irish antiquities and Gaelic literature, this was a reflection of current trends in Britain... Only at the very end of the 18th century, under the impact of revolutionary forces, did there appear some vague idea of a distinctly Irish culture.[8]

To illustrate the magnetic effect of London on any author of talent, Beckett examines the careers of the six most successful writers with Irish connections in the first half of the eighteenth century; his findings may be summarised as follows. Southerne received his early education in Dublin, but went to the Middle Temple when he was eighteen, lived in England the rest of his days, and wrote nothing which might reveal his Irish birth; Steele went to Charterhouse at twelve, then Oxford, then London, and could later write, without a trace of irony, 'I am an Englishman, born in the city of Dublin';[9] Congreve grew up in Ireland, but left by the time he was twenty, never to return; Farquhar was born in Derry and educated at Trinity, but after the success of his first play in London, none of his works was set in Ireland; and, famously, Swift, had he achieved his hoped-for success in England, would likely never have written about the trials of his native land.

The Irish literary magazines of the eighteenth century can all be divided into two categories, according to which innovative English example they copied – those which were modelled on the *Tatler* (both the *Tatler* and the *Spectator* were widely pirated in Dublin, almost from their inception; Steele himself was, of course, Irish); and those more general magazines which were modelled on the *Gentleman's Magazine* (1731). The *Tatler*-type (a two-page essay, plus two pages of gossip or news) came first – the *Examiner* (the first of all Irish literary magazines), the *Dublin Weekly Journal* (the first true Irish literary magazine, and the first to originate in Ireland), the *Intelligencer* (Swift's second, more successful attempt), and the *Publick Register* (which added a section of poetry between the essays and news). The rest of the literary magazines published in Ireland in that century were firmly in the second camp. The *Tatler*-type are all products of a dominant artistic personality (a characteristic which prefigures the Little Magazines of the twentieth century), a vehicle for his (and it was almost always 'his') opinions. The Miscellanies are usually the product of a bookseller or publisher, hack work based on pirating items from England and abroad, and often an attempt by the bookseller to cut out the editorial middleman.

The provincial market in England for all sorts of publication began to expand greatly as the century progressed and stability and prosperity increased. However, the London publishers found it increasingly difficult to communicate with these new customers. The radical new development which the *Gentleman's Magazine* introduced was to list all new books published, for the information of these provincial readers; the first book reviews, mostly the short summaries known as 'epitomes' were a natural evolution of these lists.[10] Although the Irish market was never so developed, it is not hard to see the attraction of a *Gentleman's Magazine*-type publication for the Dublin publishers; these epitomes developed into what we would now regard as 'proper' book reviews, appearing first in Tobias Smollett's *Critical Review*, from 1756.[11] In 1731 when the *Gentleman's Magazine* appeared in England, the metaphor of the 'magazine' was much fresher, and was understood to mean a storehouse of many different items, which were arrayed openly on the shelves. 'Miscellany' is also a good description of the kind of magazine which followed, and featured in many of their titles. They tend to be much less satisfying to posterity, as the lack of a defining personality, the sheer brevity of many of the items, and the padding out with contemporary ephemera (news flashes, advertisements, and so on) gives them an insubstantial quality in all but a few cases.

We can look first at the *Tatler*-type magazines. It is no accident that the first Irish literary magazine, *The Examiner* (1710–1712) was edited by that ambitious associate of Addison and Steele, Jonathan Swift. For Swift, this venture was the logical next step from the contributions he was making to the *Tatler* during the period 1710–1713 when he was in London, working as a party writer for the Tories. It represents a perfect 'missing link' between the first Irish literary magazines and their English predecessors, because Swift took his inspiration directly from source at the *Tatler*, and because his magazine straddles the two countries, being published first in London, then reprinted in Dublin. Unlike the *Tatler* it is intensely political; as Ehrenpreis says, its sole purpose was 'to damn the Whigs and praise the Tories'.[12] Because of its propagandist purpose, few of the contents are very distinguished from a literary point of view; there is nothing Irish about them.

The first true Irish literary magazine was the *Dublin Weekly Journal* (1725–1752), written and published in Dublin; again, the *Tatler* format is used, and all the pieces are signed either 'Hibernicus' (James Arbuckle, the editor) or 'To Hibernicus' (other contributors, including his fellow members of the 'New Light' circle, like Robert Molesworth and Francis Hutcheson).[13] In the *Journal*, Arbuckle says: 'we bestow the ornaments of our own Nation on our Neighbours, and then pay them at a dear Rate for the Use of them at second hand', and this is quoted in the *Oxford Companion to Irish Literature* as an espousal of 'literary nationalism'.[14] However, I think Welch's contributor is overstating his case here; 'literary nationalism' would surely have to imply some national content, sentiment, style or politics. Elsewhere (see his contributions to Powell's *Tribune* newspaper throughout 1729), Arbuckle was to argue that England's conquest of Ireland was both just and necessary. Rather, this is just the first of a long line of complaints about the economic imbalances which tempted Ireland's best to greater things in London (and did the 'Patriot' party's later campaign ever amount to much more than this sort of economic or trade grievance?). As Beckett says:

> But the pen-name was more Irish than the context, for the questions were treated in general terms, with little or no specific reference to Ireland... it provided a living for

no one but Arbuckle himself, and it is hard to think of anyone else in Ireland at that time who could gain a livelihood by literary work.[15]

Perhaps inspired by Arbuckle's success, Swift made his second attempt at a *Tatler*-type magazine, *The Intelligencer* (Dublin, 1728), this time alternating the issues with Thomas Sheridan. At this time (in contrast to his *Examiner* years when he still had high hopes of preferment in England), Swift was spending a lot of time in Ireland, principally with Sheridan in Cavan;[16] he was at the peak of his success – *Gulliver's Travels* was published in 1726, *A Modest Proposal* in 1729. Although *The Intelligencer* lasted only four months, and the quality of both paper and print is execrable, the quality of the contents was higher than anything in the *Examiner* – his defence of the *Beggar's Opera*, 'A Short View of the State of Ireland' and many other pieces of the highest quality appear.

In a direct echo of the *Examiner*, the first literary magazine to be published in Ireland outside of Dublin was the *Publick Register* (Belfast, 1741), a reprint by Henry Joy of a London title (liberally sprinkled with adverts for Joy's own products). Production values were high, and the literary content less diluted than many of its peers, but since editorial control rested in London, its appearance from Belfast is its only significance for the history of Irish literary magazines.

In any case, the day of the *Tatler*-type magazine was over in Ireland; it is impossible to state precisely why this should be, but suspicion must fall on the usual suspects – the low calibre of literary activity in Ireland at this time; poor sales; the easy availability of the English originals which cultural inferiority complexes led Irish buyers to prefer; and the fact that the booksellers and publishers saw the Miscellanies as more profitable, and an easy option which had the advantage that they did not have to deal with strong editorial personalities like Swift.

Turning now to the Miscellanies, of which the first was the *Literary Journal* (Dublin, 1744–1749). The opening editorial of this magazine contains an honest description of what the Miscellanies were about – 'to give abstracts of…foreign books…Foreign Journals…[and] English Writers'; in other words, brazen piracy of material which was not protected by copyright in Ireland. One caveat must be applied here – the use of the word piracy, while factually correct, may perhaps mislead; these magazines were not necessarily substandard, and the *Literary Journal* is a case in point. Of the five earlier Irish literary magazines discussed above, the largest ran to just sixteen pages; they were mostly small in size; and the clarity of the print and the quality of production tended to be poor. The *Literary Journal*, on the other hand, is a most impressive production, averaging two hundred pages and of the best quality. Again, all five previous Irish literary magazines were weeklies, giving them the transitory quality of a newspaper, whereas the quarterly appearances of the *Literary Journal* must have given it the feel of a journal of record. It also provided a good index of its contents: readers of the *Literary Journal* were obviously expected to keep their copies, and build them into a library. As so often, the Irish content was negligible.

Although the quality of publications like the *Literary Journal* was high, most of the eighteenth-century Irish literary magazines were far less impressive. *The Weekly*

Miscellany (Dublin, 1734–1735), while outstanding only for that fact, was the first Irish literary magazine of the *Miscellany* type and, while it may have lasted only a year, it established this new type of publication which was to achieve a dominant position in Ireland for the rest of the century. The *Magazine of Magazines* (1751–1759) wears its heart on its sleeve – its very title reads like a meta-magazine. Obviously an imitator of the *Literary Journal*, its main interest is that the publishers managed to maintain such a magazine for a run of over 200 issues, from a base in Limerick. The *Compendious Library* (Dublin, 1751–1752), was another *Literary Journal* imitator, although this time at least the debt was acknowledged as the *Compendious Library* claimed to be a 'revival' of the earlier work. It is a faithful imitation in all respects except quality. The *Dublin Library* (Dublin, 1761) is another Miscellany; the only interesting pieces to appear in it are 'A Journey Through Ireland' and 'The Manners and Customs of the Native Irish' as they are the first clear indication of late-eighteenth-century antiquarian interest in 'the matter of Ireland', which was to feature strongly in future Irish literary magazines. The *Dublin Magazine* (Dublin, 1762-1765) was yet another piratical Miscellany of no great originality, which never attempted to depart from the model in any way. Finally, *The Repository* (Dublin, 1763) perhaps gives an insight into the nakedly commercial influences at work, as it is an exact reprint, under a new name, of the *Dublin Library*, which the same printer had published only a couple of years earlier (and which was itself mostly pirated).

In a different league was the *Hibernian Magazine* (Dublin, 1771–1812). This has to be seen, with the *Anthologia Hibernica*, as the pinnacle of eighteenth-century Irish literary magazines – not only did it maintain an unbroken run of 510 issues over forty-one years, but production values were very high, and the contents remained interesting and varied throughout (even if little of outstanding literary merit appeared in its pages). In fact, the *Hibernian Magazine* stands so far above most of its peers that it appears almost to be, rather than just the apotheosis of the Miscellany, a deliberate attempt to blend the interest and variety of that type of publication with the personality and intellectual quality of the *Tatler*-type. It also has a far higher Irish content than anything previously seen, its very name seeming like a statement of a more confident nationalist position.

An indication of the new confidence (or maybe the changed political climate which it embodies) is that Irish material was included from the very start – a lot of it political or social comment, but also broader cultural material (essays on monuments like Newgrange), and coverage of Irish artistic activity which, if hardly exhaustive, was far more serious than anything which had gone before. Some of this is reportage, or reviews of current plays, but it is hard to imagine any of the *Hibernian Magazine*'s predecessors trumpeting the exclusive of a previously unpublished letter of Sterne's, for example. While the book reviews are the standard short notices of the time, they do cover the output of the Dublin publishers (and not just Walker himself). Some of the Irish literary material is more substantial, such as the six-page essay on Sterne in March 1774, but there is never any danger of its blossoming into the more heavyweight coverage which was to come in the Victorian journals. Walker had hit upon a winning formula here, whose success depended upon always keeping his readers 'diverted'.

Alongside these more impressive works, the flow of lesser Miscellanies continued. The

Weekly Magazine (Dublin, 1779), like the *Repository* and the *Compendious Library*, represents the lowest common denominator of the eighteenth century Miscellany. As the *Compendious Library* was to the *Literary Journal*, so the *Universal Magazine* (Dublin, 1789–1792) was to the *Hibernian Magazine* – a pale imitation. The *Universal Magazine* is superior to the *Compendious Library* only because its model, the *Hibernian Magazine*, is superior to the *Literary Journal*. The *Limerick Weekly Magazine* (Limerick, 1790) is another also-ran, remarkable only for two things – it shows a slight influence of Romanticism in a few of its poems, and it was produced in Limerick. 'The Gleanor' was originally a column in the *Anthologia Hibernica*, and was reprinted as *The Gleanor* (Dublin, 1793–1794). It is a piece of extreme ephemera, and it is impossible now to tell whether it was even issued as an independent publication. Although it is difficult to say, on the basis of just three issues, what sort of publication the *Monthly Miscellany* (Cork, 1796–1797) might have turned out to be, it showed early promise as a superior example of the Miscellany. As it is, its only real importance now lies in that fact that it was published in Cork. And, finally, *The Flapper* (Dublin, 1796–1797) was published by Mercier and was described by R.R. Madden[17] as 'one of the dullest' of Mercier's magazines, and it is impossible to disagree with his judgement.

The *Hibernian Magazine* may have been ahead of its time, but it was joined in the 1790s by a new generation of Irish literary magazines – more 'Patriotic', introducing the new Romantic movement in literature, and influenced by the radical ideas from France and by the United Irish movement. The *Sentimental and Masonic* (Dublin, 1792–1795) is a good example of this trend, but it reaches its peak in the *Anthologia Hibernica* (Dublin, 1793–1794). The 1790s saw a general upsurge of activity in Irish literary magazines, with substantial increases in both quality and quantity. Although most were to prove short-lived, eight new titles started up in this decade (one-third of the total for the whole century), to join the still-thriving *Hibernian Magazine*; in addition, they include some of the most interesting magazines of the century.

The *Sentimental and Masonic* was the first worthy competitor the *Hibernian Magazine* had had since it began over twenty years earlier, and it shares many of the same characteristics – a varied and diverting range of contents, good production values, and a strong mixture of Irish-related material included with the pirated copy. The former included a series of pen-portraits of famous Irishmen and poems by Sheridan, amongst more adventurous elements like the column 'The Critic' which reviewed contemporary plays and writing, or W.P. Curry's poem 'Dermod and Cathleen, or the Dying Peasant'. As with all its contemporaries, the *Sentimental and Masonic*'s output began to suffer in 1795, and it failed completely before the year was out.

The *Anthologia Hibernica* could be looked at in two ways – either as another worthy competitor to the *Hibernian Magazine*, a Miscellany whose high standards made it the only real rival to that established title apart from the *Sentimental and Masonic*, or as a precursor of the nineteenth-century Reviews, similar in aim and organisation to their eighteenth-century forerunners, but with a level of seriousness, a commitment to quality, and above all a concentration on Irish material which the older magazines could not match. The *Anthologia Hibernica* proves its superiority over its peers wherever you chose to look

– it has the brief snippets of 'Literary Intelligence', but these cover contemporary Irish publications like Wolfe Tone's pamphlet for the Catholic Committee; it has the pages of verse, but these include some of Thomas Moore's earliest works; and it has the essays on Irish antiquarian subjects, but these are sensible (no nonsense about the Lost Tribe of Israel here) and thorough.

Unlike any of its predecessors, the *Anthologia Hibernica* also has a sense of literature as more than a pleasant diversion or a list of legendary names. Its articles included a piece on J.P. Droz and the *Literary Journal* of fifty years before, a long examination of contemporary drama, and a debate on the lack of copyright protection in Ireland and its consequences. The magazine seems to have had strong connections with Trinity (Mercier, the printer, was the college bookseller), which may have contributed to its higher standards.

In Ireland, as across Europe, the early 1790s was a time of radical ferment, but while most of their contemporaries were fired by Paine or the new ideas emerging from France, the inspiration for the *Parlour Window* (Dublin, 1795) seems to have been Mary Wollstonecraft, whose 'Vindication of the Rights of Women' was published three years earlier. While every editor and publisher of a literary magazine, from Addison onwards, knew of the commercial benefits which could be reaped from attracting a female readership, the gestures made toward this half of the population were generally patronising and trivial – on the level of articles discussing whether a lady should be seen laughing in public. The tone of the *Parlour Window*'s first editorial, in contrast, is one which had not been heard in the limited world of Irish literary magazines before (and it would be many years before it was to be heard again):

> Female Authors have so many discouragements to encounter, it is no wonder they so rarely appear in Print; the general opinion is against them; People of Contracted Minds, judge hardly of them; and consider that every drop of Ink that flows from the Pen of a Woman, as so many *blots* on her character. As Writers they labour under many disadvantages, which instead of procuring indulgence, rather provoke censure, and their Writings are discovered to have many defects which are often overlooked in those of the other sex.

Its proto-feminism may have made it *sui generis*, and gives it added historical interest, but unfortunately the quality of the contents does not quite live up to the rhetoric of the editorials.

The century closes with *The Microscope* (Belfast, 1798–1800), which is somewhat reminiscent of the *Anthologia Hibernica*, albeit on a much more modest scale. *The Microscope* straddles the eighteenth and nineteenth centuries, and, as one reads it through, one can see it, issue by issue, sloughing off the tone and subject matter of the eighteenth century, and embracing Romanticism. It moves from diverting anecdotes and essays on Virgil, to articles on Cowper and Coleridge and William Drennan's 'Protest' at the Act of Union. The only ingredient lacking is a stronger commitment to Irish material, but the voice is a modern one, and looks forward to the Reviews of the following century. A more intense, critical attitude to art and artists, a new dedication to scientific method, a substantial bourgeoisie, higher standards of literacy and education; all these are prerequisites for the success of more serious literary periodicals, and none were to be in place in Ireland until the 1820s or 1830s.

Something which the *Hibernian Magazine, Sentimental and Masonic* and *Anthologia Hibernica* share is that, around 1795, they all seem to hit the brick wall of increasing repression. The *Hibernian Magazine*, although it was not forced to close, becomes a much narrower and more reactionary publication, and it also drops all Irish literature, and attacks the United Irishmen, turning its attention to the war in Europe; the *Sentimental and Masonic* declines to a halt in August 1795; while the *Anthologia Hibernica* stops dead at the start of that year. Both the *Monthly Miscellany* and *The Flapper*, although published after 1795, confirm the pattern – unlike the publications of the first half of the decade, both were at pains to present themselves as totally inoffensive and non-political publications, yet both reached to just three issues in the climate of fear and the disruption of communications and normal life.

Some impression of the political climate can be gained from a list of events in this decade: in April 1793 the Volunteers were suppressed; in May 1794 the United Irishmen were also suppressed; April of 1795 saw the establishment of a Militia; in March 1796 the Insurrection Act was passed, permitting curfews and arms searches, and establishing the death penalty for illegal oath-taking; in October of the same year Habeas Corpus was suspended; and in March 1798 martial law was imposed.[18] Across Great Britain and Ireland, Stamp Duty was raised dramatically to discourage publication, and by the end of the century the 1799 Seditious Societies Act required the registration of all presses and founts, inclusion of the printer's name on all publications, and maintenance of full records of all work carried out which could be inspected by Justices of the Peace.[19]

For most of its first ninety years, the story of Irish Literary Magazines is indeed a dreadful one, a provincial Grub Street where piratical titles which took their material direct from English or European originals are difficult to distinguish from their cannibalistic brethren who copied (or simply reprinted) each other. The honourable exceptions, the incidental outpourings of Swift's literary activities in England at one end, or the *Literary Journal* and *Hibernian Magazine* at the other, do little to lift the gloom. It is a story of false starts and deservedly short runs, until the last decade when, mirroring the political and social upheaval all around, new titles spring up at an unprecedented rate, giving voice to new constituencies (see the *Parlour Window*) or developing new formats (*Anthologia Hibernica*); in addition, two of the best magazines of the century (the *Anthologia* and *The Microscope*) were published in this decade. Unfortunately, these journals depended for their contributors and their audience on a world which was about to disappear, and the 1790s were a false dawn, whose promise would not be fulfilled for a generation.

NOTES

1 Feather, *A History*, pp. 85–87.
2 J.H. Jack, 'The Periodical Essayists', in Boris Ford (ed.), *Pelican Guide to English Literature Volume Four* (Harmondsworth, 1957), pp. 217–229.

3 J.C. Beckett, 'Literature in English' in T.W. Moody and W.E. Vaughan (eds), *Oxford New History of Ireland Volume IV* (Oxford, 1986), p. 424.

4 Beckett, 'Literature in English', p. 425.

5 Beckett, 'Literature in English', p. 426.

6 Munter, *The History*, pp. 70–71.

7 Munter, *The History*, p. 72.

8 Beckett, 'Literature in English', pp. 428–429.

9 Beckett, 'Literature in English', p. 431.

10 Feather, *A History*, pp. 110–112.

11 Feather, *A History*, p. 100.

12 Irvin Ehrenpreis, *Swift the Man, His Works and the Age*, II (London, 1962), p. 407.

13 Munter, *The History*, pp. 160–162.

14 Welch, *Oxford Companion*, p. 18.

15 Beckett, 'Literature in English', p. 440.

16 Welch, *Oxford Companion*, pp. 546–547.

17 R.R. Madden, annotation to his copy of *The Flapper* in the library, Queen's University Belfast.

18 R.F. Foster, *Modern Ireland 1600–1972* (London, 1988), p. 604.

19 Feather, *A History*, p. 92.

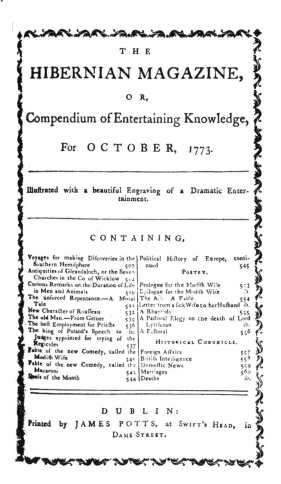

Chapter 3
Irish literary magazines, 1800–1829

Traditionally, the period between the Act of Union and the achievement of Catholic Emancipation has been regarded as something of a hiatus in the course of Irish history, an era of lassitude and aimlessness compared with the years of legislative independence and rebellion which preceded it, or of monster meetings and famine which followed. Barbara Hayley opened her evaluation of the period by saying: 'The most notable features of Ireland at the beginning of the nineteenth century were silence and apathy'.[1] A more recent generation of historians, such as Sean Connolly and George Boyce, has challenged this picture, tracing a series of important events and innovations which lie just below the surface of these apparent doldrums – the shift from tillage to pasturage, the early experiments with a national school system, or far-reaching changes in the structure of policing or the administration of government – and which contain the seeds of the more dramatic events of the mid-nineteenth century. Above all, the 'unfinished business' of Emancipation acted as a logjam on Irish society; as pressure built and built through these years, sectarian bitterness polluted national life, and when the waters finally broke, the effect was purgative. The generation which flourished between Emancipation and the Great Famine was relatively free of the extreme rancour which both preceded and followed it.

As usual, these currents in wider Irish society can be seen reflected in the literary magazines produced. On the one hand, evidence for the feeling of ennui, dislocation and frustration can easily be found, particularly in the titles published in Dublin. For example, see the essay carried across the first two issues of the *Dublin Magazine* (1820), 'Reflections on the Melancholy State of Literature in this Country':

> ...literary discussion has been abandoned, and patronage can no longer be obtained in Ireland...Our booksellers' shops are furnished with works, not of native genius or native manufacture, but imported at exorbitant prices; and we have even waived our privilege of judging these productions by our own standards of taste and feeling; our opinions, like our presses, have been proscribed, and we must import them like any other foreign luxuries.

The phrase about patronage reveals that the author is still thinking in eighteenth-century modes, and from this perspective contemporary Dublin must have seemed greatly faded from the high-point of the Ascendancy. A few years later, issue six of the *Dublin and London Magazine* (August 1825) includes a depressing and depressed account of the long history of failure of Irish literary magazines, which the author ascribes to the lack of support from Irish booksellers, the daunting competition from England, and the fact that nearly all of them were terrible! A year later the editor of *Bolster's Quarterly*, in his 'Introductory

Observations' to the first volume, laments the loss of Irish literary talent abroad since the Union, and claims that 'in Periodical writing, we...have produced absolutely nothing!', before declaring that he is about to make up the lost ground. In her 1987 piece, Hayley asserts that 'In the first three decades of the century, the only kind of magazine to flourish was political or religious', and that 'A few magazines tried to be literary and apolitical, but failed rapidly'.[2] This contrasts with the situation in England; Sullivan describes the period between 1798 and 1825 as that of 'the Romantic vanguard', one of exceptional activity, with some thirty-eight literary magazines started.[3] While some eighteenth-century-type magazines persisted for a while, a completely new standard was being set by newcomers like the *Edinburgh Review* (1802), the *Quarterly Review* (1809) and *Blackwood's Edinburgh Magazine* (1817), all of which would continue for over a century, and would involve writers of a much higher calibre than the denizens of Grub Street.

The ILMs of this period lasted only on average for twenty months, and if we except the three most successful, this lifespan drops to just ten months.[4] At the same time, while none of the magazines of these years fully achieved their promise, it is possible to see in embryo some more positive developments which were to flower so impressively in the next generation. It is true that Dublin lost the initiative at this time (only 50 per cent of the new titles emerged from there, as compared with 80 per cent during the previous century, and 70 per cent in the 1830s), but this was to some extent compensated for by a flourish of new regional titles, including one each in Lurgan and Sligo, two in Cork, and an interesting group of five in Belfast. This period is also marked by a transition in the poetry which appears, which gradually sloughs off the remains of the eighteenth-century manner and embraces Romanticism. And finally, one can catch glimpses in the best of these periodicals, like the *Dublin and London Magazine* and *Bolster's Quarterly*, of the more confidently Irish, Catholic, nationalist and above all popular magazines which would dominate the lower end of the market in the Victorian era. On the technical front, two key inventions emerged in 1798, Lord Stanhope's iron printing press and M. Robert's paper-making machine; in the period under discussion, developments of these inventions would present revolutionary opportunities.[5]

From the group published in Dublin, the two most substantial, the *Dublin Examiner* (1816) and the *Dublin and London Magazine* (1825), will be dealt with separately below; the only other magazine to emerge from Dublin at this time which stands out with any individuality is the *Irish Magazine* (1807), edited by Walter (Watty) Cox. Hayley calls this publication 'outrageously insulting to the administration and to the established church',[6] but while there were many short-lived journals at this time which engaged directly in the political debates around emancipation, many of them blatantly sectarian, this was one of the most significant; it also lay on the boundary between political magazines pure and simple, and the literary journals. However, the *Irish Magazine*'s main claim on posterity is not based on its literary items, which are few in number, and whose only lasting interest is that they exemplify the transition period in Ireland between the pre-Romantic and Romantic modes.

The lack of originality and significance of the remainder of the Dublin titles, and the seriousness with which they approached literature, is indicated by their subtitles: 'Register of History, Literature, the Arts, Science &c.'; 'General Repertory of Politics, Arts, Science, Literature & Miscellaneous Information'; 'Repertory, of Arts, Science, Literature and Miscellaneous Information'; 'Repository of Dramatic, Literary, Political, & Miscellaneous Intelligence'; 'Repertory of Philosophy, Belles Lettres and Miscellaneous Information'. As with the *Irish Magazine*, their sole interest now is in how they allow us to trace the gradual move from pre-Romantic to Romantic styles, as they increasingly focus on Scott, Moore, Byron and Shelley.

Although the group of five titles from Belfast represents the most substantial bloc of journals to be produced outside Dublin up to this point in time, it is hard to make a telling case for assigning them a distinct character. The *Literary and Mathematical Asylum* is too ephemeral a production on which to base any conclusions; and the *Rushlight*, which carries the flame for the radical agenda of the 1790s, is *sui generis* (not least in the way that it refuses to talk down to its readers, and its proto-socialism); the others all share a mild form of nationalism, moderate support for emancipation, and an interest in the Irish language and antiquities, but in this they are no different from their Dublin contemporaries. They do include an occasional piece in or about the Ulster-Scots dialect, but this does not amount to anything resembling an agenda. As a footnote, one innovation which a number of these magazines share is a rejection of the principle of anonymity: the *Belfast Monthly Magazine* and the *Literary and Mathematical Asylum* are the first Irish literary magazines to attach signatures to most of their contributions, while the *Belfast Magazine* and *Literary Journal* carries an article condemning the 'Evils' which arise from anonymity, representing a substantial turnaround from the convention of the previous century which defended anonymity as a protection against bias and outside influence.

In addition, there are a number of regional titles. Again, these are too short-lived and fleeting to draw any meaningful conclusions, beyond pointing out the importance of the *Ulster Magazine* and the *Weekly Selector* as the first Irish literary magazines to be published outside the larger conurbations, with the latter, from Sligo, being the first to emerge west of a line from Limerick to Belfast, a half of the country which has been effectively voiceless up to this point.

It helps to view the sad state of literary publishing in Ireland at this time in broader context, as publishing in the British Isles generally was reeling from the effects of sustained government pressure. Stamp duty was used ruthlessly by a succession of ministries to suppress opposition publications (more or less covert subsidy helped 'friendly' papers to survive); in Ireland 'Foster's Act' of 1784 had raised stamp duty from $\frac{1}{2}$d per copy to 1d, and the duty on advertisements from 2d per advertisement to a swingeing 1 shilling,[7] while in 1798 another penny was added to the stamp duty, and new excise duties were imposed on newsprint. Although English publishers also had to pay duty, and at a higher rate, they received a 20 per cent rebate which was not available to their Irish competitors.[8] Publishers obviously had to pass on these costs to their readers, and the high prices which were sustained throughout this period contributed to the caution and underachievement of the press. Inglis concludes that '1817 was the year in which the Irish press reached the nadir of its fortunes, and fewer people, probably, were reading newspapers in 1830 than in 1800',[9] and quotes a petition from the Dublin printers to

Parliament which claimed that, in 1830, the average sale of an Irish newspaper was only 547 copies, as compared to 3,260 for an English.[10]

This was not the only burden borne by printers and publishers. With increasing levels of education, political stability and personal wealth, demand for paper began to rise exponentially in the last decades of the eighteenth century and this, combined with the inability of existing printing and binding technologies to keep pace with the increased demand (both were still mainly manual processes at the turn of the century), also contributed to increased costs. In response, the first papermaking machine was introduced in 1807, and the steam-powered printing press in 1814, but these, of course, went first to the cutting-edge of contemporary publishing, the big London newspapers, and it took some years for the new technologies to have an impact in Ireland.[11]

In the same way that general historical trends in the period 1800–1829 can be seen as preparatory, laying the foundations upon which more dramatic change will be built by the succeeding generation, it is perhaps emblematic of this generation of periodicals that the three best examples – the *Dublin Examiner* (1816), the *Dublin and London Magazine* (1825), and *Bolster's Quarterly* (1826) – stand out primarily as harbingers of a new kind of Irish literary magazine which would only be fully realised in the 1830s and 1840s. They share most of the characteristics identified regarding the Belfast magazines (moderate nationalism, favourable to the emancipation campaign, and interested in Irish language and antiquities in a superficial and popular way); the only difference is that they take literature slightly more seriously than most of their contemporaries, for example, exploring the possibilities of longer, more thoughtful reviews.

However, the overriding impression from all the literary magazines of these three decades is of promise unfulfilled. None of them lasted for more than a few months, and the standard of original material is fairly modest and easily eclipsed by the reprints of Scott and Byron. But all of them are, firstly, livelier and more engaged with the broader world around them than most of the journals of the eighteenth century, and secondly, forerunners of the more confidently Irish, Catholic and nationalist popular literary magazines which comprise one of the main streams of the Victorian era.

NOTES

1   Barbara Hayley, 'A Reading and Thinking Nation: Periodicals as the Voice of Nineteenth-Century Ireland', in B. Hayley and E. McKay (eds), *300 Years of Irish Periodicals*, Association of Irish Learned Journals (Mullingar, 1987), p. 29.
2   Hayley (1987), 'A Reading and Thinking Nation', pp. 29, 31.
3   Alvin Sullivan (ed.), *British Literary Magazines: The Romantic Age, 1789–1836* (Westport, 1993), 'Preface', p. viii.
4   Hayley attributes the high attrition rate to: a relatively small population, low levels of literacy, a high proportion of Irish speakers, extreme poverty, and bitter political conflict which in turn divided the market – Barbara Hayley, 'Irish Periodicals from the Union to the Nation', in P.J. Drudy (ed.), *Anglo-Irish Studies II* (Bucks, 1976), p. 83.
5   John O Hayden, 'Introduction', to Sullivan (ed.), *British Literary Magazines: The Romantic*

Age, 1789–1836, p. xv.

6 Hayley (1987) 'A Reading and Thinking Nation, p. 31.

7 Brian Inglis, *The Freedom of the Press in Ireland 1784–1841* (London, 1954), p. 110.

8 Inglis, *The Freedom,* pp. 88, 144.

9 Inglis, *The Freedom,* p. 190.

10 Inglis, *The Freedom,* p. 193.

11 Feather, *A History*, pp. 129–134.

Chapter 4
Irish literary magazines, 1830–1849

If earlier scholars were tempted to write off the first thirty years of the nineteenth century in Ireland as dull and unimportant, the historian of the following two decades is in danger of being deafened by the sound of chickens coming home to roost, the whole period being coloured by our knowledge of its catastrophic climax. And while the Great Famine of 1845–1849 is undoubtedly the dominating event of these years, and the one which had the greatest impact on future political and economic development, it should not be forgotten how vibrant and vital were the preceding twenty years. It is during this time that O'Connell bestrides the scene, diverting Irish grievances and political energies away from violent confrontation and into pragmatic negotiation at Westminster for practical reform measures; and, while many of these reforms were half-hearted or ill-conceived, they did bring significant improvements to the lot of the majority of ordinary Irish people. This was the period when the new, increasingly cohesive and confident Catholic nation emerged. However, with the benefit of hindsight we can see all this taking place in the shadow of looming disaster.

When we look at the literary magazines published between 1830 and 1849 there is a strong feeling of the faltering and abortive efforts of previous decades finally coming to fruition, of a culture at last getting into its stride, to the extent that this period could almost be seen as the first Irish literary revival. To begin with, the fertility of the period is shown in the sheer number of new titles which started up, as many in these twenty years as in the whole of the eighteenth century. This fertility to some extent makes up for the short lifespans which most of these titles enjoyed: if we exclude the two great successes of the period, the *Dublin University Magazine* and the *Nation*, the average magazine lasted for only thirteen months; after the onset of the Great Famine no new title (with the exception of the *Cork Magazine*) lasted longer than two or three months, and the *DUM* and *Nation* were the only ones still in production when the blight had passed. More importantly, and although the long march of the general miscellany continues unabated, a number of completely new genres are established in Ireland: Political Magazines, like the *Citizen* and the *Nation*, which rise far above the level of the earlier sectarian rags; the Penny Magazines, good-quality populist titles like the *Dublin Penny Journal* or the *Irish Penny Magazine*; the Victorian Great Reviews, modelled on the *Edinburgh* and *Blackwood's*, such as the *Dublin University Review* and *Quarterly Magazine* and, above all, the *Dublin University Magazine*; and finally, journals which were more specialised, like the various temperance titles or the *Belfast Advertiser* and *Literary Gazette*, and the plain eccentric (see the *Larne Literary* and *Agricultural Journal*). Distribution of these magazines is still largely confined to the traditional centres – 61 per cent are from Dublin, with Belfast and Cork accounting for a further

23 per cent – and, while a few creep out into outlying towns like Larne and Athy, the *Kilrush Magazine*, clinging to the west coast of Clare, is a lonely outpost west of that imaginary dividing line stretching from Limerick to Belfast.

There is a group of miscellaneous titles, difficult to categorise. Two of these (the *Irish Temperance* and *Literary Gazette* (1836), and the *Dublin Journal of Temperance, Science and Literature* (1842–1843)) are primarily propaganda vehicles for the movement but, while their literary elements are of no intrinsic value, they do illustrate a number of important trends: the spread to Ireland of the Victorian moral complex, which saw piety, hard work, abstinence, education and culture as interrelated components of a moral person; and the spread of literacy, as both are clearly aimed at the artisan class. The *Belfast Advertiser and Literary Gazette* (1847) is also experimental, in that it was distributed free of charge. The theory was that if it was free, people would pick it up; the selection of literary extracts from good-quality sources, like the *Cork Magazine*, would encourage them to read it, including the advertisements; this would encourage advertisers to cover the costs of publication, and a virtuous circle would be formed. Unfortunately, Ireland was not quite ready for such entrepreneurship, but the fact that the attempt was made is indicative of the new climate. Finally, the *Larne Literary and Agricultural Journal* (1838–1840), while oddly reminiscent of the *Irish Homestead*, is finally *sui generis*, an ego-trip by an eccentric individual, obsessively local and a fascinating glimpse into the spread of reading clubs and literary activity into the most unlikely corners of the country.

A more cohesive class of political magazine emerged at this time: more militant, but less sectarian; less tied to narrow factions and campaigns, and with a broad national vision; and at least attempting to speak to a mass audience. The first of these was the *Citizen*, which sailed under various guises from 1839 to 1843. The refreshing breadth of its nationalism was signalled in the first issue – the need for a railway system, the iniquities of the Grand Juries, the limitations of the franchise were all discussed, alongside a ballad, stories and book reviews, to be joined in later issues by a serialised play and sheet music for 'native' tunes. It rejected the 'Mock-Irish Works' of the previous generation, while reviewing or publishing the best of its contemporaries – Moore, Carleton, Griffin, Banim and Madden. It also served as a nursery for Thomas Davis, before he founded Ireland's most important and influential political magazine, the *Nation*.

Starting in 1842, the *Nation* was also to change its name in order to survive, which it did (after a sort) for the rest of the century; however, its creative life was really over by 1845. This version of the magazine, under Charles Gavan Duffy, John Dillon and Thomas Davis, was a phenomenon: despite costing 6d, it was soon selling 10,000 copies a month;[1] it embodied the ideals of Young Ireland; it produced the most successful combination of topical news and political coverage with complementary literary material; and it helped form the political consciousness of a generation. It also

created a literature of its own, with hearty prose and stirring ballads single-mindedly aimed at inflaming Irish patriotism…an endless stream of poems perhaps too militant to be great literature, but fired by a spirit that lifts them above the hack verse of…the preceding magazines.[2]

The *Nation* was both more topical and more engaged than its predecessors; in no sense were the likes of Duffy or Dillon mere spectators of the political scene.

Of the remaining political magazines of this period, two (the *Irish National Magazine and Weekly Journal* (1846), and the *Irish Tribune* (1848)) were failures which ran for only a matter of weeks each, and the third, the *Clubbist* (1849) was, as its subtitle suggests, simply a selection of work from the radical nationalist press (the *Nation*, the *Felon*, etc.)

The genre of the Great Review was well-established in Britain and, given the habitual deference of the Irish upper-classes to anything which crossed the Irish Sea, many an aspirational library table sported a copy of *Blackwood's* or *Fraser's*. No serious attempt had been made to establish an Irish counterpart, but now the time was right. In January 1833, two new titles were launched; firstly, the *Dublin University Review and Quarterly Magazine*, which was of good quality but a little scholarly and timid, and folded after only eighteen months. At exactly the same moment, however, there also emerged the other colossus of these years, a journal as important as the *Nation* in its own field; this was the *Dublin University Magazine*, which was to have an unbroken run of forty-four years. The title was a deliberate deception, as it was never intended to be a mere university publication; on the one hand it consciously copied many of the characteristics of its models (the editorial personae, some of the features), but its success seems to have been built on an apparently incongruous mix of relentless, conservative unionism (which no doubt reassured many at those upper-class library tables in Britain, as well as in Dublin), with an equally persistent championing of the best in Irish literature. So articles in defence of the Orange Order and attacking Repeal appeared alongside the work of Mrs Hall, Le Fanu, Mangan, Carleton and Lever; Hayley claims that 'it established that an Irish literary world did exist'.[3] There were other factors which Hayley glosses over, which contributed equally to its success: the ability of most of its editors (Butt, Lever, Le Fanu); the high production values; and the backing of the major publishing house of Curry (undercapitalisation at times seems almost an obligatory quality of Irish literary magazines). Also, it cornered its market in Ireland, and was to suffer no serious rivals.

Yet another genre which emerged in fresh form in Ireland during these years was the Penny Magazine,[4] and it was to be dominated by three titles. The *Dublin Penny Journal* (1832–1836) was the first and greatest. The original editors maintained a very high standard for the first year, with scholarly articles, original material and a light touch which (for the times) was not unduly patronising (it is important to remember that most of the popular periodicals of the century were produced for the masses by their 'betters', and a certain whiff of paternalism is common). The quality and quantity of illustrations and the proudly mass-market approach give it a place as the third ground-breaking magazine of the era, after the *DUM* and the *Nation*. Hardy, although he gets a very rough ride from Hayley,[5] carried on its success, at least in his own, nakedly commercial, terms; he took it downmarket, as was his wont, but he maintained a very high circulation,[6] and secured for it a longer run than any of its competitors. Perhaps one small step down in quality was the *Irish Penny Magazine* (1833–1834). Lover's stories are not as good as Carleton's, the standard of scholarship is a little lower, and the whole is less lively and attractive; however it was the *DPJ*'s only real competition. The last in this triumvirate of innovative popular magazines is the *Irish Penny Journal* (1840–1841), again a little weaker than its predecessor, although it is saved from obscurity by the quality of its illustrations and the sprinkling of items from Mrs Hall, Lover, Carleton and the editor, Petrie. Despite being modest and derivative, the *Belfast Penny Journal* (1845–1846) is redeemed by sharing the distinguishing characteristics of all these northern magazines, a well-developed sense of its own place (embodied in poems from, and biographical sketches of, the 'Bards' of Antrim), and a broad-minded liberalism. Finally, the *Fireside Magazine* (1848–1849) is very light-weight, and can perhaps be seen as a prototype for the kind of sentimental publication with which James Duffy was to dominate the lower end of the market in the 1850s and 1860s.

Finally, there is a selection of general miscellanies. The dreary procession of minor titles continues with the *Ulster Monthly Magazine* (1845), of which little can be said since it only managed two issues; the *Dublin Monthly Magazine* (1830), a new version of the old 'cut and paste' approach, with little original material and its 'book reviews' which make exceptionally free use of quotation; and the *Dublin Literary Journal* (1843–1846), which is another lightweight, as happy to reprint pieces by Shelley and Southey as by any Irish writer. Not much better are the couple of regional magazines, whose only real importance lies in their provenance, the *Athy Literary Magazine* (1837–1838), with its oddly anachronistic features by or about Edgeworth and Goldsmith, and the *Kilrush Magazine*, poor quality and very short-lived, which originated in the small town twenty-five miles west of Ennis.

Not all the general miscellanies of the period were as bad. In fact, the *Cork Magazine* (1847–1848) is rather good, with a sophisticated level of literary analysis and a clear idea of the failings which needed to be confronted if a mature national literature was to develop, a vision frustrated by the shortness of its run. The *Irish Monthly Magazine* (1832–1834) could be seen as a successor to the *Dublin Literary Gazette and National Magazine* but its more strongly nationalist line and greater concentration on politics limit its importance as a literary magazine to the articles on subjects like copyright and censorship. The *Ulster Magazine* (1830–1831) is a very good publication, which cultivates a sense of its own locality, making it stand out from most of the titles produced further south. Here the principles of 1782 and 1798 are still celebrated, and a liberalism rejecting the excesses of both unionism and nationalism is developed; there are a number of substantial and serious articles on topics like the freedom of the press, and the stories and poems have a concrete grounding in their locality which goes some way toward compensating for their shortcomings in purely literary terms. Finally, the best of the miscellanies was the *Dublin Literary Gazette* (1830), in which the traditional Irish literary magazine, that ragbag of novelties, biographical sketches and advertisements, evolves into a new, more respectable manifestation, better-suited to the new era (though never completely shaking off its origins). In truth, the *DLG* can often be a little dull, and this is not completely offset by its 'stop-press' tone, generated by the snippets of works-in-progress and reviews of the latest publications. After five months it metamorphosed into the more political, more conservative but (in its literary content, at least) not radically different *Dublin Literary Gazette and National Magazine* (1830–1831). When Hardy took over as editor, the usual decline in quality resulted.

As with the rest of Irish society, in the literary magazines of the period 1830–1849 there is the unmistakable sense of brakes having been let off after a long interval of frustrating anticipation, only to rush headlong into the devastation of the Great Famine. Of all the dozens of Irish literary magazines examined so far only two, the *DUM* and the *Nation*, were still being published after the Famine, and both of them were much diminished. Unlike the newspapers and pamphlets of the day, the literary magazines mostly have very little to say about the holocaust which Ireland suffered between 1845 and 1849, but this is usually because they sank before they had much of a chance. The *Nation*, of course, railed against what was happening, but even the conservative, unionist *DUM* made impassioned appeals to England to send its ships and men to help.[7]

It is important in all this not to lose sight of the achievements of the golden years between 1830 and 1845. Not only were a record number of new titles being launched in a variety of stimulating new genres – as well as the less-than-stimulating general miscellany – but their distribution and sales were wider than ever before. The opening editorial to the *Ulster Monthly Magazine*, in January 1845, was claiming that at the close of the eighteenth century there were only 40,000 literate people in Ireland, yet by 1836 Hardy was claiming a circulation of 12,000 for the *Dublin Penny Journal*; in 1843 the *Nation* (perhaps more credibly) claimed sales of 10,000; and in the same year even the *DUM* (under Lever) was claiming a circulation of 4,000. Even a lesser title like the *Irish National Magazine* was being sold in thirty-three towns around Ireland, including Ballina, Ennis and Sligo, as well as in Glasgow, Liverpool, London and Manchester. At the same time, some abortive expressions of greater regional confidence were emerging. The *Larne Literary and Agricultural Journal* was reporting with interest literary and educational achievements in Doagh and Ballynure, while the *Athy Literary Magazine* was being sold in Athy itself, Ballitore, Carlow, Kilcullen, Monasterevin and Naas.

Any survey of the period must, however, be dominated by the two greatest achievements of nineteenth-century Irish literary magazines, the *DUM* and the *Nation*. Each became legendary, cultivating both a literary coterie of contributors and a large and loyal readership, while both became the first Irish literary magazines to unashamedly hold their own against the best productions of England and Scotland. Equally revealing about the lack of depth and maturity in the newly confident Irish national literary scene, this 'first' Irish Literary Revival, is the fact that neither suffered any real domestic competition during their long runs, and nor did they inspire any successors.

NOTES

1   Brian Inglis, 'The Press', in R.B. McDowell (ed.), *Social Life in Ireland 1800–45* (Dublin, 1957), p. 110. However, to put this in context, it must be remembered that in England, Sullivan gives a peak sales figure for Dickens's *All the Year Round* of 300,000!
2   Barbara Hayley, 'Irish Periodicals from the Union to the *Nation*', in P.J. Drudy (ed.), *Anglo-Irish Studies II* (Bucks, 1976), pp. 104–105.
3   Hayley (1976), 'Irish Periodicals', p. 94.

4   There were of course far more of these than I examine here. My sample is representative of the most significant examples, and avoids both what Hayley calls 'the most vulgar religious periodicals' and 'bottom-of-the-market satirical squibs' (Hayley (1976), 'Irish Periodicals', pp. 98, 102).
5   Hayley (1976), 'Irish Periodicals', p. 100.
6   Hardy claimed 40,000 copies per week; even if we assume this was exaggerated, he must surely have picked a figure which his contemporaries would not have found ludicrous.
7   D. George Boyce, *Nineteenth-Century Ireland: The Search for Stability*, New Gill History of Ireland 5 (Dublin, 1990), p. 114.

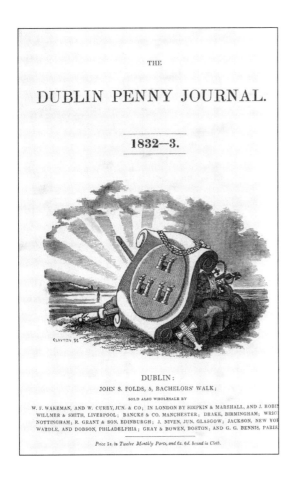

Chapter 5
Irish literary magazines, 1850–1869

The period following the Famine and the Young Ireland revolt has a very similar timbre to that which followed the 1798 Rebellion and the Act of Union. Superficially, it is another doldrums period, one of fragmentation and exhaustion when, politically, little of moment was attempted or achieved. Closer examination, however, reveals that, as in the first three decades of the century, under the surface profound social and economic changes were under way, changes which laid the foundations of the more dramatic political upheavals of the decades immediately following, and which determined their character.

The Irish literary magazines of the period, especially when compared with the best of the previous generation, are a disappointing lot. Hayley says that the 'outward-looking and self-expressive' tendencies of the earlier period are reversed, that there was a 'breakup of all patterns of Irish life and literature...the previous clearly defined stream of periodicals is dispersed...the main trend...was specialism', and that 'there was no single, unified voice abroad in the land'.[1] Surveying the wider literary scene, Flanagan asserts that 'the decades that stretch between the collapse of the Young Ireland movement and the literary revival of the 1890s fail to present a coherent cultural pattern'; this was a time when 'the catholic hierarchy and the protestant ascendancy were disinclined to nurture nationalist sentiment, and nationalism was therefore deprived of that intellectual...leadership'. 'Accordingly,' he concludes, 'there was no climate of opinion favourable to the creation of a new literary movement'.[2]

When we turn back to the literary magazines of this time, a number of trends are obvious. The bubbling fertility of 1830–1849 has gone off the boil; while the average lifespan has increased slightly (to twenty-one months, when we exclude the three longest-running titles, as opposed to thirteen months earlier), the total number of new titles is down by around 25 per cent.[3] More importantly, the innovation of the earlier period, the introduction into Ireland of new genres, has gone, and the quality of the individual titles is noticeably lower; the sense of breakup and dispersal noted by Hayley is all too obvious. As with the previous two decades, only two new magazines begun in the period 1850–1869 were to last beyond it: the *Shamrock* (1866–1922, in various manifestations) and *Kottabos* (1869–1895); neither had anything like the stature or impact of the *Dublin University Magazine* or the *Nation*. The stream of political magazines continues, but is much abated; the stimulating Penny Magazines degenerate into vehicles for Victorian sentimentality; and only one new Great Review is published. The remaining titles were devoted to specialisms of various sorts, and were usually as unadventurous as they were short-lived. The only small innovation of the period comes in the form of the *College Magazine* (1857–1858) and *Kottabos*, which, driven more by the students than by the college authorities, were early harbingers of the University Magazines which would be one of the twentieth century's most fertile sub-genres.

Another symptom of the gradual narrowing of these years is the trend in distribution. In 1800–1829 nearly 50 per cent of new magazines came from outside Dublin; in 1830–1849 this fell to under 40 per cent; and by 1850–1869 it had declined again, to less than 30 per cent. As in those two earlier periods, only one title comes from west of that invisible line running from the south-west of the country to the north-east, Tralee's *Kerry Magazine* (1854–1856). Finally, the magazines of this period gave up boasting about their wide distribution and high sales, although it is impossible to say whether this was due to increased self-confidence, or to embarrassment at the figures; only the *Irish Literary Gazette* makes a public claim (in the editorial to the third issue), of 10,000 copies sold.

The lively and occasionally stimulating Penny Magazines of the 1830s and 1840s deteriorated in these years into cosier, more sentimental magazines, aimed at family and 'fireside' reading. There are some independent instances, for example the short-lived *Dublin Journal* of 1858; the king of the Fireside Magazine, however, was the Dublin publisher of tracts, missals and pamphlets, James Duffy. Between 1847 and 1864 he published a handful of journals which, while the titles varied slightly, were in effect the same magazine in subtly different forms – *Duffy's Irish Catholic Magazine*, *Duffy's Hibernian Magazine*, *Duffy's Hibernian Sixpenny Magazine*, or the (lavishly) *Illustrated Dublin Journal* – and through these he 'invented a new kind of cosy family Catholicism'.[4] The tone of these publications was relentlessly cheerful and pious, and the literary standards woeful; their most lasting contribution is to the iconography of nineteenth-century Catholic nationalism, their covers swamped under illustrations of mitres, shadowy bards and stout blackthorns supporting even stouter peasants. (Of course, they also mirrored a wider trend in Victorian Britain – see the *Family Herald* (London, 1842) or *Leisure Hour* (published by the Religious Tract Society in London, 1852).) With the repeal of paper and stamp duties at the end of the 1850s,[5] the *Illustrated* led the way with large and striking illustrations and greater investment in paper quality, and was followed by Richard Pigott's *Shamrock*, which continued in the same vein and to the same decorative standard (for example, illustrations by Gustave Doré). The pride of this new journal, so far as contents went, was its stories, from Carleton, Kickham and, most successfully, William Lynam. After about a decade the original owner sold out to Parnell, and the *Shamrock* evolved into a more political beast.

Apart from the *Shamrock*, the representatives of the political literary magazine in this period are few in number, short in duration, and their literary standards are low in the extreme; more seriously, when compared with the productions of the previous two decades, they are insipid and uninspiring. The *Celt* (1857–1858) and the *Gael* (1861) are lacking in direction and identifiable literary style; they are poor rivals to even the faded output from the *Nation* at this time.

The situation with the Great Reviews is even sadder: the *Irish Quarterly Review* is a first-class journal, but its strengths cannot mask the fact that it is the only Great Review to join the old warhorse, the *Dublin University Magazine*, during these two decades. Its reviews are wide-ranging and thorough (if a little lacking in incisiveness for modern tastes), the standard of scholarship is high, and the bearing of the magazine is confident and totally free from provincialism and introspection; for the depth of its reviews and the seriousness of its biography, its passing after nine years is to be lamented.

Hayley claimed that the curse of these years was specialism, a narrowing of focus and ambition, and the remaining magazines of the years 1850–1869 bear her out, being aimed at extremely limited audiences. In the same article, Hayley identifies one of these specialisms, and the most productive, as 'the local magazine of more than local interest'.[6] Into this category, I would place *Francis Davis, the Belfastman's Journal*, the *Northern Magazine* and the *Ulster Magazine*, all published in Belfast. The first of these, edited by Francis Davis, is worthy but dull, and lacks a clear vision in either literature or politics; the *Northern*, edited by some students from the Queen's College is not much better; while the last has only the leavening of dialect material by David Herbison to recommend it. Similarly, the *Kerry Magazine* is never more than competent, while the *Harp* is marked by its lack of originality or ambition, and memorable only for the editorial in which it hopes to become a Catholic *Dublin University Magazine*!

In the remaining titles the focus narrows to a ludicrous extent. *Agatha* (1861–1862), while it attempts a little anodyne criticism and conventional versifying, exists primarily to promote the temperance movement. Both the protean *Irish Literary Gazette* and the *Irish Literary Advertiser* are trade papers, reams of advertisements and lists of newly published books fleshed out with perfunctory articles and literary gossip; although the *Gazette* makes more of an effort to pretend to be a real magazine, the true importance of both lies in the insight they give into the ongoing development of the book trade in Ireland, and the adverts and lists may be of use to the specialist social or economic historian, or the history of the book in Ireland. Finally, the last two specialist journals at least in some way point to new options for the future. Although the *College Magazine* (1857–1858) did not live long enough to have any lasting impact, the sort of magazine it hinted at emerged a decade later in *Kottabos*, which had the distinguished contributors (O'Grady, Graves, Wilde, at the start of their careers) and the financial backing to produce the first genuine Irish example of the University Magazine. More independent of the college, directed more by the students and their tastes, than earlier college periodicals, in its deliberate élitism and disregard for either established contemporary literary taste or sales, it foreshadowed not only the flood of University Magazines which would continue throughout the next century, but also the Little Magazine, the dominant twentieth-century genre, which was arriving in Ireland just as *Kottabos* was expiring.

After the excitement and achievements of the literary magazines of the age of O'Connell, the period under review can only be a disappointment. Although the *Irish Quarterly Review*, the *Illustrated Dublin Journal* and *Kottabos* are all worth skimming, none of them even approaches the quality or importance of the two great survivors of the previous generation, the *DUM* and the *Nation*, which, though they were still being published, were both much diminished in stature. More damning is the fact that it is not hard to think of half a dozen lesser titles from the 1830s and 1840s (including the earlier *Dublin Literary Gazette*, the *Ulster Magazine*, and both the *Dublin* and the *Irish* Penny Journals) which one would rather read. At the same time, if we disregard the tentative forays into University Magazines, no new genres were introduced into the country. Even sales do not seem to have increased as much as could have been hoped with the abolition of restrictive duties. Apart from a few flickering candles, activity was increasingly centred on the capital, and even the two longest-running titles (the *Shamrock* and *Kottabos*) were far from being trail-blazers. In this, these periodicals once again reflect and embody their time, perfectly mirroring its lack of vision or cohesion, of innovation or achievement. Partly this was due to a loss of their English market. During the century, Irish writers and publishers had come to depend on a substantial export market to the bigger island; but the horror of the Famine and its aftermath made it impossible, for a few decades at least, for the English to see Ireland as the picturesque and colourful land of their earlier imaginings. Indeed, in this period it was not merely the English political class which turned its back on Ireland, and it was to be some time before Irish writers could themselves produce a new and coherent literary programme.[7] In addition, it was during these years that English magazines became a juggernaut against which it was very difficult for provincial competitors to make any stand.[8]

NOTES

1   Barbara Hayley 'Irish Periodicals from the Union to the *Nation*', in P.J. Drudy (ed.), *Anglo-Irish Studies II* (Bucks, 1987), pp. 41, 42.

2   Thomas Flanagan, 'Literature in English, 1801–91', in W.E. Vaughan (ed.), *A New History of Ireland, V: Ireland under the Union I, 1801–70* (Oxford, 1989), p. 509.

3   Although Sullivan does not cover many Irish literary magazines, it must be noted that in his third volume, *British Literary Magazines: The Victorian and Edwardian Age, 1837–1913* (Westport, 1984), he does not consider a single Irish title from these two decades worthy of coverage.

4   Hayley (1987), 'Irish Periodicals', p. 42.

5   Stamp duty went in 1855, paper duties in 1861 (Sullivan, *British Literary Magazines*, volume three, p. xv).

6   Hayley (1987), 'Irish Periodicals', p. 42.

7   Flanagan, 'Literature in English, 1801–91', p. 509.

8   Sullivan quotes the staggering figure for the total number of English periodicals during the Victorian period of over fifty thousand individual titles (Sullivan, *British Literary Magazines*, volume three, p. xv).

Chapter 6
Irish literary magazines, 1870–1891

The Irish literary magazines of the period 1870–1891 contradict one of my implicit theses in this work, that there is a strong correlation – however difficult it might be to prove direct causation – between the level of political activity in the country, and the level of cultural activity, and so the vitality of the literary magazines. Unlike the late eighteenth century, or the 1830s, the resurrection of Irish politics in the 1870s and 1880s did not produce a corresponding surge in cultural activity, and certainly as regards Irish literary magazines, these decades see them slump to their lowest level in more than a century. Without further, and much more detailed study, it is difficult to suggest why this period should be different.

If the journals produced between 1850 and 1869 were disappointing when compared to the glories of the previous generation, they now slump even further into disunity and lack of either achievement or relevance. Thomas Flanagan's assertion quoted in Chapter 5 about the lack of any 'coherent cultural pattern' rings ever more true as this period progresses. The two writers whom Flanagan nominates as most representative of their time are Kickham, author of *Knocknagow* (1873), a pious, sentimental, pastoral novel, poorly written but full of detail and bitter Anglophobia, and Emily Lawless, whose novel *Hurrish* (1886), although full of genuine affection for the people, is concerned to show us a once happy, organic community shattered by the political and financial ambitions of demagogues. Both writers embody the myths of their own communities, one identifying the Irish 'nation' with its Catholic population, the other showing a fundamentally decent (if gullible) people who would live happily with their social superiors if undisturbed by troublemakers. Flanagan's third exemplar is the quixotic figure of Standish O'Grady, inspired to convey both what he saw as the heroic history of his country and the poetry in which it was recorded. O'Grady's work is an incoherent triumph of the imagination which led future generations to regard him as 'the father of the revival'.[1]

The average lifespan of the Irish literary magazines produced during these two decades (if we exclude a couple of obviously anomalous titles) has declined to a pitiful ten months; the number of new titles emerging is lower than at any time since the 1780s; and there are precious few signs of innovation or originality. Again, as in earlier periods, only two magazines emerged between 1870 and 1892 to live beyond the latter date: the *Irish Monthly Magazine* (1873–1954) and *Hermathena* (founded 1873). Although they are among the longest-running Irish magazines and were massively successful on their own terms, both allowed only a marginal role to literature and had little wider impact. As for the other titles, there are usually only one or two examples of each genre, making it difficult to draw any meaningful wider conclusions, and the individual journals are not distinguished in themselves. The picture in terms of distribution is even narrower – all these titles come from Dublin, making this the longest period since 1790 to have no representation from the provinces.

The closest thing to an innovation in terms of genre, *Hermathena* is Ireland's first real academic publication, produced by (and largely for) the fellows of Trinity College and concentrating on detailed examination of the classics, philosophy and theology. As such, it is an interesting sign of the development of journals in Ireland, and of the increasing sophistication of at least a certain section of the market. Unfortunately, for our purposes, for the first thirty-five or so years it largely ignores contemporary literature – in the decade before the First World War it dips its toe into the odd article on early Irish, and it is another twenty-five years before poetry makes a regular appearance.

A small cluster of periodicals whose focus is primarily religious also feature literary material in this period: the *Irish Young Man's Journal* – Protestant and extremely ephemeral; the *Irish Monthly Magazine* – an extremely important and popular Catholic title, which ran for over eighty years but for which literature (despite a sprinkling of prestigious names) was little more than superficial top-dressing; and the *Lyceum* which, although again primarily of 'Catholic interest', regularly reviewed new books and was open to literature from other countries. None of these, however, rely remotely on their literary content for their importance.

The final stage in the decline of nineteenth-century popular magazines in Ireland, from the lively penny papers of the 1830s, through to the more sickly Fireside Magazines of the 1850s, reaches its nadir here, from which point popular magazines in Ireland largely bid adieu to any relationship with the serious literature of their country. The two representatives from this period are the *Irish Monthly Illustrated Journal*, a lightweight vehicle for gossip and entertainment thinly leavened with the occasional poem, and *Irish Pleasantry and Fun*, a strange attempt to revive the popular story magazines of a generation earlier, which unfortunately also relied on the same material – Carleton, Lover and Banim.

Two journals emerged in these years embodying the Ascendancy views expressed in works such as those of Lawless: *Now-a-Days*, a substantial, if rather stolid, publication whose stirring tales of derring-do in far-flung corners of the Empire now seem almost as naïve as their hopelessly out-of-touch attempts to engage with contemporary Ireland, and the *Monitor*, an equally handsome but even more vapid production.

Only one Great Review appeared to cash in on the recent demise of the *DUM*. Although a fairly pale shadow of its inspiration, the *Dublin University Review* is nevertheless easily the best Irish literary magazine of its day. Its wide range and open mind is extremely refreshing, literature makes up a higher percentage of its contents than of any of its peers and – although is not much of a compliment – the standard of the material reproduced is also higher. Forward-looking (pieces from young writers who would soon bestride the stage) while maintaining a sense of respect for the previous generation (Davis, Ferguson), the *DUR* was also open to foreign literatures and mixed creative writing with wider cultural coverage and politics more naturally and to better effect than any of the competition. Finally, it was only the first of many Irish literary magazines in which W.B. Yeats was to try to directly intervene to influence the development of public taste and build a new paradigm for Irish literature. His hand is evident in some of the material selected (for example the piece by Mohani Chatterji), and after the depressing parade of lesser journals in these years, is a promise of much better to come.

Even the lean years after the Act of Union were more fruitful for Irish literary magazines than the period under discussion. The field is utterly fragmented and lacking in vision; the best that can perhaps be said for these periodicals is that they faithfully mirror their times. There is no sense of dialogue, on any level, between *Hermathena*, *Now-a-Days* and the *Irish Monthly Magazine*; they occupy entirely disparate and divorced worlds. The Ascendancy Magazines, seen in a sympathetic light, are poignant reminders of a doomed tribe, with their vision of a world where everything is falling into ruin, but quietly and courteously, where changes are probably for the worse but are at least slow, of 'the long late afternoon of the ascendancy'.[2] Perhaps it is sufficiently damning to note that the most prominent names to appear regularly in these titles are the non-Ascendancy likes of T.C. Irwin, Lady Wilde and, especially, Katherine Tynan and Rosa Mulholland. The pseudo-historical myth-making of Standish O'Grady, and the first publications by W.B. Yeats at least offer a hopeful glimpse into the future.

NOTES

1   Thomas Flanagan, 'Literature in English, 1801–91', in W.E. Vaughan (ed.), *A New History of Ireland, V: Ireland under the Union I 1801–70* (Oxford, 1989), p. 518.
2   Flanagan, 'Literature in English, 1801–91', p. 514.

Chapter 7
Irish literary magazines, 1892–1922

This is the second golden age of Irish literary magazines, the period of greatest fecundity and innovation since before the Great Famine, and it is grounded in two, overlapping and interlinked, movements in Irish society: the Irish Literary Revival, and the revival of militant Irish nationalism after the shock waves following Parnell's death began to subside. The titles produced range from platforms for the creators of a new theatre, through political journals with a cultural aspect, and manifestations of the growing power and ambition of the Catholic Church, to an 'All Poetry Journal'. Almost all of them share the same underlying goals: to investigate what it means to be Irish, to inculcate in Irish people a new pride in their culture and history, and to lay before them a range of models of how that Irishness should look in the future. Accordingly, the new titles of these decades largely fall into two camps, which we may call Literary Revival and Political Revival, while never overlooking the amount of 'leakage' between the two (at the most basic level, the same names – Pearse, Russell, Bigger, Stephens, Yeats – are liberally sprinkled through both camps while, more profoundly, they share the same themes and vision).

After the prolonged decline of the previous thirty or forty years, the snowballing level of activity of the new generation is exhilarating. It starts slowly in the 1890s with just three new titles, but each of these is important, both in its own right, and as the advance guard of a new development in Irish literary magazines (*Irish Homestead, Shan Van Vocht, Beltaine*). They prepared the way for the outburst of Literary Revival titles in the first five years of the new century, starting in January 1900 when, for the first time since the days of Young Ireland, the educated, national-minded citizen could choose from four literary periodicals in simultaneous publication (*Homestead, Beltaine*, the *Journal of the National Literary Society* and the *All Ireland Review*). This wave reached its peak around the end of 1904, when no fewer than eight titles – *Homestead*, the *Journal of the National Literary Society, All Ireland Review, Samhain, St. Stephen's*, the new *Dublin Penny Journal, Dana* and *Uladh* – could be found in the bookshops. Even though there was then a slight decline, at no time throughout this thirty-year period was the choice restricted to less than three or four magazines, a situation which again had not obtained since the 1830s and 1840s.

Not only were there more titles emerging, but they were also living longer; using the same calculation as for previous periods (a simple average, but minus the longest surviving, and slightly anomalous, publications) we see that average lifespan has risen from ten to thirty months. (The three excluded are *Studies*, the *Catholic Book Bulletin*, and the *Irish Homestead*; none of these was primarily literary, and all had their existence subsidised, or at least heavily supported, by cohesive outside bodies. As ever, the less literary a title, the longer it is likely to thrive.) The rate at which new magazines were emerging is at its highest since the 1840s. This level of activity also allowed for considerable diversity; for the first time in two generations, there could be more than one title in a particular genre in publication at the same time, and the resulting competition seems to have spurred editors to try to individuate their journals. Finally, for the first time since the *Ulster Magazine* of the 1860s, we see Irish literary magazines appearing other than in Dublin; this period sees one title from Athlone, one from Cork, and no fewer than three magazines published in Belfast (while the *All Ireland Review* started its life in Kilkenny).

The vitality and innovation can also be seen on a deeper level, in the revitalisation of important genres, and the introduction of completely new ones. If we exclude those titles too individual to group (such as the *Catholic Book Bulletin*, or the *Irish Review* of 1922), three clear genres emerge: College Magazines, Political Revival, and Literary Revival; each takes significant new directions in this period. There have been magazines associated in some way with universities in Ireland since at least the *Dublin University Magazine*; *Studies* and *St. Stephen's*, however, are different. The first marks the emergence of the more serious and narrowly-focused academic journal, while the latter is a new type of student magazine, less fettered by the authorities, produced by and for the students themselves (it also proclaims its kinship with the student magazines of later decades by having been suppressed by the authorities for getting too far out of their control). Under the Political Revival heading, we find the most serious and successful attempts at promoting a cultural nationalist agenda since the heyday of the *Nation*, reaching its apogee in the first *Irish Review* (1911–1914). The most significant innovation of these years, however, is to be found amongst the Literary Revival titles; *Beltaine* is the first Irish example of a Little Magazine, a type which utterly dominates the Irish literary magazines of the twentieth century, and so deserves fuller definition and discussion.[1]

The origins of the Little Magazine seem to lie in the United States. There were a few false starts in the mid-nineteenth century, including Emerson's *Dial* (1840–44), but they really took off in the last decade of that century and the first decade of the twentieth. By the end of the First World War there were dozens, including *Poetry*, *Voices* and Margaret Anderson's *Little Review*, from which the term Little Magazine seems to be derived. Already in this first flush we can find the three underlying phenomena which have found expression in the Little Magazines of every country – the avant garde in art; political radicalism, particularly of a left-wing or libertarian hue (in Ireland, this usually took the form of a radical, conservative irredentism); and regionalism, the urge of areas like the American Midwest to free themselves from cosmopolitan domination (the Revival project to create a respected culture away from London and Paris fits this model, as does *Uladh*'s abortive gesture of Ulster regionalism). As by-products of that vast phenomenon known as Modernism, and of its many sub-movements (Symbolism, Imagism), these Little Magazines embodied the principles of the sects which spawned them and acted as manifestos, falling into two broad camps: the explicit, tied to a particular movement and typically deliberately calculated to cause shock and outrage (a classic example is Tristan Tzara's *Dada* magazine); and those publications whose programmes were more subtle and expressed implicitly. These created 'a comprehensive aesthetic environment in which new developments in writing and the visual arts compound to distil an attitude, a distinctive graphic and typographic complex'.[2] A typical example is the *Yellow Book*, published in England in 1894.

Another way of looking at this new type of magazine is as a kind of privatisation of publishing, a fragmented new mode more in keeping with the new century than the decidedly public Great Reviews which held sway in the Victorian era, the obverse of their seriousness and occasional solemnity. The Little Magazines, with their (deliberately) limited but (supposedly) discriminating readership, were more specialised than those they replaced, and often determined to bring the various arts together, combining poetry, layout, typefaces and illustrations to make a unified artistic statement. Obviously they varied a great deal, but the new magazines were usually physically smaller than the standard nineteenth-century production: their rise saw the gradual emergence of the A5 format as the standard. They were also little in that they generally had much smaller circulations, minute bank balances and shorter lifespans. There are lots of possible reasons for this, including the fact that anything so intimately tied to fashion must die when the fashion changes; the editors' lack of, and disdain for, commercial sense; their consequent lack of hard cash; lack of interest among the general population; quarrelling and ego clashes among the editorial staff (none of whom would be professionals); the fact that most editors are artists who will fold a project and move on the instant they feel staleness or repetition creeping in; and finally censorship or persecution, though these have been surprisingly rare in Ireland, at least as regards purely literary publications. The obverse of this is that they frequently have ludicrously large-scale ambitions, a sense of their own uniqueness and of their mission to nurture literary talent in a subtler and more vital fashion than the large-scale, commercial press is capable of. Consequently most have an air of arrogance which is usually a direct expression of the editor's own, necessarily forceful, personality.

Taking into consideration the role they play, 'avant garde magazines' might be a more accurate description. This leaves the bigger magazines and reviews as the rear guard, less responsive (if not openly hostile) to the latest developments, or simply unaware of their existence. It is only after the Little Magazines have broken the ice that the more self-important reviews will accept new writers and movements. This division of roles became established very early in the twentieth century, with the Little Magazines as the recognised arbiters of taste and the accepted route of entry for new writers. In 1946 Hoffman, Allen and Ulrich estimated that these magazines first published some 80 per cent 'of our most important post-1912 critics, novelists, poets and storytellers',[3] and this is a role they still play today. They illustrate the importance of these Little Magazines thus:

Hemingway publishes his first story in *The Double Dealer* in 1922. Assume that the editor and a few other people read this story and like it. These people talk enthusiastically of the story and perhaps twice as many read the next Hemingway offering. Soon many admirers are talking – a snowball is rolling in the advance guard. A half-dozen Little Magazines are printing Hemingway stories and he has several thousand readers. An obscure, noncommercial press in Paris publishes his first thin volume, *Three Stories and Ten Poems*. The snowball rolls into the Scribner's office. Finally in 1926 comes *The Sun Also Rises*.[4]

The biggest and most fertile of our groupings, the Literary Revival Magazines, kicks off most suitably in 1899 with *Beltaine* – Ireland's first Little Magazine, the first of a number of titles to be associated with that other great innovation, the Irish Literary Theatre, the first of a series of dabblings in magazine editing by W.B. Yeats – a clear harbinger for the new century; its immediate English contemporaries are the *Yellow Book* (1894) and the *Savoy* (1896). *Beltaine* is the first of a cluster of Little Magazines which orbit around the figure of Yeats in these years. *Samhain*, *The Shanachie* and *A Broadside* share the same striking and refreshing visual style (reinforced by their reliance on the innovative artwork of Jack B. Yeats), and the same core pool of literary talent – Yeats himself, but also Padraic Colum, George Moore, Lady Gregory and Æ – into which peers and protégés are drawn and released (Lord Dunsany, Alice Milligan, F.R. Higgins). *Shanachie* diluted the Little Magazine paradigm somewhat in an unsuccessful attempt to produce something more popular, while Yeats's *Broadsides* are more a visually stunning personal statement than the product of a movement.

This central group spawned a number of offshoots, which took the vision in new directions. *Uladh* at first looks like a provincial homage to *Samhain*, the same visual style (with Joseph Campbell playing the Jack Yeats role), linked to the Ulster rather than the Irish Literary Theatre, and an overlapping list of contributors, but a conflict with the rather patronising metropolitan élite soon emerged which could have become quite fruitful had the magazine lived longer (and which can be seen as an ancestor of the Belfast-based magazines of the 1940s). *Dana* rejected the unifying agenda of the Revival in favour of a more modern pluralism and individualism, pointing the way for the *Dublin Magazine* and *Bell* in future years. *Aengus* adopted the Revival typographic style and physical format, but rejected the rest of the formula to concentrate purely on poetry, while the *Journal of the National Literary Society* focuses on theatre business, leaving only a peripheral role for literary pieces.

The Literary Revival Magazines are almost equalled, in numbers if not always in achievement, by their political counterparts which emerged a little later. The first of these, the *Shan Van Vocht*, is atypical, coming as it does from Belfast, being produced by women, and devoting a rather larger proportion of its space to literature than the norm, and could be seen as occupying ground half way between the political and literary. However, the political coverage has clear primacy, and most of the literary items which did appear conformed to the political agenda (marching songs, patriotic ballads, stories of penal days). The line of descent from the *Nation* is clear. The *Leader* is more typical, at least in the impression given that, rather than pursuing a sophisticated attempt at cultural politics, the literary items are grudgingly admitted as a sop, or because it is felt that they will attract readers. *An Connachtach*, the *Irish Commonwealth*, the *Red Hand Magazine* and *Banba* are broadly similar and, although they attracted some contributions from prominent, if secondary, figures like Higgins, Daniel Corkery and Francis Bigger, they do little to dilute the impression of an increasingly fevered nationalism. The best of these magazines, and indeed one of the most impressive serial publications of its day, is the *Irish Review*, the embodiment of early twentieth-century cultural nationalism. Here, and partly because the editors were prepared to allow contributions which did not toe their party line, or which even opposed it, is one of the most successful marriages of urgent, committed political journalism and good quality literature to be published in Ireland. Of course, the main figures involved in producing the *Irish Review* were themselves caught on the cusp between writing and political action; Patrick Pearse and Thomas MacDonagh produced some of the most wistful poetry to appear on these pages, alongside some of the fiercest polemics, and their high standards and editorial integrity attracted the cream of their generation. Lyrics by W.B. Yeats, illustrations by his brother Jack, articles on Irish economics and history by Kuno Meyer and Edmund Curtis, stories by George Moore and James Stephens, these two thousand-odd pages contain the best distillation of the intellectual and artistic ferment of Ireland in the years before the First World War.

The last cohesive grouping is also the smallest, and comprises those titles which had strong connections to Ireland's universities. *Hermes* was worthy, and well-produced, and short-lived. The quality of the contents of the first series of *St. Stephen's* is almost universally poor, but it does have some historical significance, and not just for its difficult relationship with James Joyce; it is the first appearance in Ireland of the modern student magazine, often superficial and puerile, and preoccupied with the minutiae of their institutions' hermetic existence, but often innovative and confrontational (and sometimes, as with *St. Stephen's*, clashing with their own authorities). *Studies* is an entirely different beast, an attempt to provide a Catholic *Hermathena* which, during its first phase up to Partition, provided a more detached and academic perspective on the concerns and products of the Revival. Creative writing is rare, and usually not by major players, but there are useful articles on Æ, MacDonagh, Pearse, James Stephens and Yeats, and reviews, including of Ernest Boyd's book on the Revival and of Stephen J. Brown on nineteenth-century fiction.

Of the remaining, miscellaneous, titles, the *National Story Magazine* is too ephemeral to comment on, while the rest are so individual they generally form groups of one. Although some have depicted Bulmer Hobson's *Irish Review* of 1922 as a new series of its illustrious predecessor, they share little more than the name, and it is of note only for a handful of interesting book reviews. *The Day* is a Cork publication which largely concentrates on the literary activities in that town, and is of no more than historical significance.

The *All Ireland Review* and *Dublin Penny Journal* hark back to nineteenth-century modes, the latter rather self-consciously claiming to be a new series of the magazine of the same title which closed in 1836. Rejecting the new format, the organic blend of writing, typography and illustration which contemporaries like *Samhain* were forging, both these titles aimed at a more populist approach; to some extent, both succeeded, running to 320 and 156 issues, respectively. The unique personality of Standish O'Grady guarantees his publication more character, and token contributions from his famous friends, but neither of them makes a substantial contribution.

Finally, we have two heavyweights of Irish serial publication, both with strong links to broadly based and influential institutions, and both as a consequence lasting longer than any mainly literary magazine could dream of (more than one thousand issues in the first instance, and some 350 in the second, both over a thirty-year period). The *Irish Homestead* was the organ of the Irish Co-Operative Movement, a pioneering organisation aimed at improving the lot of the most isolated and powerless members of Irish society. In amongst the practical advice and inspiring messages there was little room for literary material; however, the enormous number of issues means that the *Homestead* accumulated a considerable body of work, while the recruitment at an early stage of Æ as editor ensured that much of it was of the highest quality. Any purely literary Little Magazine which could boast 'The Wanderings of Oisin' and 'The Lake Isle of Innisfree', alongside material from Hyde, Somerville and Ross, Milligan, Tynan, and Æ himself would be of interest to scholars; the presence of these in such a publication indicates much about the unique character and quiet achievements of Æ. The *Catholic Book Bulletin* (which quickly became simply the *Catholic Bulletin*), was dedicated to suppressing dissent, exclusive rather than inclusive, Ultramontane rather than liberal, allying itself to power and control instead of empowering the socially excluded, and stands in diametric opposition to the *Homestead*. The poems and reviews which appeared in its pages are of no importance, but the publication itself is of enormous historical significance as the semi-official voice of a conservative church consolidating its position in Irish society, and promoting a doctrine of censorship and provincial isolation which would dominate Irish publishing for the first decades of the new Free State.

Preceded by almost half a century of underachievement, and followed by a decade of retrenchment, the period 1892–1922 stands out as one of great achievement in the field of Irish literary magazines. I have described at the start of this chapter the dizzying rush of publications which gathered pace at the turn of the century, and the unprecedented range of titles on offer; this was also sustained, and only began to ease in the last few years of this period (after a brief faltering between 1912 and 1916, when no new titles emerged). Not only were there more new magazines, from a wider range of places, and embodying more innovations, than at any time since the Famine, but the quality of some of these titles places them in the very first rank; the *Irish Homestead*, *Dana*, *A Broadside*, *Studies*, the *Irish Review* are all amongst the best magazines produced in Ireland. More than that, for the first time since the death of Young Ireland, virtually all these journals share the same world-view, a sense of commonality beneath their superficial differences. Even titles which I have classified as miscellaneous and difficult to group, like the *Homestead* or *All Ireland Review*, are still clearly Revival publications, as are more political rivals like *Shan Van Vocht*, sharing the underlying goals I outlined in my introduction (perhaps ironically, they can also be linked to a trend in England to bring politics and culture closer together while rejecting Victorian escapism and *fin de siècle* decadence, for example in the *New Statesman and Nation* (1913)). The period closes as have all its predecessors, with a withering of titles, and only two or three atypical publications surviving beyond the terminal date. But after Partition and the convulsions of civil war, the survivors regroup and attempt to carry on, albeit in an increasingly unsympathetic climate; Æ moves to the *Irish Statesman* and continues to promote the same mix of peers and protégés, and some of those influenced by him (such as Seumas O'Sullivan) start new magazines of their own. The Revival generation, their forms and achievements, continued to dominate Irish literary magazines until the start of the Second World War.

NOTES

1   The following outline is strongly influenced by Malcolm Bradbury, and James McFarlane, 'Movements, Magazines and Manifestos', in Malcolm Bradbury, and James McFarlane (eds), *Modernism 1890–1930* (Harmondsworth, 1976), pp. 192–205, and by Frederick J. Hoffman, Charles Allen and Carolyn F. Ulrich, *The Little Magazine, A History and Bibliography* (Princeton, 1946).

2   Bradbury and McFarlane, 'Movements, Magazines and Manifestos', p. 203.

3   Hoffman, Allen and Ulrich, *The Little Magazine*, pp. 1–2.

4   Hoffman, Allen and Ulrich, *The Little Magazine,* p. 14.

Chapter 8
Irish literary magazines, 1923–1939

After the frenetic activity of the previous thirty years, the period under examination marks a pause for breath during which the personalities and preoccupations of the Revival enter an extended afterlife. Although the average number of literary magazines in print throughout this period is only a little lower than during the heyday of the Revival, there is a strong sense of a falling-off, and the same peaks are never reached, in terms of quantity of titles, of quality, or of innovation. Of the new magazines, the greatest successes are the *Dublin Magazine*, the *Capuchin Annual* and *Ireland To-Day*, but none of these approaches the stature and impact of predecessors like the *Irish Statesman* or *Irish Review*. Similarly, all the titles of this period fall into previously established genres, and there are no major formal innovations. Nearly one-third of these titles are the solitary representative of their genre, reducing the fruitful effects of competition which we observed during the first twenty years of the century. The rest fall into the two best-established existing genres, Little Magazines (which has the biggest number of titles, but also the least successful individual publications) and General Magazines. In the latter category, the *Dublin Magazine* is the latest in a long line, stretching back to the *Literary Journal* of the 1740s, of such magazines, all adapting to changing tastes in each generation, while the *Ulster Review* and *Ulsterman* are lesser, provincial attempts in the same mould. *Ireland To-Day* follows in the footsteps of the *Irish Review*. The Little Magazines are faltering, and perhaps the best that can be said for *Klaxon*, *To-morrow*, *Inisfáil* and the rest, is that they include some of the most eccentric and individual journals published in Ireland, and one or two very noble failures.

Using one of our other measures of the level of activity (average lifespan, excluding the two or three exceptional publications), we see that from 1923 to 1939 the average Irish literary magazine survived for only half as long as during 1892–1922. As ever, the exceptions (*Dublin Magazine*, *Quarryman* and the *Capuchin Annual*) were among the most broadly-based, least purely literary titles and, in the latter two at least, were attached to institutions (University College Cork and the Catholic Church, respectively) which provided them with sustenance. There is also evidence, in the higher number of failures, that support for these magazines had become weaker. No fewer than a third of them managed only a single issue, while fewer than half made it into double figures.

One trend established by the Revival which was extended and strengthened in the journals of the 1920s and 1930s was the spread of publication back out into a range of towns wider than at any time since before the Great Famine. In the previous thirty years around fifteen magazines came from outside Dublin; this now more than doubles to almost forty, and the appearance of one each from Waterford and Cork, and a strong group of five from Belfast, establishes a string of publishing centres along the eastern seaboard from Belfast to Cork city.

The two regional representatives, the *Ulster Review* and *Ulsterman*, are half-hearted and of little interest. However, two general magazines from Dublin, the *Dublin Magazine* and *Ireland To-Day* mark the start and end of our period with two of the best examples of this genre. After a brief false start, Seumas O'Sullivan established the *Dublin Magazine* as a modern update of the various Museums and Repertories which had been so popular seventy, eighty or ninety years earlier, and containing the same diverting mixture of novelties, popular science, basic economics and light literature. While a solid and respectable achievement, the *Dublin Magazine*'s popular reputation is not reinforced by an examination of its contents; like most of Ireland's longer-running and commercially successful literary magazines, its popularity depended heavily on its comfortable and conservative approach, which rarely challenged its audience's expectations. It must also be said that it faced no serious competition for nearly twenty years. Nonetheless, it did much to keep the torch of literary publishing burning in Ireland during some very difficult years. *Ireland To-Day* is in many ways a direct contrast. If the *Irish Review* brought the concept of the Great Review in Ireland into the twentieth century, transforming it into a new genre, a cross between the Great Review and the Little Magazine (the 'Little Review'?), then *Ireland To-Day* is the missing link between the *Irish Review* and the apotheosis of this hybrid, *The Bell*. Like O'Sullivan's periodical it covered new developments in economics and popular science, along with many varied pieces on a wide range of topics, but its position was radical and challenging, a direct forerunner of the liberal pluralism of the best of *The Bell*. Given the discouraging political climate of these decades, its success was more substantial than a direct comparison of its couple of dozen issues with the *Dublin Magazine*'s 150-odd might suggest.

Among the Little Magazines, the *Ulster Book* and *Ulster Free Lance* are too ephemeral to justify discussion, but the others divide into two camps, both of which exemplify classic models of this genre. *Contemporary Poetry*, the first *Inisfáil*, and *On the Boiler* are all hobby horses, personal indulgences of which *Inisfáil* is probably the strangest, but only *On the Boiler* has any broader interest as another vehicle for the fertile outpourings of the brain of W.B. Yeats. *To-morrow* and the *Klaxon* are more interesting, the first (and, for some forty years, the only) Irish examples of the explicitly confrontational and polemical Little Magazine more common in continental Europe. Both were products of the same loose grouping (A.J. Leventhal, Thomas MacGreevy, Francis Stuart, Cecil Salkeld) of Young Turks, associated with Yeats and his circle but keen to take the Revival agenda further. Both magazines, in their enthusiasms, style and visual character, instantly convey the stamp of the contemporary artistic innovations (Dada, Modernism) which were sweeping the European avant garde, but which were jarringly alien in an Ireland in which the Catholic Vigilance Association and Catholic Truth Society were demanding censorship, and the Galway library board was locking up the works of Shaw.[1] The story of *To-morrow*, in particular, because of the behind-the-scenes pressures and manoeuvrings which it prompted, and the fuel which it provided to the conservative, pro-censorship lobby, reveals much about the new Ireland which was about to emerge.

The remaining magazines of this period are a somewhat rag-bag collection, one or two representatives each of a variety of well-worn genres, with little cohesion or signs of a shared agenda. In itself, this is probably as revealing of the character of the Irish literary magazines of these years as any other aspect, as nearly half of all the new titles to appear between Partition and the Second World War fall into this generalised pool. There are two populist periodicals, leaning heavily on undemanding stories, which hark back to another staple of the previous century, both (the *Hearthstone* and *Green and Gold*) only moderately successful. The UCC publication *Quarryman* is another student rag in the mould of *St. Stephen's* and the later *Northman*, and like them is dominated by tiresome and incestuous juvenilia. *Motley* is a theatre magazine which barely qualifies for inclusion here on the basis of the few original poems which it published. And the *Capuchin Annual* is the sole example from this period of the Catholic literary periodical, and a quantum leap ahead of previous examples like the *Catholic Book Bulletin*. It is far less doctrinaire and intolerant, better produced, and was extremely popular, running for over forty years and (if the editorials are to be believed) being produced in the tens of thousands at its peak. Finally, two semi-promotional publications, *An Ulster Garland* and the second *Inisfáil*, one intended to raise funds for a hospital, the other an anthology aimed at the Irish diaspora, both of which seem to have managed only a single issue.

As stated at the conclusion to the previous chapter, these two decades mark a period of retrenchment, marked mainly by frustration and lack of achievement, despite the occasional exception. Most of the figures who appeared in the magazines of the Revival carry on in these journals, few of which try to question the agenda established in the previous thirty years, so giving this period the feeling of a continuation of the Revival, an over-extension beyond its time. The twin poles of the Revival magazines, Æ and Yeats, are unchallenged, while most of the newcomers (for example O'Sullivan) are either acolytes or are deeply in their shadow. Wherever we look, at the abject failure of the few experiments like the *Klaxon* and *To-morrow*; at the steady, worthy, but somewhat unexciting achievements of the *Dublin Magazine* (at least, after its period of innovation in the 1920s and 1930s, when it began to ossify) or the *Capuchin Annual*; at the fleeting existence of many publications (especially the star of the Revival period, the Little Magazine); or at the lack of focus and direction, these two decades, as indicated earlier, clearly mark a falling-off from previous glories. However, it is important to place this in context; this is not a sustained drought like the second half of the nineteenth century, when observers could have been forgiven for thinking that the Irish literary magazine was on the verge of expiring. While the average lifespan of these publications, at fifteen months, was half that of their immediate predecessors, it is still higher than the ten months achieved in the late nineteenth century. Rather, it is a pause for breath in extremely difficult circumstances: the disruption of the Civil War (hinted at in O'Sullivan's reference to strikes disrupting paper supplies), the emergence of a new society (and one increasingly hostile to avant garde gestures and foreign influences) in the 1920s (and *To-morrow* provides us with an opening into this secret world of covert censorship), and of course the economic difficulties of the 1930s. A relatively short pause for breath, moreover, which would be followed by a period of sustained growth and achievement without parallel in the almost three centuries of Irish literary magazines. The pathfinder here is *Ireland To-Day*, precursor of a new generation which would interrogate and subvert the Revival model of Irishness, and give voice to new movements, from liberals to regionalists.

NOTES

1   Terence Brown, *Ireland, A Social and Cultural History 1922–1985* (London, 1985), p. 74.

Chapter 9
Irish literary magazines, 1940–1952

This is a curious period, one in which the most extreme ephemera (for example, 'N') coexist alongside the most substantial achievement (the *Bell*). The rate at which new titles are started is only slightly higher than between 1923 and 1939 (seventeen in twelve years, as opposed to nineteen in sixteen years), but there is a different quality to the titles and the period as a whole has more of a feeling of solidity and stability. Given the small number of new titles, the fact that this period sees the birth not only of *The Bell*, but also of *Lagan*, *Irish Writing*, *Poetry Ireland*, *Rann*, *Envoy* and *Kavanagh's Weekly* points to something stirring in the national consciousness.

The average lifespan (excluding the exceptional *Irish Writing* and *Poetry Ireland*) remains roughly the same, at around six years. These two exceptions have extended their lives, possibly indefinitely, by (after years of struggle) linking themselves to powerful institutions (national newspapers in the first case, the 'Poetry Ireland' organisation in the other). The rate of failure is lower than before, with two-thirds of these titles making it into double figures in terms of issues published.

During these years production begins to cluster into the three main urban areas, around Dublin (eight magazines), Belfast (six) and Cork (three); it is also the first time ever that more ILMs have been published outside Dublin than inside, with the greater Belfast area in particular maintaining the same level as during 1923–1939. At the same time, there is a greater divergence than ever before between the journals published in Ulster and those from the rest of the country; the bedding-in of Partition and hardening of political divisions may have contributed to this, but looking at the titles themselves it seems apparent that the radically differing experiences of the Second World War and the Emergency are the more important factor.

Of the Ulster magazines, *Ulster Parade*, *Ulster Quill* and, to a lesser extent, *Lagan*, are all heavily marked by the war, the first two dominated by an air of morale-boosting cheer, the latter carrying many contributions from those in the forces. *Lagan* and *Rann* share an Ulster Regionalist agenda which was to a large extent inspired by wartime isolation and, in a more implicit way, this vision affects *Ulster Parade*, *Quill* and *Voices* (waving the name of the province like a flag of identity has never before been so prevalent, and cannot be coincidental). *Lagan* and *Rann* are obviously the most substantial (*Ulster Voices* being clearly a dry-run for *Rann*), and pick up the baton from *Uladh* after a forty-year gap during which no important ILM appeared from the North. Their Regionalist stance has been criticised by Nationalists who have seen it as an evasive attempt to circumvent key questions of national identity, but the role it played in the North itself was crucial. After two decades since Partition, during which the siege mentality reigned and the Stormont regime attempted to impose a monolithic Ulster/Protestant/Unionist/conservative identity and culture, Ulster Regionalism stands as the first attempt by the intelligentsia within the state to propose an alternative, more inclusive vision. Their attempt was unsuccessful, but their example was extremely useful to the 1960s generation of writers in their own, more confident rebellion (in particular, Heaney and Simmons). The dynamism of this group of Ulster writers during the war years and immediately after is confirmed by looking beyond their own publications to the considerable presence they had in contemporary Dublin magazines. *The Bell* had not one but two special issues devoted to the North, not something which would have occurred to any of their Dublin predecessors.

Among the more commercial magazines, *Puck Fare*, the *Blarney Annual* and *Castle Junction* are all lightweight efforts which look increasingly dated beside their more serious contemporaries. On a rather higher level is the *Irish Bookman* which infiltrates a stream of high-quality writing into its more populist material, and it is heartening to see that this more ambitious publication was also the most successful of the four.

The *Circle* and '*N*' are minor eccentricities, and do not rate further comment. *Kavanagh's Weekly* is also *sui generis*, but far more important. In other times this might have been a light-hearted exercise, or even a messianic one (like Simmons's *HU*), but in fact it sustains an air of entrapment and despair. While this paper, and his column in *Envoy*, contain the closest thing to a statement of Kavanagh's philosophy, and while superficially the venom gives his writing an energy and drive, the whole is fatally undermined by self-loathing. In these pages, Kavanagh only attacks, he does not propose any positive alternatives, either directly or implicitly by his writing; there is little praise, and those he does see as being on his side, he is likely to turn on later. Ultimately, Kavanagh's attacks on 'buckleppin' and philistinism are as great a failure as Hewitt's regionalism, and seem to have drawn an equally apathetic response from the broader population.

The only new student magazine to emerge in these years is *Icarus*, but it is also one of the best of its type, the first of the modern university publications, more interested in the best quality new verse than in the activities of the rugby club, and free from the interference of the university authorities which censored and undermined predecessors like the *Quarryman* in its early years. Particularly as it moves into the 1960s, it seems that Alec Reid in Trinity played as important a role in fostering a new generation of literary talent as Philip Hobsbaum at Queen's, but without the same degree of recognition from posterity.

Irish Writing and *Poetry Ireland* are the two most successful purely literary magazines yet published in Ireland, and were for a time intertwined. While both started as standard Little Magazines, their increasingly imaginative efforts to stay in print show the range of forms and the vitality of the ILM in the second half of the twentieth century. Between 1953 and 1955 *Poetry Ireland* 'hitched a ride' as a supplement to *Irish Writing* which bridged a gap in its own run; in 1968 David Marcus took an even more daring leap when he launched *New Irish Writing* as a page in a national newspaper (firstly the *Irish Press*, and from 1988 the *Sunday Tribune*). Largely without editorial comment, and (while the vast majority of contributors are Irish) with a fairly soft-focus national agenda, both titles embody the evolution of the role of Irish literature from the mid-century position of marginalised oppositionism, to an institutionalised, officially tolerated and funded 'heritage' industry.

The Bell and its slightly more daring little brother *Envoy* are cultural reviews in the tradition of the *Irish Review* and *Crane Bag*. The former, in particular, has become *the* representative ILM, a shibboleth for liberal revisionists and a target for those of a different ideological bent; it is interesting in this context to note that, although it has attracted more comment than any other publication in this study, the definitive work on *The Bell* has still to be written. What can be said, without doubt, is that it marks the start of a new chapter in Irish culture, the rejection of turn-of-the-century definitions of national literature and politics after the long hangover of such values through the 1920s and 1930s, and an attempt to come to terms with a country which was increasingly urbanised and beginning to see itself not as the bearer of a unique destiny but simply as another small European state. It never managed to capture a wider Zeitgeist, to reflect and amplify a shift in popular perceptions; it always remained slightly ahead of the aspirations of the majority, and remained the monthly bulletin of enlightenment posted out to isolated individuals. Still, many of its preoccupations – seeing the North as more than simply the fourth green field, still to be saved; focusing on the weaknesses of the new state in the area of social provision; promoting pluralism against a reductionist, essentialist vision of Irishness; and seeing Ireland as a potential member of a modern Europe – are now common currency, and it has undoubtedly had a greater impact than any other ILM in the twentieth century. *Envoy* has always seemed a 'younger', trendier relative of *The Bell*; sited among the bohemian, college buzz of Grafton Street rather than the commercial respectability of O'Connell Street, and regularly taking gently satirical pot-shots at the seriousness and mundane concerns of its elder rival, *Envoy* takes one aspect of *The Bell* (its coverage of modernism in the arts, with an openness to outside influences) and makes an entire magazine of it. While *The Bell* attacked head-on the outdated nostrums of, for example, institutionalised state nationalism, *Envoy* refused to flatter them with its attention, and devoted itself to its art.

This is a period of consolidation and solid achievement. While there is no formal innovation (except perhaps in the emergence of the Theme Issue, where an entire issue of a magazine is devoted to a single subject), it is strongly marked by (largely unsuccessful) attempts to shake off the dead hand of Edwardian definitions of Ireland, its politics and culture, from the cluster of Ulster Regionalists, through the revisionism of *Envoy* and *The Bell*, to Patrick Kavanagh's personal *cri de coeur*. It is also a transitional phase since the various attempts by the intelligentsia to imagine new versions of Ireland were met with widespread hostility and resistance, but the foundations they laid were to be picked up and developed by the next generation. At the same time, the magazines themselves were striving toward a new level of complexity and maturity, looking outside Ireland for examples of best practice; the spirits of belle-lettrism, patriotic versifying and parochial amateurism may not have been banished in this era, but notice had definitely been served on them. An example of this greater ambition is the attitude to censorship. Only twenty years before, *To-morrow* had simply vanished under the weight of behind-the-scenes pressure and the *Dublin Magazine* had published articles on the subject which were at best ambivalent; the briefest look at Seán O'Faoláin's principled opposition, or Patrick Kavanagh's lacerating venom, on the same subject is enough to highlight the progress which was being made. That they were not yet receiving any substantial response from the wider society is evident in the recurring note of bitterness in much of what is written, and the practical effect of being ahead of their audience can perhaps be inferred from the regular appearance of begging notes in the editorials of the *Bell* and *Poetry Ireland* and the blunt blackmail attempt in number twelve of *Kavanagh's Weekly*.[1]

NOTE

1   The financial difficulties were made much worse by the ban on the importation of Irish publications imposed by the British Board of Trade in 1947, and the furious reaction of Irish editors only reveals how dependent they still were on the English market.

Chapter 10
Irish literary magazines, 1953–1985

After 1830–1849 and 1892–1922, this period sees the third and greatest peak of Irish literary magazines. Never before had so many new titles been started up (seventy in thirty-two years); never had so many of these (five magazines) survived beyond their own era; and never had there been such variety in form, content and style. There are Little Magazines and Reviews, sales figures (for example, *Books Ireland* or the *Linenhall Review*) higher than any in the twentieth century, and formal experimentation on a scale not seen since the early years of the century. Riding a tide of rising standards of living, state subsidy and an unparalleled expansion in higher education, ILMs in this period reached new levels of ambition and professionalism. The momentum faltered slightly in the years 1962–1967 (a fact noted by editors at the time; in the introduction to his 1983 book, Hayden Murphy talks about the mid-1960s as a time of decay, with magazines either atrophying or closing,[1] while David Marcus says much the same in the introduction to his first anthology of *New Irish Writing*)[2] when the rate of new starts begins to flag, and none of them lasts for more than a couple of years or four issues. It is as if they were pausing for breath to absorb all the changes going on around them, before going on to a new phase of achievement.

The average lifespan (even including the 1962–1967 dip) is seven years, while the five surviving titles have stretched to twenty-three years (*Books Ireland*), twenty-four years (*Cyphers*), twenty-nine years (*Fortnight*), thirty-one years (*HU*) and forty-five years (*University Review*), so far. On the other hand, a very high proportion (forty titles out of seventy) last for six issues or fewer. This could be influenced by the fact that many of the prevailing philosophies (hippy, Maoist, anarchist) did not put much value on stability and longevity, but the fact that many stretched their few issues over quite a long period of time seems to indicate that the real culprit is public subsidy. The removal of commercial pressures encourages experimentation, with no pressure to stop production if sales fall.

The geographical spread is also wider than ever, with titles published in twenty different locations all over the country, from Castlerock to Cork, and from Kilkee to Blackrock. Again, some 60 per cent are published outside Dublin, maintaining and extending the healthy anti-centralising trend seen in the previous chapter. In addition, the drifting apart of North and South seen in the 1940s goes into reverse here.

There is a small flush of local titles, which seem to be a kind of 'heritage' publishing, arising from the feeling that everyone has the right to have themselves and their place expressed in verse. The *Shannonside Annual*, *Wordsnare*, *Roscrea Writing* and *Castle Poets* are no more than that, and are mostly very poor. The *Stony Thursday Book* aims a little higher and seems to be developing a unifying agenda before it collapses, but the best of these is the *Drumlin*, which shows a real creative mind at work behind it, but which unfortunately never lived to fulfil its potential.

Among the College Magazines we find the same two main types as before, what can loosely be termed the official and the unofficial. There are a dozen of the latter – *Criterion*, *Gown*, *Q*, the *University Gazette*, *Interest*, *Gorgon*, *Sganarelle*, *Motus*, *P*, *Quarto*, *Beggar's Bridge* and *Watermark*. They are, of course, irreverent and inconsistent, but they have all to some extent learnt from the example of *Icarus* and are produced to a much higher standard than their predecessors. Most of them are only of interest because they contain the first published work by writers who later became famous (as with Seamus Heaney and *Gorgon*) and, while some (for example *Interest*, *P*) entertainingly experiment with coloured paper and radical graphics, only *Gown* (by the end of its second series, as the *Gown Literary Supplement*) and *Quarto* produce any lasting work. The 'official' magazines are represented by the *University Review*, *Acorn* and *Yeats Studies*; the last of these passed too quickly to achieve anything, and *Acorn* is mostly living in the past, but the *University Review* (particularly after 1970, when it became the *Irish University Review*) has established itself as the main talking shop of Arts Faculty academics in Ireland. It often seems a little staid and unadventurous, but its record is one of solid achievement, focusing around the central canon of Yeats, Joyce, Beckett and (more recently) Heaney, while it has performed a valuable service in its series of special issues devoted to most of the major Irish writers. In addition, there are a couple of semi-detached sub-groups of this official pack; one (which includes *New Yeats Papers* and *Writing from the Age of Swift*) comprises journals which, while not formally attached to a particular college, are still clearly specialist academic publications; the other (*Focus*, *Everyman* and the *Maynooth Review*) are religious, but share a studious, academic air, are often associated with colleges like Maynooth, and eschew the polemics of religious magazines from previous eras. This variety – and the sheer numbers, since these titles together make up some 30 per cent of the total for this period – reinforces the point about the rapid expansion of higher education, and shows the universities coming to the fore in the cultural life of the country.

The main technical innovation of these years is to be found in a group of guerrilla publications, obviously influenced by the social upheavals and political radicalism around them. Again, they break into two clear groups: the 'Roundheads' (*Broadsheet*, *Capella*, *Book of Invasions*, *Minerva*, *Neptune's Kingdom*, the *Broadsheet* from UCD, the *Austin Clarke Broadsheet* and the *Mongrel Fox*) with their ostentatiously cheap and cheery production values and earnest populism, and the 'Cavaliers' (*Mañana* and *Sganarelle* are early harbingers, but they come to a crescendo with *Ego*, *Id* and *Crab Grass*), flamboyant, anything-goes experimenters with every physical aspect of a magazine – paper of different colours and textures, surreal and drug-influenced graphics, song-sheets, plastic bags, and more. The Roundheads are clear winners in terms of the quality of the literature which they publish, but the Cavaliers' brief flourish is undoubtedly amusing.

Prestige publications, with lots of money going in to top-quality production, and produced by academics who feel that they should be able to stand alongside their international, cosmopolitan peers – this is the ideal of the cultural review. There were a couple of false starts in this genre in this period with *Nonplus* (whose purview took in everything from Sarajevo, to Heidegger and the GAA in four short issues) and the

Northern Review (which in practice was too local in its coverage), but the peak was clearly reached with *Atlantis* and the *Crane Bag*. Heavyweight commentators tackling the big issues, from Solzhenitsyn to the future of the media, underpinned by lashings of the latest critical theory and a thoroughgoing internationalism are the order of the day here. Creative writing is kept on a very tight leash, in case anyone should think them too frivolous (*Crane Bag* carried none at all). It is easy to mock these publications for the seriousness with which they carry themselves, but it is an unavoidable sign of the maturity of Irish culture that there is now a niche even for these rarefied birds, and they played a key role in developing concepts which would soon after enter the mainstream, such as Revisionism.

An interesting cluster of more commercial periodicals begins at the end of the 1970s; generally A4 size, with attractive cover photography and often leavened with local listings or reviews of television or pop music in an attempt to make the poetry more palatable. These titles (*Northern Lights*, the *Cork Review*, the *Belfast Review* and *North*) now seem a transparent response to the chill winds of Thatcherism which began to blow around that time and to the pressure to prove that the arts are not actually élitist at all, and that they can and should pay their way. As a long-term prospect they were probably doomed – most people looking for the best club to attend at the weekend are not likely to stop to read an interview with a septuagenarian poet, while serious readers of poetry will probably be frustrated at having to skip over large photographs of dog tracks or sex shops. Nevertheless, they managed to squeeze in a surprising amount of good work before commercial pressures reined them in.

Sometimes looking a little dowdy and old-fashioned beside flashier newcomers like *Crab Grass*, *Atlantis* or the *Belfast Review*, while these titles came and went the traditional Little Magazine continued to prove both its popularity (25 per cent of the total for these years) and its durability (*Threshold* lasted for thirty-three years, *Cyphers* and *HU* are still going after twenty-four and thirty-one years, respectively). There are a couple of eccentricities (the *Martello Magazine* and *Portlight*). Many (*Writers' Digest*, *Arena*, the *Holy Door*, *Words*, the *Belle* and the *Beau*) are ephemeral, amounting to two or three issues before disappearing. Others were more successful: the *Kilkenny Magazine*, *Phoenix*, the *Lace Curtain*, *Caret*, *Era* and *Tracks* were all put together with sufficient care and enthusiasm, attracted enough stimulating new writing, and seemed to be forming distinctive characters which makes it unfortunate that they did not last long enough to make a real contribution. The real achievement in this genre, however, lies in four titles which are paradigms of the type. *Poetry Galway* (better known as the *Salmon*) is the best example of a publication by and for new writers, and during its decade it provided the first appearance in print of many new writers; unfortunately, the lack of discrimination which was sometimes in evidence meant that this was often their last appearance as well. Nevertheless, it served a vital function for many years, and provided a strong platform for poetry away from the metropolitan centres. *Cyphers* is a pure poetry publication, in many ways a classic example of the genre: it has a core of committed editors, who have a very clear idea of what, for them, comprises quality poetry; its physical layout is attractive but not ostentatious, and states clearly that this is a serious enterprise; and it continues, year after year, to quietly put its wares before the public. *Threshold* was a cross between one of

Yeats's theatre magazines and yet another offspring of *The Bell*, mixing solid verse with essays about the theatre and pieces on Eastern Europe. For a while in the mid-1960s it looked as if it might become more experimental, but this soon passed and, while it was consistently interesting, *Threshold* was never really challenging, and always had a slightly old-fashioned air. The *Honest Ulsterman* is a much harder beast to tie down, but one characteristic which it has maintained is its ability to simultaneously capture the mood of the times (be that the revolutionary late-1960s, the less public and more sardonic 1970s, or the earnest and sober 1980s) while holding to a fairly consistent artistic line (a loyalty to what has been called both the 'less-deceived' school of poetry, and the 'well-made' poem). Like virtually all ILMs from Ulster, it has a strong (if implicit) regionalist flavour, and has regularly devoted space to 'archaeological' work on the likes of the Belfast Group or George Buchanan. Different editors, according to taste, keep attempting to break out into contemporary European poetry, or addressing the need for a Critical Forum, but the essential formula has remained unchanged: a predominance of poetry, most of it from the North of Ireland or its Diaspora, but with strong links out to the rest of the country and to the North of England. One interesting, but not entirely unique, feature, has been the four series of pamphlets which have been issued, providing the next step towards full publication for newer poets and a space for work in progress for the more established; pamphlets have been devoted to Dawe, Hardy, Heaney, Mahon, Muldoon, Newmann, Ormsby, Simmons and nearly fifty others.

A last group of periodicals have 'hitched a ride' on the back of outside organisations, or non-literary publications with a wider appeal. The *Dolmen Miscellany* and *Soundings* are shop windows for established publishing houses (Dolmen and Blackstaff Presses, respectively), showcase productions on which no money was spared in an attempt to present both the writers – and the companies' abilities to produce quality product – in the best possible light. The remaining three titles have circulations measured in thousands rather than hundreds and, like similar ILMs down the years, this is due to external reasons other than the simple attraction of their literary material. The *Linenhall Review* was the house journal of the distinguished Belfast library; every member of the library was entitled to a free copy of the *Review*, thus guaranteeing it a large and stable circulation. The library connection also gave it a rather bibliophile leaning, and even a slightly conservative air. *Fortnight* is a political and current affairs magazine whose editors have all, to a greater or lesser extent, recognised that social and cultural matters have an important role to play; as with many such publications, the few pages of literary material in *Fortnight* have made their impact cumulatively, over an extended period of time. *Books Ireland* is the house magazine of the Irish publishing industry, with the feel of a trade journal, but which has maintained a reputation as one of the most reliable sources of contemporaneous reviews of new Irish publications of all kinds.

The very fertility of this period makes it difficult to characterise, but some conclusions may be drawn. It was during these years that *Envoy*'s offhand boast about most writers being relaxed about their nationality and concentrating on the quality of their writing at last came true. There is an atomisation of the literary community into a series of inward-looking groups – Ulster Regionalists, new Dublin proletarians, local interest publications, academics – with the attempts at cross-fertilisation (see the *Honest Ulsterman*'s 'Critical Forum') increasingly self-conscious. The *Crane Bag*'s exclusion of creative writing seems as strategic a mistake as the *Belfast Review*'s transparent bid for 'street cred'. Nevertheless, we should not lose sight of the fact that the three decades from 1953 to 1985 represent a most remarkable climax to almost three centuries of Irish literary magazines, an outburst of quantity, quality and sheer exuberance which should be celebrated all the more for the realisation that it has been succeeded (so far as we can tell this close to the action) by a period of contraction and retrenchment.

NOTES

1   Hayden Murphy, *Broadsheet 1967–1978: Poetry, Prose and Graphics* (Edinburgh, 1983), 'Introduction'.
2   David Marcus, *New Irish Writing 1, An Anthology from* The Irish Press *series* (Dublin, 1970), 'Introduction'.

Conclusions

Looking at the Irish literary magazines launched since 1985, it seems that another cycle has begun, and that we are currently in something of a downturn. One does not have to subscribe to the conspiracy theory that the Troubles were started by Ulster writers to promote their own work, to note that the rate of new starts from the North has dropped since the end of the Hunger Strikes and the painful moves towards a political solution to the conflict. It is also apparent in a number of symptoms already seen at the start of the 1980s – the rash of more commercial, listings-type titles, for example – that a loss of direction and confidence seems to have occurred. A high proportion of magazines of all types in the 1953–1985 period were dependent on two products of the post-war consensus – the (generously funded) expansion of further education, and the belief in extensive state funding of the arts. Both these pillars have been severely shaken by the neo-liberal winds of the 1980s, and editors do not yet seem to have come up with a suitable response to the changed environment. Most of the established titles have produced Web sites, or are planning to do so; these are fairly unsophisticated as yet, but may suggest a route towards the nirvana of greater circulation and lower costs.

To summarise almost three centuries of magazine development is well-nigh impossible, but perhaps some generalisations may be ventured. The periodical works best (despite drastically personal episodes like *Kavanagh's Weekly* and Simmons's *HU*, which can only function for very short periods of time) as a form of counterpoint: opposing, even unrelated threads woven together. Some coming to the fore, then fading, an essentially democratic form. There are two successful battle-plans available to editors who wish to make an impact; firstly, the shooting star, the *Kavanagh's Weekly* which lives fast and dies young and achieves posthumous glory, and secondly the long haul, which usually involves attachment to some outside institution (a political cause, or an academic institution, for preference) which can provide indulgent funding or a captive audience, and thus the longevity which allows a cumulative importance.

Historically, the production of literary magazines is an activity of the towns on the eastern seaboard. Even when they stray outside Dublin, ILMs have tended to cluster around the shoreline from Cork to Belfast, and the reasons for this are not hard to imagine; the map on page 69 of the Oxford *New History of Ireland* shows the towns in Ireland with a population of ten thousand and over in 1831: Belfast, Carlow, Clonmel, Cork, Derry, Drogheda, Dublin, Dundalk, Galway, Kilkenny, Limerick, Newry, Sligo, Waterford and Wexford. All of these, except Galway, Limerick and Sligo are on that eastern crescent. Obviously, the mail coach routes, and later the train lines, concentrated on linking those population centres.[1] Again, the three maps on page 78 of the same volume show illiteracy rates in 1841, 1861 and 1891, and how literacy started to rise first in centres like Down and Dublin. Even as literacy rates throughout the country gradually began to rise as the nineteenth century progressed, the imbalance between east and west coasts was maintained.[2] This amounts to a rolling bandwagon of literacy, population, education, money and communications which has established patterns of development which have yet to be broken. Whether the arrival of the Internet will transform this situation remains to be seen.

Throughout this study, I have hinted at a relationship between the rise and fall in the numbers of new starts and general levels of political activity; without much more extensive research this is impossible to prove, but it is interesting to examine a chart in the same volume of the *Oxford New History*.[3] This shows the numbers of instrument makers, music printers and publishers, and reveals a gentle rise to a small peak from 1730 to 1750; then decline, but not to the old level; another rise from 1780 to a much greater peak in 1795; again a falling back, again not to the old level; another rise from 1815 to the greatest peak lasting from 1820 to 1840. A comparison with my charts in Appendix 3 shows that there may be some substance to the thesis of a direct connection between the levels of cultural and political activity.

Several commentators have identified a gap in literary studies. For example: 'Literature is studied so often in terms of writers alone, and so seldom in terms of processes, that we are not yet accustomed to considering the significance of the multifarious literary inter-relationships that book publishing entails';[4] 'We do not yet know enough to understand how publishing influences literature and how literary circumstances require the evolution of different kinds of publishing.'[5] As Görtschacher argues:

> ...we need social historians of the little magazine...Although the overwhelming majority of British literary experiments and developments first originated...in the little magazines, this exciting phenomenon has largely been neglected by literary historians and critics. With the exception of...profiles of single magazines...and synchronic studies which hardly exceed a decade...little with a more comprehensive perspective has appeared.[6]

There are dozens of fruitful possible theses in this material. There is certainly a need for an Irish version of Görtschacher's book, in which (for British Little Magazines only) he frames extensive interviews with a dozen important editors who have been active over the last forty years with a discursive introduction (definitions, history), and his own critical reviews of their magazines. Examples of other possible approaches include: looking at the history of one important publisher (Curry's, say, or Liam Miller); or at one important editor throughout a long career (for example David Marcus). Many important writers (Yeats, Heaney, Montague) have played an editorial or semi-editorial role in a number of these magazines, and it would be interesting to trace their editorials, the material they selected (and that they omitted). On a larger scale, two projects suggest themselves: firstly, using ILMs as a source to trace the history of censorship in Ireland, not only under the 1929 Act in the Free State/Republic, but stretching from the prosecutions of Swift's printers to the pressure brought to bear on the *Honest Ulsterman* by the RUC. Secondly, the relationship between ILMs and small presses, and the roles they both play in nurturing Irish writing, has still to be properly explored.

My own research represents an initial and vital cartographical exercise, which will provide others with the tools to enter this territory, and some inspiration on the paths to follow.[7]

NOTES

1   T.W. Moody, F.X. Martin and F.J. Byrne (eds), *A New History of Ireland, Volume IX: Maps, Genealogies, Lists* (Oxford, 1984).

2   In 1841, the only counties with rates in the 20 to 29 per cent band are Antrim, Carlow, Down, Derry and Dublin, while all the counties of the western seaboard, from Donegal to Wexford, have rates of 60 per cent or higher. By 1861 the rates in all counties have dropped by around 10 per cent, while by 1891 only Donegal, Galway and Mayo are in the 30 to 39 per cent band and all counties in the eastern half of the country are down to below 20 per cent.

3   Moody, Martin and Byrne, *A New History of Ireland*, Appendix VI: 'The Dublin Music Trade, 1650–1850'.

4   Tom Montag, 'The Little Magazine/Small Press Connection: Some Conjectures', *TriQuarterly* 43, 1978, p. 577.

5   Montag, 'The Little Magazine', p. 593.

6   Wolfgang Görtschacher, *Little Magazine Profiles: The Little Magazines in Great Britain* (Salzburg, 1993), p. i.

7   The cross-references I have given at the end of many of the title entries in Part 2 will provide future researchers interested in exploring this area in more depth not only with a bibliography of the primary materials, but also with the initial apparatus to begin their pursuit.

Part 2
Descriptive Bibliography

THE EXAMINER

Location:	Originally London, but reprinted by Cornelius Carter, Fish Shamble Street, Dublin
Editor(s):	Various; between numbers 14 and 45 Jonathan Swift
Dates:	14 August 1710–4 November 1712
No. of issues:	99
Average periodicity:	Weekly
Average no. pages:	4
Libraries:	BCL=Microfilm, Location 4H; NLI=Microfilm; PSPL=Gilbert Collection (London Edition); QUB=MicA/202; TCD=OL Microfilm 50; also TT.1.73; UCD=Gen 827 IR SWI (Blackwell reprint, 1957); UCG=827.5 SWI (Blackwell reprint, 1940).

Taken from a purely literary standpoint the *Examiner* is not very significant, but it is of vital importance as the 'missing link', the point at which literature first emerges into periodical publication in Ireland. It also stands as an archetype of this first, transitional phase in the development of Irish literary magazines, for it embodies all the important characteristics: although the driving force behind it during its middle and best year was a great Irish writer, it was written purely for English consumption, and reprinted in Dublin, unchanged, only as an afterthought. Nowhere in its pages is Ireland mentioned. It is primarily a newsletter, but one which – like its contemporaries – was learning to use essays and poems as padding and as a way of widening the readership. And indeed as more than that, since a number of the supposedly literary items have a pointed political subtext.

Swift's contributions to *The Examiner* (from 2 November 1710 to 7 June 1711) include some great examples of his gifts as a journalist, polemicist and propagandist, but the scanty literary items are undistinguished. The publication's sole purpose was, as Irvin Ehrenpreis observes, 'to damn the Whigs and praise the Tories', and while it seems to have enjoyed remarkable success in propping up the Oxford ministry, that brief left little room for literary development. Perceived as the voice of the Queen's ministers, according to Sullivan, it achieved substantial sales of around four to five thousand copies per issue (Britain and Ireland combined).

See Herbert Davis, *The Examiner* (Oxford, 1940; second edition 1957).
See Irvin Ehrenpreis, *Swift the Man, his Works and the Age*, volume 3 (London, 1962), pp. 581–586.
See Alvin Sullivan, *British Literary Magazines: The Augustan Age and the Age of Johnson, 1698–1788* (Westport, 1983), pp. 113–119.
See Frank H. Ellis, *Swift vs. Mainwaring, The Examiner and The Medley* (Oxford, 1985). (Includes a reprint of the magazine).

DUBLIN WEEKLY JOURNAL

Location: Dublin (printer James Carson, Dame Street)
Editor(s):   Anon. (James Arbuckle)
Dates: 3 April 1725–11 April 1752
No. of issues: 586 on microfilm (1,406 published?)
Average periodicity: Weekly
Average no. pages: 4
Libraries: BL=Document Supply Centre, 1725–1730 only; BCL=Microfilm,
                         Location 4H; NLI=Newspaper Microfilm; PSPL=Gilbert Collection;
                         QUB=MicA/208; RIA=RR Gall/Case 2/17–18; TCD=OL Microfilm
                         56 (incomplete).

[BCL, NLI and TCD all have the same microfilm (Ann Arbor, 1950), which covers the following periods: 3 April 1725–25 December 1731; 24 January 1736–11 December 1736; 1 January 1737–4 June 1737 (with substantial gaps); and 9 January 1748-11 April 1752.]

J.C. Beckett is right to nominate this (in his essay in the *Oxford New History of Ireland*) as one of the first magazines based in Ireland to make use of literature. It is very clear from the start that this is not a newsletter padded out with literary titbits, but rather the reverse: two of the four pages are taken up by what we would now call a 'column', wide-ranging and prone to digression, but containing a good deal of literary talk. The standard format is for the first two pages to be given over to a letter, essay, poem, etc., with the last two devoted to news items and a couple of advertisements.

The pieces are mostly by 'Hibernicus' (i.e. Arbuckle), with occasional replies 'To Hibernicus' (various, including Thomas Parnell and Francis Hutcheson). For the first couple of years the poems are nearly all translations or paraphrases of passages from the Bible or from the Classics (22 May 1725 – translation of an ode by Anacreon; 31 July 1725 – 'Psalm CIV. Paraphrased in Imitation of Milton's Stile'; 2 July 1726 – a translation of Horace, Book I, Ode XIII), often introduced as being of 'particular interest to the ladies'. During the period 1728–1735 these begin to be replaced by more 'original', occasional verses; from late 1728, most issues have at least one of these light verses, e.g. 'The Tea-Table' (18 January 1728), or 'On a Lady Throwing Snow-Balls' (27 January 1728). During the third and last period, 1736–1752, the amount of verse increases noticeably, e.g. numbers 9, 15 and 22 (1736) all carry two or three poems, one of which opens the magazine.

Arbuckle was educated in Glasgow; he was related to the Black family of Belfast, and his education and literary connections were Scottish. His *Journal* is obviously modelled on the *Spectator* and *Tatler*. 'But the pen-name was more Irish than the content, for the questions were treated in general terms, with little or no specific reference to Ireland; and it is significant that when they were reprinted in volume form they were published in London' (Beckett).

See J.C. Beckett, 'Literature in English, 1691–1800', T.W. Moody and W.E. Vaughan, (eds), *Oxford New History of Ireland*, volume IV, *Eighteenth Century* (Oxford, 1986), pp. 424-470.
See James W. Phillips, *Printing and Bookselling in Dublin, 1670–1800* (Dublin, 1998), p. 54.

THE INTELLIGENCER

Location:	Dublin (printer Sarah Harding, 'next door to the Crown', Copper Alley); reprinted in London, 1730
Editor(s):	Jonathan Swift and Thomas Sheridan
Dates:	11 May 1728–17 May 1729
No. of issues:	21
Average periodicity:	Weekly
Average no. pages:	8; occasionally 16
Libraries:	BL=PP.6177 (incomplete); PSPL=Gilbert Collection (number 5 only); QUB=hPR1365/SWIF; RIA=Haliday Pamphlet 78(7) (numbers 1–15, and 17–20); TCD(Old Library)=194.o.85, number 2; also 192.s.2; UCG=827.5 SWI (Clarendon Press reprint, 1992).

[Two number 20s were published, the first dated '1728', the second 17 May 1729.]

As most of the contributions to this publication are unsigned, attribution is very difficult, but in general the even numbered editions seem to have been by Sheridan, the odd by Swift (see Herbert Davis, *Jonathan Swift: Irish Tracts 1728–1733* (Oxford, 1955), and Irvin Ehrenpreis, *Dean Swift* (volume 3 of his *Swift the Man, his Works and the Age* (London, 1983)). Sheridan's numbers are, in general, more topical and less memorable than Swift's, but this is no criticism since this magazine includes some of Swift's most durable pieces. Number 3 is devoted to his devastating defence of *The Beggar's Opera*, and number 15 is a reprint of his very effective pamphlet 'A Short View of the State of Ireland'. Number 19 is only slightly less impressive, with its diatribe against the debasement of Irish coinage. The rest is still interesting: number 8 is a satirical dialogue in pseudo-heroic couplets; number 14 contains a scurrilous scatological poem; number 15 puffs the *Drapier's Letters*; and the postscript to number 18 is a brief plea from the author on behalf of his 'widow printer' (i.e. Harding).

However, *The Intelligencer* cannot be regarded as a forerunner or foundation for later magazines, since it was such a short-lived and personal project, more of a logical progression from the pamphlet as a vehicle for this great writer than a real magazine. Davis quotes a later letter from Swift to Pope on the subject: 'If we could have got some ingenious young man to have been the manager, who should have published all that might be sent to him, it might have continued longer, for there were hints enough. But the printer here could not afford such a young man one farthing for his trouble, the sale being so small, and the price one halfpenny; and so it dropped.'

See Roger McHugh, and Maurice Harmon, *A Short History of Anglo-Irish Literature* (Dublin, 1982), p. 78.

See Alvin Sullivan, *British Literary Magazines: The Augustan Age and the Age of Johnson, 1698–1788* (Westport, 1983), pp. 169–172.

See James Woolley, *The Intelligencer* (Oxford, 1992). This is a reprint.

THE WEEKLY MISCELLANY

Location: Dublin (publisher Exshaw, printer S. Powell)
Editor(s):   Anon.
Dates: 10 January 1734–4 January 1735
No. of issues: 52
Average periodicity: Weekly
Average no. pages: 4
Libraries: BL=PP.5348.d; NLI=070 w 7 (offsite, 24 hrs notice; numbers 1 (28 March 1734) to 18 (9 May 1734) only); QUB=MicA/214; TCD=OL Microfilm 245 (Microfilm of British Library copy); UCC (Microfilm).

Comes in three sections ('Discourses Political, Moral, &c', 'Literary News, or an Account of Books published', 'Summary of the News'). The literary news covers one or two pages, and is mostly short reviews and notices of works just published. Most are from London publishers, with the rest evenly divided between Paris, The Hague and Dublin. There is also an overt ideological current to this magazine – volume 1, number 8 carries 'A Letter… promoting English Protestant schools in Ireland'; number 9 has a copy of the Royal Charter promoting the same cause. Although number 10 has a dreadful poem 'On Celestial and Terrestrial Love', translated from Cardinal Bellaye, 'literary news' captures this magazine's contribution exactly, as the notices are all very short, and the whole enterprise is dully methodical, worthy rather than illuminating. If a juicy news item comes in, the literary news can be reduced to as little as half a dozen lines, or even dropped altogether. A statistical analysis of the works publicised would give some insight into the tastes of the day, even after allowing for the bias towards the printer's own books.

THE PUBLICK REGISTER: OR, THE WEEKLY MAGAZINE

Location: London, but reprinted in Belfast by Francis Joy, Bridge Street, Belfast
Editor(s):   Anon.
Dates: 3 January 1741–16 May 1741
No. of issues: 20
Average periodicity: Weekly
Average no. pages: 16
Libraries: LIN.

[The copy of this magazine in the Linenhall is Henry Joy's, and is lightly annotated by him. The British Library has a copy of the London-published original at PP.5450.]

This feels very different from the earlier newsletters, which were padded out with verses. The non-literary material never amounts to even half the magazine, and sometimes comprises as little as two or three pages. They also kept to their promise to avoid 'Quack advertisements', and almost all the advertising relates to books or pamphlets just published.

The first three sections make up the bulk of the magazine: 'Original Letters and Essays', 'Poetical Essays' and 'Records of Literature'. The first is usually given over to a light essay on subjects such as novelty, humour or 'the difference betwixt Fancy and Conceit'; section two is a few pages of poems, none of them distinguished or rising above the usual Augustan collection of translations from Horace and Virgil, insipid pastoral and weak satire, spiced with the occasional song by John Gay or passage from Milton. Section three comprises short book reviews and letters from subscribers. As is usual at this period, most of the contributions are either anonymous or pseudonymous. The *Register* seems to go into decline from issue 17, when it shrinks to twelve pages, then later to eight; finally number 20 carries an announcement of the magazine's closure.

While the contents are not of the highest quality, the *Publick Register* stands out from earlier (and not a few later) periodicals for its relatively serious approach to literature – from issue 4 onward it carried a notice hoping that it 'might become a general Vehicle for the Literati of the whole Kingdom to communicate their knowledge, and converse with each other'. Production values are quite high, with good quality paper and clear, well-spaced type. The only references to Ireland to be found in its pages (outside the advertisements for Joy's own products) are one or two passing allusions to Swift.

A LITERARY JOURNAL

Location:	Dublin (printer S. Powell)
Editor(s):	Jean Pierre Droz
Dates:	Volume 1, number 1 (October 1744)–volume 5, number 9 (June 1749)
No. of issues:	10
Average periodicity:	First 6 quarterly; next 2 biannual; last 2 annual
Average no. pages:	200
Libraries:	BL=273.g.27–31; NLI=8205 L 5; TCD(Old Library)=OLS 194.n.23–27; UCD=SC 33.D.17–18 (April 1746–June 1749 only).

In an 'Advertisement' in the first issue, the editor (a Huguenot clergyman, and a bookseller) states: 'my intention is to give abstracts of the most important foreign books... I shall choose the best abstracts to be found in the great Variety of Foreign Journals... I shall also venture some short remarks of my own... I do not mean to so confine myself as never to take notice of English Writers.' This is an excellent description of the magazine, which comprises chunks of various memoirs, treatises, pamphlets and essays. It may be hack work, but it is very thoroughly and conscientiously done, with some of the extracts and articles carrying on for over thirty pages, and being allowed to run over several issues if necessary. The 'Literary News' at the back of each issue covers Sweden, Muscovy, Poland, Prussia, Italy and France, among others. The magazine is also well indexed. By the second volume a couple of Dublin publishers have crept into the literary news.

The contents sweep from 'A Description of Lapland', through 'A Treatise Concerning the Senses', to 'Letters from Calvin', but there are only two substantial pieces on Ireland in the whole run. Volume 3, part 2 (January–March 1746) contains an abstract from *The Works of Sir James Ware, concerning Ireland*, which runs into volume 4, part 2 (September 1746–March 1747), and is mainly concerned with an antiquarian examination of such issues as the 'Druids', and their supposed Hebrew origins.

See Anon., untitled letter to editor, *Anthologia Hibernica* (October 1793), pp. 259–260.

See J.-P. Pittion, '"A Literary Journal" (Dublin, 1744–9): Reflections on the Role of French Culture in Eighteenth-century Ireland', *Hermathena* 121 (1976), pp. 129–141.

See Alvin Sullivan, *British Literary Magazines: The Augustan Age and the Age of Johnson, 1698–1788* (Westport, 1983), pp. 192–197.

See M. Pollard, *Dublin's Trade in Books, 1550–1800* (Oxford, 1989), p. 158.

See James W. Phillips, *Printing and Bookselling in Dublin, 1670–1800* (Dublin, 1998), pp. 79, 300.

THE MAGAZINE OF MAGAZINES
(Compiled from original pieces, with extracts from the most celebrated books and periodical compositions)

Location:	Limerick (printer Andrew Welsh)
Editor(s):	Anon.
Dates:	January 1751–September 1769
No. of issues:	232
Average periodicity:	Monthly
Average no. pages:	96
Libraries:	BL=PP.6180.f (incomplete); NLI=Ir 05 m 2 (incomplete); UCD=SC 32.H.13-14 (January–December 1751).

The 'Preface' to the first number condemns – no doubt for wholly altruistic reasons – the generally low quality of magazines; it also makes an explicit appeal to female readers. Tone and content are both very similar to that of J.P. Droz's *Literary Journal*, and indeed this makes a more fitting successor to that publication than the *Compendious Library* (see below). Most of the contents are again taken from other magazines and cover the usual range of subjects – historical figures, contemporary events, discoveries in science and nature, along with a sprinkling of undistinguished literary items. These include an average of ten pages of dull verse, the odd romance and eastern tale, and translations of Horace and Juvenal, although they do also publish extracts, presumably pirated, from Johnson's *Rambler*. Like the *Compendious Library* this magazine also reproduces some of the Earl of Orrery's *Remarks* on Swift. From the contents alone, it would be impossible to guess that this periodical was of Irish origin.

THE COMPENDIOUS LIBRARY: OR, LITERARY JOURNAL REVIVED

Location:	Dublin (publisher Powell)
Editor(s):	V. Desvoeux
Dates:	November/December 1751–1752
No. of issues:	Only two extant
Average periodicity:	Bimonthly
Average no. pages:	96
Libraries:	BL=1508/1065; NLI=I 6551 Dubl 1752; TCD=Gall.C.11.36, number 1 (November/December 1751 and January/February 1752 only; bound into *Miscellaneous Tracts*).

The 'Preface' to the issue for November/December 1751 declares this to be a 'revival' of the late J.P. Droz's *Literary Journal*, and follows that with a manifesto for blandness. The editor abjures passing judgement on books, rejects consulting his own taste, and promises to avoid controversy, satire, personal reflections or anything that might be 'deemed unmannerly': to a large extent he succeeds. He sticks closely to the pattern established by Droz, with substantial extracts from (mostly foreign) books, and twenty pages of 'Literary News'. The only interesting items are in the issue for January/February 1752, and comprise a sizeable extract from *Remarks on the Life and Writings of Dr Jonathan Swift* by John Boyle, Earl of Orrery (Dublin, 1752), and a complimentary review of Fielding's *Amelia*. The *Compendious Review* is neither as thorough nor as professional a production as the *Literary Journal*, and is of considerably less interest and importance.

THE DUBLIN LIBRARY: OR, IRISH MAGAZINE

Location:	Dublin (printer Dillon Chamberlaine, Smock Alley)
Editor(s):	Anon.
Dates:	1 May 1761–October 1761
No. of issues:	8
Average periodicity:	May and June, fortnightly; thereafter, monthly
Average no. pages:	56
Libraries:	NLI=J 05.

As usual with the journals of this period, the bulk of this production is made up of articles of general interest – oriental tales, 'An Essay on Laughter', 'History of the Knights of Malta' – but it also included poetry (six pages, on average) and 'Literary Articles' (two pages). The poetry is unexceptional, while the 'Literary News' usually consists of nothing more than lists of newly published works. There are only a couple of interesting items, including 'A Journey Through Ireland' (in the issue for 16–30 May 1761), and 'The Manners and Customs of the Native Irish' (July 1761).

See Richard Cargill Cole, *Irish Booksellers and English Writers 1740–1800* (London, 1986), p. 10.

THE DUBLIN MAGAZINE

Location:	Dublin (printer Wilson)
Editor(s):	Anon.
Dates:	January 1762–December 1764
No. of issues:	36
Average periodicity:	Monthly
Average no. pages:	64
Libraries:	BL=PP.6154.i; MAR=Y.8.109(2),110,111; NLI=J 05; PSPL=Gilbert Collection (January 1762–December 1764); RIA=RR Gall/36/B (as 'Wilson's Dublin Magazine'); TCD(Old Library)=159.d.27–28, 30–32; UCD=SC 44.Y.11/1 (June 1762–August 1762, and May 1764 only).

This is another fairly unimportant eighteenth-century magazine of general interest, which includes four or five pages of 'Poetry' and five or six of 'Literary Intelligence'; quite a lot of its contents, both literary and non-literary, are 'borrowed' from other publications. The poetry is of purely historical interest, the most frequent contributor being David Garrick, including a couple of his 'alterations' of Shakespeare. Also popular were a 'Miss Carter', and Charles Churchill; in terms of quality, none of them remotely approaches the occasional reprinted poem by Swift. The reviews tend to be very short, and are again mainly of historical interest; 'Ossian's' *Fingal* receives glowing praise, as does a new edition of Swift's poetry, while *Tristram Shandy* is roundly condemned.

See Richard Cargill Cole, *Irish Booksellers and English Writers 1740–1800* (London, 1986), p. 10.

THE REPOSITORY: OR, LIBRARY OF FUGITIVE PIECES

Location:	Dublin (printer Dillon Chamberlaine, Smock Alley)
Editor(s):	Anon.
Dates:	1763
No. of issues:	8
Average periodicity:	not known
Average no. pages:	56
Libraries:	NLI= Ir 828 r 8; RIA=RR Gall/36/B.

This is an exact reprint of another of Chamberlaine's magazines, the *Dublin Library*, or *Irish Magazine* (see above), published two years earlier.

THE HIBERNIAN MAGAZINE: OR, COMPENDIUM OF ENTERTAINING KNOWLEDGE
(Containing, the greatest variety of the most curious and useful subjects in every branch
of polite literature)

Location:	Dublin (publisher James Potts, Swift's Head, Dame Street; from October 1773 Peter Seguin, Stephen's Green; from June 1778 Thomas Walker, 79 Dame Street)
Editor(s):	Anon.
Dates:	February 1771–July 1812
No. of issues:	510
Average periodicity:	Monthly
Average no. pages:	56
Libraries:	BL=6154.k; LIN (incomplete); NLI=J 05; PSPL=052; QUB=MicA/180–194 (includes index at MicA/180); RIA=Mem R/Case 3/C; TCD=OO.pp.103; UCC (1777–1812 only); UCD=SC 33.J.1-15, SC 33.JJ.1-13, and SC 33.K.1-16.

The first issue opens with an account of 'the great sea-snake' by the Bishop of Bergen, but it also includes a letter of Laurence Sterne's, a 'critique' of a new play, short notices of half a dozen theatrical productions, a prose retelling of a new tragedy, two or three moral tales, and eight poems; all of which (plus the purely non-literary elements) amount to a typical edition of this magazine. Indeed, possibly the most remarkable thing about the *Hibernian Magazine* is the fact that the formula remained unchanged for so long – over forty years. After 1773 slightly more stories and the odd serialised novel appear, while the only innovation of the 1790s is the inclusion of the sheet music for a popular song or a song from one of the plays in each number. The rest of the magazine, perhaps two-thirds of each issue, is made up of the usual contents of a late eighteenth-century magazine: accounts of debates in the two parliaments, foreign news, and general and political essays.

Very little of the creative writing is worth reading; in fact, the only interest in most of the poetry is that it shows how long the influence of pre-Romantic ideals lasted in Ireland, and then the tentative emergence of a more Romantic approach. In spite of the appearance in March 1771 of the Scots ballad 'The Wife of Auchtermuchty' (complete with translation), up until the mid-1790s the pre-Romantic mode is unchallenged, the pages crowded with 'Julia's Beauty', 'Advice to the Fair', and imitations of Horace; by 1797 (alongside reports from Bantry Bay) an element of dilute Romanticism has crept in, mainly manifesting itself in an increase in the number of nature poems, although there are even a couple of more political efforts ('To Mr. Wilberforce').

Most of the prose reveals the strange fascination of the editors (or their readers) with the orient, in 'factual' anecdotes and stories, with Turkish sultans and their harems' special favourites. The first Irish subject matter appears in May 1771 in an account of an exhibition by Dublin artists, which carries over into June; the June issue also carries an account of Newgrange. This marks the start of a more serious engagement with the matter of Ireland, although this is mainly devoted to straight political coverage, including sympathetic reporting of the revolt in America, the Volunteers and (in the early stages, at least), the French Revolution and the United Irishmen. In the magazine's cultural sections we find mainly that characteristic late eighteenth-century antiquarianism: 'Essay on the Antiquity of the Irish Language' ('proving' it to be descended from Punic), extracts from 'Ossian', 'Essay on Druidical Monuments', and so on. From September 1771 the *Hibernian* carries brief book reviews, initially of books published abroad, but by 1773 also of the output of the Dublin publishers. At this time they also publish the odd radical essay by Voltaire, and a couple of more solid literary items, including a five-page extract from *Humphrey Clinker* (July 1771), a six-page essay on Sterne (March 1774), and a short essay on Richardson's *Clarissa* (February 1789).

From the early 1790s the increasing political fervour both at home and abroad pushes literature off the pages, and from 1797 the (by now very hostile) accounts of the United Irishmen, the Rebellion and its aftermath, and the French wars force the literary content into a decline from which it never really recovers.

See M. Burke, E. Clossick, P. Hanlon and J. McKenna, *Index to Walker's Hibernian Magazine*, for Fellowship of the Library Association of Ireland (nd.)
See Alvin Sullivan, *British Literary Magazines: The Augustan Age and the Age of Johnson, 1698–1788* (Westport, 1983), pp. 157–160.
See Richard Cargill Cole, *Irish Booksellers and English Writers 1740–1800* (London, 1986), pp. 10, 50, 72, 82–85, 102, 104, 105, 108, 111, 112, 118, 121, 124, 136, 140, 141, 143, 160, 178, 198.

THE WEEKLY MAGAZINE AND LITERARY REVIEW
(Containing a variety of instructive and entertaining essays, in verse and prose)

Location:	Dublin (printer John Norman)
Editor(s):	Anon.
Dates:	2 January 1779–17 April 1779
No. of issues:	16
Average periodicity:	Weekly
Average no. pages:	24, issues 1–4; thereafter 18
Libraries:	NLI=J 05.

Yet another eighteenth-century magazine which is largely constructed out of extracts from others. The first issue contains an essay on the theatre by Rousseau, an 'Elegy' by Chatterton, and a 'Song' by Goldsmith; combine this with a few general essays, and a number of very short romances, tales and 'characters', and you have a typical issue. The quality of the 'borrowed' items balances out the deadweight pieces, but only just; in all a lightweight production.

THE UNIVERSAL MAGAZINE AND REVIEW: OR, REPOSITORY OF LITERATURE
(Containing the Literature, History, Manners, Arts and Amusements of the Age)

Location:	Dublin (printer P. Byrne, Grafton Street)
Editor(s):	Anon.
Dates:	Volume 1 (1789)–volume 8 (1792)
No. of issues:	36
Average periodicity:	Monthly
Average no. pages:	100
Libraries:	BL=PP.6154.g; LIN (February, April, May and June 1789, and January 1790 only); PSPL=052 (incomplete); RIA=Mem R/Case 3/B; TCD(Old Library)=OLS L-1-792-793 (January–June 1790 and January–June 1791 only); UCD=SC 33.D.15-16 (January–June 1789 and January–June 1790 only).

The contents are the usual mixed bag, including stories ('The Parricide Punished', 'The Hermit's Cave'), letters from readers, essays ('On Dramas', 'The Passions and their Effects', 'On Gaming'), reviews (including quite a high proportion of books published in Dublin), Irish parliamentary proceedings, poetry, and domestic and foreign news. Longer stories and essays are sometimes carried over a number of issues.

The quality of both the production and the contents is quite low. The tone tends towards the less serious and the diverting, although it never sinks to the merely frivolous. The *Universal* has quite a strong Irish flavour, although this is mostly due to the coverage of the Irish parliament and domestic news (mostly agrarian unrest). The book reviews also contribute to this, as quite a few of the books are printed in Dublin, and some even have Irish subjects, as usual with eighteenth-century productions of an antiquarian nature, including archaeological finds and a treatise on Irish dress. Some Irish poems and novels are also reviewed. The creative writing is scant and none of it is distinguished.

See Richard Cargill Cole, *Irish Booksellers and English Writers 1740–1800* (London, 1986), pp. 10, 108, 111, 182.

THE LIMERICK WEEKLY MAGAZINE: OR, MISCELLANEOUS REPOSITORY

Location:	Limerick (printer George Cherry)
Editor(s):	Anon.
Dates:	19 June 1790–11 December 1790
No. of issues:	26
Average periodicity:	Weekly
Average no. pages:	8
Libraries:	NLI=J 05.

Another fairly dull 'compilation' magazine, whose 'borrowing' includes a couple of pieces by Dr Johnson which, although quite entertaining, do not make up for the rest of the items. These are mostly weak poems, whose only interest is that they show some stirrings of Romanticism, e.g. in 'Knight Walter – a legendary tale', in issue 10. In twenty-six issues, there are just two explicit references to Ireland, a description of the lakes of Killarney (number 12), and 'A Description of Ireland, written in 1500', (number 25).

THE SENTIMENTAL AND MASONIC MAGAZINE

Location:	Dublin (printer John Jones, Grafton Street)
Editor(s):	Anon.
Dates:	July 1792–August 1795
No. of issues:	38
Average periodicity:	Monthly
Average no. pages:	96
Libraries:	BL=PP.1056; LIN (1793 only); NLI=J 05; QUB=wAP3.S5; RIA=RR Gall/Case 35/F.

Despite the title, there is rarely more than one Masonic-related item per issue of this wide-ranging magazine, and that is often a poem. It is in three sections, the first (usually around fifty pages) comprising general articles (portraits of famous Irishmen, martial stories, traveller's tales, etc.), and the last (around twenty pages) a summary of parliamentary proceedings. The remaining portion is devoted to stories, poems and the occasional novel extract.

The poems touch only obliquely on Irish subjects, for example, one may be in praise of a famous politician or nobleman, another may praise a great house; there is a heavy tendency toward pastoral. Among a swarm of imitators (and almost four hundred poems were published in three years) are a handful of works by Gay, Sheridan and Gray ('The Bard' and the 'Elegy'). Only a few have any direct relation to the country in which they were written, such as the translation of a song from the Irish in August 1792, or 'Dermod and Cathleen, or the Dying Peasant' (by 'W.P. C__r__y.' who, along with 'M.E. O'Brien' contributes a large number of the poems). Similarly the reviews and articles are as likely to be on English, or even French, writers as Irish. There is less reliance on moral essays than was common earlier in the century, and more Gothic romances and oriental tales, for example 'The Friar's Tale' (July–October 1792) or 'Grasville Abbey', which ran from July 1793 until the closure of the magazine. There are anecdotal articles on earlier writers like Johnson and Goldsmith, and more serious comments on Sterne, Pope and Swift; from December 1794 to February 1795 a detailed piece, 'Remarks on a leading Sentiment in Dr. Johnson's Rambler' was serialised. The issue for September 1793 begins 'The Critic: or, Annals of the Literature of Ireland', an anonymous and fairly regular column which averaged ten pages in length. The column is varied, containing at various times reviews, notices of new books, plays or poems, plus more general remarks on contemporary writing, liberally illustrated with quotations.

The lifespan of the *Sentimental* was too short for there to be much development, although there is a definite feeling that the literature was becoming more important as time went by; the number of poems in each issue goes up from an average of eight or nine at the start to a peak of nineteen in August 1794. The critical pieces, while still few in number, were becoming slightly more serious. Unfortunately this trend was reversed as the pace of outside events increased; more space is given to coverage of the war with France and to political events at home such as the trials of William Drennan and Hamilton Rowan, at the expense of literature. Then, from about April 1795, a decline sets in: the number of poems and stories begins to fall, the literary anecdotes disappear, and the general articles become more trivial.

See Richard Cargill Cole, *Irish Booksellers and English Writers 1740–1800* (London, 1986), p. 119.

ANTHOLOGIA HIBERNICA: OR, MONTHLY COLLECTIONS OF SCIENCE, BELLE-LETTRES, AND HISTORY

Location:	Dublin (printer Edward Mercier, 31 Anglesea Street)
Editor(s):	Anon.
Dates:	January 1793–December 1794
No. of issues:	24
Average periodicity:	Monthly
Average no. pages:	80
Libraries:	BL=251.1.12-15 and G.415-61 (two copies; North Library); LIN; NLI=J Ir 8205 a 2; PSPL=052; QUB=hAP3.A6; RDS=LR I 050; RIA=RR/Gall/35/G/24-27; TCD=V.k.64-67; UCC; UCD=26.E.1-4 (Special Collection).

This is one of the best Irish literary magazines of the eighteenth century. The standard of scholarship is high, and it takes its subjects seriously; there is a good admixture of Irish material, and the layout, illustrations, and the quality of the paper and printing are all very good. At the back of each issue are two sections, 'Literary Intelligence' (short notices of new books, including from number 4 onward a subsection on 'Irish Literature' which, for example, includes a favourable notice of Wolfe Tone's pamphlet for the Catholic Committee), and 'Poetry', which covers new poems submitted to the magazine, plus a fair amount of reprinted material. The former averages four pages in length (or over one hundred pages over the run of the magazine), the latter averages nine pages, or well over two hundred pages in total. The poetry, with one or two exceptions, is very much of the eighteenth century, with a great number of translations from the classics (especially Horace), epigrams, and a very Augustan approach to pastoral. It is largely undistinguished, although a few stand out (those by Thomas Moore, or Burns's 'Tam O'Shanter'). The more general literary coverage includes essays on translation, a long essay on contemporary drama (which continues through twelve issues), and a short piece on Shakespeare, as well as more eccentric items such as league tables rating the genius of different writers (Homer and Shakespeare tie for first place!).

Every issue carries a fairly substantial essay on an Irish subject, such as the Irish language (this is a much more sensible piece than those which appeared earlier in the century, with no claims of descent from Hebrew or Punic), ancient Irish laws and customs, ruins and great houses, and so on. The introduction to such an essay in number 5 (May 1793) states 'Anything in the line of Irish antiquities cannot be displeasing'. There is also a fair amount of Irish literary material, for example a reminiscence on the Rev. J.P. Droz (editor of *A Literary Journal*, see above), a letter of Goldsmith's, a couple of pastoral poems with titles like 'The Irish Peasant', some very early poems of Thomas Moore, and even three or four poems or songs in Irish, some with translations, some not. There is also a very interesting open letter on the (lack of) Irish copyright laws.

Anthologia Hibernica had strong connections with Trinity College, and a much more active readership than earlier magazines, with a large number of letters, notes and queries from them appearing in its pages, as well as many of the more formal contributions. In its second year there is a slight change of tone, with the emphasis shifting away from the literary, and more space given to both political commentary (essays on the workings of parliament, or on slavery, for instance), and new developments in science and mathematics. As usual, there is no hint that issue 24 was to be the last.

See M. Pollard, *Dublin's Trade in Books, 1550–1800* (Oxford, 1989), pp. 91–93, 143.
See Mary Helen Thuente, *The Harp Re-strung, The United Irishmen and the Rise of Irish Literary Nationalism* (New York, 1994), pp. 74–79, 83, 110.

THE GLEANOR: A PERIODICAL WORK

Location:	Dublin (printer Edward Mercier, Anglesea Street)
Editor(s):	Anon.
Dates:	1 December 1793–1794?
No. of issues:	5?
Average periodicity:	?
Average no. pages:	6
Libraries:	NLI=IR 824 s 3 (bound into Sir William C. Smith, *Miscellanies in Prose*); PSPL=052; QUB=hAP3.M6 (bound into *Miscellanies in Prose*); RIA=RR Gall/36/F.

This is a selection from a column which appeared in numbers twelve to twenty-one of *Anthologia Hibernica*. Whether it ever appeared as a magazine on its own is very doubtful. It is more likely that it was used by Mercier to pad out *Miscellanies in Prose*. In any case the contents are not of outstanding quality, mostly satirical, including a mock-heroic poem, false letters claiming to be from readers, and a great deal of student humour.

THE PARLOUR WINDOW
(Containing original essays, poetry and part of An Instructive Tale)

Location:	Dublin (printer J. Whitworth, Exchange Street)
Editor(s):	Anon.
Dates:	1795
No. of issues:	7
Average periodicity:	Weekly?
Average no. pages:	40
Libraries:	NLI=J 05; TCD=OLS 186.0.30, number 2 (numbers 1–6 only, bound into *Murphy's Ethicks*).

The first ILM aimed primarily at a female readership, issue 1 begins with an explicitly feminist editorial: 'Female Authors have so many discouragements to encounter, it is no wonder they so rarely appear in Print; the general opinion is against them; People of Contracted Minds, judge hardly of them; and consider that every drop of Ink that flows from the Pen of a Woman, as so many *blots* on her character. As Writers they labour under many disadvantages, which instead of procuring indulgence, rather provoke censure, and their Writings are discovered to have many defects which are often overlooked in those of the other sex.'

A typical issue contains a short essay, favourably comparing the new novel with the old romance, three or four poems (usually lightweight and romantic), and an extract from *Caroline of Abbeyville, An Instructive Tale* (which takes up nearly half of the magazine). This latter confirms the proto-feminist approach, with the heroine's frequent philosophical musings, rather self-consciously laced with references to recent astronomical discoveries and foreign literature.

Caroline is set in England, and in all seven issues the only direct mention of Ireland is the translation in number 5 'Sonnet from the Irish'. Nevertheless, this is one of the more interesting and innovative of eighteenth-century Irish literary magazines, and also one of the least derivative; it is one of the few whose short lifespans are to be regretted.

THE FLAPPER, A PERIODICAL WORK

Location:	Dublin (publisher and printer Richard E. Mercier and Co., 31 Anglesea Street)
Editor(s):	Anon.
Dates:	2 February 1796–4 February 1797 (although flyleaf to bound volume says 2 February 1796–10 September 1797, neither copy I have examined actually contains any extra material)
No. of issues:	75
Average periodicity:	Twice-weekly
Average no. pages:	4

Libraries: BL=629.1.7; BCL=I/052.[1] FLAP; NLI=IR 05 f 4; also a selection
                            bound into IR 824 s 3, Sir William C. Smith, *Miscellanies in Prose*);
                            PSPL=052; QUB=hAP3.M6 (*Miscellanies in Prose*); RIA=RR
                            Gall/36/F (2 copies); TCD=TT.c.52.

A selection of pieces from this is bound, together with selections from two other Mercier
periodicals, in a volume called *Miscellanies in Prose*, published by Mercier in 1804. The
copy in QUB is extensively annotated; a later owner attributed these notes to Dr R.R.
Madden. At one point in these notes he describes *The Flapper* as 'one of the dullest [of
Mercier's magazines]', and only three of the issues reproduced in this selection have any
merit. Number 4 (13 February 1796) is devoted to an eight-page discussion on the nature
and standing of the periodical essay; numbers 58 (10 December 1796) and 66 (11
February 1797) are given over to a twenty-five-page critique of Johnson's criticism of
Pope's epitaphs. This is a detailed and thorough rebuttal of Johnson's remarks, although
a little dry.

See Richard Cargill Cole, *Irish Booksellers and English Writers 1740–1800* (London,
    1986), p. 26.

THE MONTHLY MISCELLANY: OR, IRISH REVIEW AND REGISTER

Location: Cork (printer James Haly)
Editor(s):   Anon.
Dates: April 1796–June 1796
No. of issues: 3
Average periodicity: Monthly
Average no. pages: 104
Libraries: NLI=J 05.

This is divided into five sections, of which the most interesting are 'Poetry, original and
selected' (around eight pages), and the 'Review' (eighteen pages, including four or five
pages of 'literary notices', i.e. lists of new publications). The poetry is generally weak, but
the reviews are more worthwhile; one of the publications reviewed is Paine's *Age of
Reason*. The other sections (e.g. 'Original Correspondence') sometimes include an
interesting piece, e.g. 'On the cultivation of Irish history'. It is impossible to draw
significant conclusions on the basis of just three issues, but *The Monthly Miscellany* could
have been one of the better magazines published in Ireland in the eighteenth century. It was
serious, but not pompous, the contents were of a reasonable quality, and the whole effort
much more professional than the norm.

THE MICROSCOPE: OR, MINUTE OBSERVER

Location:	Belfast (printer Joseph Smyth, High Street)
Editor(s):	Anon.
Dates:	Volume 1, number 1 (May 1799)–volume 2, number 12 (December 1800)
No. of issues:	21 (including a Supplementary Number, December 1800)
Average periodicity:	Monthly
Average no. pages:	48
Libraries:	BCL=I/094.1[1] SMYT; LIN; NLI=Ir 6551 Belf 1800 (1800 only; two copies); QUB=hAP4.M7; TCD(Old Library)=159.c.35 (1800 only).

The first issue is prefaced by 'To The Public', where it is described as a 'lucrative plan of intellectual commerce', where the Augustan age is described in historical terms, and where the very un-Augustan assertion is made that contemporary Addisons may be at that moment trapped behind a plough. Both this preface and the magazine itself suffer greatly from 'cultural cringe': the preface states their intention to publish local writing 'though we cannot equal ... the authors of the English classes', and ends with the self-conscious (if understandable, given contemporary events) reassurance that 'nothing offensive either to the civil Power, to propriety, or to Christianity shall find a place in this publication'.

This tension between an appeal to pre-Romantic and conservative certainties and the desire to produce something local and new runs throughout *The Microscope*'s brief run. The first issue is entirely given over to the classic late eighteenth-century mix of moral essays, 'characters', anecdotes and so on; in the second a couple of poems by (anonymous) local writers and a serialised novel creep in; in issue 3 essays on Milton and Virgil are balanced by an extract from Coleridge's 'Tears in Solitude'. It is not until number 7 (November 1799) that any explicitly Irish subjects appear, in the form of an essay 'Memoirs of Farquhar'.

Gradually the implicit Romanticism becomes more coherent; the 'characters' begin to be of French or American politicians, mild essays opposing slavery or even the impending Union appear, and titles like 'The Hermit of Mont-Blanc' or 'The Ghost' emerge among the poetry. The issues of July, August and November 1800 carry a quite substantial piece on Cowper, reproducing some of his poems. The best piece to appear in *The Microscope* is William Drennan's 'Protest' in March 1800, rejecting the Union.

Otherwise, the connection with contemporary Ireland is weak: none of the poems have Irish themes, and the subjects of the essays are either long dead or politically 'safe' (e.g. the fifteen pages devoted to Goldsmith in December 1800). Most of the contents are worthy rather than stimulating, and overall the magazine has the feel of a very promising enterprise stifled by the political climate in which it was forced to operate.

See John Killen, *An Index to The Microscope (1799) and to the Belfast Literary Journal (1816)* (Belfast, 1994). This is a first-class author and subject index to the two magazines, with microfiche copies of the full runs bound into the back.

THE ULSTER MAGAZINE: OR, EDIFYING AND INTERESTING MISCELLANY

Location: Lurgan (printer Robert Crawford)
Editor(s):   Anon.
Dates: January–June 1804
No. of issues: 6
Average periodicity: Monthly
Average no. pages: 72
Libraries: LIN; NLI=I 6551 Lurgan (February 1804 only); PSPL=052.

This is a current affairs magazine, concentrating on events in France, but it does have one section, 'Original and Select Poetry', at the back of each issue. Some thirty poems were published over the six issues, none of them distinguished. The journal closed due to insufficient sales – in fact, only eighty names appear in the list of subscribers; however, it remains the first Irish literary magazine to be produced outside of the biggest towns.

THE CYCLOPÆDIAN MAGAZINE, AND DUBLIN MONTHLY REGISTER OF HISTORY, LITERATURE, THE ARTS, SCIENCE &C.

Location: Dublin (printer Thomas Burnside, Dame Street)
Editor(s):   Anon.
Dates: January 1807–December 1808
No. of issues: 24
Average periodicity: Monthly
Average no. pages: 64
Libraries: BL=PP.6167; MAR=Y.9.70,71; NLI=J 05; PSPL=052; RIA=MEM R/Case 3/K; TCD=P.vv.1.N.2-4, 5 (November 1807, July 1808 and September 1808 only; bound into volume entitled *Irish Magazines*).

A minor magazine, very clearly organised into a number of sections, only three of which are of interest – 'Literature, Science and the Fine Arts', 'The Drama' and 'Poetry'. The first is a dozen pages of short and superficial book notices; the second comprises some ten pages of short notices of current plays, along with some theatre gossip; and the last is three or four pages of poetry, 'original and selected'. While issue 1 reprints 'Helvellyn', by Sir Walter Scott, the dominant poet of *The Cyclopædian* is Thomas Dermody, who has a piece in virtually every issue. None of the books reviewed are of more than historical interest, the reviews themselves are too short, and few of the poems stand out.

THE IRISH MAGAZINE, AND MONTHLY ASYLUM FOR NEGLECTED BIOGRAPHY

Location: Dublin (publisher Walter Cox)
Editor(s):   Walter Cox
Dates: 1 November 1807–December(?) 1815
No. of issues: 98
Average periodicity: Monthly
Average no. pages: 48
Libraries: BL=PP.6154.m; LIN (incomplete); NLI=J 05 (1807–1809 only); PSPL=052 (1809–1815); QUB=hAP4.I6 (incomplete); RIA=RR G/36/C; TCD=V.k.69–76; UCD=SC 33.N.1–4 (November 1807–November 1810, and January–July 1815 only).

An infamous sectarian publication – Sir Robert Peel (admittedly a not entirely unbiased witness), claimed that its sole purpose was 'to ferment a bitter hatred against England'; in 1810 it produced the illustrations of claimed brutalities during 1798 (pitch-cappings and floggings) which were to be reprinted again and again for decades. A typical issue is mainly made up of accounts of Catholic martyrs, bishops and saints, along with a fair scattering of miscellaneous pieces on subjects ranging from piracy to fashion. However, at the end of each issue there is a short section, from four to six pages in length, dedicated to poetry: 'Where wild Drumard's bless'd abbey lies/In ruins, awfully sublime;/Exhibiting to wanderers wise,/The ravages of changeful time,/ Dwelt a recluse...' ('The Recluse', April 1808). The poetry is of fairly low quality, although it is interestingly caught between the Gothic (see example above), and traditional eighteenth-century modes (see 'Lucia & Corydon', September 1808). By the end of 1809 one can detect the first stirrings of that strain of Irish versifying best exemplified by Thomas Moore, and represented here by many anonymous efforts with titles such as 'To Erin', 'The Harp' and 'The Patriot's Grave'.

By 1811 the magazine has taken a definite move downmarket, with the general articles becoming more sectarian and the poetry more popular, with more and more ballads and patriotic songs appearing; there is also less poetry in each issue, and from 1813 onward, some issues have no poems at all.

See Séamus O Casaide, 'Watty Cox and His Publications', *Bibliographical Society of Ireland Publications* 5 (1935), pp. 17–38.

See Barbara Hayley, 'A Reading and Thinking Nation: Periodicals as the Voice of Nineteenth-Century Ireland', in Barbara Hayley and Enda McKay, *300 Years of Irish Periodicals* (Mullingar, 1987), p. 31.

See Brendan Clifford, *The Origins of Catholic Nationalism, Selections from Walter Cox's 'Irish Magazine'* (Belfast, 1992).

THE MONTHLY PANTHEON: OR, GENERAL REPERTORY OF POLITICS, ARTS, SCIENCE, LITERATURE, AND MISCELLANEOUS INFORMATION

Location:	Dublin (printer J. Stockdale and Sons, Abbey Street, publisher Gilbert and Hodges)
Editor(s):	Anon.
Dates:	June 1808–November 1809
No. of issues:	18
Average periodicity:	Monthly
Average no. pages:	80 (occasionally longer)
Libraries:	LIN (June 1808–May 1809); NLI=J 05; PSPL=052; RIA=Mem R/3/J; TCD=P.w.1 (December 1808, February 1809 and November 1809 only; bound into volume entitled *Irish Magazines*); UCD=SC 32.N.5–7.

A general repertory indeed, with the overwhelming bulk of each issue dedicated to historical sketches, scientific discoveries, parliamentary proceedings, and so on. But from the start there were a couple of pages each given over to poetry and to reviews of new publications. The poetry soon grows to five or six pages, and a kind of Romanticism very indebted to Thomas Moore predominates, although strangely it lacks the nationalist element. The literary contents of the *Pantheon* gradually evolve – by October short romances and tales appear, usually claiming Moorish or Spanish origins; from January 1809 some more extensive reviews appear, e.g. one of 'Ossian'; and by the following May, more general literary articles emerge, 'on novel writing', or female authors. The November 1808 issue contains a very obvious and patronising play for female readers, and related articles (advice and tales 'for the Ladies') begin to be published. By the following summer, tentative hints of nationalism have emerged, first in mild political pieces, then in translations from the Irish, although this never reaches the original poetry. In general, the literary items are only of historical interest.

THE BELFAST MONTHLY MAGAZINE

Location:	Belfast (publisher Smyth and Lyons, High Street)
Editor(s):	William Drennan
Dates:	1 September 1808–31 December 1814
No. of issues:	77
Average periodicity:	Monthly
Average no. pages:	82
Libraries:	BCL=I/094.1[1] SMYT (3 issues only); BL=PP.6180.c; LIN; NLI=J 05; QUB=hAP4.B4; RIA=RR/Gall/35; TCD=AA.ss.28; UCD=SC 32.H.3-12 (September 1808–December 1812 only).

A good, solid, general magazine, covering contemporary politics, Irish antiquities, farming, new discoveries and social gossip, with a regular literary content, and edited by one of the outstanding radical figures of his generation. An unusual feature is that many of the articles (although none of the poems) are signed. Each issue contains a list of new publications, reviews of some of these, and some poetry; together these amount to about two dozen pages. In addition, there is the occasional essay on Ovid and 'Persian' or 'Spanish' tale. The first issue carries a review of Scott's poem 'Marmion'. The only interesting poems to appear are the long narrative 'The O'Nial' [*sic*] in issue 3, and 'My Ain Fire-Side', an Ulster-Scots dialect piece in issue 8. The poetry in the magazine is an uncomfortable mixture of eighteenth-century ('Epistle to a Young Man Going to College to Study Physic') and nineteenth-century modes ('Written in a Grove'). The *Belfast Monthly*'s tone is mildly nationalist, favourable to reform on the 'Catholic Question', interested in the Irish language and antiquities, although the tone of many of the pieces published, and the names of most contributors, imply that the audience was mostly Protestant. From 1809 the literary content begins to decline, both in quality and in quantity, with the book reviews suffering particularly and soon being dropped completely. An interesting magazine, although not terribly important from a literary viewpoint.

See Norman Vance, *Irish Literature: A Social History – Tradition, Identity and Difference* (Oxford, 1990), p. 100.
See Mary Helen Thuente, *The Harp Re-strung, The United Irishmen and the Rise of Irish Literary Nationalism* (New York, 1994), p. 197.

THE WEEKLY SELECTOR: OR, SLIGO MISCELLANEOUS MAGAZINE

Location: Sligo (printer and publisher A. Bolton, Castle Street)
Editor(s):   Anon.
Dates   :   18 February 1812–31 April 1812
No. of issues: 9
Average periodicity: Weekly
Average no. pages: 8
Libraries: NLI=P 2393 (volume entitled *Pamphlets*).

Each issue of this small magazine carries a serialised story, a general article (most often biographical), a few letters and news items, and three or four poems on the back page. The quality of most of the contributions is very poor, and the main importance of this magazine is as evidence of the spread of literacy, communications and civil society out from the main towns to the more provincial areas of the island.

See Robert May, 'Rare Sligo Magazine', *Irish Book Lover*, 6 (1914), pp. 56–57.
See Brian McKenna, *Irish Literature 1800–1875* (Detroit, 1978), p. 24.

THE DUBLIN MAGAZINE: OR, MONTHLY MEMORIALIST

Location: Dublin (printer R. Smith, College Green)
Editor(s):   Anon.
Dates: November 1812–December 1813
No. of issues: 12
Average periodicity: Monthly
Average no. pages: 64
Libraries: BL=PP.6156.lb; NLI=J 05; TCD=OLS 198.0.15 (last two issues missing).

The literary content of this production is slight. At the start it is confined to three or four pages of poems; then the occasional tale appears, mostly very short although one ('Hawthorne Cottage') stretches to ten issues and sixty-eight pages. The April and May 1813 issues carry a substantial article on Scott's *Rokeby*. By June 1813 a more Irish tone has crept in, manifested for example in a description of the lakes of Killarney with an accompanying long poem, or in a short piece on Swift; however, this is always balanced by eulogistic sketches of Wellington or George III, a schizophrenia which we see in a number of journals of this period.

THE MONTHLY MUSEUM; OR, DUBLIN LITERARY REPERTORY, OF ARTS, SCIENCE, LITERATURE, AND MISCELLANEOUS INFORMATION

Location: Dublin (printer and publisher Espy and Cross, 9 Bedford Row)
Editor(s):   Anon.
Dates: Number 1 (October 1813)–number 15 (December 1814)
No. of issues: 15
Average periodicity: Monthly
Average no. pages: 64
Libraries: BL=PP.6168; LIN (1 issue only); NLI=J 05; RIA=Fr C/Sect 5/1/B; TCD=Press B.4.24 (complete); also EE.r.28 (Vol 1, October–May only); UCD=SC 32.G.15 (October 1813-September 1814 only).

Each issue includes a couple of pages of verse, a list of newly printed books, and a handful of short book notices; nothing is of lasting merit.

See John S. Crone, 'The Monthly Museum', *Irish Book Lover*, 6 (1914), pp. 43–45.

THE BELFAST LITERARY JOURNAL
(Containing original essays, on various subjects, in literature)

Location:	Belfast (printer George Berwick)
Editor(s):	Anon.
Dates:	Volume 1, number 1 (1 April 1816)–volume 1, number 6 (10 June 1816)
No. of issues:	6
Average periodicity:	Fortnightly
Average no. pages:	32
Libraries:	BCL=I/094.1[1] SMYT (bound into M. M'Dermott Original Miscellaneous Pieces); LIN.

Each number carries a handful of short articles ('On the Music of the Belfast Theatre', 'On Newton's Rules'), a couple of pages of 'Original Poetry', a biographical sketch and the occasional moral tale. The second half of the magazine is taken up with domestic and foreign news, reports of trials, etc. The only interesting item is 'Man was made to Smile', a poem by James Orr in the fifth issue; otherwise the contents are very lightweight, the poems and stories of only historical or topographical interest.

See John Killen, *An Index to The Microscope (1799) and to the Belfast Literary Journal (1816)* (Belfast, 1994). This is a first-class author and subject index to the two magazines, with microfiche copies of the full runs bound into the back.

THE DUBLIN EXAMINER: OR, MONTHLY JOURNAL OF SCIENCE, LITERATURE AND ART

Location:	Dublin (publisher Hodges and McArthur, printer Thomas Reilly, College Green)
Editor(s):	Anon.
Dates:	May 1816–January 1817
No. of issues:	9
Average periodicity:	Monthly
Average no. pages:	80
Libraries:	BL=PP.6169; NLI=J 05; RIA=Moore Lib 3/E; TCD=Gall.M.14.3; UCD=SC 44.Y.16/4 (December 1816–January 1817 only).

The first Irish literary magazine to clearly shake itself free of the preceding century, the *Examiner* clearly belongs to the new era – good quality print (using a variety of the new typefaces available) on good paper, and a bolder, more outgoing approach; it is perhaps emblematic that their literary hero seems to be Byron. The most interesting feature of this journal is its reviews, which are far longer than had previously been the norm, which quote liberally from the works under review, and which are far closer to the modern idea of a book review than the 'literary notices' of an earlier age. The average review covers twelve pages, and subjects include: Byron's 'The Siege of Corinth' (issue 1), Scott's *The Antiquary* and Leigh Hunt's 'The Story of Rimini' (issue 2), Edward Fitzsimons's *Irish Minstrelsy* (issue 3), Moore's *Melodies* and Bunting's *Ancient Music of Ireland* (issue 4), and Charles Maturin's *Bertram* in issue 5. Some of these reviews are interesting in their own right, and of more than historical importance.

There is also some poetry, by Moore, Scott and Byron, but more often by their imitators. Often it is both derivative and sentimentally patriotic – 'The Dying Patriot to his Mistress', or 'The Emigrant'. Finally, there is a scattering of more general literary pieces, including 'Moore's suppressed Preface to *The Irish Melodies*', and an essay comparing Scott with Tasso. A long essay in the sixth issue helps to pinpoint the *Examiner*'s audience, since it is clearly in favour of Catholic Emancipation, but the tone implies a Protestant readership. This is a very good magazine by the standards of Irish literary magazines up to that point, and it is ironic, therefore, that the last issue carries a notice that they are closing due to poor sales.

THE LITERARY AND POLITICAL EXAMINER

Location: Cork (printer John Bolster, Patrick Street)
Editor(s):   Anon.
Dates: February–April 1818
No. of issues: 3
Average periodicity: Monthly
Average no. pages: 64
Libraries: BL=PP.6159.c (no. 1 only); NLI=JP 4712; TCD (Old Library)=OLS.200.o.48 (February and March 1818 only).

There is not really enough in the three surviving numbers on which to base an opinion, although the *Examiner* could have been quite interesting, as indicated by a substantial review of Scott's *Rob Roy*, a good article on Irish antiquaries, a sonnet ('On Flatterie') by Sir Walter Raleigh, and a handful of translations from the Irish.

See Barbara Hayley, 'Irish Periodicals from the Union to the Nation', in P.J. Drudy (ed.), *Anglo-Irish Studies* II (Cambridge, 1976), p. 84.

THE CRITIC: OR, WEEKLY REPOSITORY OF DRAMATIC, LITERARY, POLITICAL, & MISCELLANEOUS INTELLIGENCE

Location: Dublin
Editor(s):   Anon.
Dates: 19 December 1818
No. of issues: 1

Average periodicity: Weekly?
Average no. pages: 16
Libraries: NLI=JP 4712.

A very ephemeral production, the only surviving issue carries some notices of new publications and theatre productions, and a five-page review of *Florence McCarthy* by Lady Morgan.

THE DUBLIN MAGAZINE: OR, GENERAL REPERTORY OF PHILOSOPHY, BELLES LETTRES, AND MISCELLANEOUS INFORMATION

Location: Dublin (printer W. Folds, 88 Great Strand Street)
Editor(s):   E.W.M. Rice and W.G. Cole (attr. S.J. Brown, Hayley)
Dates: January–December 1820
No. of issues: 12
Average periodicity: Monthly
Average no. pages: 80
Libraries: BL=PP.6154.lc; NLI=J 05; PSPL=052; RIA=Fr C/2/3/E-G; TCD=OO.s.40, 41; UCC.

Concentrating mainly on scientific and natural discoveries, with a little politics, this also has eight to ten pages of poetry plus one substantial review in each issue, padded out with the occasional short piece of literary interest. The major reviews – and these can often go to twelve pages or more – include one interesting piece on *Ivanhoe*; the May issue has remarks on Byron, the November on Shelley. The poetry, none of which is very good, is heavily influenced by Byron, Moore and Scott, especially the ballads.

One interesting essay which is carried across the first two issues is 'Reflections on the Melancholy State of Literature in this Country', which embodies what seems to have been a general feeling in the years after Union (see Part 1, Chapter 3).

See Barbara Hayley, 'Irish Periodicals from the Union to the Nation', in P.J. Drudy (ed.), *Anglo-Irish Studies* II (Cambridge, 1976), p. 86.
See Barbara Hayley, 'A Reading and Thinking Nation: Periodicals as the Voice of Nineteenth-Century Ireland', Barbara, Hayley and Enda McKay (eds), *300 Years of Irish Periodicals* (Mullingar, 1987), p. 31.

THE LITERARY AND MATHEMATICAL ASYLUM

Location: Belfast (publisher Joseph Smyth)
Editor(s):   Mathew M. Meagher
Dates: 1 November 1823

No. of issues: 3? (LIN has number 2, which includes replies to issues raised in
                        number 1, and promises of number 3)
Average periodicity: Weekly?
Average no. pages: 70
Libraries: LIN.

The main claim to fame of this interesting, if slight, production is that it is the first Irish
literary magazine to explicitly name its editor. The *Asylum* also assumes a wider spread of
literacy than in the immediate past; the tone is more popular than in earlier journals, and
this and the contents of some of the pieces imply that they are appealing to a wider social
range. The magazine carries belles-lettres ('On Perseverance in Literary Pursuits') and a
great deal of verse, none of it good. Most of the contributors have also signed their names.

THE RUSHLIGHT: A WEEKLY LITERARY PUBLICATION

Location: Belfast (printer and publisher Clark and Hope (numbers 1–24),
                        then Luke M. Hope, Ann Street (numbers 25–41))
Editor(s):   Luke Mullen Hope
Dates: Volume 1, number 1 (5 December 1824)–volume 1, number 41 (9
                        September 1825)
No. of issues: 41
Average periodicity: Weekly
Average no. pages: 8
Libraries: BCL=I/094.1[1] RUSH (numbers 2–40); BL(Colin); LIN; NLI=J 05
                        (first issue missing).

This magazine can be seen as a very efficient propaganda vehicle, but it also has some
literary merit. Radical essays are concealed amongst biography and travel writing, and
while there is lots of poetry, much of it is of a Romantic type, and reinforces the political
message. It lives up to its promise to be entertaining – 'diverting', for example in its use
of new printing technology (decorative fonts, etc.), but is really more substantial than that.

    The first seven numbers open with 'Notes Editorial', a witty and irreverent diary full of
comments and sideswipes at other contemporary newspapers and magazines. There is also
a more serious vein of radical talk which runs through the entire magazine, whether in the
'Political Conversations', or in more general essays, touching on Paine, Cobbett, early
trade unions, Wolfe Tone or Daniel O'Connell; for example, an essay on 'the female
character' by Mary Wollstonecraft runs over several issues.

    The first eleven issues carry the occasional poem among the essays, but from number
12 onward these are gathered together into a one or two page section at the back. Most of
the poems are anonymous (in both senses of the word), although some are reasonable
examples of high Romantic nature poetry, but among them there are verses from Crabbe,
Swift, Byron, Wordsworth and, above all, Moore. There is some, inconsequential, prose,

and also a little criticism, covering Byron, Poet's Corner, *The Belfast Magazine* (a rival), Moore's Melodies, the Dublin Library and Burns. From issue 30, one or two short reviews of Irish books appear. As usual, there is no indication that the end is nigh, except for a complaint about subscribers not paying up!

Bound into the back of the BCL volume are pp. 5–14 of something called *Ghost of the Rushlight*; it is almost identical to the original, in tone, contents and layout, although as the front page is missing, no more details can be given. The catalogue dates it to December 1826.

See F.J. Bigger, 'The Rushlight and the Irish Rushlight', *Irish Book Lover,* 3 (1912), p. 115.
See Barbara Hayley, 'Irish Periodicals from the Union to the Nation', in P.J. Drudy (ed.), *Anglo-Irish Studies* II (Cambridge, 1976), p. 88.
See Mary Helen Thuente, *The Harp Re-strung, The United Irishmen and the Rise of Irish Literary Nationalism* (New York, 1994), p. 198.

THE BELFAST MAGAZINE AND LITERARY JOURNAL

Location:	Belfast (publisher Morgan Jellet, Commercial Buildings)
Editor(s):	Anon.
Dates:	January–July 1825
No. of issues:	6
Average periodicity:	Monthly
Average no. pages:	96
Libraries:	BCL=I/094.1[1] FINL; BL=PP.6180.ca; LIN; NLI=Ir 6551 Belfast (April 1825 only; bound into *Belfast Pamphlets* 1–5); PSPL=052; QUB=hAP4.B45; TCD=54.u.79 (offsite – 24 hours' notice).

The subject matter of this journal is largely Irish, with the occasional piece on Boccaccio or Athens very much the exception, and it covers topography, antiquarianism, history and literature. The first poem in the first issue ('To the Shamrock') is a typical example: 'Oh, emblem of a disunited land!/By nature planted on a land so fair'. There are also a number of Carletonesque tales and sketches. The most prolific contributor of both poems and articles – and so possibly the editor – is a William Knox.

See Barbara Hayley, 'Irish Periodicals from the Union to the Nation', in P.J. Drudy, *Anglo-Irish Studies* II (Cambridge, 1976), p. 85.
See Barbara Hayley, 'A Reading and Thinking Nation: Periodicals as the Voice of Nineteenth-Century Ireland', Barbara Hayley and Enda McKay (eds), *300 Years of Irish Periodicals* (Mullingar, 1987), p. 31.

THE DUBLIN AND LONDON MAGAZINE

Location: Dublin (printer Joseph Robins Jun., Lower Ormond Quay) and
                       London (printer James Robins and Co., Paternoster Row)
Editor(s):   M.J. Whitty (attr. Power, S.J. Brown and McKenna)
Dates: March 1825–June 1828
No. of issues: 40
Average periodicity: Monthly
Average no. pages: 48 (March 1825–December 1826); 112 (January 1827–?); 48 (?–
                       June 1828)
Libraries: BL=PP.6191   (incomplete);   LIN=N10963   (1825   only);
                       MAR=P2.6.8(10,11); NLI=Ir 05 d 3 (July–December 1827 missing);
                       RIA=Fr C/1/3/C; TCD=N.1.47-49.

Living up to the promise made in the preface to the first issue, this is 'no scissors and paste work'. It takes a populist line, and in pursuit of this maintains a determinedly lightweight tone, which undermines its increasingly interesting contents; publishing no more than a smattering of poems, its mainstay is a diet of peasant tales and book reviews. Whether this was in pursuit of sales at home, or to broaden its appeal to specifically include an English audience (an indicator of the new market in England for a certain kind of Irishry which was to become increasingly significant in later decades), is impossible to tell; certainly the figures claimed (e.g. a circulation of five thousand is mentioned in the preface to the bound volume produced at the end of the first year) are impressive enough to bury any embarrassment that such a high-quality magazine could only be produced jointly with a London publisher. The fate of the *Dublin Examiner*, 1816 is perhaps an instructive comparison – its attempt to use the best quality paper and illustrations, and the newest printing technology, while restricting itself to Irish distribution, foundered due to poor sales. The much larger catchment area was obviously important, but it is also suggested in this magazine that English readers had more highly developed tastes.

The reviews can be quite substantial (fourteen pages is not unusual), and typically cover such titles as Cruikshank's *Tales of Irish Life*, Moore's life of Sheridan, or Thomas Croker's *Fairy Legends and Traditions of the South of Ireland*. An exception is the mammoth review of Wolfe Tone's memoirs and journals which spreads across two issues in 1827, and is sixty-three pages long. Each issue of the *Dublin and London* contains an Irish tale, including some by William Carleton and John Banim, and this develops (from February 1826) into the serialisation of a number of novels by Banim, including *The Whiteboy* and *The Orangeman*. (S.J. Brown claims that many of the stories were contributed by the editor, under a variety of pseudonyms). A four-part feature in 1828 outlines the history of literature in the Irish language.

The *Dublin and London* starts out by flirting with Irish nationalism, for instance, praising O'Connell while expressing worries about some of his more hot-headed allies, and gradually this political identification hardens, with an essay on Emmet and the Tone review, and the increased contribution from writers such as Banim.

See D.J. O'Donoghue, untitled piece in *Irish Book Lover*, 8, p. 53.

See Barbara Hayley, 'Irish Periodicals from the Union to the Nation', in P.J. Drudy, *Anglo-Irish Studies* II (Cambridge, 1976), p. 89.

See John Kelly, *The Collected Letters of W.B. Yeats*, Volume 1: 1865–1895 (Oxford, 1986), p. 81.

BOLSTER'S QUARTERLY MAGAZINE

Location:	Cork (publisher J. Bolster, Patrick Street)
Editor(s):	Anon. (John Windele-Power)
Dates:	February 1826–October 1827
No. of issues:	8
Average periodicity:	Quarterly
Average no. pages:	96
Libraries:	BL=PP.6180.ea; NLI=Per 05 (offsite– 24 hours' notice); PSPL=052; QUB=hPR8817/1-2 (1834 reprint, under the title *Tales and Legends of Ireland*, printer Thomas Hurst, London); RIA=RR Gall/35/E; TCD=54.u.49-51 (offsite – 24 hours' notice).

The tone of this magazine is very worthy, but a little dull. The most interesting thing about it is the (for the time) highly Irish nature of the contents, but this is undermined as the subject matter is treated as being 'polite', 'interesting' or 'diverting'.

The format, as laid out in the first issue, is fifteen to twenty poems, a couple of general articles, a biographical sketch, an essay on 'Sir Walter Scott in Ireland', chapter one of a serialised novel (*The Protege*), and some general literary news. The tales include 'Tiarna na Clanna Mac Diarmuidh' (number 3), 'Recollections of an Absentee' (number 5), 'The Geraldines, A Story of the South' (number 6), and 'The Legend of Carrig-na-ceat' (number 8). Among the best of the essays are 'Irish Arts and Artists' (number 5), and criticism of Moore (number 7) and Dermody (number 8). The standard of the poetry is fairly poor.

See Patrick Power, article in *Cork Historical and Archaeological Society Journal*, 14, 1939, pp. 59–60.

See Mary Helen Thuente, *The Harp Re-strung, The United Irishmen and the Rise of Irish Literary Nationalism* (New York, 1994), p. 198.

THE DUBLIN LITERARY GAZETTE: OR; WEEKLY CHRONICLE OF CRITICISM, BELLES LETTRES, AND FINE ARTS

Location:	Dublin (publisher W.F. Wakeman, 9 D'Olier Street, printer John S. Folds, 56 Great Strand Street)
Editor(s):	Samuel Lover

Dates:	2 January 1830–26 June 1830
No. of issues:	26
Average periodicity:	Weekly
Average no. pages:	16
Libraries:	BL=PP.6154.o; LIN; NLI=IR 05 d 5, another at J 05; PSPL=052; QUB=hAP4.N2; RIA=RR Gall/36/F and Moore Lib 4/G; TCD=OLS L-3-390 & 391; UCC; UCD=SC 32.u.17.

The first issue of this journal opens with the traditional address to the public which declares its seriousness of purpose, and bewails the lack of any magazine in Ireland dedicated to literature: contrasting Ireland with other countries, the writer says 'we have . . . to create the taste we seek to gratify'.

The format is established in this first issue: a tale by Mrs S.C. Hall, followed by five pages of book reviews, two pages each of short book notices, miscellaneous items (poems, notices of other magazines or of plays), and finally a couple of pages of adverts. The *Gazette* sticks firmly to this formula throughout its run. It covers a wide range of publications in its pages, though the brevity of most reviews means they tend to be quite superficial; this, along with the adverts and miscellaneous items, gives the whole something of the flavour of a literary newspaper. The poetry is unremarkable, derivative high Romanticism, with very little Irish content; the best is found in the occasional sonnets by Sir Aubrey de Vere. Charles Lever, then still a medical student, contributed 'Notes from a Rambler' anonymously (Sullivan).

While the reviewers sometimes throw in envious references to the forty or fifty pages others are given to cover a new novel in, say, *Blackwood's* or the *Edinburgh Review*, the *Gazette* grows more confident as it progresses, adopting a slightly higher literary tone, and including more poetry. For once an Irish magazine lived up to its promise to be unsectarian and to avoid politics, although it is written from a position securely within British (and indeed Imperial) life and culture.

Number 3 carries a review of Gerald Griffin's *The Rivals*; number 4 has Carleton's 'Confessions of a Reformed Ribbonman' (which would later become 'Wildgoose Lodge') and a review of Moore's life of Byron; number 9 has 'The Three Tasks', also by Carleton; while number 14 reviews his *Traits and Stories*. There is an interesting article on the London Irish in number 11. Number 25 notifies the readers of the impending change of title.

See Alvin Sullivan, *British Literary Magazines: The Romantic Age, 1789–1836* (Westport, 1983), pp. 112–114.

Continued as:

DUBLIN LITERARY GAZETTE AND NATIONAL MAGAZINE

Location:	Dublin (publisher National Magazine Office, 9 Cecelia Street, printer W.F. Wakeman, 9 D'Olier Street; also printed in London and Edinburgh)

Editor(s):   Samuel Lover; from November 1830 Philip Dixon Hardy.
Dates: Volume 1, Number 1 (July 1830)–volume 10, number 2 (April 1831)
No. of issues: 10
Average periodicity: Monthly
Average no. pages: 124
Libraries: BL=PP.6154.o; NLI=IR 05 n 1; QUB=hAP4.N2; RIA=Mem R/Case
                  3/K; UCD=SC 32.u.18-19.

This is a much more forthrightly British publication than its predecessor; published simultaneously in Dublin, London and Edinburgh, it is firmly Royalist, Tory and Anglican, with more of its pages given over to politics. The short notices of books and plays are replaced by fewer, longer reviews. Otherwise the format remains much the same: a dozen or so poems, two or three tales (mostly Irish, but also 'Venetian' or other exotica), a couple of pages of book reviews and a couple of biographical pieces. A new regular poet appears alongside Sir Aubrey de Vere, a Miss Jewsbury.

The Irish material comes in three forms – highly Unionist political comment, sentimental views of peasant customs or the landscape, and the occasional antiquarian piece. From around December 1830 the literary content goes into decline, with more general and political articles crowding in, and a return to the shorter 'Critical Notices'. At the same time, there is a little more openness about the contributors, with more signed pieces; the editor's name appears for the first time in January 1831.

In issue 3, between one of Mrs Hall's sketches and a handful of translated Greek and German poetry, there is an interesting comparative review of Mrs Hall's *Sketches of Irish Character* and Carleton's *Traits and Stories*. Number 3 contains a review of Schiller's 'An die Freunde' and a sixteen-page article on Shelley. Number 8 has substantial articles on 'Scottish and Irish Popular Poetry' and Lover's *Legends and Stories of Ireland*; number 19 has 'Eman Oge, A Translation from an Original Irish Story'; and number 10 'The Landlord and the Tenant' by Carleton.

See Barbara Hayley, 'Irish Periodicals from the Union to the Nation', in P.J. Drudy (ed.), *Anglo-Irish Studies* II (Cambridge, 1976), p. 89–90.
See Barbara Hayley, 'A Reading and Thinking Nation: Periodicals as the Voice of Nineteenth-Century Ireland', Barbara Hayley and Enda McKay (eds), *300 Years of Irish Periodicals* (Mullingar, 1987), pp. 33–34.

THE DUBLIN MONTHLY MAGAZINE: A LITERARY AND THEOLOGICAL MISCELLANY

Location: Dublin (printer and publisher Tyrrell, Lower Sackville Street)
Editor(s):   Anon.
Dates: January–June 1830
No. of issues: 6
Average periodicity: Monthly

Average no. pages: 88
Libraries: BL=PP.6154.la; NLI=J 05; PSPL=820.5; RIA=Hal.T.454/12;
                      TCD=EE.r.26.

According to a notice which appeared in the last issue (September 1829) of the *Dublin
Family Magazine; or, Literary and Religious Miscellany*, this is a continuation of that title
with a new co-editor, and with 'the literary character of the magazine...very considerably
raised'.

   The bulk of this short-lived magazine is made up of extracts from new books, which are
sometimes quite substantial, covering a wide range of subjects – biography, travel, and so
on. The general standard of these is fairly high, although the tone is kept light and
entertaining. Every issue also has some religious content (poems, biblical exegesis),
although there is no polemic or sectarianism.

   The most important literary contents are the stories and tales, which are in the style of
either Carleton or Scott. These include 'A Night with the Whiteboys', 'The Hedge School',
'The Wedding in the Mountains', and 'Lord Connor of Inniskillen; A Story of 1641'. The
poetry is mostly very weak Romanticism (see 'A Father's Lament for his Child', number
1), although it does include Wordsworth's 'To a Skylark'. Each issue rounds off with
'Sights of Books', half a dozen pages of short reviews, mostly Irish, which are heavy on
quotation and very light on analysis.

See Barbara, Hayley, 'Irish Periodicals from the Union to the Nation', in P.J. Drudy (ed.),
   Anglo-Irish Studies II (Cambridge, 1976), p. 88.

THE ULSTER MAGAZINE

Location: Belfast (printer Joseph Smythe, 34 High Street)
Editor(s):   C.H. Teeling
Dates :   January 1830–October 1831
No. of issues: 23
Average periodicity: Monthly
Average no. pages: 64
Libraries: LIN; NLI=J 05 (January 1830–February 1831 only);
                      QUB=hAP4.U42.

This is one of the best Irish literary magazines to date, avoiding the perennial traps of
pomposity, boredom and sectarianism. The tales and poems have a local particularity
which makes them distinctive, and the whole enterprise is driven by a very modern
manifestation of the desire for democracy and fairness. While no individual works of
genius stand out, the general standard is very good. The articles on issues like censorship,
and the book reviews, all have an air of good sense and authority.

   The *Ulster Magazine* feels very different from its Dublin contemporaries, Protestant or

Catholic. The opening editorial is a paean to the province of Ulster, looking back with pride to the ideals of 1782, and rejecting both imperialism and sectarianism; the first poem in the first issue is 'The Rebel's Grave', an elegy to '98. It carries the usual quota of Irish tales but these are set in specific, named areas of the Ulster countryside, rather than 'in the West'. Number 1 also contains a 'Sketch of the Life of Thomas Russell', and from then on barely an issue goes past without some coverage of the characters and events of the 1780s and 1790s, reminding us how long those events echoed in the province's imagination. This magazine embodies a generous liberalism which goes far beyond the rising tide of Irish nationalism, and is as likely to speak out against anti-Semitism as perfidious Albion, or in favour of the Great Reform Bill or greater opportunities for women.

The second issue has a stimulating essay on the 'Diffusion of Popular Literature', and a review of Moore's life of Byron, while number 3 has a first-class essay on the 'Liberty of the Press' which was prompted by a contemporary legal action, but broadens into a reasoned argument against the use of the libel laws as the primary instrument of censorship. From the fourth issue, extracts from other journals begin to appear, such as the *Edinburgh Review* or the *London University Magazine*. That number also contains a clearly thought out survey of Irish literature which, unlike many of its predecessors, does not merely extol the glories of the Middle Ages and deplore the subsequent fall, but isolates the primary reasons for that fall as the military subjugation of Ireland, the attempt to impose the Reformation by force, and the total alienation of the bulk of the population from such cultural institutions as Trinity College. The author links the emergence of a new literature in English to increasing political freedom during the eighteenth century, and ends by welcoming a new dawn.

The Irish nationalist element becomes slightly stronger from issue 5, with more poetry modelled on Sir Samuel Ferguson, and more tales of long-dead chieftains (see 'An Irish Battle-Song', in number 7 – 'Oh, fling out your banner! and free let it wave,/ The standard of Erin, the flag of the brave'). Number 13 begins a regular series of Ulster ballads ('The Rescue of the Mare', 'Una Phelimy'), and also has a review of periodical literature which claims to detect a change of climate. The author says that previously Irish literary magazines were simply 'a repository for fugitive productions, which could not properly be given to the world as distinct works', but now editors are pleasantly surprised that writers of the first rank are producing work primarily for serial publication. Another of the cogently argued essays, 'Taxes on Knowledge', appears in issue 15, this time condemning the imposition of Stamp Duty on magazines and newspapers. Rather poignantly, the twenty-first number carries an editorial which refers to the fact that all Irish literary magazines to date have foundered after a short time, apologises for production problems with the *Ulster Magazine*, and promises that it will have a long and stable future.

See Mary Helen Thuente, *The Harp Re-strung, The United Irishmen and the Rise of Irish Literary Nationalism* (New York, 1994), p. 198.

IRISH MONTHLY MAGAZINE OF POLITICS AND LITERATURE

Location: Dublin (printer Joseph Blundell, Nelson Lane)
Editor(s):   Anon.
Dates: May 1832–September 1834
No. of issues: 29
Average periodicity: Monthly
Average no. pages: 96
Libraries: LIN (November 1832 only); NLI=J 05; PSPL=052; RIA=FR
                     C/2/3/A; TCD=EE.r.23-25.

For its first year or so, each issue contains a handful of poems (by 'Carolan', 'Alfieri' or 'Conla'), some legends and sketches, and a couple of very short and dry book reviews; 'The Children of Usnach', a poetic drama, is serialised in issues 2, 3 and 4. In this period, the most interesting things to appear are more general articles, including a survey of earlier Dublin magazines in issues 1 and 2; an attack on the extension of copyright in issue 5; and an impassioned attack on government censorship in issue 7.

From early 1833, it becomes steadily more radical, attacking restrictions on Catholics and the Union; drops first to sixty-six pages, then sixty-two, then fifty-eight. It then settles into a steady pattern of three or four political pieces, three or four poems, a couple of tales or sketches, per issue.

As we move into 1834, the tone seems to be moving back toward literature, with the appearance of 'The Burial of the Tithe', by Lever, 'The Sun-Stroke, by the author of The Collegians' [i.e. Griffin], a translation of a long poem by Schiller and an article on Carleton. Unfortunately, publication is halted before this is given a chance to develop.

A very interesting magazine, not least because of the insights it grants us into the wider issues involved in publishing at this time, including copyright, commercial pressures and government censorship.

See Barbara Hayley, 'Irish Periodicals from the Union to the Nation', in P.J. Drudy, *Anglo-Irish Studies* II (Cambridge, 1976), p. 91–92.
See Barbara Hayley, 'A Reading and Thinking Nation: Periodicals as the Voice of Nineteenth-Century Ireland', Barbara Hayley and Enda McKay (eds), *300 Years of Irish Periodicals* (Mullingar, 1987), p. 34.
See Mary Helen Thuente, *The Harp Re-strung, The United Irishmen and the Rise of Irish Literary Nationalism* (New York, 1994), p. 198.

THE DUBLIN PENNY JOURNAL

Location: Dublin (printer and publisher John S. Folds, 5 Bachelor's Walk (June
                     1832–June 1833), then Philip Dixon Hardy (July 1833–June 1836))
Editor(s):   Charles Otway and George Petrie; from July 1833 Philip Dixon Hardy

Dates: Volume 1, Number 1 (30 June 1832)–volume 4, Number 208 (25
                        June 1836)
No. of issues: 208
Average periodicity: Weekly
Average no. pages: 8
Libraries: BL=PP.6315; LIN; MAR=Y.3.6 (1832–33); NLI=Ir 05 d 10;
                        PSPL=052; QUB=hqAP4.D3; RDS=NL51; RIA=RR Gall/36/F;
                        TCD=WW.f.19, 20; UCC (Microfilm); UCD=MICJ 050; UCG=052.

A very attractive popular journal which is liberally illustrated with engravings of the Irish
landscape, maps and diagrams; the quality of these is further improved after 1834 when a
new steam printing press was ordered from Glasgow. Any remaining eighteenth-century
cobwebs are shaken off with this truly nineteenth-century production – the quantity and
quality of illustrations, the use of the latest technology to keep the price down, the wide
distribution (it was sold in eleven towns in Ireland, six more in Britain, three in the United
States, and in Paris) and the large circulation (Hardy claimed twelve thousand in his
farewell address) all declare that we are firmly into the new age of greatly improved
communications and mass readerships. Even so, the production and distribution of such a
publication on a weekly basis was a substantial achievement for Ireland at the time.

The tone of the magazine is appropriately light and entertaining, but never frivolous, and
the matter of Ireland is tackled with total confidence – tales, legends, translations from the
Irish (often accompanied by the originals), history, topography – all are covered with an
assurance and lightness of touch, and completely lacking any sense of cultural cringe. It is
interesting that this is in a magazine which is obviously so intimately tied into the modern
British network of distribution and communications.

Each short issue contains an Irish tale, myth or legend (usually abridged from someone
like Carleton, and often a reprinting of something which had originally appeared
elsewhere) and one or two poems, including some of J.C. Mangan's earliest work (often a
translation from the Irish, or German) or a piece by a distinguished writer like Goldsmith
or Moore. When P.D. Hardy took over as editor in July 1833, he took the *Journal* slightly
downmarket, and the nationalist tone became slightly stronger, but the most obvious effect
on the contents was the increased amount of (fairly dull) verse.

The 'Preface' to the first bound volume begins with the customary stress on 'the brief
existence' which was the common fate of Irish literary journals, listing the main obstacles
to be overcome as the middle and upper classes' 'deep-rooted prejudice against what was
home-bred and national', and the reluctance of booksellers at home to stock Irish
magazines. The Preface to volume 4 (June 1836) carries Hardy's announcement that he is
closing the magazine, due to his own ill-health.

See Philip Dixon Hardy, *Pic Nics from the Dublin Penny Journal, being a Selection from
   the Legends, Tales and Stories of Ireland* (Dublin, 1836) (Libraries: BL=012612.df.24
   (outhoused); NLI=J 823; and QUB=hPR8876/4). A selection of the best literary items
   from the *Dublin Penny Journal*, illustrated by many drawings from the same source.

See Anon., 'The Dublin Penny Journal', *Dublin University Magazine*, 15 (1840), pp. 112–128.

See James Hayes, 'Old Popular Pennyworths', *Irish Book Lover*, 2 (1911), pp. 149–151.

See Barbara Hayley, 'Irish Periodicals from the Union to the Nation', in P.J. Drudy (ed.), *Anglo-Irish Studies* II (Cambridge, 1976), pp. 99–100.

See Jacques Chuto, 'Mangan, Petrie, O'Donovan, and a Few Others: The Poet and the Scholars', *Irish University Review*, 2, 2 (Autumn 1976), pp. 169–187, *passim*.

See C.P. Hyland, *A Topographical Index to Five Nineteenth Century Literary Periodicals*, 'printed by the author' (1979). Indexes the illustrations.

See Roger McHugh and Maurice Harmon, *A Short History of Anglo-Irish Literature* (Dublin, 1982), pp. 108, 122.

See John Kelly, *The Collected Letters of WB Yeats*, Volume 1: 1865–1895 (Oxford, 1986), p. 79.

See Barbara Hayley, 'A Reading and Thinking Nation: Periodicals as the Voice of Nineteenth-Century Ireland', in Barbara Hayley and Enda McKay (eds), *300 Years of Irish Periodicals* (Mullingar, 1987), p. 38.

THE DUBLIN UNIVERSITY MAGAZINE

Location:	Dublin (publisher William Curry Jun. and Co.; from April 1846 James McGlashan; from January 1856 McGlashan and Gill; from April 1856 Hodges, Smith and Co.; from June 1858 Alex. Thom and Sons; from February 1860 William Robertson; from July 1861 William H. Smith & Son; from October 1861 George Herbert; from January 1876 W. Ridings; from July 1877 Hurst & Blackett, London. Printer Folds? (attr. Houghton))
Editor(s):	Charles Stanford; from August 1834 Isaac Butt; from December 1838 James McGlashan; from April 1842 Charles Lever; from June 1845 James McGlashan; from July 1845 John F. Waller; from January 1856 Durham Dunlop; from November 1856 Cheyne Brady; from July 1861 J.S. Le Fanu; from July 1869 Charles F. Adams; from June 1873 Durham Dunlop; from July 1877 Keningale Cook
Dates:	Volume 1, number 1 (January 1833)–volume 90, number 540 (December 1877)
No. of issues:	540
Average periodicity:	Monthly
Average no. pages:	114
Libraries:	BL=PP.6155; LIN; MAR=YR (incomplete); NLI=Ir 05 d 11; PSPL=052; QUB=hAP4.D81; RDS=NL54; RIA=Mem R/Case 3; TCD=Gall.EE.18.95-131; UCD=SC 32.K.1-18, SC 32.L.1-17 and SC 32.M.1; (1833–1850); J 820 (1851–1873) UCG=378.155 (PS, from 1856); UCC=incomplete.

The *Dublin University Magazine* (*DUM*) is one of the most important of all Irish literary magazines, superlative by any measure, be it circulation, longevity or impact on the wider culture. For contemporaries, it had additional significance, in that it was seen as the starting pistol for a new era in Irish culture, the big success which definitively broke the run of inferior, short-lived failures which had prevailed since the Union; this success was all the sweeter as the *DUM* was from the start distinctively Irish in character. It had its origins in the fallout from the Great Reform Bill; the authorities in Trinity College were felt by many to be overly sympathetic toward reform, and a group of radical young conservative dons and students decided to act as an ultra-Protestant internal opposition. This group included Isaac Butt, Samuel Ferguson and Caesar Otway, and their ambitions very quickly spread beyond the narrow confines of Trinity politics; the *DUM* would be much more than simply a university magazine, it would have popular appeal, and hold its own among the great British journals (*Fraser's*, *Blackwood's*) on which it was clearly modelled.

In broad outline, the DUM aped much of its exemplars' mix of contents (the balance between politics and literature), and their prevailing editorial tone (a kind of self-congratulatory and endlessly self-referential facetiousness); they also, as Sadleir puts it: 'during the first years of its existence carried anonymity, pseudonymity and mystery generally to annoying extremes'. The borrowings even extend to the editorial personae ('Anthony Poplar'), and the 'Portrait Gallery' of illustrious figures (frequently contributors and editorial staff!). More interesting is its complex, ambiguous position at the nexus of Britishness and Irishness. In a way which embodied the internal contradictions of the Anglo-Irish Ascendancy from whose heart it emerged, the *DUM* was militantly patriotic to the British Empire, while preoccupied with the minutiae of petty local squabbles; British enough to be unthreatening, but definitively Irish in its attitudes. Its second editor, Butt, who firmly established the magazine during his time in office, was a staunch Orangeman, but from the start he enlisted Irish writers, regardless of their personal background (most famously Carleton, but also John Sheridan Le Fanu, Mrs Hall, Lever, and even Mangan). In a famous and influential article in November 1833 ('A Dialogue between the Head and Heart of an Irish Protestant'), Ferguson crystallised this position; the Irish Protestant, 'deserted by the Tories, insulted by the Whigs, and envied by the Dissenters' could contribute, could perhaps even survive, by being aware of 'the Irish history of centuries'. Ferguson's own contribution, both to this project and to the *DUM*, was significant, and in this magazine alone he published important articles and poems, including some two dozen translations from the Irish.

The first editor was the Rev. Charles Stuart Stanford, and during his time the title was more closely linked to Trinity, and slightly undergraduate in style. However, the speed of its maturation, and its growing success can be seen in the fact that Curry's, the most commercially astute of contemporary publishers, stepped in to take it over and invest in its future after only a year of operation. In particular, it became the 'property' of their energetic and persuasive managing director, James McGlashan, and his first move was to replace the self-effacing Stanford with Butt, who immediately increased the length and depth of the articles and introduced a more mature tone. In a key article ('Past and Present State of Literature in Ireland', number 9, 1837) Butt published a manifesto for literature as the vehicle by which Irish Protestants could not only overcome their inferiority complex regarding England, but also establish beyond doubt their claim to be 'real' Irishmen. He backed this up by attracting as regular contributors during his time Lover (briefly), Carleton, Mangan, Lever and Le Fanu. The importance of the *DUM* as a platform can be measured by the fact that Carleton (whose *Traits and Stories* had been published by Curry's) chose to first serialise five of his novels, including *The Black Prophet* there; or that, by the time of his death, Mangan had contributed nearly 500 poems, including his 'Literae Orientales' ('versions' of Arabic, Persian and Turkish 'originals') and 'Anthologia Hibernica' (from the Irish). Butt left the magazine in November 1838, and McGlashan seems to have carried on alone for a while.

The next, and most successful editor of the *DUM*, was Charles Lever; he was certainly the most flamboyant, with a populist style (he steadily increased the amount of fiction, for example) which took the magazine from an already respectable claimed circulation of 2,500 (number 17, 1841) to its peak of around 4,000 copies per month. A weakness, which initially appeared his greatest strength, was that this success relied heavily on Lever's own contributions (his *Confessions of Harry Lorrequer* had been serialised 1837–1840, and more contributions appeared during his editorship, including *Arthur O'Leary* and the exploits of his popular character, Jack Hinton). Lever gave the *DUM* more of an international dimension and greater variety in its contents but, despite his enormous success with the public, he was attacked by the intelligentsia for taking the magazine downmarket; he also did not get on well with some of his contributors (Carleton stopped writing for the *DUM* in 1841, not to return for six years) and, more importantly, with McGlashan, and in 1845 they argued and Lever departed, leaving McGlashan once again to sustain the title alone.

McGlashan's next appointee, John Francis Waller, seems to have had no fresh ideas of his own, and made few changes save a move toward a more lightweight tone; they lost some key contributors (Mangan had died, and Butt and Ferguson simply moved on), and the successors (e.g. both Sir William and Lady Jane Wilde) were not of the same standard. In these years (1845–1861) the *DUM* rather lost its way, with a succession of short-term editors and a slightly vague identity, and things looked bleak in the extreme in 1855 when McGlashan went bankrupt and sold the title to a firm of London proprietors (who in turn sold it on only three months later). This led to a dilution of its Irish identity, and has been suggested as a reason why it took almost two years to acknowledge the horror of the Famine; however, this ignores the fact that most contemporary Irish literary magazines did the same. To Waller's credit, by 1847 the *DUM* had begun a vigorous campaign for action, and even mellowed its attitude slightly toward some Young Ireland figures.

There is an assumption amongst some commentators (see McBride's thesis), that the *DUM* was only of importance during its first two decades, but this ignores its amazing revival in 1861. An old contributor, now a highly popular figure in Irish letters, Sheridan Le Fanu, bought the title, and immediately reverted to Lever's formula, making the magazine once again more Irish in tone, and increasing the number of serialised novels; and once again this worked, and the *DUM* returned to mass popularity. He serialised some of his best work – *The House by the Churchyard*, *Uncle Silas* – and infected the staid old title with his own enthusiasms, for the supernatural, mysticism and folktales. Unfortunately, Le Fanu also repeated Lever's key weakness, and this regained popularity was once again dependent on the contributions of the editor. After Le Fanu's retirement in 1869 a steady decline set in (Sadleir refers to these as 'years of melancholy ineffectiveness', lightened only briefly by the appearance of the first poems by the young Oscar Wilde); the title was once again sold to another London proprietor, and by 1877 panic seems to have set in, exemplified by the change of title (see below).

Why did the *DUM* succeed so spectacularly where an entire generation of its predecessors had so dismally failed? Firstly, it managed to combine fire in the belly (from the Trinity radicals), with practical business sense (McGlashan), and an appeal to the all-important English market, which gave it a sound commercial footing. Secondly, it was lucky in its timing, coinciding with the emergence of Daniel O'Connell and a new, more confident assertion of Irish national pride which not only gave the Ascendancy conservatives a bogeyman around whom they could unite, but also encouraged them to assert their rights to that pride in being Irish. Above all, the strength of its literature provided the bedrock both of its identity and of its popular success, and that very success was its greatest legacy, establishing beyond question the right of Irish culture to assert itself in public, and that an Irish literary world could actually exist, and inspiring others by its example. (It is perhaps ironic that, despite all the criticism of them from the Dublin/Trinity insiders, it was under the two outrageous outsiders, Lever and Le Fanu, that the magazine reached its peaks.) Its uniqueness lay in its ability to combine reactionary politics (and there is a vein of shocking invective running through the *DUM* supporting every lost cause of the nineteenth century – opposition to a Catholic university, to Catholic Emancipation, to tenant rights, etc.) with the feeling that 'whatever its politics, it seems to stand for Ireland and to speak to Ireland' (Hayley, 1976, p. 96). This sense of absolute authority allowed it to rebuke 'the insensitivity of England to Irish concerns' (McBride, p. 8), which in turn led even its political opponents in Ireland to afford it a grudging respect. Finally, in the confusion and lack of conviction of its dotage, it could be said that the *DUM* continued to embody the Ascendancy class from which it sprang.

Continued as:

THE UNIVERSITY MAGAZINE, A LITERARY AND PHILOSOPHICAL REVIEW

Location:	London (publisher Hurst & Blackett)
Editor(s):	Keningale Cook
Dates:	January 1878–1880
No. of issues:	32
Average periodicity:	Monthly; from July 1880, quarterly
Average no. pages:	112
Libraries:	QUB=AP4.D9 (Basement); TCD=Gall.GG.19.23-28.

In this incarnation the former *DUM* is a shadow of its old glory, publishing little of distinction, and little of that Irish; the sum amounts to not much more than a couple of articles by T.H. Huxley and John Ruskin, and a poem by Christina Rosetti.

See Anon., 'A Note on the *DUM*', *Dublin Penny Journal*, 2 (1834), p. 285.

See Anon. (Isaac Butt), 'The Close of the Year', *Dublin University Magazine*, 6 (1835). An account of the founding of the magazine.

See William Carleton, 'The Dublin University Magazine and Mr Lever', *The Nation* (7 October 1843).

See anonymous article in *Irish Book Lover*, 10 (1913), pp. 75–79.

See Michael Sadleir, 'The Dublin University Magazine: the History, Contents and Bibliography', *Bibliography Society of Ireland Journal*, 5, 4 (1938), pp. 59–82.

See Walter Houghton, *The Wellesley Index to Victorian Periodicals 1824–1900*, 5 volumes (Toronto, 1966–1989), pp. 193–370 (essay plus index).

See double issue of the *Long Room*, numbers 14 and 15 (1976), which was devoted to the *DUM*.

See Jacques Chuto, 'Mangan, Petrie, O'Donovan, and a Few Others: The Poet and the Scholars', *Irish University Review*, 2, 2 (Autumn 1976), pp. 169–187, *passim*.

See Barbara Hayley, 'Irish Periodicals from the Union to the Nation', in P.J. Drudy (ed.), *Anglo-Irish Studies* II (Cambridge, 1976), pp. 94–96.

See Roger McHugh and Maurice Harmon, *A Short History of Anglo-Irish Literature* (Dublin, 1982), pp. 91, 95, 98, 99, 112, 117.

See Alvin Sullivan, *British Literary Magazines: The Romantic Age, 1789–1836* (Westport, 1983), pp. 119–123.

See A.C. Partridge, *Language and Society in Anglo-Irish Literature* (Dublin, 1984), pp. 138, 175, 253, 255–256.

See Seamus Deane, *Celtic Revivals* (London, 1985), p. 98.

See John Kelly, *The Collected Letters of WB Yeats*, Volume 1: 1865–1895 (Oxford, 1986), pp. 74, 75n, 79, 81, 85.

See John P. McBride, 'The Dublin University Magazine: Cultural Nationality and Tory Ideology in an Irish Literary and Political Journal, 1833–1852', PhD Thesis (TCD, 1987).

See Barbara Hayley, 'A Reading and Thinking Nation: Periodicals as the Voice of Nineteenth-Century Ireland', Barbara Hayley and Enda McKay (eds), *300 Years of Irish Periodicals* (Mullingar, 1987), pp. 35–36.

See W.J. McCormack, *Dissolute Characters, Irish Literary History through Balzac, Sheridan Le Fanu, Yeats and Bowen* (Manchester, 1993), pp. 45, 46, 60, 84–85, 95, 98, 143, 160, 184, 185.

See Roy Foster, *Paddy and Mr Punch* (London, 1993), pp. 26, 62, 283.

See W.J. McCormack, *From Burke to Beckett: Ascendancy, Tradition and Betrayal in Literary History* (Cork, 1994), pp. 6, 89, 139, 141, 142, 144, 148, 149, 153, 161n, 175, 187, 199.

Subject index in William Frederick Poole, *Poole's Index to Periodical Literature*, revised edition (Gloucester, MA, 1963).

An author index appears in Richard J. Hayes (ed.), *Sources for the History of Irish Civilisation: Articles in Irish Periodicals*, 5 vols (Boston, 1970).

THE DUBLIN UNIVERSITY REVIEW, AND QUARTERLY MAGAZINE

Location:	Dublin (publisher Grant and Bolton, then W.F. Wakeman, 9 D'Olier Street, printer P.D. Hardy, Cecelia Street)
Editor(s):	Anon.
Dates:	Volume 1, number 1 (January 1833)–volume 1, number 4 (November 1833); New Series, volume 1, numbers 1 and 2 (January and November 1834)
No. of issues:	6
Average periodicity:	Quarterly (first four), then biannual
Average no. pages:	235
Libraries:	BL=PP.6164, and PP.6165 (two copies); NLI=J 05; QUB=hAP4.U51 (vol 1, 1833, only); RIA=RR Gall/36/D; UCD=SC 32.H.1 (vol 1, numbers 1 (January 1833) and 2 (April 1833) only).

The preface to the first issue, 'To the Reader', begins with the traditional declaration 'That hitherto all attempts have failed which aimed at establishing in Ireland a purely Literary Periodical, is known to the Public Generally.' The author discounts as reasons the lack of talent, money or good editors, and instead puts the blame on the small number of regular contributors, asserting that the *Review*'s contacts with the University will save it.

The *University Review* is a magazine which does not seem to know its own mind. The format and design imply a relative of the great nineteenth-century reviews, and the first couple of numbers start well, with top-class writers (Carleton), solid literary articles and reviews, and a good range of topics. But it quickly falters, and by number 4 we have been overrun by a curious mixture of tedious academia ('On a General Method of Expressing the Paths of Light') and lightweight articles ('Recollections of the Kingstown Caves'). Amongst essays on Greek tragedy, astronomy and the Dublin University we find a handful of stories by Carleton ('Neal Malone' in issue 1 is the best); substantial reviews of Maxwell's *Wild Sports of the West*, Carleton's *Traits and Stories*, and Michael Banim's *The Ghosthunter*; and a good deal of Romantic poetry, most of it by 'W.R.H', and mostly a long way after Moore.

See Barbara Hayley, 'Irish Periodicals from the Union to the Nation', in P.J. Drudy (ed.), *Anglo-Irish Studies* II (Cambridge, 1976), p. 97.
See Barbara Hayley, 'A Reading and Thinking Nation: Periodicals as the Voice of Nineteenth-Century Ireland', Barbara Hayley and Enda McKay (eds), *300 Years of Irish Periodicals* (Mullingar, 1987), p. 37.

THE IRISH PENNY MAGAZINE

Location:	Dublin (printer and publisher Thomas and John Coldwell, 50 Capel Street)
Editor(s):	Samuel Lover (attr. Hayley)
Dates:	Volume 1, Number 1 (5 January 1833)–volume 2, Number 2 (11 January 1834); New Series Volume 2, Number 1 (1 January 1842)–volume 2, Number 13 (26 March 1842)
No. of issues:	67
Average periodicity:	Weekly
Average no. pages:	8
Libraries:	BL=PP.6193.k (incomplete); LIN; NLI=I 05 i 16; PSPL=052; QUB=hqAP4.I5; RIA=RR Gall/36/F; TCD=OLS L-3-792.

Similar in format and subject-matter to the *Dublin Penny Journal* of the same year, although slightly more 'respectable' in tone – and also not so lively nor so interesting. The *Magazine* makes much of the contributions of Lover, which are in two areas, his illustrations to the series 'The Antient History of Ireland' [*sic*], and the 'Irish Legends, Tales and National Proverbs, written and illustrated expressly for this work', both of which continue through the complete run of this magazine. Each issue also carries a poem, most of which are entirely undistinguished. Some of Lover's contributions are very amusing, although they are not in the same class as the stories which Carleton supplied to the *Dublin Penny Journal*. Most of the illustrations, and a few of the contributions, are signed. The second series in the 1840s is little different from the first.

See James Hayes, 'Old Popular Pennyworths', *Irish Book Lover*, 2 (1911), pp. 149–151.
See Barbara Hayley, 'Irish Periodicals from the Union to the Nation', in P.J. Drudy (ed.), *Anglo-Irish Studies* II (Cambridge, 1976), p. 102.
See C.P. Hyland, *A Topographical Index to Five Nineteenth Century Literary Periodicals*, 'printed by the author' (1979). Indexes the illustrations.
See Roger McHugh and Maurice Harmon, *A Short History of Anglo-Irish Literature* (Dublin, 1982), p. 108.
See Barbara Hayley, 'A Reading and Thinking Nation: Periodicals as the Voice of Nineteenth-Century Ireland', in Barbara Hayley and Enda McKay (eds), *300 Years of Irish Periodicals* (Mullingar, 1987), p. 38.

THE NEW BELFAST MAGAZINE

Location:	Belfast (publisher Magill and Jardine, 6 Ann Street)
Editor(s):	Anon. ('conducted by the students of the Royal Academical Institution')
Dates:	December 1833–April 1834

No. of issues: 5
Average periodicity: Monthly
Average no. pages: 48
Libraries: LIN; QUB=pLH5.N5.

In spite of its source, this is in no way a 'student' magazine, but rather a very professional, confident production. While no famous names appear, and while some of the contents are 'borrowed' from *Blackwood's*, the standard is generally good. The 'Literary Papers' include 'The History of Reviewing', a substantial piece on Schiller, and a good article on Wordsworth's sonnets (in which he is described as 'a man who, till very late years, required defence'), although there is nothing specifically Irish. Some of the 'Tales, Sketches, &c.', for example 'Barney Fudaghan' are very passable efforts in the style of Carleton's earliest. None of the 'Literary Notices' address Irish subjects, although they do include, for instance, a reasonable defence of Harriet Martineau. The poetry is sparse, only a couple of dozen poems in all, and uninspiring, although the song which ends the final issue ('My native hills, sae far away') is charming. The tone is serious, though not unduly so, and progressive, embracing moderate nationalism and a defence of women writers.

THE IRISH TEMPERANCE AND LITERARY GAZETTE

Location: Dublin
Editor(s):   Anon.
Dates: 12 November 1836–31 December 1836
No. of issues: 8
Average periodicity: Weekly
Average no. pages: 4
Libraries: BL(Colin).

This is really a newspaper of the Irish Temperance movement, about half of whose pages are taken up with notices, advertisements, texts of speeches, etc., and the rest with (very) short stories and poems. The former are all heavily moralising (about honest farmboys who throw away their land after succumbing to the demon drink) and the latter tend to be grandiloquent hymns to the movement:

> Hail to thee, Nymph, Health's goddess, hail!
> To Thee our *Paeans* swell the gale –
> Naiad of pure translucent rill,
> What joys each beating bosom fill...
> > 'To Temperance'

Perhaps the best thing that can be said about the paper is that, unlike many at the time, it largely resists the temptations of sectarianism.

THE ATHY LITERARY MAGAZINE

Location: Athy (printer and publisher T. French, Market Square)
Editor(s):   Anon.
Dates: 14 November 1837–13 March 1838
No. of issues: 18
Average periodicity: Weekly
Average no. pages: 8
Libraries: RIA=H.PAM.1692.

A fairly lightweight 1d production, 'adapted' as its first editorial says, 'to all classes, but more especially the middle orders'. It is mostly made up of anecdotes, topographical sketches, etc., with a smattering of short tales and light verses. It feels very old-fashioned for 1837, closer in spirit to some of the magazines published in Dublin before the Union. Its importance lies in its being published in a small market town, and its contents are perhaps indicative of the more conservative tastes of those with less exposure to the world of Trinity and the Dublin theatres. The most interesting contributions are: 'Comparison of Watches' by Maria Edgeworth (number 4); a short essay on Goldsmith's 'Deserted Village' (number 6); and 'The Reg'lar Fat Man', from *The Pickwick Papers* (number 14). Most of the, fairly weak, verse is by Moore O'Connor.

LARNE LITERARY & AGRICULTURAL JOURNAL

Location: Larne (printer and publisher William McCalmont)
Editor(s):   William McCalmont
Dates: 1 November 1838–October 1840
No. of issues: 24
Average periodicity: Monthly
Average no. pages: 8
Libraries: BCL; LIN.

A highly eccentric, but worthy, hobby-horse, run entirely by McCalmont. Only the last two pages carry articles on farm issues and agricultural improvement, the bulk of the magazine being devoted to anecdotes, topography, poems and stories. Most of the poetry is by local writers from Larne, Doagh, Ballynure and Belfast, and a good deal of it is by James McHenry or by McCalmont himself; unfortunately, none of it is very good. A few of the tales and stories are also by local writers, although many more are lifted from English magazines, e.g. *Blackwood's*.

The focus is entirely local, rather than national or even regional, and there seems to be no embarrassment about covering aspects of the area's Gaelic past. The *Journal*'s main importance is in the insight it gives us into the spread of civil society beyond the major towns, and of literacy, wealth and the demand for literature into rural areas, in articles such as that on the Doagh Bookclub in the first issue.

THE CITIZEN; A MONTHLY JOURNAL OF POLITICS, LITERATURE AND ART

Location:	Dublin (printer and publisher P. Doyle, Crow Street) and London (from March 1841, printer and publisher Samuel Machen, D'Olier Street; from January 1843, publisher T. O'Gorman, Upper Ormond Quay)
Editor(s):	Anon.
Dates:	November 1839–February 1841
No. of issues:	40
Average periodicity:	Monthly
Average no. pages:	72
Libraries:	BL=PP.6180; NLI=Ir 05 c 3; PSPL=052; RIA=RR Gall/36/B; TCD=VV.x.35-39, and 66.e.39-41 offsite (November 1839–May 1840, and January–December 1841 only); UCC; UCD=SC 44.P.11/2 (September and December 1840 only); UCG=052 PS.

This is primarily a political magazine; for example in the first issue, an argument for a national railway for Ireland, a condemnation of Grand Juries, and a discussion of the franchise take up more than half the pages. Nevertheless, the editors obviously placed cultural politics high on the agenda, and that issue also includes 'Rosalie; A Ballad'; the 'Literary Register' (later 'Our Monthly Review'), a ten-page section devoted to short reviews; and two stories, 'Tales of the Village' and 'Charlie Maloney; or Mischance, and No Mistake'. The second issue carries a seven-page review of Moore's 'Alciphron'. From the start of 1841 they also publish a couple of tunes in each issue, under the heading 'The Native Music of Ireland'. In June 1840 they published Carleton's 'The Parent's Trial', and the following month reviewed Lady Morgan's *Woman and her Master*; the July number also has an obituary of Griffin and begins publication of a play by Banim.

Continued as:

THE CITIZEN: OR, DUBLIN MONTHLY MAGAZINE

Location:	Dublin (printer and publisher Samuel Machen, D'Olier Street)
Editor(s):	Anon.
Dates:	March 1841–December 1841
No. of issues:	10
Average periodicity:	Monthly
Average no. pages:	50
Libraries:	BL=PP.6180; NLI=Ir 05 c 3; PSPL=052; RIA=RR Gall/36/B; TCD=VV.x.35-39, and 66.e.3941 offsite; UCC; UCG=052 PS.

In March 1841 the title and printer change, and the contents shift even more strongly towards politics; 'Our Monthly Review', for instance, is dropped. Some significant literary items are still published, however, including 'Moll Roe's Marriage' by Carleton, a number of translations (e.g. from Goethe), and a good review of Carleton's *The Clarionet and other tales* (October 1841).

Continued as:

THE DUBLIN MONTHLY MAGAZINE; BEING A NEW SERIES OF THE CITIZEN

Location:	Dublin (printer and publisher Samuel Machen, D'Olier Street)
Editor(s):	Anon.
Dates:	January–December 1842
No. of issues:	12
Average periodicity:	Monthly
Average no. pages:	88
Libraries:	BL=PP.6180; LIN; NLI=Ir 05 d 8; QUB=hAP4.D4 (January–June 1842 only); RIA=RR Gall/36/B; TCD=VV.x.35-39; UCG=052 PS.

This manifestation is larger, and feels less overtly political. A typical menu for each issue would be a handful of patriotic poems, topographical sketches and general essays, the series 'Memoirs of Native Artists', and the serialised novels *Macklin; or, the Son's sacrifice* and *The Clandestine Marriage*. In July and August 1842 they reviewed R.R. Madden's *The United Irishmen*. Packaged with the *DMM* was *The Native Music of Ireland*, a separate page with the sheet music for two or three songs.

Continued as:

THE DUBLIN MAGAZINE AND CITIZEN

Location:	Dublin (publisher T. O'Gorman, Upper Ormond Quay)
Editor(s):	Anon.
Dates:	January–April 1843
No. of issues:	4
Average periodicity:	Monthly
Average no. pages:	42
Libraries:	BL=PP.6180; NLI=J 05.

For these last four issues it is divided into three sections – firstly, four or five prose pieces, including a story or novel extract; four or five pages of the 'Native Music of Ireland'; and a couple of pages of 'Temperance Band Music'. Nothing of any lasting interest was published.

The *Citizen* stands in a John the Baptist relationship to the *Nation* – a clear break with what went before, harbinger of the new era of more sophisticated, self-confident nationalism which the later title was to embody (see its ongoing campaign against Mrs Hall and other 'Mock-Irish Works'); it also provided Thomas Davis with his journalistic training-ground before he went on to co-found the *Nation*.

See Barbara Hayley, 'Irish Periodicals from the Union to the Nation', in P.J. Drudy (ed.), *Anglo-Irish Studies* II (Cambridge, 1976), p. 104.
See Barbara Hayley, 'A Reading and Thinking Nation: Periodicals as the Voice of

Nineteenth-Century Ireland', in Barbara Hayley and Enda McKay (eds), *300 Years of Irish Periodicals* (Mullingar, 1987), p. 40.

See Mary Helen Thuente, *The Harp Re-strung, The United Irishmen and the Rise of Irish Literary Nationalism* (New York, 1994), pp. 197, 199.

THE IRISH PENNY JOURNAL

Location:	Dublin (printer and publisher Gunn and Cameron, 6 Church Lane)
Editor(s):	George Petrie
Dates:	4 July 1840–26 June 1841
No. of issues:	52
Average periodicity:	Weekly
Average no. pages:	8
Libraries:	BL=PP.6285; LIN; NLI=J 05; PSPL=052; QUB=hAP4.I41; RIA=RR Gall/36/F; TCD=V.f.17; UCG=052 (PS).

Opens with 'To our readers', an editorial bemoaning the lack of 'a cheap literary publication for the great body of the people of this country', saying that while London alone has more than twenty penny magazines, Ireland has none; the only doubt expressed is whether the Irish can afford such a publication. Each issue has a short story or character sketch by Martin Doyle or 'Mrs. Hall' (and, in passing, it is interesting how these sketches have moved downmarket: a staple of the eighteenth-century gentlemen's magazines, by this date they are only found in the popular penny magazines), a poem (most often by 'JUU' or 'M'), a topographical sketch, and a handful of historical anecdotes, legends, proverbs, etc.

An interesting sign of development in the genre is that around half of the pieces are signed, while some Irish poems (in a series 'Ancient Irish Literature') are given in both the original and translation. The most outstanding contributions are 'Deaf and Dumb', a story by Mrs Hall (number 12); 'Song' by Lover (number 9), and a regular series of stories by William Carleton (including 'The Irish Fiddler', number 6; 'The Country Dancing-Master', number 9, and 'The Irish Matchmaker', number 15).

The run is closed by another 'To our readers', in number 52. The overall tone is sentimental rather than overtly political, and while individual items are necessarily short the leavening of good writing from Carleton, Lever, etc. makes it quite a satisfying read, and one of the more substantial penny magazines.

This title was reissued in 1842 by James Duffy.

See James Hayes, 'Old Popular Pennyworths', *Irish Book Lover,* 2 (1911), pp. 149–151.

See Barbara Hayley, 'Irish Periodicals from the Union to the Nation', in P.J. Drudy, *Anglo-Irish Studies* II (Cambridge, 1976), p. 103.

See Jacques Chuto, 'Mangan, Petrie, O'Donovan, and a Few Others: The Poet and the Scholars' *Irish University Review*, 2, 2 (Autumn 1976), pp. 169–187, *passim*.

See C.P. Hyland, *A Topographical Index to Five Nineteenth Century Literary Periodicals*, 'printed by the author' (1979). Indexes the illustrations.

See Roger McHugh and Maurice Harmon, *A Short History of Anglo-Irish Literature* (Dublin, 1982), pp. 108, 122.

See Barbara Hayley, 'A Reading and Thinking Nation: Periodicals as the Voice of Nineteenth-Century Ireland', in Barbara Hayley and Enda McKay (eds), *300 Years of Irish Periodicals* (Mullingar, 1987), pp. 38–40.

See Norman Vance, *Irish Literature: A Social History – Tradition, Identity and Difference* (Oxford, 1990), p. 142.

See Roy Foster, *Paddy and Mr Punch* (London, 1993), p. 4.

THE DUBLIN JOURNAL OF TEMPERANCE, SCIENCE AND LITERATURE

Location: Dublin (printer Typographic Total Abstinence Society (1842) and George R. Tracy, 32 Lower Sackville Street (1843), publisher Typographic Total Abstinence Society (numbers 1–8); T Gegg, 8 Lower Abbey Street (8 – volume 2, number 6); T. Le Mesurier, 8 Lower Abbey Street (volume 2, number 7–volume 2, number 19); George R. Tracy, 32 Lower Sackville Street (volume 2, number 20–volume 2, number 27))

Editor(s):   Anon.

Dates: 30 April 1842–29 April 1843

No. of issues: 53

Average periodicity: Weekly

Average no. pages: 16

Libraries: BL=PP.6192.b; LIN (30 April 1842–15 October 1842 only); NLI=J 05; PSPL=052; QUB=hAP4.D5; TCD=54.u.65 (30 April 1842–15 October 1842 only).

'To our readers', in the first issue, bemoans the fact that Ireland 'has not yet successfully sustained even one periodical devoted to the practical interests of her industrious millions', and blames this on Irish people buying foreign publications in preference to Irish. The magazine is broadly based, intending to divert and instruct, so there are articles on the Daguerreotype, education, Mechanics Institutes, and so on, as well as romances, tales, and poems. Their favourite authors seem to be Thomas Furlong (poetry) and Edward Walshe (prose); the standard of the writing is entirely unexceptional. As well as opposing the consumption of alcohol, they opposed capital punishment and slavery; however the poor level of writing leaves it feeling worthy but dull.

THE NATION, A WEEKLY JOURNAL OF POLITICS, LITERATURE AND THE ARTS

Location: Dublin (publisher 'The Proprietor', 12 Trinity Street)
Editor(s):   Anon. (Thomas Davis, C.G. Duffy, etc.)
Dates: Volume 1, number 1 (15 October 1842)–volume 6, number 304 (29 July 1848); banned from August 1848 to August 1849; volume 7 ('New Series Volume 1'), number 1 (1 September 1849–volume 11, number 17 (25 December 1852)
No. of issues: 477
Average periodicity: Weekly
Average no. pages: 16
Libraries: BL(Colindale)= Microfilm; NLI=Newspaper Floor; PSPL=079.415; QUB=MicA/568-573 (15 October 1842–25 December 1852; microfilm of NLI copy); RIA=RR Gall/Case 4/F/9–20; TCD=IN.19.1-7; UCC=15 October 1842–25 December 1852; UCD=MICJ 941.5.

[NLI copy, Volume 6, number 303 has handwritten on it: 'On Friday 21st July the Police entered the Printing Office of the Nation and seized every copy of the Publication for the 29th (No. 304) – they also seized every printer and inkman found in the place and sent them to Newgate – therefore not a single copy of the paper reached the public – all were lodged in the Castle – (Except the Copy on this pile which escaped).']

The mouthpiece of the Young Ireland movement, the *Nation*, quickly became a legendary success, galvanising a new form of cultural nationalism and selling more than 10,000 copies per issue, though its subsequent reputation has obscured the fact that a wider range of opinions was allowed expression in its pages than many imagine. It followed a standard newspaper format, with lots of advertisements, news from abroad, sections on the courts, births, marriages, and deaths. The first editorial was a suitably ringing declaration of first principles, on the surface plangently radical, but in a more subtle way announcing Davis's ideal of an Irish identity more inclusive and less sectarian than that of the early years of the nineteenth century: 'With all the nicknames that serve to delude and divide us . . . there are, in truth, but two parties in Ireland: those who suffer from her national degradation, and those who profit by it . . .'. He added the hope that: 'our kindred love of letters will often induce [writers] to turn with us from the study of mankind in books, to the service of mankind in politics . . .'.

Each issue has a couple of pages devoted to literature – poems, notices, and the famous 'Songs of the Nation'. Most of this conforms to the reputation, that is, rousing and populist rather than of great artistic quality, but there are a few surprises. In keeping with the spirit of the enterprise, there are many cases of creative writers slipping easily from polemic to poetry and back again; Davis is probably the best example of this, but Carleton also contributed both tales and a couple of non-fiction pieces (1843–1846). The main players also contribute a series of substantial essays, including Davis's own 'Nationalism'. After the failure of the Young Ireland rising in 1848, the *Nation*'s contributors split into various factions, each with its own organ; a fairly moderate group (including Gavan Duffy, Lady

Wilde and A.M. Sullivan) began the second series of the *Nation*, which continued in fits and starts until the end of the century, although after 1852 it was but a shadow of its former self, with greatly reduced sales and impact, and devoted primarily to Duffy's Tenant League.

The *Nation*'s secret may be that it combines the best aspects of its contemporaries: it publishes many of the best Irish writers of its day (as the *DUM* did); it promoted the new, more sophisticated cultural nationalism (like the *Citizen*); and it educated, informed and entertained the working-classes (as in the best of the Penny magazines). It also, of course, brought a couple of completely new qualities of its own – primarily its direct engagement (Davis, Dillon and Duffy were not mere reporters, but also important actors on the Irish political stage), and it was also one of the first Irish magazines to create a literature of its own. These muscular ballads and tales, 'racy of the soil', were to be criticised by a later generation for confusing patriotism with quality, but at its best (e.g. in Davis himself, and Ferguson and Mangan) it provided an inspiration and foundation for much that was to be achieved during the Revival (see, amongst other strong work, Mangan's 'Siberia' and 'Dark Rosaleen', both of which first appeared here).

This 'afterlife' of diminishing echoes leads to great confusion in the indexes and commentaries, Hayley gives the dates of the *Nation* as 1842–1876, while Welch gives 1842–1848, 2nd series 1849–1896. I have not examined these later titles as they had only a fraction of the importance or impact of the original, and added nothing to its literary achievement. This variety of pale shadows was published throughout the following fifty years: as *The Nation* from 1882 to 11 July 1891, as *The Irish Catholic and Nation* from 18 July 1891 to 6 June 1896, *The Nation* again from 13 June 1896 to 5 June 1897, and finally as *The Daily Nation* from 12 June 1897 to 31 August 1900.

Another important way in which the lasting cultural impact of the *Nation* can be gauged is by examining the many spin-offs which were produced. These included *The Spirit of the Nation* (edited by Duffy), two volumes of verses from May and November 1843, and which grew to acquire a mythic stature in Nationalist culture second only to the *Nation* itself; by November the first volume had been reprinted, and an American edition published; by 1870, these volumes had been reprinted fifty times (see Kelly, 1994, p. 439; see Thuente, pp. 194, 200–1, 213, 217, 218, 221, 224, 225). There was also *The Voice of the Nation; a manual of national identity*, 1844; *Squibs and Crackers*, 1853 (humorous pieces from the paper); *Easy Lessons* [in Irish], 1860; *The New Spirit of the Nation*, Martin McDermott, 1894; and *Selection from 'Poets of the Nation'*, 1900. There were in addition numerous one-off reprints of essays and so on. This constant recycling of the people and pieces from the *Nation* built into a myth of super-committed nationalism. If it is hard to imagine the popular nationalism of the early twentieth century taking the form it did without the example of the *Nation* and its prime agents, it is equally hard to imagine the more sophisticated magazines of that period, like the 1911 *Irish Review*, without that same example.

See Matthew Russell, 'Signatures in the Old Nation Newspaper', *Irish Monthly,* 17 (1889), pp. 502–506 and 609–612.
See Kevin McGrath, 'Writers in The Nation 1842–45', *Irish Historical Studies,* 6 (1949), pp. 189–223.

See Richard J. Loftus, *Nationalism in Modern Anglo-Irish Poetry* (Wisconsin, 1964), p. 8, 21, 131, 288n, 321n.

See Barbara Hayley, 'Irish Periodicals from the Union to the Nation', in P.J. Drudy (ed.), *Anglo-Irish Studies* II (Cambridge, 1976), p. 104–105.

See William Bradley, 'The Poetry of the Nation, 1842–1848', PhD thesis (University of London, 1977).

See Roger McHugh and Maurice Harmon, *A Short History of Anglo-Irish Literature* (Dublin, 1982), pp. 94, 108–110, 127, 132.

See A.C. Partridge, *Language and Society in Anglo-Irish Literature* (Dublin, 1984), pp. 121–122, 124, 137, 165–166, 174.

See Seamus Deane, *Celtic Revivals* (London, 1985), p. 21.

See John Kelly, *The Collected Letters of W.B. Yeats*, Volume 1: 1865–1895 (Oxford, 1986), pp. 13n, 29n, 31n, 52n, 66n, 70n, 72n, 77, 83n, 99, 102, 122, 123, 125, 132n, 148, 156, 204, 205–208, 210, 217, 218, 297, 298n, 299, 311, 334n, 483, 484.

See Barbara Hayley, 'A Reading and Thinking Nation: Periodicals as the Voice of Nineteenth-Century Ireland', in Barbara Hayley and Enda McKay (eds), *300 Years of Irish Periodicals* (Mullingar, 1987), pp. 40–41.

See Norman Vance, *Irish Literature: A Social History – Tradition, Identity and Difference* (Oxford, 1990), p. 132.

See W.J. McCormack, *From Burke to Beckett: Ascendancy, Tradition and Betrayal in Literary History* (Cork, 1994), pp. 142, 173.

See John Kelly, *The Collected Letters of W.B. Yeats*, Volume 3: 1901–1904 (Oxford, 1994), p. 439.

See Mary Helen Thuente, *The Harp Re-strung, The United Irishmen and the Rise of Irish Literary Nationalism* (New York, 1994), pp. 193–197, 200–230.

See Declan Kiberd, *Inventing Ireland* (London, 1995), p. 22.

See John Kelly, *The Collected Letters of W.B. Yeats*, Volume 2: 1896–1900 (Oxford, 1997), pp. 387n, 547n, 567n.

THE DUBLIN LITERARY JOURNAL, AND SELECT FAMILY VISITOR, FOR THE DISSEMINATION OF USEFUL KNOWLEDGE

Location:	Dublin (printer W. Nolan, Upper Sackville Street, publisher Joshua Abell, 27 Eustace Street)
Editor(s):	Joshua Abell
Dates:	1 April 1843–1 February 1846
No. of issues:	35
Average periodicity:	Monthly
Average no. pages:	16
Libraries:	BL=PP.6193.1; NLI=J 05; PSPL=805; RIA=RR Gall/36/F; TCD=BB.ff.40.

This magazine is in five clearly defined sections: book reviews, accounts of literary and scientific meetings, miscellanea, poetry and advertising. There are a few significant poems – 'A Severe Winter's Night' by Shelley, 'The Complaint of the Poor' by Southey, 'On a Visit to Wordsworth' by Sir Aubrey de Vere – and many insignificant ones, including those by Abell himself. Although no major books are covered, the reviews are informative, if short. The literary world covered by the *Journal* is Britain, including Ireland as an integral part; no discussion of politics or religion appears. The 'Dissemination of Useful Knowledge' is, in fact, a good description of both its achievement and its limitations.

THE ULSTER MONTHLY MAGAZINE, AND LITERARY MISCELLANY

Location:	Belfast (printer Robert F. Ward, Waring Street, publisher E.H. Lamont, Donegall Place Buildings)
Editor(s):	Anon.
Dates:	January–February 1845
No. of issues:	2
Average periodicity:	Monthly
Average no. pages:	32
Libraries:	LIN; RIA=RR Gall/36/E.

An 'Introductory Address' in the first issue claims that they are starting up because '. . . (with the exception of the old *Belfast Magazine*) every effort of the kind has hitherto failed', which they blame on the traditional causes of cultural cringe, and the public's unfortunate preference for works from England and Scotland; this piece also claims that, at the end of the eighteenth century, forty thousand people in Ireland were literate. As it only lasted for two issues, it is impossible to know how the magazine would have developed. The first issue contained an article on 'Early Native Poetry of Ireland', a traveller's tale, two ballads by Frances Brown, a couple of general essays, and notices of new books published; the second has the end of the essay on early native poetry, a 'War Ode to Osgur', and a few dull essays.

THE BELFAST PENNY JOURNAL, A NATIONAL MISCELLANY OF ORIGINAL AND SELECTED LITERATURE

Location:	Belfast (printer J. M'Lornan and Co., William Street South, publisher William Pollack, 62 North Street)
Editor(s):	Anon.
Dates:	17 May 1845–26 December 1846
No. of issues:	82
Average periodicity:	Weekly
Average no. pages:	16

Libraries: BCL=I/094.1[1] MULL (volume 1, number 1, 17 May 1845–volume 2, number 30, 12 December 1846 only); LIN (volume 1, number 1, 17 May 1845–volume 1, number 50, 16 May 1845 only); QUB=hAP4.B46 (incomplete).

This carried the slogan, 'Interesting to all – Offensive to None', and the first editorial chimed with those modest ambitions, simply hoping that the *Journal* might sell enough copies to break even; it does, however, call for contributions from local writers, and it is the positive response to this call which makes the *Journal* worth reading. A relatively small group of writers, all locally based, provides the bulk of the material published, a group which includes: Thomas Elliott, Thomas Henry, Frances Brown, William Keenan, John Herbison and David Herbison; and the magazine has a distinctly Antrim feel about it, with many of the contributions containing authentic local detail. In October 1845 they embarked on a series of short 'Sketches in Ulster', of local characters and life, and short biographies of some of the 'Bards', such as James Orr. Their opinions are liberal, against prize-fighting, and for working-class education.

By Autumn 1845, the *Journal* had got into its stride, maintaining a steady level of quality week after week, leavened with the occasional reprint, e.g. Dickens's 'The Cricket on the Hearth', or 'From the Arabic, by P.B. Shelley'; however, by the following summer a number of that core group of writers had moved on, and the magazine's successful formula begins to look a little stale. The last number contains a small notice, 'To Our Readers': 'With the Present number of the Belfast Penny Journal it shall cease for the present, until other arrangements are made to bring out another series'. Although most of the contributions are workmanlike rather than inspired, still this is a pretty good effort, readable and consistent.

THE IRISH NATIONAL MAGAZINE AND WEEKLY JOURNAL OF LITERATURE, SCIENCE, AND ART

Location: Dublin (publisher T. Le Mesurier, 8 Lower Abbey Street)
Editor(s): Anon.
Dates: 16 May 1846–15 August 1846
No. of issues: 14
Average periodicity: Weekly
Average no. pages: 16
Libraries: BL=PP.6193.f; NLI=Ir 8205 i 4 (bound with *Holmes' Defence of 'The Nation'*); PSPL=805.

Despite its title, primarily a political magazine, whose declared aim was to 'diffuse throughout this land the principle of NATIONALITY'. Each issue carries one or two short tales of Irish life, a handful of poems (the only major name is Griffin), and a literary article; this latter includes 'The Literary Resources of Dublin' (literary history), 'Swift, Sheridan and Delaney', and 'Sketches of Irish Poets – Thomas Dermody'. A serious and well put together magazine, but the brevity of the individual pieces, and the unrelenting political bias undermines its worth.

See Richard Kearney, 'Between Politics and Literature: The Irish Cultural Journal', *Crane Bag,* 7, 2 (Autumn 1983), pp. 160-171. Mentions *National Magazine.*
See Barbara Hayley, 'A Reading and Thinking Nation: Periodicals as the Voice of Nineteenth-Century Ireland', in Barbara Hayley and Enda McKay (eds), *300 Years of Irish Periodicals* (Mullingar, 1987), p. 41.

THE BELFAST ADVERTISER AND LITERARY GAZETTE

Location: Belfast
Editor(s):   Anon.
Dates: 5 November 1847–31 December 1847
No. of issues: 9
Average periodicity: Weekly
Average no. pages: 4
Libraries: BCL=Microfilm, Location 1A; BL(Colin).

Newspaper size and shape, distributed free. Most of the features and the literary articles are taken from other magazines, including *Blackwood's*, *Cork Magazine* and the *Dublin University Magazine.*

The first issue contains, along with notices of new magazines, two poems and a short story, and a 3,000-word essay on 'The Novels and Novel Writers of Ireland', reprinted from the *Cork Magazine.* This is a good, quick survey of the subject, touching on the Banims, Carleton, Lover and Lever. This is typical of the contents and tone of the gazette. By number 4 the story ('Sophia Robartes's Flirtations') has reached nearly 8,000 words; number 6 carries a short extract from *Dombey and Son*; while number 8 has 'The Raven', by 'Edgar A. Poe, an American poet'.

The Belfast Advertiser is one of the more successful attempts at presenting literature in this popular way – or of using stories and poems to mark out a trade paper from the crowd and draw a wider audience. The quality of the contributors is rather higher than usual, and there is no feeling of pandering to the crowd or patronising them.

THE KILRUSH MAGAZINE, AND MONTHLY JOURNAL OF LITERATURE AND USEFUL INFORMATION

Location: Kilrush (printer and publisher J.A. Carroll, 42 Frances Street)
Editor(s):   William M. Downes

Dates: May 1847–August 1847
No. of issues: 4
Average periodicity: Monthly
Average no. pages: ?
Libraries: BL=1866.a.18(4), no.1 only; NLI=Ir 8205 k 1.

The NLI copy is a selection, printed in 1852, of this small magazine's contents; the introduction says it foundered in the middle of the Famine. There is poetry by Downes, Griffin and Byron, and some anonymous tales and legends of the West. Poorly printed, and spiced with articles on the wonders of the turnip, it is still important as an example of the spread of literary and other magazines to what even the editor describes as a remote spot. All four issues were republished by Carroll in 1852 as a single volume, *An Old Friend (with a new face) to which is added a monthly journal of literature and information.*

THE CORK MAGAZINE

Location: Cork (publisher Bradford and Co., Patrick Street)
Editor(s):   Joseph Brenan
Dates   :   November 1847–December 1848
No. of issues: 14
Average periodicity: Monthly
Average no. pages: 64
Libraries: BL=1609/470; NLI=J 05; PSPL=052; RIA=Fr Crypt/Sect1/2/E; TCD=Gall.KK.3.33,34.

This publication contains a few poems, but is mostly given over to literary articles, and to long, serialised stories and novels. The opening editorial, 'A National Literature for Ireland', is a self-explanatory manifesto which declares that 'no country can be anything better than a province, where a National Literature is wanting'. It praises Griffin, Carleton, Lover, Drennan and Edgeworth as giants of the past, and nominates Davis as their successor. The first issue also contains a good essay, 'The Novels and Novel Writers of Ireland', a quite sophisticated analysis claiming that Ireland has not yet produced a great novelist, and that the works of Banim, Carleton, Lever, etc. are all spoilt by caricature, stage Irishry and weak plots. Other contributions include a translation of 'The Seven Chords of the Lyre' by George Sand, the serialised stories 'The Last Lord of Beara' and 'Judith O'Donoghue – A Tale of the South of Ireland', and some poems by Martin MacDermott.

The articles are generally more impressive than the creative pieces but, by keeping the political comment within reasonable bounds, it is far more convincing in its attempt to sustain a new wave of Irish national literature than, for example, the slightly hysterical *Irish National Magazine* of the previous year.

See M. Holland, 'The Cork Magazine and its Writers', *Journal of the Ivernian Society,* 7 (1915), pp. 142–146.

See D.J. O'Donoghue, 'The Cork Magazine', *Irish Book Lover*, 6 (1915), pp. 125–127 and 7 (1915), p. 103.

See Brian McKenna, *Irish Literature 1800–1875* (Detroit, 1978), p. 34.

THE IRISH TRIBUNE

Location:	Dublin (printer Denis Hoban, 11 Trinity Street)
Editor(s):	Anon.
Dates:	Volume 1, number 1 (10 June 1848)–volume 1, number 5 (8 July 1848)
No. of issues:	5
Average periodicity:	Weekly
Average no. pages:	16
Libraries:	BL(Colin)=Microfilm (full run, some pages missing from number 3); NLI=Microfilm 58 (first issue only).

This is more a pro-Repeal newspaper than a magazine, devoting most of its coverage to news and political articles. All five issues carry patriotic ballads, while the second has a poem from Mangan and the first three serialise 'The Evil Eye', a short story by Carleton. The most regular poetic contributor is John Savage.

See Brian McKenna, *Irish Literature 1800–1875* (Detroit, 1978), p. 35.

THE FIRESIDE MAGAZINE; A WEEKLY JOURNAL OF ENTERTAINING LITERATURE

Location:	Cork (printer and publisher John Jesse and Co., 6 Cumberland Street)
Editor(s):	Anon.
Dates:	2 December 1848–6 January 1849
No. of issues:	6
Average periodicity:	Weekly
Average no. pages:	8
Libraries:	TCD=OLS 188.n.24, number 10 (first five issues only).

Another very lightweight 1d magazine, carrying one or two weak verses ('Our Parish'), a legendary tale, and a serialised story ('Ulic O'Regan' by Miss S. O'Sullivan). Like the *Athy Literary Magazine* its only claim to importance comes from its being published outside Dublin; also like the *Athy*, it is very conservative in its approach.

THE CLUBBIST, CONSISTING CHIEFLY OF A SELECTION OF POEMS FROM THE PAGES OF THE SUPPRESSED JOURNALS

Location: Dublin (printed at 171 Great Britain Street)
Editor(s):   Mathew Fannin
Dates: 1849
No. of issues: 3
Average periodicity: Not known
Average no. pages: 16
Libraries: BL=PP.6162.

Fannin reveals the purpose of his magazine in his editorial to the first issue, where he states that its object is 'to give the patriotic poor Irish Literature at the cheapest rate'. The contributions are all either anonymous, pseudonymous (with pen names ranging from 'Sliabh Cuilinn' (John O'Hagan, according to McKenna), to 'One of the State Prisoners'), or simply initialled (McKenna identifying 'JCM' as Mangan). They are taken from a number of sources, including *The Felon*, *The Nation* and (surprisingly) the *Dublin University Magazine*.

The poems are classic Young Ireland ballads, whose titles reveal all: 'The Place Where Man Should Die', 'Oh! For a Steed', 'Song of Lamentation for the Premature Death of Owen Roe O'Neill', 'A Felon's Chaunt', while the rare essays are in similar vein (see 'Memoir of John Mitchel', in issue 2).

All bar one of the verses are in clunking rhyming couplets, and almost all are crippled by sentimentality, stilted 'poetic' diction and lack of originality in subject matter, tone and imagery; for example, 'Doubts' by 'M MacD', (3rd stanza):

> Where is now my land belovéd?
> Wo is me! wo is me! –
> Not with banner in the air,
> And her keen sword flashing bare–
> Oh! in chains and shame she's lying–
> Wo is me!

is far from the worst.

See Brian McKenna, *Irish Literature 1800–1875* (Detroit, 1978), p. 35.

FRANCIS DAVIS, THE BELFAST MAN'S JOURNAL

Location: Belfast (printer and publisher John Henderson, 13 Castle Place)
Editor(s):   Francis Davis
Dates: 5 January 1850–23 March 1850
No. of issues: 12
Average periodicity: Weekly

Average no. pages: 16
Libraries: BL=PP.6193; LIN; NLI=J 05; PSPL=805 (bound with *Irish National*
                      Magazine and Weekly Journal); TCD=Gall.NN.15.3, no.8.

'Our Plans and Prospects', in the first issue, reads: '. . . the working-classes of Belfast, have more than once or twice possessed the opportunity of supporting a native literary periodical; but for some reason . . . ye have ever been the last to receive, and the first to decline, any and every thing of the stamp . . .' Most of this periodical seems to have been written by Davis himself; he places the blame for previous failures in Ireland in equal measure on the poor quality of previous magazines, and on cultural cringe. Unfortunately, the contents of the *Journal* do not exactly live up to this ringing plea. An article on Goldsmith is carried over three issues, and one on Swift appears in number 12; 'The Power of Love, A Tale of '98' by L. Maria Child graces issue 5; while number 10 has a review of Denis Florence MacCarthy's *Ballads, Poems and Limericks*. By 1850, Goldsmith and Swift were not exactly the cutting edge of Irish literature, and the verdict on the magazine as a whole must be that it is worthy but dull.

See Barbara Hayley, 'A Reading and Thinking Nation: Periodicals as the Voice of Nineteenth-Century Ireland', in Barbara Hayley, and Enda McKay (eds) *300 Years of Irish Periodicals* (Mullingar, 1987, p. 42.
See Norman Vance, *Irish Literature: A Social History– Tradition, Identity and Difference* (Oxford, 1990), p. 133.

DUFFY'S FIRESIDE MAGAZINE, A MONTHLY MISCELLANY

Location: Dublin (printer J.M. O'Toole, 13 Hankins Street, publisher James
                      Duffy, 7 Wellington Quay)
Editor(s):   Dr Reynolds
Dates: November 1850–October 1854
No. of issues: 48
Average periodicity: Monthly
Average no. pages: 30
Libraries: BL=PP.6193.c; LIN; NLI=J 05; QUB=hAP4.D85; RIA=Fr C/3/D;
                      UCC (1851–1852 only); UCG=052 (PS).

The editorial in the first issue proclaims: 'A Fireside Magazine, like the fireside itself, should be filled with gentle thoughts, kindly feelings, calm reflections and pleasant associations.' In its four years, it carried a number of serialised novels, including 'The Irish Privateer', '"Maitland; or, The Mystery" by a well-known Irish novelist', and 'Adventures of an Irish Giant', by 'the late Gerald Griffin'; some short book reviews; and a few poems, mostly very poor, with the most frequent contributors William Bernard MacCabe and some who preferred to remain anonymous ('S.N.E.', 'W.N.S.'). Unfortunately, *Duffy's Fireside* achieved the ambitions laid out at its start, and the contents remained bland and inoffensive.

See Matthew Russell, 'Anonymities Unveiled: Contributors to Duffy's Fireside Magazine', *Irish Monthly*, 20 (1892), pp. 319–326.
See D.J. O'Donoghue, 'Duffy's Fireside Magazine', *Irish Book Lover*, 7 (1915), pp. 47–48.
See Donat O'Donnell, 'The Catholic Press, A Study in Theopolitics', *The Bell*, 10, 1 (June 1945) pp. 30–40.
See Thomas Wall, 'Catholic Periodicals of the Past', *Irish Ecclesiastical Record*, 102 (1964).
See Barbara Hayley, 'A Reading and Thinking Nation: Periodicals as the Voice of Nineteenth-Century Ireland', in Barbara Hayley and Enda McKay (eds), *300 Years of Irish Periodicals* (Mullingar, 1987), p. 42.

THE IRISH QUARTERLY REVIEW

Location:	Dublin (printer Browne and Nolan, 21 Nassau Street, publisher W.B. Kelly, 8 Grafton Street; also Simpkin and Co., London, and Oliver and Boyd, Edinburgh)
Editor(s):	Anon.
Dates:	March 1851–January 1860
No. of issues:	36
Average periodicity:	Quarterly
Average no. pages:	180, rising through 220 and 240 to 360 in its last year
Libraries:	BL=PP.6157; LIN; MAR=YR (incomplete); NLI=Ir 05 i 17; PSPL=052 (1852–1855 only); QUB=hAP4.I61; RIA=RR Gall/35/B; TCD=OLS 186.q.34–49; UCC=1851–1856; UCG=052 (PS, incomplete).

This is an excellent magazine, well produced and serious about literature, but not pompous. It is mostly devoted to general articles on a wide range of subjects, including the Irish court system, the Tenant League, Irish painting and the development of the British Empire, but it also gives considerable space to what might be regarded as classic Victorian book reviews – relatively restrained in their judgements (at least compared with the factionalism of earlier journals), very thorough, and built on extensive quotation. There is no trace of provincialism in this magazine; they are not apologetic about giving serious coverage to MacCarthy or Griffin, while keeping their readers up to date with the latest French poetry or US novelists. The only deficiency in the *Review* is that it carries very little creative writing, beyond the occasional light verse.

Issue 3 contains a typically substantial, discursive review of 'Poetical Literature of the Past Half-Century', while issue 4 has a similar piece on Maria Edgeworth; number 7 introduces the portmanteau review with 'Poets of Yesterday and Today', looking at six collections, including three by Bulwer Lytton. An even longer review of Russell's memoirs of Thomas Moore is spread across numbers 9 and 10, while an extensive, 200-page biographical study of Banim runs from issue 14 to issue 21. Number 20 carries a review of collections of poetry from Thomas Davis, Griffin and Francis Davis; number 28 of two collections by William Allingham, and issue 34 a 100-page critical biography of Lady Morgan.

This is certainly one of the most convincing examples of the grand review to have emerged in Ireland up to this time, and it would not be embarrassed in the company of the London and Edinburgh reviews it so obviously sought to emulate.

See Barbara Hayley, 'A Reading and Thinking Nation: Periodicals as the Voice of Nineteenth-Century Ireland', in Barbara Hayley, and Enda McKay (eds), *300 Years of Irish Periodicals* (Mullingar, 1987), p. 42.

Subject index in William Frederick Poole, *Poole's Index to Periodical Literature*, revised edition (Gloucester, MA, 1963).

An author index appears in Richard J. Hayes, *Sources for the History of Irish Civilisation: Articles in Irish Periodicals*, 5 vols (Boston, 1970).

THE NORTHERN MAGAZINE

Location: Belfast (printer McCormick and Robie, 35 Donegall Street, publisher Henry Greer, High Street)
Editor(s):   Anon.
Dates: March 1852–February 1853
No. of issues: 12
Average periodicity: Monthly
Average no. pages: 30
Libraries: BCL=I/094.1[1] MACC; BL=PP.6180.b; LIN; NLI=J 05; QUB=hAP4.N77.

From 'We Make a Beginning', issue 1: 'This magazine is now started by a number of young men, principally students in the Queen's College, whose observations have led them to think that Belfast is of sufficient size to support a monthly magazine, and Ulster of sufficient literary standing to require one.' The magazine inevitably has the feel of a student production, a sometimes immature tone and a tendency toward self-conscious displays of erudition. The first issue shows a typical mix, comprising some weak satire, an essay on Roman Britain, three workmanlike poems, a review of Longfellow's 'The Golden Legend', and a folk-tale. Despite essays on Irish towns and Irish topics in some of the poetry, contributors have a habit of referring to contemporary happenings in England as 'our internal politics'. The issue for December 1852 has a good review of

Drummond's *Ancient Irish Minstrelsy*, while February 1853 sees a gushing review of '"Poets and Poetry of the Nineteenth Century" by the Earl of Belfast'. 'Our Farewell Word' in the last issue states that: 'The graver and more important pursuits of life, mercantile, collegiate and professional, demand from us...such undivided attention that this, the pleasant recreation of last year, must be discontinued', which perhaps reveals why the magazine failed to establish any strong identity, or to make any serious contribution to Irish literature.

See Barbara Hayley, 'A Reading and Thinking Nation: Periodicals as the Voice of Nineteenth-Century Ireland', Barbara Hayley and Enda McKay (eds), *300 Years of Irish Periodicals* (Mullingar, 1987), p. 42.

THE KERRY MAGAZINE: A MONTHLY JOURNAL OF ANTIQUITIES, POLITE LITERATURE, CRITICISM, POETRY

Location:	Tralee (printer and publisher Ferdinand Charles Panormo, 25 Lower Castle Street)
Editor(s):	Anon.
Dates:	1 January 1854–1 December 1856
No. of issues:	36
Average periodicity:	Monthly
Average no. pages:	16, rising to 20
Libraries:	BL=PP.6193.b; QUB=hAP4.K4; NLI=Ir 94146 k 1; RIA=RR Gall/36/F; TCD=HH.r.67-69.

The prospectus for this journal proclaims a desire to produce something more elevated than the existing Kerry newspapers and political magazines, and to provide a platform to show the beauties and positive side of the county, as well as to trumpet them to outsiders. Each issue starts with a main article, usually on Kerry's antiquities; then some letters; a couple of 'original' poems; a more general literary piece (e.g. 'Selections from the English Poets', which covered Crabbe and Tennyson, amongst others); and finally a short tale. The literary efforts are workmanlike, at best, and it is hard to believe that they contributed much to the *Magazine*'s popularity. Its importance obviously comes from its being a good quality, regular, non-political magazine, from a small town in the west of the country, which found enough of an audience to last for three years.

See Barbara Hayley, 'A Reading and Thinking Nation: Periodicals as the Voice of Nineteenth-Century Ireland', in Barbara Hayley and Enda McKay (eds), *300 Years of Irish Periodicals* (Mullingar, 1987), p. 42.

An author index appears in Richard J. Hayes (ed.), *Sources for the History of Irish Civilisation: Articles in Irish Periodicals*, 5 vols (Boston, 1970).

THE CELT. A WEEKLY PERIODICAL OF IRISH NATIONAL LITERATURE

Location: Dublin (publisher John O'Daly, 9 Anglesea Street)
Editor(s):   'A Committee of the Celtic Union' (though S.J. Brown identifies the
                     'chief editor' as a Dr Cane)
Dates: 1 August 1857–26 December 1857, and supplement 31 December
                     1857; March 1858–August 1858
No. of issues: 22 as a weekly, 6 as a monthly
Average periodicity: Weekly, then monthly
Average no. pages: 16, then 48
Libraries: BL=PP.6173; NLI=J 89162 and Ir 8916205 c 1; PSPL=052; RIA=Fr
                     Crypt/Sect 1/2/D; TCD=Gall.D.20.22.

The first editorial says that both wealth and education have increased rapidly in Ireland, but that the first is due to the reduction in population after the Famine, and that the education given in National Schools is basic, non-nationalist and un-Catholic. While it was a weekly, the main preoccupation was politics, and the literary content was kept fairly low, mainly patriotic ballads like 'The Felons of '48', although there are a few more interesting items, like a couple of poems in the Irish language, with translations; 'The poet Moore's Letter to the Students of Trinity College'; 'An Exile's Death' by Robert Emmet; and Mangan's translation of the 'Lament for Owen Roe O'Neill'. The monthly was slightly less political, but unfortunately the quality of the literature declined; the poems tended to be less than purely national, and a number of romances were published, like 'The Knights of the Pale' in the first monthly issue. Although an article in August 1858 ends with 'To be continued', the NLI copy is marked 'Complete'.

[see McKenna – continued as *The Celt: An Irish Catholic National Monthly Magazine*, Dublin, pub. O'Kelly, August–November 1859, ed. John Thomas Campion]

See Matthew Russell, 'Signatures in the Nation and the Celt', *Irish Monthly*, 17 (1889), pp. 609–612.
See Roy Foster, *Paddy and Mr Punch* (London, 1993), p. 269.
See John Kelly, *The Collected Letters of W.B. Yeats*, Volume 3: 1901–1904 (Oxford, 1994), pp. 155n, 375.

An author index appears in Richard J. Hayes, *Sources for the History of Irish Civilisation: Articles in Irish Periodicals*, 5 vols (Boston, 1970).

IRISH LITERARY GAZETTE, A WEEKLY JOURNAL OF NATIONAL LITERATURE, CRITICISM, FICTION, INDUSTRY, SCIENCE AND ART

Location: Dublin (publisher and printer Robert M. Chamney, 86 Middle Abbey
                     Street; also printed in Cork (Samuel M. Peck, South Mall) and
                     Belfast (John Henderson, 13 Castle Place))

Editor(s):   Anon.
Dates: Volume 1, number 1 (1 August 1857)–volume 1, number 22 (26 December 1857); then changes to *The Irish Literary Gazette and National Reformer*, volume 2 (new series), number 1 (2 January 1858)–volume 2, number 4 (23 January 1858); then back to original title, volume 2, number 27 (30 January 1858)–volume 2, number 44 (29 May 1858); then to *Irish Literary Gazette, A Monthly Miscellany of National Literature, Criticism, Fiction, Industry, Science and Art*, number 45 (1 July 1858); then to *Irish Literary Gazette, A Monthly Pictorial Journal of National Literature, Criticism, Fiction, Industry, Science and Art*, number 46 (1 August 1858)–number 50 (1 December 1858); then to *The Irish Literary Gazette and Register of Facts and Occurrences Relating to Literature, the Sciences, & the Arts*, number 1 (November 1860)–number 11 (September 1861)
No. of issues: 61
Average periodicity: Weekly (until 29 May 1858), then monthly
Average no. pages: 16; then 20; then 14; then 32; then 32; then 48
Libraries: LIN (1 August 1857–26 December 1857); NLI=J 05 and Ir 05 i 45; PSPL=052; RIA=Top Floor Room 5/5/B; TCD=Gall.X.3.14,15 (incomplete); UCC (incomplete).

Densely printed in double columns, this has the feel of a trade paper. Each issue opens with a couple of pages of 'Literary Intelligence' (gossip about writers and publishers), and closes with three or four pages of lists of books published at home and abroad, and half-a-dozen pages of advertising. In between there were many general essays, plus a few on literary subjects. Amongst the articles on drawing, the rights of women and the topographical sketches, there are usually one or two short verses, a handful of very short book reviews and a serialised novel. There is also a diary of the wider literary world (a notice that Dickens has embarked on a tour of the USA, for example).

The incarnation of January 1858 gives the impression of two completely separate magazines bound together, although the literary section carries on as before. In July of the same year, the magazine shrinks from roughly A4 size to roughly A5, but again there is no change in the content.

In its final incarnation the nationalist politics are dropped, and it becomes more of a standard Victorian review – a couple of pages of literary intelligence, a serialised novel, a short piece on English periodicals, a longer one on George Sand's last work; the rest is general pieces on George Fox or exploration in Africa. In this incarnation it almost loses its Irish character.

Although the literary standard was low, this magazine has some importance as a source of information on contemporary literature and publishing; the most significant author to appear in its pages was 'W. Allingham', on 27 February 1858, though his poem, 'Venus of the Needle', is poor.

THE COLLEGE MAGAZINE

Location: Dublin (printer M.H. Gill, University Press, publisher William
                     McGee and Co., 18 Nassau Street)
Editor(s):   Anon.
Dates: October 1857–March 1858
No. of issues: 6
Average periodicity: Monthly
Average no. pages: 64
Libraries: LIN; NLI=Ir 3784105; QUB=hAP4.C8; TCD=Gall.M.19.64.

An odd little curiosity, this, with a strange mixture of contents: a retelling of the 'Ballad of
Damayanti' (from the Mahabharata) alongside ten pages of Irish proverbs; a good
introductory essay to Shelley followed by one on lycanthropy. Despite the fact that there
are some interesting items, like the three translated Heine poems in the first issue, the tone
remains uncertain, and it is never clear who the intended audience is supposed to be.

THE ATLANTIS: A REGISTER OF LITERATURE AND SCIENCE

Location: Dublin (printer John F. Fowler, 3 Crow Street) and London
                     (publisher Longman, Brown, Green, Longman and Roberts)
Editor(s):   John Henry Newman and William K. Sullivan; from volume three,
                     Newman, Sullivan and Peter LePage Renouf; from   volume 6,
                     Sullivan and Renouf; from volume 8, Bartholomew Woodlock.
Dates: Volume 1, number 1 (January 1858)–volume 8 (February 1870)
No. of issues: 8
Average periodicity: Twice-yearly; from volume 5, irregular
Average no. pages: 252
Libraries: BL=PP.6159; NLI=Ir 05; also J 8205; PSPL; QUB=hAP4.A81
                     (volumes 1 (1858), 2 (1859) 3 (1862), and 4 (1863) only);
                     TCD=32.dd.72; another at Gall.I.25.28-32; UCD.

[Subtitle 'Conducted By Members of the Catholic University of Ireland'.]

A 'Prospectus' was issued, which declared that: 'The object of the work...is to serve
principally as the repository and memorial of such investigations in Literature and Science,
as are made by the members of the new Catholic University of Ireland...'.

   The tone of *Atlantis* is extremely dry and academic (Houghton says that this was
deliberate, that Newman wanted it to prove how seriously the new university should be
taken); the first issue has no editorial nor prefatory material of any kind, but launches
straight into a paper (signed by the Very Rev J.H. Newman, DD, himself) on 'The Mission
of the Benedictine Order', while the rest is heavyweight scientific papers (on geology,
chemistry, etc.), by contributors whose names include Joule and Pasteur.

The only contributions which could be described as literary are: an article by Thomas Arnold on 'The Genius of Alcibiades', a couple of Spanish plays, introduced and translated by D.F. McCarthy, and an 'Ode on the Foundation of the New Building for the Catholic University of Ireland' by Aubrey de Vere. More interesting are the translations (with parallel originals) of an Irish poem, 'The Vengence of Connal Cearnach', also by de Vere, and of a handful of myths (including 'The Sick-bed of Cuchulainn, and the only Jealousy of Emer') by Eugene O'Curry.

Most of the actual editing was done by Sullivan, but Newman was the driving force behind the venture, and this resulted in a self-consciously serious and strait-laced academic journal. There was an inevitable clash between Newman's desire for an austere, even difficult, academic publication and the Catholic bishops who, in response to poor sales, kept the funding tight. Eventually, Newman himself left both the university and Ireland, and the *Atlantis* petered out.

See Rev C. Stephen Dessain, *The Letters and Diaries of John Henry Newman* (Oxford, 1961–1977), vols. XVII, XVIII and XIX, *passim.*

See Brian McKenna, *Irish Literature 1800–1875* (Detroit, 1978), p. 37.

See Walter Houghton, *The Wellesley Index to Victorian Periodicals 1824–1900*, 5 volumes (Toronto, 1966–1989), Volume 3, pp. 53–61 (essay plus index).

See John Kelly, *The Collected Letters of WB Yeats*, Volume 3: 1901–1904 (Oxford, 1994), pp. 136n, 144.

An author index appears in Richard J. Hayes, *Sources for the History of Irish Civilisation: Articles in Irish Periodicals*, 5 vols (Boston, 1970).

Continued as:

THE LYCEUM. A MONTHLY EDUCATIONAL AND LITERARY MAGAZINE AND REVIEW

Location:	Dublin (publisher Keating and Co., 4 Lower Ormond Quay, printer Browne and Nolan, 24 Nassau Street; from October 1891 printed and published 99–96 Middle Abbey Street; from February 1893 printed and published 54 Eccles Street)
Editor(s):	Fr Thomas Finlay; from 1887 edited jointly with William Magennis; from 1891, Magennis alone
Dates:	Volume 1, number 1 (September 1887)–volume 7, number 77 (February 1894)
No. of issues:	77
Average periodicity:	Monthly
Average no. pages:	Volumes 1 and 2, 32; vols 3 and 4, 24, vols 5 and 6 vary widely, but average 16
Libraries:	RIA=RR Gall/36/E (incomplete); TCD=38.f.116–118 (offsite; 24hrs' notice); UCC (1 February 1890–1 December 1893 only); UCD=J 050.

Despite the gap of some seventeen years, the *Lyceum* was intended to carry on the work of the *Atlantis*, and was founded by the occupational descendants of Newman and Sullivan, a group of professors at University College in Stephen's Green (Fr T.A. Finlay, Fr O'Carroll, and Fr George O'Neill who, with Fr Peter Finlay, wrote the entire first number). They were joined by William Magennis, Thomas Arnold and others, 'to promote a higher Catholic literature, to discuss questions of scientific and literary interest from the Catholic point of view, and under guidance of Catholic teaching to contribute something... to the solution... of the great problems...', and this editorial declaration is also a direct echo of the 'Prospectus' for *Atlantis*.

As it clearly states in the first editorial, the *Lyceum*'s main concern was with Catholic education, and the vast majority of the contents were concerned with theological issues, or with the establishment of the Catholic university. However, it did carry regular reviews of new publications, such as Katherine Tynan's *Shamrocks*, or *Red Hugh's Captivity* by Standish O'Grady. There were also literary articles, although these were more often devoted to Russian literature than Irish, covering Gogol, Dostoievsky and Turgenev. In July 1890, they began to publish a sonnet in each issue, but these were usually anonymous in more than one sense. Finally, in February 1894, it was announced that the *Lyceum* would close, and be absorbed into the *New Ireland Review*.

[Houghton says 'an Annual was published in 1914.']

An author index appears in Richard J. Hayes, *Sources for the History of Irish Civilisation: Articles in Irish Periodicals*, 5 vols (Boston, 1970).

Continued as:

THE NEW IRELAND REVIEW, A CATHOLIC MAGAZINE OF SOCIAL, AGRARIAN AND LITERARY INTEREST

Location:	Dublin (publisher New Ireland Review, 29 Lower Sackville Street, printer Sealy, Bryars and Walker, Middle Abbey Street, Dublin; from volume 22 the publisher's address changes to 29 Lower O'Connell Street, and from volume 23 to 94 Middle Abbey Street)
Editor(s):	Fr Thomas Finlay
Dates:	Volume 1, number 1 (March 1894)–volume 34 (January 1911)
No. of issues:	203
Average periodicity:	Monthly
Average no. pages:	64
Libraries:	BL=PP.6158.e; LIN (two copies, both v. incomplete); NLI=Ir 05; RIA=RR Gall/40/G (incomplete); TCD=34.p.1-34 (offsite, 24 hrs' notice); another at Gall.6.f.45–50; QUB= hAP4.N53 (v. incomplete, but has volume 1).

The opening editorial marks the profound changes in Ireland, for example the emergence of farmers as owners of their land, and the improvements in education, and declares the

NIR's determination to provide a forum for the new thinking which would be needed. Although it was intended as the successor to the *Lyceum*, the *NIR*'s mixture of politics, patriotic history and practical advice (e.g. on subjects such as butter-making), with a sprinkling of poems, reviews and articles, means that it reads instead like a more conventional, more simply nationalist, *Irish Statesman*.

While its contents were predominantly political and economic in character (indeed, the backbone of the magazine was the series of strong political statements by D.P. Moran, later reprinted as *The Philosophy of Irish-Ireland*), it did publish articles on a variety of literary and cultural topics: the Cuchulainn saga (by Æ), on Sir Charles Gavan Duffy, the Irish Literary Theatre, Hamlet (Edward Dowden), the 'Irish Literary Renaissance and the Irish Language' (George Moore), and on a series of Irish writers, including Allingham, Ferguson, Goldsmith, Mangan, Moira O'Neill, Swift and Canon Sheehan. There was some original poetry, e.g. by Eva Gore-Booth, but by far the most significant of these cultural productions, paralleling Moran's in importance and impact, is Douglas Hyde's serialisation of the 'Religious Songs of Connacht'.

See Rudi Holzapfel, 'A Survey of Irish Literary Magazines from 1900 to the Present Day', M Litt thesis (Trinity College Dublin, 1964), p. 3.
See Maurice Harmon, *Select Bibliography for the Study of Anglo-Irish Literature and Its Backgrounds* (Dublin, 1977), p. 142.
See John Kelly, *The Collected Letters of WB Yeats*, Volume 1: 1865–1895 (Oxford, 1986), pp. 433, 437, 446.
See Peter Denman, 'Ireland's Little Magazines', Barbara Hayley and McKay Enda (eds), *300 Years of Irish Periodicals* (Mullingar, 1987), p. 127.
See Roy Foster, *Paddy and Mr Punch* (London, 1993), pp. 264–265, 276.
See John Kelly, *The Collected Letters of WB Yeats*, Volume 3: 1901–1904 (Oxford, 1994), pp. 174n, 426n.
See John Kelly, *The Collected Letters of WB Yeats*, Volume 2: 1896–1900 (Oxford, 1997), pp. 242n, 375n, 379n, 484n, 516n, 562n, 563n, 564n, 565n, 569, 689.

An author index appears in Richard J. Hayes, *Sources for the History of Irish Civilisation: Articles in Irish Periodicals*, 5 vols (Boston, 1970).

Continued as:

NEW IRELAND, AN IRISH WEEKLY REVIEW

Location:	Dublin (publisher 65 Middle Abbey Street, printer Wood Printing Works, Fleet Street)
Editor(s):	Anon.
Dates:	Volume 1, number 1 (15 May 1915)–volume 8, number 20 (20 September 1919); 'New Issue' volume 1, number 1 (27 May 1922)–volume 1, number 6 (1 July 1922).
No. of issues:	230; 'New Issue' 5

Average periodicity: Weekly
Average no. pages: 16
Libraries: LIN (v. incomplete); TCD=IN.20.114-IN.20.119 (incomplete);
                    QUB=hpqAP4.A6 (incomplete).

This is really a Nationalist paper, which carries the occasional poem and book review, e.g. volume 1, number 1 has a poem by Tynan. By volume 3 the title changed to *Ár n-Éire, New Ireland*, and it became more and more militant; given some of its contents, it is not surprising that it was suppressed from 18 October 1919 to 3 December 1921. Volume 4, number 6 carries a poem by Padraic Gregory; number 24 a poem by F.R. Higgins and a review by 'Daniel Corkerry' [*sic*]; poems also appear by Alice Milligan and Constance Markievicz. In volume 7, number 13 there is an article by Joseph Campbell. The second series (1922) is anti-Treaty and even more militantly political and non-literary.

[QUB Catalogue says this was then continued as *Old Ireland* (Glasgow), no details given.]

See John Kelly, *The Collected Letters of WB Yeats*, Volume 2: 1896–1900 (Oxford, 1997), pp. 259n, 265n, 411n.

THE DUBLIN JOURNAL: AND PEOPLE'S MISCELLANY OF LITERATURE, SCIENCE AND ART

Location: Dublin (publisher Robinson and Co., 81 Great Britain Street)
Editor(s):   Anon.
Dates: 9 January 1858–6 March 1858
No. of issues: 9
Average periodicity: Weekly
Average no. pages: 16
Libraries: LIN; NLI=J 05.

The 1850s was not the golden age of Irish literary periodicals, and this is another largely unremarkable family magazine of the period. Two stories are serialised, 'Ellen Kavanagh; A Legend of the Barrow', and 'Bryan O'Regan, The Sporting Irish Gentleman' by the author of the 'Guide to the Blackwater in Munster'; a few weak verses also were published. No indication is given in the magazine itself that it was about to close.

THE IRISH LITERARY ADVERTISER

Location: Dublin (publisher McGlashan and Gill)
Editor(s):   Anon.
Dates: 15 December 1858–15 December 1859
No. of issues: 13
Average periodicity: Monthly

Average no. pages: 16
Libraries: BL=PP.6490.d; TCD=O.oo.45.

According to the 'Prospectus' on the first page of the first issue, this journal will be 'entirely devoted to Announcements connected with Literature and the Fine Arts...for *gratuitous* circulation'. Each issue is packed with advertisements, publicising around twenty-four publishers in each issue, mostly with full or half page advertisements. The front cover states the minimum circulation as 1,500 copies: the question must be asked, does the existence of this publication say good things about the state of Irish publishing, or does its short life say something bad about it?

From issue 2 onward it includes two or three pages of 'Literary News', mostly puffs and pre-announcements of coming books, with the odd, very short, extract from the most impressive, e.g. Sir John Gilbert's *History of Dublin*. From June it carries two or three pages of 'New Works', a straight list of all Irish books published in the previous month. As usual, number 13 gives no indication of it's being the last.

THE HARP: AN IRISH CATHOLIC MONTHLY MAGAZINE

Location: Cork (publisher Roche, 10 Marlboro' Street)
Editor(s):   Michael Joseph McCann
Dates: March 1859–October 1859
No. of issues: 8
Average periodicity: Monthly
Average no. pages: 48
Libraries: NLI=J 05; TCD=PP.6159.b.

Roughly half of each issue is taken up with an account of an Irish battle (Boyne, Limerick, Athlone); another quarter with miscellaneous articles, e.g. 'Facts of Catholic Interest'; the remainder was devoted to various literary enterprises: serialised romances, literary articles, and so on. Most of these are of little interest, apart from a short, bitter article on Irish periodicals in number 3, and a review of Drennan's poems, in which a few are reproduced, in number 5. The seventh issue carries an (unintentionally) hilarious editorial in which their ambition to be a Catholic *Dublin University Magazine* is revealed.

Continued as:
THE IRISH HARP: A MONTHLY MAGAZINE OF NATIONAL AND GENERAL LITERATURE

Location: Wexford (printer Godwin and Nelthercroft, Dublin, publisher 'New
                      Irish Serial Publication Co.')
Editor(s):   M.J. McCann
Dates: March–April 1863; January–February 1864
No. of issues: 4
Average periodicity: Monthly

Average no. pages: 48
Libraries: BL=PP.6193.e; NLI=I 05 i 8; PSPL=052.

This was even less adventurous, and the title had entered into a terminal decline; the last two issues were published in England.

THE ULSTER MAGAZINE AND MONTHLY REVIEW OF SCIENCE AND LITERATURE

Location: Belfast (publisher C.H. McCloskie, 35 Ann Street)
Editor(s):   Anon.
Dates: January 1860–February 1864
No. of issues: 50
Average periodicity: Monthly
Average no. pages: 64
Libraries: LIN; NLI=Ir 05 u 1; QUB=hAP4.U4 (January–December 1860; January, February and April–August 1862; April, June–August, December 1863; January and February 1864)

Despite the presence of some material from Francis Davis, and quite a lot from David Herbison, this remains a very lightweight, 'family'-type magazine, dominated by weak stories and general articles.

DUFFY'S HIBERNIAN MAGAZINE: A MISCELLANY OF LITERATURE, SCIENCE AND ART

Location: Dublin (printer and publisher James Duffy, 15 Wellington Quay)
Editor(s):   Martin Haverty
Dates: July 1860–December 1861
No. of issues: 18
Average periodicity: Monthly
Average no. pages: 48
Libraries: BL=PP.6193.d; LIN; NLI=J 05; PSPL=820.5; QUB=hAP4.H6; RIA=Fr C/1/3/E; TCD=Gall.D.20.24–26; UCC (1860–1863 only); UCG=052 (PS, 1862–1864).

This is stuffed with romantic history ('The O'Donnells in Exile'), topography ('A Day Among the Twelve Pins'), and gently nationalist ballads ('The Battle of Manning Ford' by Robert D. Joyce). The best aspects are the short book reviews, e.g. of a biography of Lady Morgan, and the contributions from Carleton, including *The Rapparee*, which is serialised across issues 2 to 6, and *The Double Prophecy*, across issues 7 to 14; it remains of interest as the embodiment of the Catholic, Nationalist, middle-class and middle-brow taste of its time. S.J. Brown identifies Lady Wilde as an anonymous contributor.

Continued as:

DUFFY'S HIBERNIAN SIXPENNY MAGAZINE

Location: Dublin
Editor(s):   Anon.
Dates: January 1862–June 1864
No. of issues: 18
Average periodicity: Monthly
Average no. pages: 96
Libraries: as above, except TCD=Gall.D.30.1–5.

Despite its high price, and the presence of a sketch by Carleton in the September 1862 issue, this is a very downmarket publication, dominated by light and romantic fiction, with 'How I Married a Countess' a typical title.

Continued as:

THE HIBERNIAN MAGAZINE

Location: Dublin (publisher John F. Fowler, 3 Crow Street; also London, Burns and Lambert)
Editor(s):   Anon.
Dates: July–December 1864
No. of issues: 6
Average periodicity: Monthly
Average no. pages: 64
Libraries: NLI=J 05; TCD=Gall.D.30.1–5.

Carries a Gothic serial, 'The Untenanted Graves', by Charles Kickham, some pieces on travel and biography, and the occasional poor sample of verse; Lady Wilde was a contributor, but the hand of Thomas Irwin is most strongly evident.

See John Kelly, *The Collected Letters of WB Yeats*, Volume 1: 1865–1895 (Oxford, 1986), p. 207.
See Barbara Hayley, 'A Reading and Thinking Nation: Periodicals as the Voice of Nineteenth-Century Ireland', Barbara Hayley and Enda McKay (eds), *300 Years of Irish Periodicals* (Mullingar, 1987), p. 45.

THE GAEL; A NATIONAL WEEKLY JOURNAL OF IRISH HISTORY, LITERATURE, ARTS, &C.

Location: Dublin (printer and publisher Stephen Bolger)
Editor(s):   Anon.
Dates: 1 June 1861 and 8 June 1861

No. of issues: 2
Average periodicity: Weekly
Average no. pages: 16
Libraries: TCD(Old Library)=190.q.1.

An unremarkable collection of derivative 'Keltick' verses and glowing tributes to the past glories of Irish literature, a possible clue to this magazine's exceptionally short lifespan may be found in its first editorial: 'For all the drawbacks and short-comings, we offer the excuses of a beginner – haste and imperfect preparation. In future numbers we hope to be able to make up for the failures of this one.'

See John Kelly, *The Collected Letters of WB Yeats*, Volume 1: 1865–1895 (Oxford, 1986), pp. 11n, 14n, 15–17, 19n, 20n, 21, 30–33, 42, 43, 82.
See John Kelly, *The Collected Letters of WB Yeats*, Volume 3: 1901–1904 (Oxford, 1994), p. 109n.
See John Kelly, *The Collected Letters of WB Yeats*, Volume 2: 1896–1900 (Oxford, 1997), pp. 625–627.

THE ILLUSTRATED DUBLIN JOURNAL, A WEEKLY MISCELLANY OF AMUSEMENT AND POPULAR INFORMATION

Location: Dublin (publisher James Duffy, 7 Wellington Quay, printer Pattison Jolly, 22 Essex Street West)
Editor(s): Anon.
Dates: 7 September 1861–17 May 1862
No. of issues: 37
Average periodicity: Weekly
Average no. pages: 16
Libraries: BL=PP.6315.b; LIN; NLI=J 05; PSPL=052; QUB=hqAP4.I3; TCD=OLS L-2-118.

A lavishly illustrated, light journal, with many diverting articles on subjects from astronomy to duck shooting, which nevertheless includes: Carleton's 'The Miller of Mohill'; and 'Lord Ulla's Lesson', 'The Invasion' and 'Suil Dhuv, the Coiner' by Griffin. It remains, however, of more interest to the social than the literary historian.

See C.P. Hyland, *A Topographical Index to Five Nineteenth Century Literary Periodicals*, 'printed by the author' (1979). Indexes the illustrations.
See Barbara Hayley, 'A Reading and Thinking Nation: Periodicals as the Voice of Nineteenth-Century Ireland', Barbara Hayley and Enda McKay (eds), *300 Years of Irish Periodicals* (Mullingar, 1987), p. 45.

AGATHA: A MAGAZINE OF SOCIAL REFORM AND GENERAL LITERATURE

Location:	Dublin (publisher John Robertson, 3 Grafton St, printer Porteous and Gibbs, 18 Wicklow St)
Editor(s):	Anon.
Dates:	October 1861–June 1862
No. of issues:	9
Average periodicity:	Monthly
Average no. pages:	36
Libraries:	BL=PP.6158.b; TCD=Gall.CC.12.79.

Primarily a promoter of the Temperance movement, although a good deal more sophisticated than the *Dublin Journal of Temperance* (1842–1843, see above). A handful of weak verses can be found in its pages, although they at least refrain from preaching. The same is almost all that can be said for *At Home and Abroad*, the superficial novel of manners and family life which is serialised through the complete run. A number of critical articles are slightly better, although even the longest – including one on Coleridge, by 'Madame Ernestina', and others on Thackeray and Tennyson, by Horace Saltoun – amount to no more than basic introductions.

THE SHAMROCK, A NATIONAL WEEKLY JOURNAL OF IRISH HISTORY, LITERATURE, ARTS, & CO.

Location:	Dublin (printer and publisher William O'Brien, 33 Lower Abbey Street)
Editor(s):	T.R. Herrington (McKenna; Holzapfel)
Dates:	13 October 1866–21 February 1922
No. of issues:	2,879
Average periodicity:	Weekly
Average no. pages:	16
Libraries:	BCL=I/052.[1] SHAM (6 October 1866–30 September 1871; 7 October 1876–29 September 1877; 4 June 1877–1 June 1889); BL(Colin) (Number 464 (4 September 1875), and Number 876 (28 July 1883) – Number 2,386 (10 August 1912) only); continued as *The Shamrock and Irish Emerald* (Number 2,387 (17 August 1912)–Number 2,733 (19 May 1917)); NLI=Ir 05 s 4; PSPL=052; RDS=NL72; RIA=Fr C/Sect 6/2.

A 1d, popular story magazine which, because of its longevity and quality, may stand as an exemplar of the type. Most issues start with a brief verse, and include a couple of short articles of general interest, but from the start its priorities are clear as the first issue is dominated by four serialised novels; in time, as these conclude, they are seamlessly replaced by new titles, and the stories are often good (see 'The Weird Woman of Tavnimore' by Carleton (starts issue 82), or Kickham's 'Knocknagow' (starts number 181)). The Nationalist credentials are proved by articles on Emmet and '98.

As with other popular publications, the most remarkable characteristic is how little they tinkered with the original formula. In 1872, they begin 'Lessons in Gaelic' and, soon after, the Famine and the Fenians are added to the patriotic material; but the stories continue to dominate, with the same roster of authors to the fore – T.C. Irwin and, above all others, William Lynam with his comic creation, Mick McQuaid. This stage-Irish saga begins in 1867, with 'Mick McQuaid's Conversion', when Lynam's military rank is given as Captain; it continues through Lieutenant-Colonel Lynam's many contributions in the 1880s and 1890s; and even his death in 1894 does not stop the proprietors reprinting old McQuaid stories and unearthing unpublished ones. Meanwhile, other authors update their locations, e.g. to mention the Franco-Prussian War, but in all other respects remain unchanged.

The original owner, Richard Piggott, sold his interest in the *Shamrock* in 1879 to the Irish National Newspaper and Publishing Company (owned by Parnell and the Land League), when it swung towards more straightforward political coverage. In the 1890s, the Nationalist tone grows stronger; the cover story for number 1,408 (2 October 1893) concerns the 'Dark Doings of Dublin Castle'– informers, conspiracies and brutal treatment of prisoners. In different guises (e.g. the *Shamrock and Irish Emerald*, 1912–1922) it continued into the 1920s, but by the turn of the century, the *Shamrock* had lost its way, plunged downmarket, and become irrelevant from any literary standpoint.

See P.S. O'Hegarty, article in *Irish Book Lover*, 25 (1937), p. 31.
See Rudi Holzapfel, 'Irish Literary Magazines from 1900 to the Present Day', M Litt thesis
    (Trinity College Dublin, 1964), p. 1.
See John Kelly, *The Collected Letters of WB Yeats*, Volume 1: 1865–1895 (Oxford, 1986),
    p. 16n.
See John Kelly, *The Collected Letters of WB Yeats*, Volume 2: 1896–1900 (Oxford, 1997),
    pp. 539n, 540n, 653n.

KOTTABOS, A COLLEGE MISCELLANY

Location:	Dublin (printer Porteous and Gibbs, 18 Wicklow Street, publisher William McGee, 18 Nassau Street)
Editor(s):	Robert Yelverton Tyrrell
Dates:	Trinity 1869–Hilary 1881; New Series Hilary 1888–Michaelmas 1895
No. of issues:	60
Average periodicity:	Triannual
Average no. pages:	30
Libraries:	BL=PP.6163 (incomplete); LIN; NLI=Ir 3784105 k 1; QUB=hPN6099.6.K7 (incomplete); TCD=Gall.1.g.86, no.5; UCG=808 (PS, incomplete).

This college magazine has a decidedly elitist tone, with no compromises made to either popular taste or to contemporary literature; instead, the literary content (around 40 per cent of the total) is made up of poetry translations, from Goethe, Shakespeare, Tennyson and many others, into Latin and Greek (and very occasionally French or German). It would be easy to write *Kottabos* off as having made no contribution to Irish writing, if it were not for the list of contributors, which includes: J.P. Mahaffy, Standish O'Grady, Alfred P. Graves, Edward Dowden, W.C.K. Wilde, O. O'F.W. Wilde and T.W.H. Rolleston.

See T.W. Rolleston, 'Kottabos and Some of its Poets', *Irish Fireside,* 1 (1887), pp. 121–122 and 154–155.

See R.Y. Tyrrell, *Echoes from Kottabos* (London, 1906). An anthology.

See pseudonymous article by 'T.C.D.', 'Kottabos', *Irish Book Lover* 6, 5 (December 1914), pp. 71–73; which explains the name: [it] 'was discovered by Tyrrell in a fragment of Euripides, and referred to a game played by the ancient Greeks in their literary Symposia'.

An author index appears in Richard J. Hayes, *Sources for the History of Irish Civilisation: Articles in Irish Periodicals*, 5 vols (Boston, 1970).

THE IRISH YOUNG MAN'S JOURNAL, LITERARY, SOCIAL AND SCIENTIFIC

Location:	Dublin
Editor(s):	Anon.
Dates:	July 1871–November 1871
No. of issues:	5
Average periodicity:	Monthly
Average no. pages:	16
Libraries:	BL=1866.b.9 (4).

The motto of this production is 'Duty is Ours – Results are God's', and it was linked to the Irish 'Young Men's Associations'; the contents are correspondingly Christian and improving, although the effort is always made to maintain a high tone. Among essays (really sermons in disguise) on 'Independence of Character' and the Scottish Covenanters, there are book reviews, translations from Horace, and around a dozen poems. The poetry is mostly very weak, romantic and derivative ('Moonlight', 'The Turret Window'), and occasionally just eccentric, as in the suggested, 'improved' version of 'God Save the Queen'.

HERMATHENA, A SERIES OF PAPERS ON LITERATURE, SCIENCE AND PHILOSOPHY, BY MEMBERS OF TRINITY COLLEGE, DUBLIN

Location:	Dublin (publisher Edward Ponsonby, 116 Grafton Street, printer 'At The University Press', Ponsonby and Murphy), and London

	(Longman's, Green and Co., Paternoster Row); from 1881, publisher changes to Hodges, Figgis and Co., 104 Grafton Street, printer University Press, Ponsonby and Weldrick; in 1922, Hodges and Figgis move to 20 Nassau Street, and printer is Ponsonby and Gibbs; in November 1945 Hodges and Figgis move to 6 Dawson Street. In May 1952, London publication is dropped
Editor(s):	J.K. Ingram (1873–1888), A. Palmer (1888–1898), L.C. Purser (1898–1904), J.I. Beare (1904–1914), E.H. Alton (1919–1937), W.A. Goligher (1937–1942), W.B. Stanford (1942–1962), E.J. Furlong (1962–?)
Dates:	1873–present
No. of issues:	164 (to Summer 1998)
Average periodicity:	Annual (1873–1937), biannual (1937–1961), triannual (1962–present)
Average no. pages:	110
Libraries:	BCL=IR; BL=PP.6159.aa; LIN (very incomplete); NLI=I 8805 h 1; PSPL=052; QUB=LF909.H5; RDS=NL53 (incomplete); RIA=Fr C/1/2–4/TS; TCD=159.s, also OLS L-4-788–825; UCC=Summer 1875 onwards; UCD=J 800; UCG=378.1 (PS until 1950, then Open Access)

Although *Hermathena* has had a long and distinguished history, it has only fitfully dipped its toes into the genre of literary magazine. Indeed, during its long first phase (from 1873 to 1930), it concentrated almost exclusively on the classics, theology and philosophy, with virtually no literary input (from 1910 we find the occasional piece on early Irish literature, e.g. F.W. O'Connell's piece on Merriman in volume 13, number 5, 1905).

During the magazine's second phase, from 1931 to 1961, it includes around ten pages of 'Kottabistae' in each issue, and even an occasional literary article, such as A.J. Leventhal's 1938 essay on Rimbaud, Peter Allt's articles in 1943 and 1944 on Yeats, or Sir Peter Coghill's 1952 piece on Somerville and Ross.

The period during which *Hermathena* really justifies its classification as a literary magazine ran from 1962 to 1980, and particularly after the title was relaunched in 1964. This period saw the publication of (amongst other material of lesser interest): essays on George Moore and Edward Martin by F.S.L. Lyons, on Carleton and on Louis MacNeice by Terence Brown, on Synge by T.R. Henn, and on Beckett by A.J. Leventhal; and reviews of Vivian Mercier's *Irish Comic Tradition*, of *Sean O'Casey: the man behind the plays* and of Michael Farrell's *Thy Tears Might Cease*. There was also a Yeats number (Autumn 1965), with half a dozen essays, including one on the Cuchulainn plays by Brendan Kennelly, three poems by Kennelly (very little original verse appeared), plus a review of Norman Jeffares's book on George Moore by Edna Longley. Spring 1967 saw the publication of a Swift number with four substantial articles, and a Kennelly poem, while the Centenary issue (Summer 1973), included a poem from Beckett, plus a review of Gregory's *Our Irish Theatre*. The latter part of this period, after 1974, saw contributions from W.J. McCormick (on Banim), Norman Jeffares (on Goldsmith), and Declan Kiberd (on Synge).

Even during this phase, the majority of the contents are still concerned with theology and the classics, and literary items represent a very small proportion of the total. When, around 1980, *Hermathena* entered its fourth phase, the literary content went into a serious decline, from which it has not yet recovered; during the entire decade of the 1980s, apart from a few short book reviews, the only issue of substantial interest is that dedicated to Beckett (Winter 1986), which carries articles by Jeffares, McCormick, Kiberd, Brown and Mercier, alongside poems from Derek Mahon and Kennelly.

See Gerry Smyth, *Decolonisation and Criticism: The Construction of Irish Literature* (London, 1998), pp. 138–141.

The British Library has an anonymous *Index of Contributors to Hermathena, 1873–1943*, 1944, at 11914.b.35.
E.J.J. Furlong, *Index to 'Hermathena', 1944–1964* (Dublin, 1965).
An author index (up to 1969) appears in Richard J. Hayes, *Sources for the History of Irish Civilisation: Articles in Irish Periodicals*, 5 vols (Boston, 1970).

THE IRISH MONTHLY ILLUSTRATED JOURNAL

Location:	Dublin (printer Alley and Co., 9 Ryder's Row, publisher M'Glashan and Gill, Sackville Street)
Editor(s):	Thomas Caulfield Irwin
Dates:	January 1873–April 1873
No. of issues:	4
Average periodicity:	Monthly
Average no. pages:	32
Libraries:	NLI=J 05; PSPL=052.

A very lightweight production which sprinkles throughout its pages of gossip and biography, poems, serialised stories and brief notices of books. The best things here, by a long way are: 'Related Souls' by Lady Wilde, 'Old Times, Old Times!' by Griffin, and Mangan's 'Soul and Country'.

THE IRISH MONTHLY MAGAZINE

Location:	Dublin (publisher M'Glashan and Gill, 50 Upper Sackville Street)
Editor(s):	Rev. Matthew Russell, 1873–1912
Dates:	July 1873–September 1954
No. of issues:	973

Average periodicity: Monthly
Average no. pages: 60
Libraries: BL=PP.6158.d; LIN (1914–1930 missing); NLI=microfilm, shelved
                       with newspapers; PSPL=820.5 (1887; 1891; 1895–1902);
                       QUB=hAP4.I5;   RDS=NL192–196;   RIA=FrCrypt/2/3/A;
                       TCD=21.p.1-63; UCC (incomplete); UCD=J 820 (1879–1954).

A landmark of Irish publishing, the *Irish Monthly* changed little over the course of more
than eighty years, but always managed to obtain regular injections of fresh new blood to
sustain it. Primarily a Catholic magazine, it published a steady trickle of creative writing
of the highest order, and it can best be summarised by the following quotation from its first
editorial and by a survey of the writers published. Under the motto 'Catholic Ireland', the
first issue begins: 'On the Feast of the Adorable Heart of Jesus, to which our country was
solemnly consecrated on the Passion Sunday of this year of grace 1873, this Irish Monthly
Magazine of religious literature enters on the discharge of its holy functions as a memorial
and a remembrancer of that national consecration...' However, after the first two years,
during which religious material made up almost the entire contents, leavened by the
occasional poem by Aubrey de Vere and a serialised novel 'Jack Hazlitt', by the author of
'Ailey Moore', the title of the magazine changed to: *The Irish Monthly: A Magazine of
General Literature*, and the Catholic tone was slightly watered down. Serialised novels by
Rosa Mulholland appear at this time, and she was to remain a mainstay for many years;
also occasional contributions from Æ, D.F. MacCarthy and Oscar Wilde.

   From 1878, the literary content begins to rise, with the appearance of 'The Holy
Ground', by Griffin, and a couple of pages of short book reviews; in 1880 another long-
term contributor joins them, under the name of 'Katie Tynan'; despite this, the main
contributors remain Mulholland, MacCarthy and Russell himself, and the tone is still
strongly Catholic and middle-brow. These years see them publishing a short story of
Kickham's, and a scoop – a fragment of Mangan's autobiography. In 1886 there are three
poems by Yeats, and the newly renamed Katherine Tynan joins Mulholland as one of their
most regular contributors. Still, it must be remembered that these well-known writers
formed only a small percentage of the material presented, and did little to shift the
magazine from its regular diet of popular fiction, lives of the saints and devotional verse.

   The 1890s and early 1900s see a drop in standards, with the disappearance of Yeats,
Tynan, and the others, to be replaced by the likes of Dora Sigerson and Agnes Romilly
White, and the *IMM* seems to be completely out of touch with contemporary literature;
during the First World War the only significant writer to appear is 'A.P. Graves'. It is at
this time that Russell retires as editor, after thirty-nine years in the job. However, showing
the resilience to which it must owe its long life, the end of the war saw another renewal,
with the appearance of regular articles on the likes of Daniel Corkery and Ethna Carbery
by writers such as Aodh de Blacam; in addition the Irish language makes its first
appearance, alongside translations of the poems reproduced; but otherwise the poetry and
stories have not recovered their earlier vigour, despite the appearance in 1923 of
'Persephone' by 'Gerard Hopkins, S.J.'.

In the 1930s the Irish language disappears; stories by Michael McLaverty appear with increasing regularity, and there are regular columns from de Blacam and Cathal O'Byrne; once again, during wartime, the original literature drops out of sight; after the end of hostilities, it re-emerges, and during the last few years we see names like Hubert Butler, Benedict Kiely and Brian Friel. This time, however, it was a false dawn, and in September 1954 it is announced that '...publication of *The Irish Monthly* is to be temporarily discontinued...'

See L. McKenna, *Irish Poems Appearing in 'The Irish Monthly'* (1930).

See Donat O'Donnell, 'The Catholic Press, A Study in Theopolitics', *The Bell* 10, 1 (June 1945) pp. 30–40.

See Rudi Holzapfel, 'A Survey of Irish Literary Magazines from 1900 to the Present Day', M Litt thesis (Trinity College Dublin, 1964), p. 2.

The British Library has an *Index to the first twenty-five volumes of the Irish Monthly, from July, 1873, to December, 1897* (1899), at PP.6158.d.

Subject index in William Frederick Poole, *Poole's Index to periodical literature*, revised edition (Gloucester, MA, 1963).

An author index appears in Richard J. Hayes, *Sources for the History of Irish Civilisation: Articles in Irish Periodicals*, 5 vols (Boston, 1970).

NOW-A-DAYS, CONTAINING NOVELS, SHORT TALES, SKETCHES, ADVENTURES, BIOGRAPHIES, ETC., ETC.

Location:	Dublin
Editor(s):	Anon.
Dates:	July 1874–December 1874
No. of issues:	6
Average periodicity:	Monthly
Average no. pages:	128
Libraries:	BL=PP.6159.ab; NLI=828 N 13.

This magazine is dominated by prose, with substantial stories, serialised novels and travellers' tales taking up most of its pages. The sparse poetry (a dozen poems in over 750 pages), falls into two distinct camps, the muscular ballad and the sub-Tennysonian, and none of it has any Irish characteristics, imagery or subject-matter.

The same can also be said of the prose, which is more likely to be set in far-flung, romantic corners of the Empire, or in the drawing-rooms of London. There are exceptions: *Lean Kine*, a rousing novel which combines absentee landlords, agrarian violence, the Famine and the '48 Rebellion with a patronising sympathy for the deserving poor and a strongly Unionist standpoint ('the only commodities that there seemed money to buy in the country were deadly weapons and powder. Food for the gun seemed to be thought more precious than food for the body'). 'The Strange Schooner', by Rosa Mulholland, is a slight but oddly effective tale of loss and loneliness on Inis Bofin. One serialised novel, *The Living Dead*, takes up over 250 pages (nearly one-third of the total magazine) with an interminable tale of moose-hunting and romance in the wilds of Canada.

The whole production is crippled by its strong Empire-loyalist politics (see the serialised *Adventures in South Africa*), which constantly undermine the tentative gestures towards Irish subjects. This is best seen in 'On Keltic Poetry' (November 1874), which is a substantial essay outlining the development of poetry in Ireland, but in which the appreciation of the 'sensuous' and 'graceful' elements are torpedoed by remarks on 'the want of deep mental grasp' in the Irish, and the summing-up which proclaims that Irish poetry has no hope of achieving real success until it cleanses itself of all 'party spirit' and 'national feeling'.

THE MONITOR: AN ILLUSTRATED DUBLIN MAGAZINE

Location: Dublin (publisher Joseph Dollard, Dame Street)
Editor(s):   Anon.
Dates: January–December 1879
No. of issues: 12
Average periodicity: Monthly
Average no. pages: 80
Libraries: BL=PP.6154.d; NLI=Ir 05 m 4; PSPL=283.05; TCD=Gall.I.34.44.

A substantial and handsome production, very 'Anglo' in tone, the *Monitor* is evenly split between historical and biographical essays, and literary material. This includes some insipid Victorian lyrics by T.C. Irwin (editor of the *Irish Monthly Illustrated Journal*), a few serialised tales, a number of essays by different hands on Thomas Moore, and a couple of essays on the technique of poetry. Overall, it is a triumph of production style over content.

IRISH PLEASANTRY AND FUN

Location: Dublin (M.H. Gill and Son, Upper Sackville Street)
Editor(s):   Anon.
Dates: December 1881 is all NLI has
No. of issues: Part 2 is all NLI has
Average periodicity: Monthly?
Average no. pages: 48
Libraries: NLI=Ir 8205 p 20.

Despite the title and garish colour frontispiece, the body of this magazine is completely set in rather intimidating uninterrupted double columns. It includes 'The Little Weaver of

Duleek Gate', 'Paddy the Piper' and 'King O'Toole and Saint Kevin' by Lover; 'The Hare-Hound and the Witch' by Michael Banim; 'Othello at Drill' by Lever; and 'Phil Purcel the Pig Driver' and 'Shane Fadh's Wedding' by Carleton. One curiosity about this magazine, which must contribute to its very old-fashioned feel, is that all the above were dead by 1881.

See Anon., *Irish Pleasantry and Fun: A selection* (Dublin, 1892).

THE DUBLIN UNIVERSITY REVIEW: A MONTHLY MAGAZINE OF LITERATURE, ART AND UNIVERSITY INTELLIGENCE

Location: Dublin (publisher 'The Review', 94–96 Middle Abbey Street, printer Sealy, Bryars and Walker)
Editor(s):   T.W. Rolleston
Dates: February 1885–June 1887
No. of issues: 29
Average periodicity: Monthly
Average no. pages: 86
Libraries: BL=Cup.400.h.2; MAR=X4.3.45; NLI=IR 05 d 12; PSPL=378.05 (volume 1, number 1 (March 1885)–6 (July 1885), and illustrated supplement only); QUB=hAP4.D7 (volume 1, number 7 (August 1885)–volume 2, number 12 (December 1886) only); RIA=Mem R/Case 3/K; TCD=Gall.FF.17.124–126; UCC (1885 only); UCD=J 050.

In three main sections: articles, creative writing and miscellaneous (letters, short reviews, university activities). The articles mostly fall into two camps, politics and culture, and the mix is very wide-ranging and liberal, allowing Conservatives, Home Rulers, Socialists and Theosophists (Mohani Chatterji) to have their say amongst non-partisan biographies and articles on education. They remained true to the declaration on their title-page, 'an organ for the thoughtful and candid discussion, by cultured Irishmen, irrespective of creed or party...'. The cultural articles include general subjects ('Nature and Art'), but also pieces on Thomas Davis, 'A Plea for the Irish Language', and Yeats's article on 'The Poetry of Sir Samuel Ferguson' (November 1886).

The creative writing includes: a Kottabos section (up to December 1885, the usual translations to and from the classics); occasional poems (including from Tynan, J. Todhunter, A.P. Graves and, most often, W.B. Yeats); and prose, including Turgenev's novel *On the Eve*, which was serialised from November 1885 to September 1886. The quality of the creative writing is, of course, varied, but sometimes excellent (e.g. Yeats's 'Mosada', June 1886).

All in all a very good, open-minded, enquiring magazine, which maintained high standards throughout its short life.

See Roger McHugh and Maurice Harmon, *A Short History of Anglo-Irish Literature*, Dublin, 1982, p. 126.

See John Kelly, *The Collected Letters of WB Yeats*, Volume 1: 1865–1895 (Oxford, 1986), pp. 9n, 10n, 12n, 16n, 32, 40, 98n, 362, 481, 493, 508, 517.

See Roy Foster, *Paddy and Mr Punch* (London, 1993), pp. 34–35.

See John Kelly, *The Collected Letters of WB Yeats*, Volume 2: 1896–1900 (Oxford, 1997), pp. 107, 169n, 203n, 626, 627n, 571n.

An author index appears in Richard J. Hayes, *Sources for the History of Irish Civilisation: Articles in Irish Periodicals*, 5 vols (Boston, 1970).

THE IRISH HOMESTEAD: A WEEKLY NEWSPAPER FOR FARMYARD, FIELD AND FIRESIDE

Location:	Dublin (publisher The Irish Co-Operative Newspaper Society, 2 Stephen's Green, printer Cahill and Co., 35 Great Strand Street)
Editor(s):	T.P. Gill; H.F. Norman; from August 1897 George Russell (Æ)
Dates:	9 March 1895–8 September 1923
No. of issues:	1,062
Average periodicity:	Weekly
Average no. pages:	16
Libraries:	BL(Colin) (volume 2, number 1 (7 March 1896)–volume 2, number 52 (27 February 1897), and volume 3, number 43 (1 January 1898)–volume 29, number 51 (30 December 1922) only); LIN (14 January 1912–July 1918 only); NLI=LB 05 i 14; QUB=hPR5271/ SELE (*Selections from the Contributors to 'The Irish Homestead'*, Gerrard's Cross, 2 vols., 1978); RIA=Fr C/2/10; UCC (incomplete).

Founded by Horace Plunkett as the organ of his Irish Agricultural Organisation Society, and concentrating on agricultural issues. Although the *Irish Homestead* included a two-page 'Fireside Section' from the start, it was intended as a general column of interest to farmers' wives; so, although they started off in the first issue with a short piece on Christina Rosetti, it was mostly dedicated to household tips, and was dropped altogether in mid-1896.

Æ came on board with a bang in volume 3, number 24 (14 August 1897), opening a new section 'Homestead Readings' with 'The Wanderings of Oisin', and for the next four years he carried on publishing a wide and varied selection from the main writers of the day – Plunkett, O'Grady, Tynan, Hyde, Somerville and Ross, Milligan, Carbery – as well as Yeats (27 November 97 has 'Lake Isle of Innisfree'), and a few poems of his own. This fertile period ended with the 1901 Christmas Supplement, which included contributions from most of those listed above. Even though, in terms of the percentage of the paper they took up, and even of the absolute quantity of material published, the literary content was small, the quality was astonishingly high, and unique in putting this level of literature in front of the *Homestead*'s primary audience, that is, small farmers in every part of the country.

From 1902, there is no regular slot for literature, and the quantity of literary material published declines, but individual stories and poems continued to appear, with contributions from Edmund Gosse, Hyde, Milligan, Moira O'Neill, Somerville and Ross, and Tynan; in addition the Christmas Supplements continued until 1910. In 1904, three abridged versions of stories which would appear in *Dubliners* were published; as Ellmann relates (*James Joyce*, Oxford, 1959, p. 171) Joyce was originally commissioned to provide six stories, but the editors asked him to stop after the third because of complaints from their readers!

In the last period, from 1911 onwards, the original material virtually disappears (although a 'Song', from *Chamber Music* was published 17 August 1912), and the interest shifts to the short book reviews which were published until the closure of the magazine. These covered many of the significant publications of these years – Stephens's *The Hill of Vision* and *The Crock of Gold*, Synge's *Works*, Campbell's *Irishry*, Hone's biography of Yeats, Ledwidge's *Songs of the Fields*, Padraic Colum's *Anthology of Irish Verse*, and so on. As with most newspaper-type publications, the huge number of issues means that, even though little space was given to literary items, the cumulative total is impressive: Summerfield lists over one hundred literary pieces by Æ alone; the last issue, 8 September 1923, announces the coming incorporation into the *Irish Statesman*.

See Richard J. Loftus, *Nationalism in Modern Anglo-Irish Poetry* (Wisconsin, 1964), pp. 99, 102.

See Henry Summerfield, *Æ – Selections from the Contributions to 'The Irish Homestead'* (Gerrard's Cross), 1978.

See Roger McHugh and Maurice Harmon, *A Short History of Anglo-Irish Literature* (Dublin, 1982), p. 213.

See John Kelly, *The Collected Letters of WB Yeats*, Volume 3: 1901–1904 (Oxford, 1994), pp. 259, 274, 276.

See Declan Kiberd, *Inventing Ireland* (London, 1995), p. 494.

Continued as:

THE IRISH STATESMAN

Location:	Dublin
Editor(s):	Warre Bradley Wells; from 1923 George Russell (Æ)
Dates:	28 June 1919–19 June 1920, and 15 September 1923-12 April 1930
No. of issues:	344
Average periodicity:	Weekly
Average no. pages:	16
Libraries:	BCL=Microfilm, location 5D; BL(Colin) (originals and microfilm); LIN; PSPL=052; QUB=qAP4.I6, also MicA/AP4.I6; RIA=Fr C/2/3/G; TCD=Per 80–410; UCD=MICJ 320 EMS20–28

The *Irish Statesman* was founded by Horace Plunkett, its intention to promote nationalism and agricultural improvement, but it also carried stories (by Shan Bullock, Brinsley MacNamara, Forrest Reid, Lennox Robinson, E. Œ. Somerville and James Stephens), poems (by Æ, R.N.D. Wilson, Jack B. Yeats and W.B. Yeats) and reviews of works by Stephen Gwynne, Thomas Hardy, Reid, Richard Rowley, Oscar Wilde and Yeats (some of the reviewers are quite distinguished, e.g. Shaw on Chesterton). Under Wells literary material makes up around 10 per cent of the total. Publication was then suspended during the worst of the fighting in the Anglo-Irish War.

Plunkett then raised money in America to revive the title, and Russell merged it with *Irish Homestead*, which he was editing for Plunkett; the literary content goes up to perhaps 15 or 20 per cent of the total: however, there is still the same dizzying mix, which gives us dairying next to drama, and beekeeping next to politics. It was his connections with the Irish Agricultural Co-operative Society and with Plunkett which brought Æ the offer to take over, which he accepted after receiving guarantes of editorial freedom. He also contributed, under his own name and a variety of pseudonyms, including 'GAL', 'OLS', 'Querist', 'LME', 'RIE' and 'YO'. Many (see Smith) see the *Statesman* as Æ's greatest and most substantial achievement: he carried the torch for the literary revival and for pluralist values during these years, he discovered and supported new writers, and he kept the magazine going through fourteen volumes, 344 weekly issues and an estimated ten million words. Contributors under his aegis included: Colum, Edmund Curtis, de Blacam, Monk Gibbon, Oliver St. John Gogarty, Gregory, Gwynne, F.R. Higgins, Sean O'Casey, Frank O'Connor, Seán O'Faoláin, Liam O'Flaherty, Standish O'Grady, Forrest Reid, Robinson, Shaw, James Stephens, Tynan and W.B. Yeats. Ironically, the sheer bulk of print has now obscured his achievement; some have skimmed this mountain, but few have really read and appreciated, and there is a serious need for a judicious selection.

A hostile review in late 1927 led to a series of vituperative letters and, in late 1928, a libel suit. Although this ended without the jury being able to agree a verdict, the costs were to bankrupt the *Statesman* (Welch, in the *Oxford Companion*, says that, at the time of the libel action, its American financiers were suffering in the Wall Street Crash).

See Richard J. Loftus, *Nationalism in Modern Anglo-Irish Poetry* (Wisconsin, 1964), pp. 17, 43, 99, 102, 104, 122, 244, 247.

See Edward Doyle Smith, 'A Survey and Index of the Irish Statesman (1923–1930)', dissertation (University of Washington, 1966).

See Roger McHugh and Maurice Harmon, *A Short History of Anglo-Irish Literature* (Dublin, 1982), pp. 213, 236–237.

See Richard Kearney, 'Between Politics and Literature: The Irish Cultural Journal', *Crane Bag,* 7, 2 (Autumn 1983), pp. 160–171.

See Norman Vance, *Irish Literature: A Social History– Tradition, Identity and Difference* (Oxford, 1990), p. 218.

See Roy Foster, *Paddy and Mr Punch* (London, 1993), pp. 35, 111, 291, 314n.

See John Kelly, *The Collected Letters of WB Yeats*, Volume 2: 1896–1900 (Oxford, 1997), pp. 716, 718.

See Brian Fallon, *An Age of Innocence: Irish Culture 1930–1960* (Dublin, 1998), p. 82.

NLI has (at Ir 05 i 55), 'The Irish Statesman, *Index 1919–20, 1923–29*' (a photocopy of the indexes which were originally bound into the start of each volume of the magazine).

There is an author, subject and title index in Edward Doyle Smith, 'A Survey and Index of the Irish Statesman (1923–1930)', dissertation (University of Washington, 1966).

THE SHAN VAN VOCHT (*AN T-SEAN BHEAN BHOCHT*).
A NATIONAL MONTHLY MAGAZINE

Location:	Belfast (published 65 Great George's Street; printer J.W. Boyd, 5–9 Academy Street)
Editor(s):	Alice L. Milligan (with Anna Johnston from volume 3)
Dates:	Volume 1, number 1 (15 January 1896)–volume 4, number 3 (6 March 1899)
No. of issues:	39
Average periodicity:	Monthly
Average no. pages:	16
Libraries:	BCL=Microfilm, location 5D, E; BL=PP.6313.ab and Colin (microfilm); LIN; NLI=Ir05s5; PSPL=052; QUB=hAP4.S4; TCD=Newspaper Room.

An annotation on the fly-leaf of the PSPL copy identifies the following contributors:

Hi Many	John T. Kelly
Iris Olkyrn	Alice Milligan
Ethna Carbery	Anna Johnston
Mac	James MacManus
MPR	Maurice P. Ryle
TOR	T. O'Neill Russell
B	Francis Joseph Bigger
Hi Fiachra	William Rooney
Brian	John T. Kelly
UIO	Thomas Nally

[The QUB copy is in three bound volumes, each with a basic two-page index; volume 2 also includes a four-page supplement, *Songs for the Centenary*, with words for half a dozen '98-related songs and a picture of Wolfe Tone. This is a gift copy, inscribed by Milligan and Johnston.]

While primarily a political journal, the twenty-four stories and seventy-nine poems make up more than half the contents; most pieces are unsigned or pseudonymous (see below), but each issue always includes one or two items from Iris Olkyrn (Milligan), Ethna Carbery (Johnston), and Alice Furlong. From late 1896 P.J. McCall becomes a regular contributor. Other contributions of note include: a poem by Hyde (4 September 1896);

another by Lionel Johnston (4 December 1896); an article by James Connolly (8 January 1897); and a serialised reprint of R.R. Madden's *Memoir of Henry Joy McCracken*.

Some of the poetry is in Irish, occasionally with a translation; most is rousing, rather than of high quality, and includes many of the marching songs and ballads ('Oh! Erin', etc.) for which Milligan and Johnston are best known. Stories are of 'the West', 'fairy' tales, tales of penal days, etc. All material is subordinated to the national and political agenda; the almost obsessive subject-matter is the Fenians and (understandably, given the centenary and the Ulster connection) 1798. For example, through 1898 they try to record, month by month, the events of one hundred years before.

The magazine is remarkable mainly for having been published in Belfast at that time, a strong, natural flowering of the national mood rarely associated with Belfast, and this isolation may explain their obsessive concentration on the topics listed above. Of course, it is also remarkable for having been founded, edited and administered by two women. The only point on which they show any independence from the Dublin-set cultural agenda of the time is in the occasional acknowledgement of the North's industrial heritage and achievements.

See C.L. Innes, '"A voice in directing the affairs of Ireland": *L'Irlande libre, The Shan Van Vocht and bean na h-Eireann*', in Paul Hyland and Neil Sammells (eds), *Irish Writing, Exile and Subversion* (London, 1991), pp. 146–158.

See Helen Meehan, 'Shan Van Vocht' in *Ulster Local Studies,* 19, 1 (Summer 1997), pp. 80–90.

See John Kelly, *The Collected Letters of WB Yeats*, Volume 2: 1896–1900 (Oxford, 1997), pp. 59, 87n, 102n, 103n, 128n, 178n, 181, 413n, 425n, 705.

BELTAINE, AN OCCASIONAL PUBLICATION

Location:	Dublin ('At the *Daily Express* office') and London ('at the sign of the Unicorn')
Editor(s):	W.B. Yeats
Dates:	May 1899–April 1900
No. of issues:	3
Average periodicity:	Occasional
Average no. pages:	22
Libraries:	BL=PP.5938.e; LIN; NLI=LO; PSPL=820.5; QUB=hPN2602.B4; RIA=Fr Crypt/1/1/F; TCD=190.q.101, nos.1–3; UCC=1970 reprint; UCD=Gen 822.09 IR BEL (1970 reprint); UCG=792 (PS).

A very slight publication, whose contents are more those of a theatrical than a literary magazine *Beltaine* is, nevertheless, of immense historical importance, due to its role as 'The Organ of the Irish Literary Theatre', to its being edited by Yeats, and to an adherence to the standard definition (non-commercial, unity of typography and contents, etc.) which gives it the best claim to be the first Irish Little Magazine.

Yeats himself is the most frequent contributor, including both essays and poems; other pieces are by Lionel Johnson, Moore, Edward Martyn, Milligan and Gregory. The third and last number (April 1900) is devoted to a single, long, rambling essay by Yeats, '"The Last Feast of the Fianna," "Maeve", and "The Bending of the Bough" in Dublin'.

See F.J. Hoffman, Charles Allen and C.F. Ulrich, *The Little Magazine: A History and a Bibliography* (Princeton, 1946; reprinted New York, 1967), p. 236.

See Rudi Holzapfel, 'A Survey of Irish Literary Magazines from 1900 to the Present Day', M Litt thesis (Trinity College Dublin, 1964), p. 4.

See B.C. Bloomfield, *Beltaine* (London, 1970) (reprint of all issues, plus short introduction).

See Roger McHugh and Maurice Harmon, *A Short History of Anglo-Irish Literature* (Dublin, 1982), p. 148.

See John Kelly, *The Collected Letters of WB Yeats*, Volume 3: 1901–1904 (Oxford, 1994), pp. 67n, 72, 74–77, 82, 95, 100, 211, 225n, 250, 259.

See Declan Kiberd, *Inventing Ireland* (London, 1995), p. 146.

See John Kelly, *The Collected Letters of WB Yeats*, Volume 2: 1896–1900 (Oxford, 1997), pp. 210n, 224n, 274n, 321n, 333n, 340n, 347n, 349n, 353n, 359n, 383n, 390n, 391, 393, 398, 399n, 400n, 404n, 410n, 414, 421n, 428, 483n, 484, 489n, 492n, 496, 525, 532, 589, 594, 598, 689.

An author index appears in Rudi Holzapfel, 'A Survey of Irish Literary Magazines from 1900 to the Present Day', M Litt thesis (Trinity College Dublin, 1964).

An author index appears in Richard J. Hayes, *Sources for the History of Irish Civilisation: Articles in Irish Periodicals*, 5 vols (Boston, 1970).

A basic author index appears in Marion Sader, *Comprehensive Index to English-Language Little Magazines 1890–1970* (Millwood, 1976).

JOURNAL OF THE NATIONAL LITERARY SOCIETY OF IRELAND

Location:	Dublin (publisher D.J. O'Donoghue and Co., 19 Lincoln Place (from 1902, 31 South Anne Street); printer Corrigan and Wilson, 24 Upper Sackville Street)
Editor(s):	Anon.
Dates:	Volume 1, number 1 (1900)–volume 1, number 4 (1904); volume 2, number 1 (1916)
No. of issues:	5
Average periodicity:	Irregular
Average no. pages:	68
Libraries:	BCL; LIN (volume 1, number 1 and volume 1, number 4 only); NLI=Ir 8206n1 (volume 2 only); QUB=PR8702.N2 (volume 1, number 3 and volume 2, number 1 only); RIA=Fr C/1/6/E; TCD(Old Library)=196.n.1, number 3; UCG=800 (PS, incomplete).

This is a dry and earnest production, stuffed with articles on folklore riddles and the importance of Celticising Ireland, each issue rounded off with the facts and figures of the Society's Annual Report. Amongst all this we find pieces on 'St. Patrick as a Man of Letters', Maria Edgeworth, Goldsmith and Celtic Hymns, as well as poems by Jane Barlow, Dora Sigerson Shorter and Mangan. However, as a purely literary magazine, divorced from its historical role and associations with major Revival figures, it is of little importance, with much more space given over to lists of lectures given to the society each year, and of its officers and members, than to either contemporary literary material or to discussion of it.

See John Kelly, *The Collected Letters of WB Yeats*, Volume 2: 1896–1900 (Oxford, 1997), p. 341n.

An author index appears in Richard J. Hayes, *Sources for the History of Irish Civilisation: Articles in Irish Periodicals*, 5 vols (Boston, 1970).

ALL IRELAND REVIEW

Location:	Kilkenny (printer and publisher O'Grady, High Street; from January 1903 printer Sealy, Bryars and Walker, 94 Middle Abbey Street, Dublin).
Editor(s):	Standish O'Grady
Dates:	Volume 1, number 1 (6 January 1900)–volume 6, number 52 (21 April 1906)
No. of issues:	320
Average periodicity:	Weekly
Average no. pages:	8; 12 from January 1903
Libraries:	BL(Colin) (full run); NLI=Ir 05 A 4 (Volume 4, number 3 (3 January 1903)–volume 5, number 53 (31 December 1904) only); PSPL=052; QUB=hfDA900.A4 (volume 1, number 1 (6 January 1900)–volume 3, number 43 (27 December 1902) only); RIA=RR Gall/Case 5/33; TCD=42.b.104–106; UCG=052 (PS, incomplete).

In format and tone, more a Saturday morning paper than a literary magazine, yet scattered throughout its many short issues are a large number of contributions from the main literary figures of the day. Apart from O'Grady's own serialised pot-boilers, there are poems by Yeats, Æ, Moira O'Neill, James H. Cousins, John Todhunter, Ethna Carbery, John Eglinton, Joseph Campbell and Alice Milligan; a short article on the theatre by Yeats (11 April 1903); and extracts from Moore's *The Untilled Field* (in June 1903). The personality of the editor comes across with a strength and individuality which is more reminiscent of a magazine than a newspaper. A curiosity, whose combination of format, contents, tone and lightweight nationalism make it feel very out of time in the context of *Samhain*, *Uladh*, and so on, and more like a production of twenty years earlier.

See Rudi Holzapfel, 'A Survey of Irish Literary Magazines from 1900 to the Present Day', M Litt thesis (Trinity College Dublin, 1964), p. 6.

See Edward A. Hagan, Standish James O'Grady and the All-Ireland Review, PhD Thesis (State University of New York, 1977).

See Roger McHugh, and Maurice Harmon, *A Short History of Anglo-Irish Literature* (Dublin, 1982), pp. 124, 149.

See John Kelly, *The Collected Letters of WB Yeats*, Volume 3: 1901–1904 (Oxford, 1994), pp. 76n, 167, 168n, 259n.

See W.J. McCormack, *From Burke to Beckett: Ascendancy, Tradition and Betrayal in Literary History* (Cork, 1994), p. 234.

See John Kelly, *The Collected Letters of WB Yeats*, Volume 2: 1896–1900 (Oxford, 1997), pp. 123n, 148n, 453, 497n, 520n, 552n, 571, 576n, 592n, 601, 602n.

THE LEADER, A REVIEW OF CURRENT AFFAIRS, POLITICS, LITERATURE, ART AND INDUSTRY

Location:	Dublin (Cahill and Co., 35-37 Gt. Strand Street)
Editor(s):	Anon.
Dates:	Volume 1, number 1 (1 September 1900)–volume II, number 26 (24/8/1901) covered; ran until August 1971
No. of issues:	(36 covered)
Average periodicity:	Weekly
Average no. pages:	16
Libraries:	BL(Colin) (Volume 2, number 1 (2/3/1901)–volume 39, number 7 (20 September 1919); New Leader volume 1, number 1 (15 November 1919)–volume 2, number 3 (5 June 1920); Leader volume 40, number 18 (12 June 1920)–volume 71, number 8, (August 1971); NLI=LB 05 L2; PSPL=052 (volume 63 (1931)–volume 83 (1941) only); TCD=Newspaper Room.

More Nationalist newspaper than literary magazine, the literary content is slight: the first issue carries letters of support, including those from Hyde, Martyn and Yeats; in October of that year they ran a number of articles on contemporary Irish drama; and in November there was a piece on Yeats. An article on 'The Brooke–Rolleston Anthology' published early in January 1901 sparked off a fierce debate, which continued for most of the month, and includes a reply to his detractors from Rolleston himself. All these pieces, however, are quite short, and from February 1901 the *Leader* becomes increasingly Nationalist, the tone more intolerantly Catholic, and the literary content all but disappears.

ST. STEPHEN'S, A RECORD OF UNIVERSITY LIFE

Location:	Dublin (printers Sealy, Bryars and Walker, Middle Abbey Street (1901–1904).
Editor(s):	Hugh Kennedy (June 1901–November 1902); F.E. Hackett (December 1902–June 1903); T.M. Kettle (December 1903–June 1904); CP Curran (November 1904–April 1905); John E. Kennedy (November 1905); F. Cruise O'Brien (February 1906–May 1906).
Dates:	Volume 1, number 1 (June 1901)–volume 2, number 12 (May 1906).
No. of issues:	24
Average periodicity:	Irregular
Average no. pages:	20
Libraries:	NLI=Ir 3784105s1 (incomplete); TCD=Per 90-347; UCC=incomplete; also 1970 reprint; UCD=SC 33.0.3 (1901–1906); UCG=059.9162 (PS, incomplete).

Predominantly a standard student magazine, filled with notices from the clubs and societies of the college, its main (if not its only) importance, despite publishing an article by Patrick Pearse (June 1901) and an interview with Canon Sheehan (February 1902), was that it rejected Joyce's essay 'Day of the Rabblement' in October 1901 (and continued to gently banter Joyce as 'The Mad Hatter'), then accepted his essay on Mangan for the issue of May 1902. The opening editorial of the 1960 revival claims that this series was closed down in May 1906 by the College authorities for supporting Nationalist students who attempted to disrupt ceremonies at the College.

See Rudi Holzapfel, 'A Survey of Irish Literary Magazines from 1900 to the Present Day', M Litt thesis, (Trinity College Dublin, 1964), p. 8.
An author index appears in Richard J. Hayes, *Sources for the History of Irish Civilisation: Articles in Irish Periodicals*, 5 vols (Boston, 1970).

Continued as:

ST. STEPHEN'S, LITERATURE AND OPINIONS

Location:	Marian Printing Co., 32 Portland Place, Binn's Bridge (Trinity 1960); Cityview Press, 32 Portland Place (Michaelmas 1960); The Earlsfort Press Ltd. (Trinity 1965–Hilary 1968); Dominick Press, Eccles Street (1971).
Editor(s):	James Boylan (Trinity 1960); Anon. (Michaelmas 1960–Trinity 1961); Leslie Faughan (Michaelmas 1964–Hilary 1965); John Boyle (Trinity 1965); Philip Meyler (Michaelmas 1966–Trinity 1967); James Macken (Michaelmas 1967–Hilary 1968); Brian Earls (Trinity 1969), Vincent Deane (Michaelmas 1969).
Dates:	Series Two: Un-numbered, Trinity 1960–Trinity 1965; 'Series II, No.

10', Michaelmas 1966–No.19, Hilary 1971.

No. of issues:	19
Average periodicity:	3 times/year
Average no. pages:	48 (1960–1965); 40 (1966–1971)
Libraries:	NLI=1960–77=Ir 3784105 s 5 (partially incomplete); QUB=hPR 8700.S2 (Series 2, numbers 13 (Michaelmas 1967), 18 (Trinity 1970) and 19 (Hilary 1971 only); TCD=Per 90–347; UCC=incomplete; also 1970 reprint; UCD=J 820; UCG=059.9162 (PS, incomplete).

Visually, very much of its time (angular, abstract cover art, contents all in lower case). The contents are fairly undistinguished, the main item of interest is the 'Writer at Work' feature, in which Thomas Kinsella, Hugh Leonard, Richard Murphy, Kennelly, Seamus Heaney, Mary Lavin and Patrick Boyle provide brief profiles of themselves. An interesting article on 'Joyce at the University' runs across Michaelmas 1960 and Trinity 1961. There are one or two stories by, e.g., Desmond Hogan, and occasional poems by Richard Ryan, Anthony Glavin, MacDara Woods, Michael Hartnett, Paul Durcan and Thomas Dillon Redshaw. The editorial for Trinity 1965 complains that 'Literary talent in UCD is declining', and despite a new stiff and glossy cover from Michaelmas 1966, the editorial in the last issue condemns the poor quality of most of their contributions. Perhaps this was inevitable when they limited themselves to students of UCD only. The opening editorial of the 1974 volume confirms that this series expired in 1971, after 19 issues.

See M.H., 'Brief – but not very passionate', *Awake,* 6, 8 (29 February 1964), p. 7. Short review of a contemporary issue of *St. Stephen's.*
See Rudi Holzapfel, 'A Survey of Irish Literary Magazines from 1900 to the Present Day', M Litt thesis , (Trinity College Dublin, 1964), p. 73.

Continued as:

ST. STEPHEN'S

Location:	Elo Press Ltd. (1974–1977)
Editor(s):	Kieran Kehoe (1974–1976); Patrick King (1977)
Dates:	volume 3, number 1 (1974)–volume 3, number 3 (1976); 2 unnumbered issues in Summer and Winter 1977
No. of issues:	5
Average periodicity:	Annual
Average no. pages:	74 (1974–1976); 36 (1977)
Libraries:	LIN (volume 3, number 3 (1976) only); NLI=1960–77=Ir 3784105 s 5 (partially incomplete); QUB=hPR8700.S2 (volume 3, numbers 1 (1974), 2 (Spring 1975) and 3 (1976) only); RIA=Fr C/5/2/G Misc Box S–Z (volume 3); TCD=Per 90–347; UCC=incomplete; also 1970 reprint; UCD=J 820 (1960–1986); UCG=059.9162 (PS, incomplete).

This was published at 7 Hollybank Avenue, Sandford Road, Dublin 6, and edited initially by Kieran Kehoe (with a Board which also included Gerard Fanning and Colm Tóibín). Obviously casting their net wider than the previous incarnation, the contents are far superior, including: essays by Richard Kearney and Conor Kelly (on the poetry of Heaney and Mahon); fiction by Tom MacIntyre, Fred Johnston and Neil Jordan; and poetry by Harry Clifton, Gerald Dawe, Gerard Fanning, Heaney, Neil Jordan, Aidan Carl Matthews, Maeve McCaughan, John Montague, James Simmons and Colm Tóibín. There are also some book reviews which are too short to say very much. Less of a college rag and more a proper literary magazine, this is a good Little Magazine, capturing well the flavour of literary activity in Dublin in the mid-1970s.

All issues since 1960 have been A5; now it switches to A4 for two issues in Summer and Winter 1977. The quality of the contents is very poor, and both issues are marked '©The Editor'; the emphasis is much more on graphics, and the whole feels like an exercise in self-indulgence.

See Gerald Dawe, untitled review of *St. Stephen's, Fortnight,* 130 (July 1976), p. 14.

Continued as:

ST. STEPHEN'S

Location:	Publisher and printer not given
Editor(s):	Michael Ross (1986)
Dates:	Un-numbered issue, 1986
No. of issues:	1
Average periodicity:	Annual?
Average no. pages:	44
Libraries:	TCD=Per 90-347; UCD=J 820 (1960–1986); UCG=059.9162 (PS, incomplete).

A single issue, mostly devoted to college politics, but it does carry an interview with Tom Murphy.

SAMHAIN

Location:	Dublin (printer and publisher, numbers 1–4 Sealy, Bryars and Walker, Middle Abbey Street; then Maunsel and Co.)
Editor(s):	W.B. Yeats
Dates:	October 1901–December 1906; and November 1908
No. of issues:	7
Average periodicity:	Occasional
Average no. pages:	38
Libraries:	BL=PP.5196.h; LIN (October 1901, October 1902, October 1903 and

November 1905); NLI=Ir 8228 s 1; PSPL=820.5; QUB=hPN2602.S1;
RIA=Fr C/5/1/G (also some in Gold Room); TCD=190.q.101,
nos.4–9; UCC (incomplete; also 1970 reprint); UCD=J 890;
UCG=059.9162 (PS, incomplete).

Obviously carrying on where *Beltaine* left off – a stylish cover, and striking typefaces –
and the same remarks apply; this is also very much a theatrical magazine, but historically
important. The contents include Yeats discussing the plans of the Irish Literary Theatre, or
individual plays by George Moore, Martyn, Æ, and of course himself. There are many bold
declarations – '...a dramatic movement which will not die has been started' (Yeats,
'Windlestraws', 1, p. 3); '...the Irish Literary Theatre has done more to awaken
intellectual life in Ireland than Trinity College...' (Moore, volume 1, p. 13). Although the
way they are presented is loose and disorganised, Yeats's thoughts here on theatre and on
the role of the writer mark a crucial stage in his development.

An innovation this time, which makes it more of a literary magazine, is that it included
the texts of the plays, as listed below:

Volume 1 (Oct 1901)	Douglas Hyde's *Twisting of the Rope*, with a translation by Lady Gregory
Volume 2 (Oct 1902)	Hyde's *The Lost Saint*, with translation by Gregory
Volume 3 (Oct 1903)	Hyde's *The Poorhouse*, trans. Gregory
Volume 4 (Dec 1904)	Synge's *In the Shadow of the Glen*, and Gregory's *The Rising of the Moon*
Volume 5 (Nov 1905)	Gregory's *Spreading the News*, with Irish translation
Volume 6 (Dec 1906)	Gregory's *Hyacinth Halvey*
Volume 7 (Nov 1908)	Gregory's *Dervogilla*

By the time the seventh issue was out, the *Arrow* had taken over the role of platform for
the National Theatre. Number 8 carries lists of all the 'Dates and Places of the First
Performances of Plays Produced by the National Theatre Society and its Predecessors'.

See F.J. Hoffman, Charles Allen and C.F. Ulrich, *The Little Magazine: A History and a
Bibliography* (Princeton, 1946); reprinted New York, 1967, p. 236.
See D.D. O'Mahony, 'Samhain– 1904', *Blarney Magazine* 14 (Summer 1958), pp. 17–19.
See Rudi Holzapfel, 'A Survey of Irish Literary Magazines from 1900 to the Present Day',
M Litt thesis, (Trinity College Dublin, 1964), p. 9.
See B.C. Bloomfield, *Samhain* (London, 1970; all issues reprinted with introduction).
See Roger McHugh and Maurice Harmon, *A Short History of Anglo-Irish Literature*
(Dublin, 1982), pp. 150, 152, 154, 170.
See Alvin Sullivan, *British Literary Magazines: The Victorian and Edwardian Age,
1837–1913* (Westport, 1984), pp. 376–379.

See John Kelly, *The Collected Letters of WB Yeats*, Volume 3: 1901–1904 (Oxford, 1994), pp. 72n, 74n, 76n, 78, 95n, 100, 115, 116, 129n, 147, 149n, 173, 175n, 183n, 220n, 221n, 228, 229, 230, 234, 235, 250, 255, 266n, 271, 289n, 290n, 320n, 356n, 365n, 381, 390n, 413, 424–426, 430, 431, 434–436, 438, 439n, 448, 462, 572n, 593n, 597n, 612n, 614n, 619n, 622, 624, 638n, 648, 673, 687, 689, 690.

See Declan Kiberd, *Inventing Ireland* (London, 1995), pp. 128, 164.

An author index appears in Rudi Holzapfel, 'A Survey of Irish Literary Magazines from 1900 to the Present Day', M Litt thesis (Trinity College Dublin, 1964).

An author index appears in Richard J. Hayes, *Sources for the History of Irish Civilisation: Articles in Irish Periodicals*, 5 vols (Boston, 1970).

DUBLIN PENNY JOURNAL, A MAGAZINE OF ART, ARCHAEOLOGY, LITERATURE AND SCIENCE

Location:	Dublin (printer and publisher W.F. Dennehy, 90 Middle Abbey Street)
Editor(s):	W.F. Dennehy (attr. Holzapfel)
Dates:	Volume 1, number 1 (5 April 1902)–volume 3, number 52 (25 March 1905)
No. of issues:	156
Average periodicity:	Weekly
Average no. pages:	16
Libraries:	BL(Colin)=5 April 1902–25 March 1905; LIN (volume 1, number 1 (5 April 1902)–volume 1, number 52 (28 March 1903) only); NLI=Ir 05 d 10; PSPL=052; QUB=pAP4.D8 (volume 3, numbers 20 and 21 (13 August 1904 and 20 August 1904) only); RIA=C/12/1/N; TCD=50.a.92–94.

From 'To Our Readers', first issue: 'Of late there has been witnessed in our midst…a renaissance of interest in matters…affecting the development of the intellectual and material resources of the country…'; it also claims to be the successor to the *Dublin Penny Journal* of 1832–1836.

This is a clear and attractive popular production, with good (if slightly old-fashioned) illustrations; each one contains a handful of verses, 'Literary Notes' (gossip about, e.g. the new novel George Moore is working on), and a short story– amongst a great deal of material on Irish history and topography. The poets appearing include William D. Gallagher, Minna Irving and Sir William Wilde; the storytellers Francis Joseph Bigger and K.F. Purdon; these were the biggest names they attracted and, despite the nearly 500 poems and 150 stories which appeared, the enduring feel of the *Journal* is of a lightweight production. None of the names which appear went on to greater things.

See Rudi Holzapfel, 'A Survey of Irish Literary Magazines from 1900 to the Present Day', M Litt thesis (Trinity College Dublin, 1964), p. 10.

DANA, AN IRISH MAGAZINE OF INDEPENDENT THOUGHT

Location: Dublin (publisher Hodges, Figgis and Co., Ltd., printer Hely's, Dublin; also published London, David Nutt)

Editor(s):   Frederick Ryan and John Eglinton (pseudonym of William Kirkpatrick Magee)

Dates: Volume 1, number 1 (May 1904)–volume 1, number 12 (April 1905)

No. of issues: 12 issues

Average periodicity: Monthly

Average no. pages: 32

Libraries: LIN; NLI=IR 05 d 1; PSPL=052; QUB=hAP4.D25 (reprint only); RDS=NL51; RIA=Fr C/1/3/D; TCD=54.p.168; UCC (1970 reprint); UCD=J 050.

Dana was perhaps a magazine ahead of its time: while paying ambiguous tribute to the 'worthy' tutelary deity of Irish cultural nationalism, Thomas Davis, the 'Introductory' essay to the first issue challenges the shibboleth of unity and calls for individual expression in Ireland. While more cosmopolitan influences can be detected – Matthew Arnold, and perhaps Thoreau and Whitman – the real avatar of *Dana* is Æ, and a vein of slightly fey idealism runs through it. It was to be another two decades before more journals took up the torch for humanist, internationalist individualism in Ireland, and even then it was to remain a minority taste.

Around a quarter of the contents (including some fine polemics) seem to have been contributed by the editors, as themselves or under pseudonyms; F.M. Atkinson was responsible for 'A Literary Causerie' in each issue; and the most frequent remaining contributors included Colum, Æ himself, and his acknowledged follower, Seumas O'Sullivan. While the editors' opinions may be judged from some of their own contributions – nominating 'The Midnight Court' as 'The Best Irish Poem', attacking the Catholic Church and Gaelic revivalism in similar terms, and promoting such novel concepts as 'Intellectual Freedom' – their quality is seen in how they juxtaposed those ideas with sincere defences by other pens of the very windmills at which they tilted.

Other contributors include Eduard Dujardin (an influence on Joyce), Cousins, Stephen Gwynn, George Moore (who also contributed under the pseudonym 'Paul Ruttledge'), Gogarty, T.W. Rolleston and (with one 'Song') 'James A Joyce'. The editors of *Dana* share with their peers at *St. Stephen's* the distinction of having rejected a more important submission from Joyce, in this case 'the manuscript of a serial story', which would later metamorphose into *A Portrait of the Artist* (see Eglinton).

See John Eglinton, 'The Beginnings of Joyce', *Irish Literary Portraits* (London, 1935), p. 136.

See F.J. Hoffman, Charles Allen and C.F. Ulrich, *The Little Magazine: A History and a Bibliography* (Princeton, 1946); reprinted New York, 1967, p. 237.

All 12 issues were reprinted in a single volume by Lemma Publishing Corporation, New York, 1970.

See Rudi Holzapfel, 'A Survey of Irish Literary Magazines from 1900 to the Present Day',
    M Litt thesis (Trinity College Dublin, 1964), p. 11.
See Alvin Sullivan, *British Literary Magazines: The Victorian and Edwardian Age,
    1837–1913* (Westport, 1984), pp. 103–110.
See Peter Denman, 'Ireland's Little Magazines', Barbara Hayley and Enda McKay (eds),
    300 Years of Irish Periodicals (Mullingar, 1987), pp. 125–126.
See John Kelly, *The Collected Letters of WB Yeats*, Volume 3: 1901–1904 (Oxford, 1994),
    pp. 24n, 132n, 576n, 630, 639, 640, 658–659.

An author index appears in Rudi Holzapfel, 'A Survey of Irish Literary Magazines from
    1900 to the Present Day', M Litt thesis (Trinity College Dublin, 1964).
A basic author index appears in Marion Sader, *Comprehensive Index to English-Language
    Little Magazines 1890–1970* (Millwood, 1976).
An author index appears in Rudi Holzapfel, *Author Index 3*, Carraig Books Ltd.
    (Blackrock, 1985), pp. 13–18.

ULADH

Location:	Belfast (publisher Ulster Literary Theatre, 109 Donegall Street; printer Davidson and McCormick, 54 King Street)
Editor(s):	Bulmer Hobson (attr. Holzapfel); G.M. Reynolds (attr. Denman)
Dates:	November 1904–September 1905
No. of issues:	4
Average periodicity:	Quarterly
Average no. pages:	32
Libraries:	BL=PP.5109.ab; LIN; NLI=Ir 8205 u 1; PSPL=820.5; QUB=hAP4.U2; RIA=Fr C/Sect 5/2/E.

Just as the Ulster Literary Theatre was a Northern echo of recent developments in Dublin,
so *Uladh* was their version of Yeats titles like *Samhain* and *Beltaine*. Ironically (given that
it came from the North), *Uladh* can be seen as representing the fullest flowering of the
Little Magazine during the Irish Literary Revival – a striking production, with a brown
cover like *Samhain*, but an even more confident synthesis of drama, poetry, typography,
and illustration. Prose pieces begin with specially designed wood-cut first letters, Irish
language items are in an attractive, Celticised font, the whole liberally sprinkled with
drawings and illustrations, large and small. *Uladh* is given extra interest by the tension at
its core between their inherited Revivalist values and the truth of the situation in the North.
Describing cities as 'more a stumbling-block to the right intellectual and artistic progress
of the country...' must have read rather better in Sligo than in Belfast.

It includes poetry by Æ, Joseph Campbell, Colum, Bulmer Hobson and Alice Milligan;
articles by Francis Joseph Bigger, Joseph Campbell, Roger Casement, James Connolly and
Forrest Reid; and a few short plays by Campbell and Lewis Purcell.

The plays are often derivative; the poetry variable though occasionally good; the articles often stimulating and of enduring interest (see review of *Dana*, volume 1, number 3); and the best of the illustrations (mostly by Campbell) remain fresh and charming. The whole is even more than the sum of these parts, in the first rank of Irish literary magazines, and one of the best from Ulster.

See F.M. Atkinson, 'A Literary Causerie', *Dana*, 1, 8 (December 1904), pp. 252–254.
See Anon., 'A Literary Causerie', *Dana*, 1, 12 (April 1905), pp. 381–382.
See Rudi Holzapfel, 'A Survey of Irish Literary Magazines from 1900 to the Present Day', M Litt thesis (Trinity College Dublin, 1964), p. 12.
See Roger McHugh and Maurice Harmon, *A Short History of Anglo-Irish Literature* (Dublin, 1982), p. 162.
See Peter Denman, 'Ireland's Little Magazines', Barbara Hayley and Enda McKay (eds), *300 Years of Irish Periodicals* (Mullingar, 1987), p. 127.
See Tom Clyde, 'Uladh, Lagan and Rann: The "Little Magazine" comes to Ulster', in Eve Patten, *Returning to Ourselves* (Belfast, 1995), pp. 145–153.

An author index appears in Richard J. Hayes, *Sources for the History of Irish Civilisation: Articles in Irish Periodicals*, 5 vols (Boston, 1970).

THE SHANACHIE, AN IRISH MISCELLANY ILLUSTRATED

Location:	Dublin (publisher Maunsel and Co., 96 Middle Abbey Street, printer Sealy, Bryars and Walker)
Editor(s):	Joseph M. Hone (Holzapfel)
Dates:	Summer 1906–Winter 1907
No. of issues:	6
Average periodicity:	Triannual
Average no. pages:	64
Libraries:	BL=PP.C.127.d.l; LIN (volume 1, numbers 1 and 2 (1906), and volume 2, number 3 (March 1907) only); NLI=Ir 828 s 1; PSPL=820.5; QUB=hAP4.S5; TCD=77.s.26; UCC.

This is an attractive production, boasting a coloured card cover with a large illustration, and also illustrations (sometimes tinted) inside. It is an entirely literary magazine, and has no discernible 'programme' or political agenda.

The first issue (not numbered), carries stories by Shaw (from 1885), and George A. Birmingham; poems by Colum, W.B. Yeats ('Against Witchcraft' and 'The Praise of Deirdre'), and A.P. Graves; an essay by Lord Dunsany and a short play by Lady Gregory, as well as some fine illustrations by, amongst others, Joseph Campbell and Jack B. Yeats. Unusually, this high standard was maintained, if only for a short run; while later issues contained more work by unknowns, amongst this can still be found poems by Æ; a story by Birmingham; articles by Synge and Æ; and illustrations by Jack B. Yeats and William Orpen.

Continued as:

THE SHANACHIE, AN IRISH ILLUSTRATED QUARTERLY

The last four issues contained material from Jane Barlow, Birmingham, Colum, Cousins, Dunsany, O'Sullivan, Orpen, Synge, Jack B. Yeats and W.B. Yeats.

The quality of this magazine is astonishingly high, in every department, poems, stories, illustrations, articles. However, it is not an integrated artistic production like *Uladh*, where fonts, layout, etc. blend into an organic whole; rather, it feels like a sincere attempt to reach out to the masses, without undue compromise. One of the best Irish literary magazines, despite its short life.

See F.J. Hoffman, Charles Allen and C.F. Ulrich, *The Little Magazine: A History and a Bibliography* (Princeton, 1946); reprinted New York, 1967, p. 238.
See Rudi Holzapfel, 'A Survey of Irish Literary Magazines from 1900 to the Present Day', M Litt thesis (Trinity College Dublin, 1964), p. 13.
See John Kelly, *The Collected Letters of WB Yeats*, Volume 3: 1901–1904 (Oxford, 1994), p. 269n.

An author index appears in Rudi Holzapfel, 'A Survey of Irish Literary Magazines from 1900 to the Present Day', M Litt thesis (Trinity College Dublin, 1964).

THE ARROW

Location:	Dublin (publisher Abbey Theatre, printer Hely's Limited, Printers, Dame Street)
Editor(s):	W.B. Yeats
Dates:	Volume 1, number 1 (20 October 1906)–volume 1, number 5 (25 August 1909)
No. of issues:	5
Average periodicity:	Irregular
Average no. pages:	8
Libraries:	BCL; NLI=Ir 391941 a 2; PSPL=820.5 (incomplete); RIA=Gold Room 11 D (2 issues only); TCD=Yeats Per 3.

A handsome production, in a slate grey cover with a bold woodcut of a queen and wolfhound. In his first editorial, Yeats says that the *Arrow* is 'not meant as a substitute [for *Samhain*] ... It will interpret or comment on particular plays, make announcements, wrap up the programme and keep it from being lost, and leave general principles to Samhain'. And this is exactly what it does. Most of the text is by Yeats himself, with occasional contributions from Gregory, short commentaries on plays which the Abbey has or will be producing, lists of plays produced to date, plus advertisements. There is little of purely literary interest, and *Arrow*'s lasting importance rests on number 3 (23 February 1907), which reprints Yeats's famous speech in defence of Synge's *Playboy of the Western World* at the Abbey debate after the riot; number 4 (1 June 1909) is also dominated by this issue.

See Rudi Holzapfel, 'A Survey of Irish Literary Magazines from 1900 to the Present Day', M Litt thesis (Trinity College Dublin, 1964), p. 14.

Continued as:

THE ARROW, W.B. YEATS COMMEMORATION NUMBER

Location:	Dublin (publisher Abbey Theatre, printer Wood Printing Works)
Editor(s):	Lennox Robinson
Dates:	Unnumbered issue, Summer 1939
No. of issues:	1
Average periodicity:	–
Average no. pages:	24
Libraries:	BL=PP.5224.ek; BCL; NLI=Ir 391941 a 2; PSPL=820.5; QUB=hpPR5906/3; TCD= 96.d.192.

Published to commemorate Yeats's death, and containing valedictory articles by, amongst others, Gordon Bottomley, Austin Clarke, Gogarty, Richard Hayes, F.R. Higgins, John Masefield and Lennox Robinson. There are also four pages of paintings and cartoons of Yeats, including famous images of the poet by his brother Jack, and by Max Beerbohm.

See F.J. Hoffman, Charles Allen and C.F. Ulrich, *The Little Magazine: A History and a Bibliography* (Princeton, 1946); reprinted New York, 1967, p. 238.
See Rudi Holzapfel, 'A Survey of Irish Literary Magazines from 1900 to the Present Day', M Litt thesis (Trinity College Dublin, 1964), p. 47.
See Alvin Sullivan, *British Literary Magazines: The Victorian and Edwardian Age, 1837–1913* (Westport, 1984), pp. 23–25.

An author index appears in Richard J. Hayes, *Sources for the History of Irish Civilisation: Articles in Irish Periodicals*, 5 vols (Boston, 1970).
A basic author index appears in Marion Sader, *Comprehensive Index to English-Language Little Magazines 1890–1970* (Millwood, 1976).
An author index appears in B.C. Bloomfield, *An author index to selected British 'little magazines', 1930–1939* (London, 1976).

HERMES. AN ILLUSTRATED UNIVERSITY LITERARY QUARTERLY

Location:	Dublin (publisher UCD, printer Sealy, Bryars and Walker)
Editor(s):	Anon.
Dates:	Number 1 (February 1907)–number 4 (February 1908)
No. of issues:	4
Average periodicity:	Quarterly
Average no. pages:	32
Libraries:	BL=PP.6155.c; NLI=IR 3784105 h 1; RIA=Top Floor Room 5/5/A; TCD=49.bb.21.

This was the first literary magazine to emerge from the National University, and its intention was to publish material from all four colleges; its editors explicitly modelled their efforts on *Kottabos*. The first issue contains an appreciation of Yeats's poetry, and short reviews of books by Stephen Gwynn, James H. Cousins and Æ's *By Still Waters*; the second a poem by Cousins and an article on Baudelaire; the third a highly positive review of Joyce's *Chamber Music*; and the last a piece on Shaw's dramatic works. The production values are high, but the contents are less than thrilling, and the short run frustrates any grander aspirations they may have had.

An author index appears in Richard J. Hayes, *Sources for the History of Irish Civilisation: Articles in Irish Periodicals*, 5 vols (Boston, 1970).

AN CONNACHTACH/THE CONNACHTMAN: A BILINGUAL JOURNAL DEVOTED TO THE NATIONAL REVIVAL

Location:	Athlone (printer The Athlone Printing Works Co. Ltd., Westmeath Independent Office, Athlone)
Editor(s):	Anon.
Dates:	Volume 1, number 1 (July 1907)–volume 1, number 11 (May 1908)
No. of issues:	11
Average periodicity:	Monthly
Average no. pages:	16
Libraries:	BL=PP.6193.o (incomplete); NLI=IR 8205 c 3; QUB=qAP4.C7; TCD=IN.20.101; UCD=STORE 820; UCG=052.1 (PS).

About half of this paper is in Irish, and it is mostly as described in the subtitle (with a revealing reference in the first editorial to the new nationalism as 'the *faith* of Sinn Féin' [my emphasis]. However, it did print a handful of poems, in both Irish and English, by the likes of Thomas MacDonagh, Alice Milligan and Alice Furlong, as well as a 'National Hymn' by Mangan, and a review of Colum's collection, *Wild Earth*. The last issue carries a notice of a public meeting to discuss incorporating *An Connachtach* as a limited company; obviously this was not as successful as was hoped.

See Rudi Holzapfel, 'A Survey of Irish Literary Magazines from 1900 to the Present Day', M Litt thesis (Trinity College Dublin, 1964), p. 16.

A BROADSIDE

Location:	Dundrum (publisher Dun Emer Press, Dundrum, Co. Dublin)
Editor(s):	W.B. Yeats, with sisters E.C. Yeats and S.M. Yeats
Dates:	Volume 1, number 1 (June 1908)–volume 7, number 12 (May 1915)
No. of issues:	84
Average periodicity:	Monthly
Average no. pages:	4
Libraries:	BL=PP.6158.fa; NLI=LO; PSPL=784.3; TCD(Old Library)=Press A, Cuala A.c.1a-84a.

Produced in a limited run of three hundred copies, this is a gem of Irish serial publication whose slight size belies its superb production values. Each issue comprises on average one full-page illustration (black and white), plus two quarter-page illustrations, all by Jack B. Yeats, which range from mildly amusing to quite stunning. The smaller illustrations are usually coloured, and the vibrancy of those colours is often startling. In homage to its vernacular inspiration each issue also carries one or two poems in the ballad style (either traditional ('The Night Before Larry Was Stretched'), cowboy ('Streets of Laredo'), or original). Some of these are anonymous, others are by a dazzling array of authors, including John Masefield, James Stephens, Sir Walter Raleigh, Lady Gregory, Seamus O'Sullivan, Thomas Davis, Colum and Mangan.

Continued as:
BROADSIDES. A COLLECTION OF OLD AND NEW SONGS (NEW SERIES)

Location:	Dublin (Cuala Press, 133 Lower Baggot Street)
Editor(s):	W.B. Yeats, with F.R. Higgins (volume 1), Dorothy Wellesley (volume 2); Musical Editor Arthur Duff
Dates:	Volume 1, 1935; volume 2, 1937
No. of issues:	24
Average periodicity:	Monthly
Average no. pages:	4
Libraries:	BCL=I/784.8 BROA (1971 reprint); BL=PP.6158.fa; PSPL=784.3; QUB=hqPR8858/2 (Irish University Press reprint, 1971); TCD(Old Library)=Press A, Cuala A.55, also Yeat A.a.58.

The first issue starts with a four-page foreword, 'Anglo-Irish Ballads' by Higgins and Yeats. Each issue carries two ballads, with music and an illustration, and is marked '300 copies only'. The poems are by Colum, Lynn Doyle, Bryan Guinness, Higgins, R.A.

Milliken, Frank O'Connor, Stephens and Yeats, and one original is usually paired with one traditional. Illustrations by Jack B. Yeats, Maurice McGonigal and others are used lavishly.

Continued as:

BROADSIDES. A COLLECTION OF NEW IRISH AND ENGLISH SONGS (NEW SERIES)

This volume starts with a two-page foreword 'Music and Poetry' by Yeats and Dorothy Wellesley. Poems by Belloc, Gordon Bottomley, Colum, De La Mare, Gogarty, Higgins, O'Connor, Edith Sitwell, Stephens and Yeats; the same illustrators are used again. As with earlier series, these are delightful productions, visually vivid and arresting . All in all, a marvellous indulgence.

See F.J. Hoffman, Charles Allen and C.F. Ulrich, *The Little Magazine: A History and a Bibliography* (Princeton, 1946); reprinted New York, 1967, p. 371.
See Liam Miller, 'The Dun Emer Press', *Irish Book* 2, 3/4 (Autumn 1963), pp. 81–90. Mentions *A Broadside*.
See Jack B. Yeats, *Broadside Characters: Drawings* (Dublin, 1971).
See Wayne McKenna, 'WB Yeats, W.J. Turner and Edmund Dulac: The *Broadsides* and Poetry Broadcasts', Warwick Gould, *Yeats Annual No.8* (1991), pp. 225–234.
See John Kelly, *The Collected Letters of WB Yeats*, Volume 3: 1901–1904 (Oxford, 1994), pp. 251n, 271n, 299n.

THE CATHOLIC BOOK BULLETIN, A MONTHLY REVIEW OF CATHOLIC LITERATURE

Location:	Dublin (printer and publisher M.H. Gill and Son Ltd, 50 Upper O'Connell Street)
Editor(s):	Anon.
Dates:	Volume 1, number 1 (January 1911)–volume 29, number 12 (December 1939)
No. of issues:	348
Average periodicity:	Monthly
Average no. pages:	48; from January 1926, 80
Libraries:	BL=PP.211.de (outhoused); LIN (incomplete); NLI=Ir 05 c 2; PSPL=282.415; QUB=BX801.C4; RIA=Fr C/4/7/E-F; TCD=71.g.104–139; UCC; UCG=282 PS (incomplete).

Established with the blessing of the church hierarchy to help guide the readers of Ireland away from sinful influences and toward wholesome, church-approved material ('...sanctioned and approved to the last page by the Catholic ecclesiastical authorities...', first editorial), the editors approached their mission with a zeal which sometimes bordered on delusion, e.g. in an article on great poetry in the first issue which explicitly includes Wordsworth because 'we seem to trace in the great poet a latent germ of Catholicity'. The *Catholic Book Bulletin* (which become the *Catholic Bulletin and Book Review* from its third issue) became the Bible of Catholic Nationalism: not the Nationalism of Pearse, let alone Connolly, but the right-wing, conservative, strongly Gaelicised, selectively patriotic beliefs which were to become the official ideology of the Free State. Literary material is limited to about one poem per issue, plus the odd book review, both of a 'religious' or devotional nature. In their second year, they began to publish lists of approved books, suitable for Catholic readers and libraries, the beginnings of a trend which would result in the establishment of the Censorship Board a decade later. In August 1912 they carry a good review of the first meeting of the National Literary Society. Despite its huge sociological and historical importance, the terms of reference of the *Catholic Bulletin* divorced it almost entirely from all that was interesting, stimulating or important in writing, whether in Ireland or abroad. It is not too much of an exaggeration to state that not a single important book was reviewed in its pages, nor did there appear a single poem or story from any author of note. To students of literature, it must represent a powerful negative presence, and an example of the kind of thing against which Irish writers had to struggle during these years.

See Terence Brown, *Ireland, A Social and Cultural History 1922–1985* (London, 1985), pp. 62–63; 71–72.
See Roy Foster, *Paddy and Mr Punch* (London, 1993), pp. 15, 35, 304.
See W.J. McCormack, *From Burke to Beckett: Ascendancy, Tradition and Betrayal in Literary History* (Cork, 1994), pp. 9, 212, 312–319, 377.

An author index appears in Richard J. Hayes, *Sources for the History of Irish Civilisation: Articles in Irish Periodicals*, 5 vols (Boston, 1970).

THE IRISH REVIEW, A MONTHLY MAGAZINE OF IRISH LITERATURE, ART & SCIENCE

Location: Dublin (publisher The Irish Review Publishing Company, 12 D'Olier Street, printer John Falconer, 53 Upper Sackville Street; reprinted in London, Edinburgh and Paris)
Editor(s):   David Houston (1911–1912); Padraic Colum (1912–1913); Joseph Plunkett (1913–1914). Associate Editor 1911–1914 Thomas MacDonagh.
Dates: March 1911–November 1914
No. of issues: 42
Average periodicity: Monthly
Average no. pages: 52; July–November 1914 60
Libraries: BL=PP.6158.ea; LIN; NLI=Ir 05 i 20; PSPL=052; QUB=hAP4.I65 (incomplete), also MifB.I65; RDS=NL51; RIA=Fr C/1/5/F; TCD=OLS 186.n.52-55; UCD=MICJ 820; UCG=052 (PS, incomplete).

This is a first-class review, which brings the genre in Ireland firmly into the twentieth century. A dull cover conceals a full-page plate at the start of each issue, attractive layout and a clear typeface. The quality of the contents – particularly for the first two years – is as high as any literary magazine ever published in this country. The issues for 1911 and 1912 contain plates of works by William Orpen, Æ, John B. Yeats and, most often, Jack B. Yeats; stories by George Moore, Colum and James Stephens (whose main contribution, 'Mary', serialised over eleven issues, later developed into his novella, *Hunger*); and, above all, poems by the cream of their generation, Stephens, Colum, Thomas MacDonagh, Joseph Campbell, Corkery, Pearse, Æ, Seumas O'Sullivan, Emily Lawless and W.B. Yeats. Even minor articles on history or economics are by contributors of the stature of George A. Birmingham, Maud Gonne, Edmund Curtis, Martyn, Forrest Reid and Kuno Meyer. While the poetry is not always of the very highest quality, it often does not fall far short of it. The least that can be said of any piece in any issue during these initial years is that it is of historical interest; many are much more than that.

From the end of 1912 there is a noticeable decline and an over-reliance on contributions from Corkery (stories and poems) and Plunkett (whose verse, along with that of MacDonagh and Pearse, dominates the poetry of the last two years). However, there is still room for stimulating articles (on Strindberg, by Mary Colum), some charming poetry by Stephens, and short reviews of important new books. The decline is quantitative also – at its height (January, February or August 1912) good quality literature made up more than half the magazine; during the rest of 1912, a quarter; but from the start of 1913 on, it is reduced to just four or five pages. An important feature of this last phase of the magazine is the appearance in every issue of carefully chosen examples, by Pearse, of Irish poetry (Raftery, etc.), alongside Pearse's own translations.

The *Irish Review* is, of course, the most forceful and celebrated example of the interface between cultural politics and the rather more risky traditional kind, and the preoccupations of the editor and major contributors begin to impinge more forcefully from June 1914, when the first of several versions of a proposed manifesto for the Irish Volunteers appeared. The next issue was a compound one, covering July and August, and came with a four-page supplement describing the Howth gun-running episode, signed 'Thomas MacDonagh, Company Commander'. The final issue (September–November 1914) has an editorial explaining that issues have had to be run together partly because of the large financial losses due to being cut off from overseas markets during the war, and partly because everyone involved has been so busy with the Volunteers. Within two years, of course, Pearse, Plunkett and MacDonagh were to put their theories into dramatic practice.

The quality of the material which appeared in the *Irish Review* throughout 1912 and into 1913 is astounding – no contemporary Irish magazine could touch it, and only a few from any era have come close. At the same time as they were publishing important literature, their other articles were stimulating and varied, a world away from any narrow propaganda sheet: land purchase, the Royal Hibernian Academy, the civil service, Feminism, forestry and congested districts all came under their notice, while a platform was given to non-believers such as 'an Ulster Imperialist' (July 1913) and Ernest Boyd (see his article on 'The Jingoism of the Gael', April 1913).

See Richard J. Loftus, *Nationalism in Modern Anglo-Irish Poetry* (Wisconsin, 1964), pp. 125, 136, 201, 307.

See F.J. Hoffman, Charles Allen and C.F. Ulrich, *The Little Magazine: A History and a Bibliography* (Princeton, 1946); reprinted New York, 1967, p. 373.

See Rudi Holzapfel, 'A Survey of Irish Literary Magazines from 1900 to the Present Day', M Litt thesis (Trinity College Dublin, 1964), p. 21.

See Roger McHugh, and Maurice Harmon, *A Short History of Anglo-Irish Literature* (Dublin, 1982), p. 201.

See Peter Denman, 'Ireland's Little Magazines', Barbara Hayley and Enda McKay (eds), *300 Years of Irish Periodicals* (Mullingar, 1987), pp. 127–128.

See Roy Foster, *Paddy and Mr Punch* (London, 1993), p. 36.

See Declan Kiberd, *Inventing Ireland* (London, 1995), p. 200.

M. Griffin, *Index to The Irish Review, for the Fellowship of the Library Association of Ireland*, nd.

An author index appears in Rudi Holzapfel, 'A Survey of Irish Literary Magazines from 1900 to the Present Day', M Litt thesis (Trinity College Dublin), 1964.

An author index appears in Richard J. Hayes, *Sources for the History of Irish Civilisation: Articles in Irish Periodicals*, 5 vols (Boston, 1970).

An author index appears in Rudi Holzapfel, *Author Index 3*, Carraig Books Ltd. (Blackrock, 1985), pp. 19–35.

STUDIES: AN IRISH QUARTERLY REVIEW OF LETTERS, PHILOSOPHY AND SCIENCE

Location:	Dublin (publisher M.H. Gill and Son, Ltd., 50 Upper O'Connell Street, printer Sealy, Bryars and Walker, 86 Middle Abbey Street; from March 1913 publisher The Educational Company of Ireland, Ltd., reprinted London and Melbourne; from volume 3 (1914) also reprinted in St. Louis; overseas reprints stop from 1950 until The Academic Press in London began to reprint in Autumn 1966; from March 1953 publisher The Talbot Press; in Spring 1975 moves to self-publishing (Studies, 35 Lower Leeson Street) to cut costs; from 1985, printer The Nationalist, Carlow; from 1993, printer Leinster Leader)
Editor(s):	Fr Corcoran (1912–Summer 1914); Fr P.J. Connolly (1914– Autumn 1950); Fr Roland Burke Savage (Winter 1950–Winter 1967); Fr James Meehan (Spring 1968–1975); Fr P.J. O'Connell (1976–1984); Fr Brian Lennon (1984–1990); Fr Noel Barber (1991 onwards)
Dates:	Volume 1, number 1 (March 1912) – still ongoing
No. of issues:	(to Winter 1997) 344
Average periodicity:	Quarterly
Average no. pages:	186 (1912–1943); 154 (1944–1966); 108 (1967–1983); 90; (1984–1993); 110 (1994 onwards).
Libraries:	BCL=IR; BL=PP.6156.ab; LIN; NLI=Ir 05 s 7; PSPL=052; QUB=hAP4.S9; RDS=NL51; RIA=RR Gall/39/C-F; TCD=Per 820; UCC; UCD=J 050; UCG=800.

Studies has long been the prime organ of the Irish Jesuits, and is yet another example of a long-running and successful Irish literary magazine whose format and contents have changed only subtly over many years. An article entitled 'Studies: 1912–1962' by Fr James Meehan appeared in volume 51, which explicitly places *Studies* in the context of the 'last issue of *New Ireland Review* [which] appeared in February 1911 ... like the *Lyceum* before it ... both journals looked back to Newman's *Atlantis*. They were a portion of the Jesuit achievement in the old University college. Now, in 1911, that College had been reconstructed. . . . ' This ties in with the foreword to the first number of *Studies*, which says that after the recent reorganisation of the University system, it seems fitting to produce a review to 'give publicity to scholarly work ... appealing to a wider circle of cultured readers than strictly specialist journals', and while it could be argued that in practice, certainly in later years, *Studies'* audience has been mainly academic, such a manifesto at least implied confidence in the existence of such 'cultured readers'. (In my following comments, it is important to stress that I only mention articles and reviews of literary significance, and that these never formed more than a small part of *Studies'* contents; the bias was always heavily towards the classics, while covering a wide range of topics, including history, archaeology, law, and science.)

After a brief start-up period (volumes one and two) which saw a couple of interesting reviews (*The Crock of Gold* and *The Hill of Vision*) and an article on Irish literature by Pearse, *Studies* embarked on its first phase, lasting from volume 3 (1914) to volume 12 (1923). During this time it carried on investigating the writers and concerns of the Revival: articles and reviews are focused on Æ, Thomas Davis, Thomas MacDonagh, Pearse, Stephens, Dunsany and Yeats; Ernest Boyd's book on the Revival is reviewed along with the work of Stephen J. Brown on nineteenth-century fiction, and the major publications during these years by Corkery. Each issue carried three or four original poems, and the most frequently published poet was Tynan.

A rather bleak new phase began with volume 13 (1924), during which literature almost dropped from view. No new poetry was published, and while books by or about the old Revival war-horses (Shaw, Corkery, Stephens, Carbery, Martyn, Colum and Yeats) were still reviewed, it was rare for more than one to appear per year. In some years, no mention was made of either contemporary or of Irish writing apart from obituaries (e.g. of Æ and Yeats). A few signs of life appear toward the end of this period (a review of Estyn Evans's *Irish Heritage* in 1943, or of books by Lavin in 1944 and 1946, or of Ellman's *Yeats, The Man and the Mask* in 1950), but the story remains much the same until the mid-1950s.

Studies' third (and current) phase begins 1956 when a new tone, much more in touch with current events and the outside world, emerges; in addition, the work of contemporary writers and critics is increasingly featured. This phase kicks off in volume 45 with articles by Vivian Mercier on criticism and on Joyce, and is confirmed two years later when two poems by Patrick Kavanagh mark the first appearance of original poetry since 1923. Articles and reviews, although still only a small portion of the whole, begin to feature Montague, Kavanagh, John Jordan and Kinsella; Pearse Hutchinson, Kinsella, Montague and Kavanagh also continue to contribute new poems. A new confidence is apparent from volume 52 (1963), when there is greater coverage of contemporary English and American writing. Augustine Martin and Denis Donoghue begin to contribute regular articles on Lavin, Yeats, Irish theatre and the 'Poetry of 1916', and the reviews are further strengthened in 1967 by the addition of Maurice Harmon to the team. More new books get short reviews, including those by McGahern, Hewitt, Brian Moore, Mahon and Simmons. However, in more recent years (from, say, the late 1970s) literature has again been accorded less importance, and the articles begin to focus on the glories of the past (Forrest Reid, George Moore, Joyce, Gogarty, Yeats, Synge), although there is the occasional review of a new book by Heaney or interview with Eavan Boland. This may be connected with the move announced in Summer 1984 away from the old miscellany approach towards themed issues.

Even during peak periods poetry never accounted for more than 2 or 3 per cent of the total contents, and most of the book reviews are short, subsumed into multiple, 'portmanteau' reviews of 'Recent Irish Books'. Still, the run of nearly 350 issues over 85 years means that a wide range of useful material can be found in the pages of *Studies*.

See Rudi Holzapfel, 'A Survey of Irish Literary Magazines from 1900 to the Present Day', M Litt thesis (Trinity College Dublin, 1964), p. 22.

See Brian Fallon, *An Age of Innocence: Irish Culture 1930–1960* (Dublin, 1998), pp. 198, 235.

See Gerry Smyth, *Decolonisation and Criticism: The Construction of Irish Literature* (London, 1998), pp. 137–138.

E.M. Kerrigan, *Index to Studies vols. 1–20*, produced by UCD library? (UCD=800, with bound run of Studies)

Aloysius O'Rahilly, *Studies: General index of Volumes 1–50, 1912–1961* (Ros Cré, 1966).

An author index (up to 1969) appears in Richard J. Hayes, *Sources for the History of Irish Civilisation: Articles in Irish Periodicals*, 5 vols (Boston, 1970).

THE 'VARSITY TATLER

Location: Belfast (publisher The Queen's University of Belfast Students' Representative Council, printer The Stevenson Printing Co., 40 Donegall Street)

Editor(s):   Anon.

Dates: Christmas 1912

No. of issues: 1?

Average periodicity: Unknown

Average no. pages: 20

Libraries: LIN; QUB(Arc)=876.

An extremely slight production, containing four short prose pieces and four light verses amongst lots of advertisements, this was primarily a fundraising vehicle for charity.

THE QUARRYMAN, CONDUCTED BY THE STUDENTS FOR THE STUDENTS

Location: Cork (publisher and printer 'Quarryman' Offices, Shandon Printing
                       Works)
Editor(s):   Anon.
Dates: UCC archive has: (bound volumes) volume 1, number 1 (December
                       1913)–volume 4, number 7 (May 1917); another volume 1, number 1
                       (March 1929)–Hilary 1963; (loose copies) volume 2, number 3 (June
                       1931); March 1935; March 1945; December 1948; April 1950; Spring
                       1952; Golden Jubilee Issue, Hilary 1963. These are all held in 'Box 8',
                       in the archive, although they do not appear in the catalogue!
No. of issues: Impossible to estimate, due to large gaps in all holdings
Average periodicity: Monthly, then quarterly, then one per term
Average no. pages: 24, rising to 32, then (in 1950s) 72
Libraries: BL=PP.6159.da (incomplete); LIN (March 1946); NLI=Ir 3784105 q
                       7 (1929–1940); TCD=Per 90439 (incomplete); UCC Archive

For most of its long life, *Quarryman* has been a typical student rag, filled with pictures of
Gaelic football teams, weak doggerel about exam week, and crude satires on students and
staff. It is indicative that out of twenty-seven pieces collected in the anthology (see below),
only three were originally published before the Second World War, and one of these was
by Frank O'Connor, a 'Guest Writer'. Among the photos of hurling teams and the light
satirical verses lies the occasional more serious piece: 'Peadar O'Donnell and the National
Integrity', by 'E.J.S.' (volume 2, number 3, March 1932); and 'The New Irish Novelists',
by 'J.H.' and a Frank O'Connor story 'Seagulls' (both in volume 2, number 6, June 1932).
The conservatism of the institution was no doubt at times crippling: an editorial from 1929
says that '...students must not expect us to print their views on contentious subjects...'.
By the 1950s the literary contributors were taking their work more seriously, although the
quality was not much improved. The main improvement of the 1960s is in production
quality, with a brighter, bigger format and lots of photographs.

See Rudi Holzapfel, 'A Survey of Irish Literary Magazines from 1900 to the Present Day',
   M Litt thesis (Trinity College Dublin, 1964), p. 38.

Continued as:

THE QUARRYMAN

Location: Cork ('A publication of the CTM, UCC'; printer City Printing Works,
                       Cork)
Editor(s):   Various; 1973 issue edited by Patrick Crotty
Dates: UCC archive has: 1965–1973, in 'Box 5' of the archive (NB – not in
                       the catalogue)
No. of issues: Impossible to estimate, due to large gaps in the holding
Average periodicity: Annual

Average no. pages: 68
Libraries: UCC.

The editorial to the 1965 issue declares that they intend to move towards being a serious literary magazine; they partially succeed, in that there is more literary material, and the contributors take their task more seriously. Unfortunately, the quality is not much better, the list of significant items stretching to: a short article by Keane (1967), poems by Robert Welch and Gabriel Rosenstock, and an article by Welch. By the 1970s, they began to solicit material from established writers, often with Cork connections, and this gleans work from Sean Lucy, Montague, Longley, Paul Muldoon and Durcan.

Everything of interest which was published in the first sixty years of this journal is included in the slim 1972 anthology, including stories by 'Guest Writers' O'Connor (1932) and Brendan Behan (1962), another by Eiléan Ní Chuilleanáin (also 1962), also a short prose piece by John B. Keane (1963).

See Davis Coakley and Mary Horgan (eds), *Through the Eyes of Quarryman* (Cork, 1972).

Continued as:

QUARRYMAN

Location: Cork (publisher Students' Union, UCC, printer Eagle Printing)
Editor(s):   Greg Delanty
Dates: UCC archive has: 1980–1984 (1981 missing)
No. of issues: 5?
Average periodicity: Annual
Average no. pages: 48
Libraries: UCC; LIN.

Finally, *Quarryman* matures as a literary periodical. A glossy, professional image combines with a good selection of poetry (mostly by outside, established writers): Dawe, Durcan, Patrick Galvin, Kennelly, Kinsella, Montague, Francis Stuart, Matthew Sweeney; the 1982 number reprints the Behan piece which first appeared in 1962.

THE DAY (AN LÁ)

Location: Cork (printer Shandon Printing Works, Robert Street)
Editor(s):   Thomas Dennehy (attr. Holzapfel)
Dates: 17 March 1916–21 December 1918
No. of issues: 9
Average periodicity: Irregular
Average no. pages: 16
Libraries: NLI=Ir 8208 d 1, numbers 1–9; TCD=120.gg.34, numbers 7–9; UCC; UCD=J 050.

This is a publication of 'The Twenty Club', which dedicated itself to injecting some life into the arts in Cork. The magazine includes reviews of publications by Cork writers, and of plays produced in the town, along with some verse and stories. The quality is low enough to make it of only historical interest; although Corkery was associated with the club, unfortunately he does not seem to have contributed to their publication. It largely kept to its promise to be 'A Non-political Journal of Local Art and Literature'. Holzapfel suggests that Standish O'Grady and Gerald MacNamara may have been involved in its production.

See Rudi Holzapfel, 'A Survey of Irish Literary Magazines from 1900 to the Present Day', M Litt thesis (Trinity College Dublin, 1964), p. 23.

THE IRISH COMMONWEALTH, A MONTHLY REVIEW OF SOCIAL AFFAIRS, POLITICS AND LITERATURE

Location: Dublin (publisher The Irish Commonwealth Publishing Co. Ltd., 30–32 Eustace Street, printer Brindley and Son, Eustace Street)
Editor(s):   Aodh de Blacam
Dates: Volume 1, number 1 (March 1919)–volume 1, number 3 (May 1919)
No. of issues: 3
Average periodicity: Monthly
Average no. pages: 64
Libraries: BL=PP.6158.dc; NLI=Ir 8205 i 1; QUB=hpAP4/1–3; RIA=Fr C/1/6/C Misc Box I-K; UCG=052 (PS).

The first issue contains an essay by Ernest A. Boyd, 'The Drift of Anglo-Irish Literature', on recent trends, and a poem by Rowley; the second another essay from Boyd, 'Making the Drama Safe from Democracy', on Yeats's plays, a poem by Higgins, and 'The Despised Aisling', an essay by Corkery; and the final issue another Higgins poem, an anecdote of Belfast life by Bigger, and an essay on the Revival by de Blacam. Obviously, three issues is far too few from which to draw any meaningful conclusions, but on the evidence the *Irish Commonwealth* was intended to be firmly in the tradition of radical general reviews such as the *Irish Review*, *Dana*, and *Ireland To-Day*, but was not in their league. The focus is too narrow, the tone too earnest and the politics narrowly socialist (bound into the back of the QUB copy of issue one is an eight-page section 'Songs of the Workers' Republic', which includes 'A Rebel Song' by Connolly and 'The International').

See Rudi Holzapfel, 'A Survey of Irish Literary Magazines from 1900 to the Present Day', M Litt thesis (Trinity College Dublin, 1964), p. 25.

An author index appears in Richard J. Hayes, *Sources for the History of Irish Civilisation: Articles in Irish Periodicals*, 5 vols (Boston, 1970).

AENGUS, AN ALL POETRY JOURNAL

Location:	Dublin (printer Wood Printing Works, Fleet Street; last issue Abbey Press, Great Peter Street, London)
Editor(s):	HO White (issue 1); then Francis Stuart
Dates:	Midsummer 1919–July 1920
No. of issues:	4
Average periodicity:	Irregular
Average no. pages:	8
Libraries:	NLI=IR 8205 A 1; TCD=99.d.207.

True to its title, there is no editorial, no advertising, nothing but a frontispiece and a series of poems in each issue, in a large, clear type. Contributors include Rowley, F.R. Higgins, E.R. Dodds and R.N.D. Wilson. The last issue (marked 'New Series') is reduced to pocket-size (6in x 4in) and printed in London.

See F.J. Hoffman, Charles Allen and C.F. Ulrich, *The Little Magazine: A History and a Bibliography* (Princeton, 1946); reprinted New York, 1967, p. 255.

See Rudi Holzapfel, 'A Survey of Irish Literary Magazines from 1900 to the Present Day', M Litt thesis (Trinity College Dublin, 1964), p. 26.

An author index appears in Rudi Holzapfel, 'A Survey of Irish Literary Magazines from 1900 to the Present Day', M Litt thesis (Trinity College Dublin, 1964).

An author index appears in Rudi Holzapfel, *Author Index 3*, Carraig Books Ltd, (Blackrock, 1985), pp. 41–43.

THE RED HAND MAGAZINE

Location:	Belfast (publisher W. Forbes Patterson, 316 Crumlin Road ('And at 48 Ingram Street, Glasgow'), printer Kirkwood and Co., 127 Stockwell Street, Glasgow)
Editor(s):	W. Forbes Patterson
Dates:	Volume 1, Number 1 (September 1920)–Volume 1, Number 4 (December 1920)
No. of issues:	4
Average periodicity:	Monthly
Average no. pages:	64
Libraries:	BCL=Microfilm, location 5E; NLI=P 2503 (volume 1, number 1, September 1920 only); QUB=hAP4.R3 (volume 1, number 1 (September 1920) and number 2 (October 1920) only; RIA=Fr C/5/1/F; TCD=86.rr.125; UCC=Microfilm.

A very unusual production, as perhaps indicated by its extraordinary cover, a gaudy merging of Blake's Great Architect with the red hand of Ulster. Despite appearances, the editorial position is a variation on Pearsian nationalism: '...if we be Irish we cannot be British. To us, in so far as it is Irish, every thing is clean and sweet and good, and in so far as it is English, every Irish growth is blighted.'

While most of the magazine is taken up by slightly unhinged, apocalyptic Nationalist rants, space is made for some, uniformly poor, verses. The literary editor was P.S. O'Hegarty, and a clear idea of their approach can be seen in the first editorial – 'For those who do not understand the driving force behind Irish Republicanism we have included "The Faith of Our Fathers" and "The Passion of Padraic Pearse". Any sane reader will draw the obvious moral that all the power of man-made force cannot destroy this spirit which is in truth The Right Hand of God.'!

Contributors include F.J. Bigger and Eoin MacNeill; there are articles by Aodh de Blacam and Corkery, and others on 'The Irish Theatre', and reviews, including one of Helen Waddell. A handful of poems appears in each issue, some in Irish; the best is Yeats's 'The Happy Townland' (reprinted shorn of its title). The tone is extreme Republicanism, with a dash of populist Socialism.

In November it moved to the Glasgow office; a 'Notice' says that the Belfast offices were raided by the police. At the same time an editorial defends the magazine against accusations of being 'too literary'. The last issue is marked 'To be continued', though BCL has no more issues.

See Rudi Holzapfel, 'A Survey of Irish Literary Magazines from 1900 to the Present Day', M Litt thesis (Trinity College Dublin, 1964), p. 27.

An author index appears in Richard J. Hayes, *Sources for the History of Irish Civilisation: Articles in Irish Periodicals*, 5 vols, (Boston, 1970).

GREEN AND GOLD, A MAGAZINE OF FICTION, & C.

Location:	Waterford (printer and publisher 50 O'Connell Street)
Editor(s):	Alan Downey
Dates:	December 1920–March/May 1926
No. of issues:	22
Average periodicity:	Quarterly
Average no. pages:	82
Libraries:	BL=PP.6180.r; NLI=IR 05 g 2; PSPL=820.5.

A commercial short-story magazine, containing a good deal of instantly forgettable material, but worthy of note on three counts. Firstly, it was printed and published in Waterford; secondly, its bold use of striking designs on the cover; and thirdly, the 'star names' which it attracted. These include Æ, George A. Birmingham, de Blacam, Colum, Corkery, James Stephens and Tynan.

See Rudi Holzapfel, 'A Survey of Irish Literary Magazines from 1900 to the Present Day', M Litt thesis (Trinity College Dublin, 1964), p. 28.

An author index appears in Rudi Holzapfel, 'A Survey of Irish Literary Magazines from 1900 to the Present Day', M Litt thesis (Trinity College Dublin, 1964).

An author index appears in Richard J. Hayes, *Sources for the History of Irish Civilisation: Articles in Irish Periodicals*, 5 vols (Boston, 1970).

An author index appears in Rudi Holzapfel, *Author Index 3*, Carraig Books Ltd, (Blackrock, 1985), pp. 45–56.

BANBA

Location:	Dublin (publisher Banba, 73 Lower Mount Street)
Editor(s):	Eamon O'Duibhir (attr. Holzapfel)
Dates:	Volume 1, number 1 (May 1921)–volume 3, number 3 (July/August 1922)
No. of issues:	27
Average periodicity:	Monthly
Average no. pages:	76
Libraries:	BL=PP.6158.gb; NLI=IR 05 b 1; QUB=hAP73.B3; RIA=Gold Room/9/D; TCD=35.bb.45,46; UCC.

The main contributors to this, whose names appear in almost every issue, include Brinsley MacNamara, George Shiels, Corkery, Higgins and de Blacam; there are also occasional pieces from Martyn, O. Henry and R.N.D. Wilson. The tone is an odd mixture of militant nationalism and chatty popular journalism (including several cowboy stories). After a quite promising start, halfway through the run the literary content veers rapidly downmarket into low populism.

See Rudi Holzapfel, 'A Survey of Irish Literary Magazines from 1900 to the Present Day', M Litt thesis (Trinity College Dublin, 1964), p. 29.

THE NATIONAL STORY MAGAZINE

Location:	Dublin (printer Dollard, Printinghouse, publisher National Story Magazine, 2–5 Wellington Quay)
Editor(s):	F.R. Higgins
Dates:	July 1922 is all NLI has
No. of issues:	Volume 1, number 1 is all NLI has
Average periodicity:	Unknown
Average no. pages:	86
Libraries:	NLI=Ir 8205 p 20 (July 1922 only).

A lightweight and populist magazine, as indicated by the inclusion of 'To Laugh or Not To Laugh' by 'Dr. Sidesplitter'; however, it also carries contributions by Tynan and Doyle, and also, more unusually, P.G. Wodehouse. No further comments can be made on the basis of just one issue.

THE IRISH REVIEW OF POLITICS, ECONOMICS, ART AND LITERATURE

Location: Dublin (publisher 78 Harcourt Street, printer O'Loughlin, Murphy and Boland Ltd., 111–112 Upper Dorset Street)
Editor(s):   Bulmer Hobson
Dates: Volume 1, number 1 (28 October 1922)–volume 1, number 6 (6 January 1923)
No. of issues: 6
Average periodicity: Fortnightly
Average no. pages: 12
Libraries: NLI=Ir 05 i 19; RIA=Fr C/Sect 6/2; TCD=85.a.115;

[Some indexes claim this as a 'New Series' of the Plunkett/ Pearse/ MacDonagh *Irish Review* (1911–1914).]

Although it has a strong whiff of official backing (what else could have moved them to run a column in every issue explaining the new state's financial system?), there is some literary content. Although constricted by the limited space available, this is generally well balanced and well chosen. Mostly it comprises short book reviews, with Eimar O'Duffy the most frequent reviewer; it is a useful source of contemporary reviews of books by the likes of Lynn Doyle, Eugene O'Neill, and W.B. Yeats, and O'Duffy also royally ties himself in knots in a review of *Ulysses* (volume 1, number 4). There is also a little poetry, including a ballad by Alice Milligan.

See Rudi Holzapfel, 'A Survey of Irish Literary Magazines from 1900 to the Present Day', M Litt thesis (Trinity College Dublin, 1964), p. 30.
See untitled article in *The Irish Book*, 1, 2 (1959).

An author index appears in Rudi Holzapfel, 'A Survey of Irish Literary Magazines from 1900 to the Present Day', M Litt thesis (Trinity College Dublin, 1964).
An author index appears in Richard J. Hayes, *Sources for the History of Irish Civilisation: Articles in Irish Periodicals*, 5 vols, Boston, 1970.
An author index appears in Rudi Holzapfel, *Author Index 3*, Carraig Books Ltd, (Blackrock, 1985), pp. 37–40.

THE DUBLIN MAGAZINE

Location:	Dublin (publisher Dublin Magazine, 2–5 Wellington Quay, printer Dollard Printinghouse (August 1923–March 1925); then publisher changes to Dublin Publishers Ltd., 9 Commercial Buildings and London, Elkin Mathews, and printers to Cahill and Co., Parkgate Printing Works)
Editor(s):	Seumas O'Sullivan
Dates:	Volume 1, number 1 (August 1923)–volume 3, number 1 (August 1925)
No. of issues:	25
Average periodicity:	Monthly
Average no. pages:	Fluctuates for first year, then settles down to average 70
Libraries:	BL=PP.6180.ibd; LIN; MAR=YR (1927–1948); NLI=Ir 8205 d 4; PSPL=052; QUB=hAP4.D1; RDS=NL52; RIA=Fr C/2/3/E–G; TCD=Gall L.28.10–39; UCD=J 820; UCG=052 (PS).

[NB. Editorial to volume 10, number 3 (Autumn/ Winter 1973/1974) says the archive of O'Sullivan's *Dublin Magazine* material is in TCD.]

This first series established a distinctive style from the start, with its blue cover and drawing of a Regency couple; the tone throughout is one of respectability; the layout is good, and clear. Each main story is accompanied by an illustration (some by Jack B. Yeats) and articles often have photographs; many of the illustrations are very striking woodcuts. The first two issues carry an apology, which perhaps reveals something of O'Sullivan's aspirations: 'Owing to strike conditions, the supply of special paper ordered for use in "The Dublin Magazine" has not reached us in time for these numbers.'

The list of contributors includes many famous names of the day: Hilaire Belloc, Austin Clarke, Colum, Corkery, Doyle, John Eglinton, Monk Gibbon, F.R. Higgins, Micheál Mac Liammóir, John Masefield, Rutherford Mayne, George Moore, O'Flaherty, Luigi Pirandello, Robinson and James Stephens.

In summary, the *Dublin Magazine* in its first incarnation maintains a very civilised, 'quality' air, but is a little dull and unoriginal. O'Sullivan's refusal to stand up to his printers and publish Leventhal's *Ulysses* review at this time also does not reflect well (see *Klaxon*, below).

Continued as:

THE DUBLIN MAGAZINE, A QUARTERLY REVIEW OF LITERATURE, SCIENCE AND ART

Location:	Dublin (publisher Dublin Magazine, 80 Rathmines Road, printers Alex. Thom and Co., Ltd.; with number 4 (October–December 1926) publisher moves to 2 Crow Street)
Editor(s):	Seamus O'Sullivan

Dates: Volume 1, number 1 (January–March 1926)–volume 33, number 2
                                (April–June 1958)
No. of issues: 130
Average periodicity: Quarterly
Average no. pages: 76
Libraries: BL=PP.7617.rn; LIN (incomplete); NLI=Ir 8205 d 8; PSPL=820.5;
                                QUB=hAP4.D8; RIA=Fr C/2/3/E–G; TCD=Old Library; UCC
                                (1928–1958); UCD=J 820; UCG=052 (PS, incomplete).

This new series has almost no illustrations and more book reviews. The 'Editorial' to the first issue says that the magazine will now expand to cover other subjects, like science and economics; also, that its 'freedom will be construed entirely in conformity with spiritual principles'. This gives a prospectus uncannily like that of the nineteenth-century *Museums* or *Repertorys*, including general pieces with titles like 'Twenty Years Ago' and 'A Note on Light' to accompany its polite literature. It also reveals O'Sullivan's attitude towards censorship; throughout 1929, a number of comments appear in various contexts, including some by O'Sullivan himself, and the verdict is that generally it is a good thing, if only it is handled carefully.

Contributors include Beckett, Betjeman, John Boyd, George Buchanan, Herbert Butler, Joseph Campbell, Clarke, Colum, Edmund Curtis, Leslie Daiken, J. Lyle Donaghy, Lord Dunsany, Eglinton, Monk Gibbon, St. John Gogarty, Hewitt, Higgins, Kavanagh, Lavin, A.J. Leventhal, both MacDonaghs, McLaverty, James Stephens and W.B. Yeats. However, we should not be misled by the presence of one or two non-Revival or more confrontational writers: Beckett is represented by three poems and two short book reviews, McLaverty, Roy McFadden and Montague by just a handful of poems. This does not quite amount to self-censorship, but certainly some careful selection occurred.

In 1930, a series of bibliographies of Irish writers begins (Æ, Synge, Moore, etc.), while there is regular commentary on current French literature. Through 1932, the magazine maintains a fairly positive note on Joyce, e.g. in a review by Colum of *Haveth Childers Everywhere* in volume 6, number 3. And in 1936 Leventhal intrudes a couple of features on Dada and Surrealism in a new regular feature on art. However, like a number of previous Irish literary magazines, the *Dublin Magazine*'s success was based on conservatism, not innovation. From 1926, when O'Sullivan had established his successful formula, he stuck with it; the address, printer, cover, structure, tone and mix of contents hardly varied in thirty years and, despite the nods to France and Russia, it remains a provincial magazine. By the late 1940s, the parade of Crabbe and Vaughan, Swift and Allingham, with a sprinkling of poems from R.N.D. Wilson, Colum and Ewart Milne is looking very stale and tired. From 1950, room is made for more poems by Northerners like McFadden and Hewitt, and there is some innovation (pieces on Lorca, poems by R.S. Thomas, and (in volume 26, number 2) the full text of *Diarmuid and Grania*) but it was too late to make any real difference – the very last issue contains a translation from Rilke, a poem by Milne and a piece on Æ. New Romantics, Regionalism, Poetry of the Pylons, all flashed by leaving no lasting mark.

See Sean O'Faoláin, '1916–1941: Tradition and Caution', *The Bell*, 2, 1 (1941), p. 6.

See F. J. Hoffman, Charles Allen and C.F. Ulrich, *The Little Magazine: A History and a Bibliography*, (Princeton, 1946); reprinted New York, 1967, p. 387.

See Rudi Holzapfel, 'A Survey of Irish Literary Magazines from 1900 to the Present Day', M Litt thesis (Trinity College Dublin, 1964), p. 31.

See Rudi Holzapfel, 'A Note on the Dublin Magazine', *Dublin Magazine*, 4, 1 (Spring 1965), pp. 18–27.

See Terence Brown, *Ireland, A Social and Cultural History 1922–1985* (London, 1985), pp. 167, 226.

See Richard Burnham, 'Seumas O'Sullivan and The Dublin Magazine', PhD Thesis (UCD, 1977).

See Roger McHugh and Maurice Harmon, *A Short History of Anglo-Irish Literature* (Dublin, 1982), pp. 217, 221.

See Dillon Johnston, *Irish Poetry After Joyce* (Notre Dame, 1985), p. 41.

See Denman, Peter, 'Ireland's Little Magazines', Barbara Hayley, and Enda McKay (eds), *300 Years of Irish Periodicals* (Mullingar, 1987), p. 130.

See Edna Longley, '"It is time that I wrote my will": Anxieties of Influence and Succession', in Warwick Gould and Edna Longley (eds), *Yeats Annual No. 12* (London, 1996), pp. 117–162 *passim*.

See Brian Fallon, *An Age of Innocence: Irish Culture 1930–1960* (Dublin, 1998), pp. 13, 48, 51, 74, 78, 101, 102, 104, 105, 109, 113, 115, 118, 120, 121, 129, 130, 150, 223, 231–232, 234, 241, 259.

See Gerry Smyth, *Decolonisation and Criticism: The Construction of Irish Literature* (London, 1998), pp. 133–136.

See Edna Longley, '"Between the Saxon Smile and Yankee Yawp": Problems and contexts of Literary Reviewing in Ireland', Jeremy Treglown, and Bridget Bennett, *Grub Street and the Ivory Tower: Literary Journalism and Literary Scholarship from Fielding to the Internet* (Oxford, 1998), p. 207.

UCD Library has *The Dublin Magazine Index, vol.1 to vol. XV* (covers 1926–1940) at J820.

TCD library has a *Dublin Magazine Index 1926–52*, at OL 052.09415 DUB1.

An author index appears in Rudi Holzapfel, 'A Survey of Irish Literary Magazines from 1900 to the Present Day', M Litt thesis (Trinity College Dublin), 1964.

Rudi Holzapfel, *An Index of Contributors to The Dublin Magazine* (Dublin Museum Bookshop, 1966).

Author and (limited) subject index appears in Stephen H. Goode, *Index to Commonwealth Little Magazines* (New York and London, 1966).

An author index appears in Richard J. Hayes, *Sources for the History of Irish Civilisation: Articles in Irish Periodicals*, 5 vols (Boston, 1970).

Basic author index appears in Marion Sader, *Comprehensive Index to Commonwealth Little Magazines 1964–74*.

Continued as:

THE DUBLINER

Location:	Dublin (publisher New Square Publications, Ltd, No.3 TCD, Dublin 2, printer Irish Printers Ltd., 64 Aungier Street; from number 2, printer Athlone Printing Works; from volume 3, number 1, printer The Three Candles Ltd., Aston Place, Dublin 2; from volume 3, number 4, printer Mercury Press Ltd., Aston Place, Dublin 2)
Editor(s):	Donald Carroll (with five assistant editors); from number 2, Bruce Arnold; from volume 3, number 1, Rivers Carew and Timothy Brownlow
Dates:	Volume 1, number 1 (November–December 1961)–volume 3, number 4 (Winter 1964)
No. of issues:	14?
Average periodicity:	Bimonthly; volumes 2 and 3 quarterly
Average no. pages:	24 (issue 1), 56 (issues 2 and 3), then 80
Libraries:	BL=PP.7617.rn; LIN (incomplete); NLI=Ir 8205 d 8; PSPL=820.5; QUB=hAP4.D8; RIA=Fr C/2/3/E–G; TCD=OLS L-3-731, no.5; UCD=J 820; UCG=052 (PS, incomplete).

After Carroll's anomalous first issue (much larger in size, only 24 pages long, and carrying the unlikely declaration in its opening editorial that it is 'designed for an eclectic taste', will contain articles of deliberately limited interest, and will eschew consistency), the *Dubliner* made strenuous efforts to present itself as the continuation of O'Sullivan's *Dublin Magazine*. When Bruce Arnold took over as editor with the second number, he produced his own editorial explicitly stating this ambition, and that he would moderate the original eclecticism to focus more on Irish matters. Despite the presence of an ee cummings poem, he immediately makes good that claim with articles on 'The Poetry of WB Yeats', on censorship (by Frank O'Connor) and George Moore (Colum), and in fact the *Dubliner* does feel like a younger relation of the earlier *Dublin Magazine*, but a little more literary, a little less staid. With a good mix of reviews and original poetry, the quality improved steadily with each issue, with good essays on 'Proust and Joyce', on Æ, Beckett, Clarke, Francis Ledwidge, MacNeice, O'Casey, Somerville and Ross, and James Stephens; poetry by Eavan Boland, Clarke, Colum, Hamburger, Richard Kell, Kennelly, Longley, MacDiarmuid, Mahon, Ewart Milne, Montague, Richard Murphy and Jon Silkin; many short book reviews by the likes of Kennelly and Boland; as well as articles on topics such as Irish painters, or life in Ireland during the Second World War, the occasional story, and a fragment of autobiography by Robert Greacen.

With volume 3, number 2 the *Dubliner* began to mutate into its final form, gaining the device (the head of the goddess of the River Liffey, from the Custom House), which would adorn the cover until 1974. Two issues later comes an editorial announcement that, with the approval of Seumas O'Sullivan's widow, from Spring 1965 the publication will become *The Dublin Magazine*.

See Rudi Holzapfel, 'A Survey of Irish Literary Magazines from 1900 to the Present Day',
M Litt thesis (Trinity College Dublin, 1964), p. 76.

See Peter Denman, 'Ireland's Little Magazines', Barbara Hayley and Enda McKay (eds),
300 Years of Irish Periodicals (Mullingar, 1987), p. 139.

An author index appears in Rudi Holzapfel, 'A Survey of Irish Literary Magazines from
1900 to the Present Day', M Litt thesis (Trinity College Dublin, 1964).

See David Elyan and Rudi Holzapfel (eds), *The Dubliner, Vol.1, No.1–Vol.3, No.4, An
Index to Contributors* (New Square Publications, 1965).

A brief index appears in *The Dublin Magazine*, 4, 1 (Spring 1965).

Author and (limited) subject index appears in Stephen H. Goode, *Index to Commonwealth
Little Magazines* (New York and London, 1966).

An author index appears in Richard J. Hayes, *Sources for the History of Irish Civilisation:
Articles in Irish Periodicals*, 5 vols (Boston, 1970).

Continued as:

THE DUBLIN MAGAZINE

Location:	Dublin (publisher New Square Publications, Ltd., No.3 TCD, Dublin 2, from volume 8, number 1, publisher moves to 2–3 Duke Street, Dublin 2, from volume 9, number 1, publisher moves to 'Elstow', Knapton Road, Dun Laoghaire; printer Three Candles Ltd, Aston Place, Dublin 2; from volume 7, number 3 and 4, printer Leinster Leader Ltd, Naas)
Editor(s):	Rivers Carew and Timothy Brownlow; from volume 8, number 1, John Ryan (associate editor Kevin O'Byrne); from volume 8, number 7, to volume 10, number 2, 'Consultant Editor' Anthony Cronin
Dates:	Volume 4, number 1 (Spring 1965)–volume 10, number 3 (Autumn/Winter 1973/1974)
No. of issues:	25
Average periodicity:	Triannual (varies)
Average no. pages:	104; rising to 126
Libraries:	BL=PP.7617.rn; LIN; QUB=hAP4.D8 (incomplete); TCD=Gall M.37.57-63; UCD=J 820; UCG=052 (PS).

The mix of features does not undergo any radical change. The same core group of poets
(Boland, Clarke, Colum, Kennelly, Longley, Mahon, Montague) is supplemented by
several from the older generation (C. Day Lewis, Norman Dugdale, R.S. Thomas and
Kathleen Raine) and only a couple of new names (including Ní Chuilleanáin and Heaney).
The book reviews continue to be dominated by Boland and Kennelly, the only significant
addition (apart from the occasional piece by Michael Longley or Heaney) being Edna
Longley. Nevertheless, the magazine continues to improve and by volume 5 it has become
a first-class publication, at least as good as O'Sullivan's, and among the best of Irish
literary magazines.

There is a steady flow of good-quality articles on (mostly) Irish authors, now often supplemented by a short and useful bibliography: on Allingham, Auden, Colum, F.R. Higgins, Joyce, Kavanagh, Kennelly (by Edna Longley), Kinsella, Mary Lavin, MacNeice (Michael Longley), George Moore, O'Casey, Swift and Yeats (by Boland, Jeffares, Raine and Henn, amongst others). There is usually a story in each issue, the best of which is by Aidan Higgins, and while the editors maintain another of O'Sullivan's crusades, by keeping open a window on contemporary Europe with pieces on subjects like Kurt Weill, they also introduce some modest innovations, including themed issues. There are issues dedicated to Yeats's centenary, the Easter Rising, Swift's tercentenary and Kavanagh.

John Ryan took over as editor with volume 8, and signalled a fresh approach by dropping the 'formerly "The Dubliner"' tag from the cover. Of the previously published poets, only Montague, Ní Chuilleanáin, Kennelly and Dugdale continue to make regular appearances, and are joined by a wave of new writers: Anthony Cronin, Durcan, Michael Foley, John Wilson Foster, Greacen, John Heath-Stubbs, Pearse Hutchinson, John Jordan, Tom MacIntyre, William Oxley, Richard Ryan, Knute Skinner, Eithne Strong and MacDara Woods. Again, the magazine now feels a little more oriented towards prose; there are articles on Cronin, Joyce, Heaney, Kiely (J.W. Foster), George Moore, O'Flaherty, Brian O'Nolan, Bram Stoker, Francis Stuart, Swift, Synge, Dylan Thomas, Wilde and Yeats, by new contributors like Richard Kell; more, and better, stories (by Dominic Behan, Cronin, Desmond Hogan, Jordan, Kiely and George O'Brien); and many book reviews, in which the old faithfuls (Kennelly, Ní Chuilleanáin) are joined by, for example, Terence Brown.

See F.J. Hoffman, Charles Allen and C.F. Ulrich, *The Little Magazine: A History and a Bibliography* (Princeton, 1946); reprinted New York, 1967, p. 387.
See James Hogan, untitled article in the *Lace Curtain,* 1 (1969), pp. 35–38.
See Terence Brown, *Ireland, A Social and Cultural History 1922–1985* (London, 1985), p. 167, 226.
See Peter Denman, 'Ireland's Little Magazines', Barbara Hayley and Enda McKay (eds), *300 Years of Irish Periodicals* (Mullingar, 1987), p. 140.

An author index (up to 1969) appears in Richard J. Hayes, *Sources for the History of Irish Civilisation: Articles in Irish Periodicals*, 5 vols (Boston, 1970).

THE KLAXON, AN IRISH INTERNATIONAL QUARTERLY

Location:	Dublin (printed and published 179 Great Brunswick Street)
Editor(s):	Lawrence K. Emery (pseudonym of A.J. Leventhal); Holzapfel also suggests an editorial role for F.R. Higgins
Dates:	Winter 1923/1924
No. of issues:	1
Average periodicity:	Quarterly (intended)

Average no. pages: 28
Libraries: BL=PP.4881.tc; LIN; NLI=Ir 805 k 2; QUB=hAP4.K6; TCD=OLS;
                      JOH 138 no.13.

Ireland's first (and last?) fiercely Modernist magazine, with homages to Dada and Picasso and a strong internationalist commitment, the *Klaxon* was swimming against the stream in the Ireland of its day, and not just the forces of church and state, but also the new literary establishment. Levanthal's prime reason for producing this spirited one-off was the refusal of the *Dublin Magazine*, under pressure from their printers, to print his long review of *Ulysses*. This forms the centrepiece of *Klaxon* (under the Emery pseudonym), but it also includes another important piece, a translation of *The Midnight Court* by Percy Arland Ussher, as well as a photograph of an African carving, a poem from Higgins, and a personal essay by Thomas MacGreevy – and then it is gone. Stylish, provocative, promising, but evidently too strong for its contemporaries.

See Rudi Holzapfel, 'A Survey of Irish Literary Magazines from 1900 to the Present Day',
   M Litt thesis (Trinity College Dublin, 1964), p. 33.

An author index appears in Rudi Holzapfel, 'A Survey of Irish Literary Magazines from
   1900 to the Present Day', M Litt thesis (Trinity College Dublin, 1964).

THE ULSTER REVIEW, A PROGRESSIVE MONTHLY OF INDIVIDUALITY

Location: Belfast (publisher Ulster Review, 2 Victoria Square, printer Wm.
                      Sweeney, 153 Upper North Street)
Editor(s):   Alfred S Moore (June 1924–November 1925); J.R. Gregg (December
                      1925–April 1926)
Dates: Volume 1, number 1 (June 1924)–volume 2, number 10 (March/April
                      1926)
No. of issues: 22
Average periodicity: Monthly
Average no. pages: 24
Libraries: NLI=Ir 05 u 6; PSPL=052; QUB=pfAP4.U4 (volume 1, number 1,
                      volume 1, number 9 and volume 2, number 9 only).

Despite the bold title, this was quite a harmless – if occasionally eccentric – mix of articles on house coal and the Border, Belfast Corporation and international business, leavened with regular (if slight) literary pieces. The latter included poems by Padraic Gregory and Richard Rowley; reviews of books by Shane Leslie and Denis Ireland; and articles by F.J. Bigger, Richard Hayward, Leslie, Forrest Reid, Rowley and Doyle covering such topics as St. John Ervine, William Conor, Carleton and Rutherford Mayne. There is also a respectful interview with Arthur Conan Doyle. The *Ulster Review* is a pleasant, if unadventurous, read, and a perfect reflection of the mild frustrations and modest ambitions of the Belfast literary scene of the 1920s.

TO-MORROW

Location:	Dublin (publisher To-morrow, 13 Fleet Street); printed by Whitely and Wright Ltd, 30 Blackfriars Street, Manchester because no Irish printer would take it on
Editor(s):	'H. Stuart' (Francis Stuart) and Cecil Salkeld
Dates:	Volume 1, number 1 (August 1924)–volume 1, number 2 (September 1924)
No. of issues:	2
Average periodicity:	Monthly
Average no. pages:	8
Libraries:	BL=PP.7611.cac; NLI=LO; PSPL=079.415; RIA=Fr C/Sect 6/2 Misc. Newsp. Box; TCD=202.U.1, numbers 1A and 1B.

A famous victim of censorship, *To-morrow* – from the same loose grouping which produced the *Klaxon* – is starkly laid out, tabloid size, and very striking. The first issue contained, in addition to the two stories which caused such offence (Robinson's 'The Madonna of Slieve Dun' and O'Flaherty's 'A Red Petticoat'), Yeats's 'Leda and the Swan', poems from F.R. Higgins, R.N.D. Wilson and Campbell, an article on modern art with accompanying lino-cut by Salkeld, and a review of O'Flaherty's *The Black Soul* by Emery. Although signed by Salkeld and Stuart, the editorial to the first issue is actually by Yeats (attr. Holzapfel, Welch). Normally, such a collection of famous names would have been enough to guarantee a favourable reception for a new magazine, but the controversy over the two stories was enough to quickly bury *To-morrow*. The second, and last, issue carried an essay on Daumier by Arthur Symons, poems by Wilson, Higgins and Blanaid Salkeld, an essay by Iseult Stuart, an article on emerging poets by Emery – and an editorial by Stuart saying that they will continue the fight.

It was not to be, and it is impossible to tell on the basis of just two issues how it might have developed; it is unlikely that this level of quality could have been maintained for long, but *To-morrow* remains a work of great promise frustrated, and there is more artistic merit in its two issues than in all twenty-seven of the conformist *Banba* combined.

See Rudi Holzapfel, 'A Survey of Irish Literary Magazines from 1900 to the Present Day', M Litt thesis (Trinity College Dublin, 1964), p. 39.
See Terence Brown, *Ireland, A Social and Cultural History 1922–1985* (London, 1985), pp. 74–75.
See Daniel J. Murphy, *Lady Gregory, The Journals Volume I* (Gerrards Cross, 1978), pp. 563; 584; 590–593; 599; 605; 609; *passim* 670–675.
See F.J. Hoffman, Charles Allen and C.F. Ulrich, *The Little Magazine: A History and a Bibliography* (Princeton, 1946); reprinted New York, 1967, p. 275.
See Peter Denman, 'Ireland's Little Magazines', Barbara Hayley and Enda McKay (eds), *300 Years of Irish Periodicals* (Mullingar, 1987), p. 128.
See W.J. McCormack, *From Burke to Beckett: Ascendancy, Tradition and Betrayal in Literary History* (Cork, 1994), pp. 313, 317, 370.

An author index appears in Rudi Holzapfel, 'A Survey of Irish Literary Magazines from 1900 to the Present Day', M Litt thesis (Trinity College Dublin, 1964).

CONTEMPORARY POETRY, A MONTHLY PUBLICATION DEVOTED TO THE YOUNGER POETS OF THE ENGLISH LANGUAGE

Location:	Dublin (printer William Calton, 43 Dame Street (1925); then Goodridge Ltd., 9 Lower Baggot Street)
Editor(s):	George Edmund Lobo
Dates:	Volume 1, number 1 (March 1925)–volume 1, number 3 (May 1925); then number 1 (Spring 1926)–number 5 (1927)
No. of issues:	8
Average periodicity:	Monthly; then quarterly
Average no. pages:	20; then 16
Libraries:	BL=PP.5126.k; NLI=Ir 82189 c 83; TCD=98.d.112 (24 hours' notice).

An 'Announcement' in the first issue states its dedication to the 'interests of the poets who are as yet unknown to a reading public', and its intention to ignore established names. The cynical might suspect that the unknown poet Lobo was most interested in promoting was himself (Holzapfel suggests convincingly that most of the contributions were by Lobo, under a variety of pseudonyms), but in any case nothing of any consequence was published. From Spring 1926 the journal shrinks in size, and changes into *Contemporary Poetry and Song, The Organ of the Younger and More Thoughtful Poets*, whose publisher is Lobo himself (at 9 Lower Baggot Street). The final issue carries a bitter little editorial, announcing the end of the run.

See Rudi Holzapfel, 'A Survey of Irish Literary Magazines from 1900 to the Present Day', M Litt thesis (Trinity College Dublin, 1964), p. 35.
See F.J. Hoffman, Charles Allen and C.F. Ulrich, *The Little Magazine: A History and a Bibliography* (Princeton, 1946); reprinted New York, 1967, p. 276.

An author index appears in Rudi Holzapfel, 'A Survey of Irish Literary Magazines from 1900 to the Present Day', M Litt thesis (Trinity College Dublin, 1964).
An author index appears in Rudi Holzapfel, *Author Index 3*, Carraig Books Ltd., (Blackrock, 1985), pp. 57–58.

THE NORTHMAN

Location:	Belfast (publisher QUB, printer T.H. Jordan, 47–49 Upper Church Lane)
Editor(s):	Anon.
Dates:	Volume 1, number 1 (December 1926)–volume 3, number 6 (Summer 1932)

No. of issues: 18
Average periodicity: Quarterly
Average no. pages: 44
Libraries: BL=PP.6180.ch (incomplete); LIN (volume 1, number 1 (December 1926)–Volume 1, number 5 (March 1928); volume 2, number 1 (December 1928)–volume 2, number 4 (December 1929); volume 3, number 1 (January 1931)–volume 3, number 6 (Summer 1932); NLI=Ir 3784105 n 4 (incomplete); QUB=qLH5.N8; TCD=126.h.91 (v. incomplete)

Starting out like so many other student rags, full of reports from the clubs and facetious jokes, in its second volume some verse and prose by the students begin to appear. However, in this first incarnation, the story of the *Northman* as a literary magazine is little more than a listing of the material published in its pages by the young John Hewitt, the only significant writer they attracted. Either under his name, or the initials 'J.H.H', he contributed twenty-seven poems, eight stories, four book reviews and obituaries of Vachel Lindsay and D.H. Lawrence.

Continued as:

THE NEW NORTHMAN

Location: Belfast (publisher 'Publication Committee (SRC) at the Queen's University of Belfast', printer T.H. Jordan, 47–49 Upper Church Lane)
Editor(s):   Anon.; from volume 9, number 2, John Gallen and Robert Greacen
Dates: Volume 1, number 1 (Winter 1932)–volume 9, number 3 (Autumn 1941)
No. of issues: 27
Average periodicity: Triannual
Average no. pages: 26
Libraries: LIN (volume 6, number 1 (Spring 1938)–volume 6, number 3 (Autumn 1938); volume 9, number 3 (Autumn 1941); NLI=Ir 3784105 n 3; QUB=qLH5.N8; UCG=052.1 (incomplete).

Despite the change of name, through the 1930s the contents carry on much as before, with the only pieces of note still the occasional poem or story by Hewitt (although volume 2, number 1 (Winter 1933–1934) does carry a short article on poetry by J.C. Beckett). However, the most significant part of the *Northman*'s history begins in 1940 with a bloodless coup by a new generation of poets – Greacen, McFadden, Alex Comfort, May Morton, John Gallen – who contribute a couple of dozen poems, two or three stories, and some interesting articles over the next couple of years. The latter include one on the Apocalyptic Movement by Henry Treece and another on Yeats by Denis Ireland (volume 11, number 1). Volume 9, number 2 sports the subtitle 'Ulster's only literary magazine', as well as Gallen and Greacen as editors.

Continued as:

THE NORTHMAN

Location:	Belfast (publisher Student Representative Council, Queen's University Belfast, printer T.H. Jordan, 47–49 Upper Church Lane)
Editor(s):	W.N. Howe and A.B. Morrison; from volume 12, number 1, Dorothy Eagleton and Michael Cochrane; from volume 14, number 3, Grizel Christie and Michael Cochrane; from volume 15, number 1, A.G. Donaldson; from volume 15, number 2, H. Kacser and R.B. Tate; from volume 16; number 1, I.S. MacBeath and W.H.C. Smith; from volume 16, n4, D. O'Neill and J.K. Devlin; from volume 17, number 1, E. Jackson, J.K. Devlin and D. O'Neill
Dates:	Volume 11, number 2 (Winter 1942–3)–volume 17, number 1 (Spring 1950)
No. of issues:	22
Average periodicity:	Triannual
Average no. pages:	32
Libraries:	LIN (volume 11, number 2 (Winter 1942–1943); volume 13, number 1 (Autumn 1944); QUB Centenary Number, 1945; volume 14, number 3 (Spring 1946); volume 15, number 1 (Autumn 1946)–volume 15, number 2 (Winter 1946) only); QUB=qLH5.N8 (last few years (1941–1950) are not bound, and about five issues are missing); RIA=AP 1945 (QUB centenary issue only).

With the reversion to the original name, the fightback begins (see the editorial to volume 11, number 2, which expresses a desire to return to a more populist stance) and, although the new breed still appears, it does so less and less frequently. Still, in these last years one may find worthwhile material: articles such as 'A Survey of Ulster Writing', Greacen (volume 11, number 2), or 'A Note on Contemporary Ulster Writing', McFadden (volume 15, number 2); stories by Denis Ireland, McFadden and Gerard Keenan; a handful of poems, by new writers like Barbara Hunter, as well as by Greacen, McFadden and so on. The issue celebrating the centenary of Queen's in 1945 is particularly good, with contributions from most of the old hands, and the obituary article and poems for John Gallen (volume 15, number 3) are also of good quality. However, the editorial to the last number carries an ominous warning that the magazine is in trouble.

See A.G. Donaldson, 'Editorial', *Northman*, 15, 1. (A reply to an attack on the *Northman* in *Lagan*, by John Boyd).

See Robert Greacen, untitled article in *The Bell,* 5, 5 (February 1943), pp. 397–399.

See Norman Vance, *Irish Literature: A Social History – Tradition, Identity and Difference* (Oxford, 1990), p. 218.

THE HEARTHSTONE, THE STORY MAGAZINE OF IRELAND

Location: Dublin (publisher 68 Upper O'Connell Street, printer Brunswick Press)
Editor(s):   Anon.
Dates: Volume 1, number 1 (May 1927)–volume 5, number 12 (April 1932)
No. of issues: 60
Average periodicity: Monthly
Average no. pages: 28
Libraries: BL=PP.6193.kb (incomplete); NLI=Ir 05 h 1; RIA=Fr C/1/5/A, Misc Box DH (incomplete).

An undemanding commercial venture whose aims can quickly be grasped from the presence of a good deal of advertising for Catholic publications and references to 'healthy reading', and from the appearance in almost every one of the first twelve issues of those stalwarts of pre-Revolutionary Celticism, Alice Furlong and Ethna Carbery. It was obviously a considerable success, and occasionally printed a more substantial item, e.g. a long story by Corkery (April 1928), or shorter pieces by Tynan (January 1932) or Cathal O'Byrne (February 1932). Generally, however, its aims were low and its sales were high.

See Rudi Holzapfel, 'A Survey of Irish Literary Magazines from 1900 to the Present Day',
    M Litt thesis (Trinity College Dublin, 1964), p. 36.

AN ULSTER GARLAND 1928, AN OCCASIONAL PUBLICATION IN AID OF THE HOSPITAL FOR SICK CHILDREN BELFAST

Location: Belfast (printer McCaw, Stevenson and Orr, Ltd, The Linenhall Works)
Editor(s):   Editorial committee (including Forrest Reid)
Dates: 1928
No. of issues: 1?
Average periodicity: Unknown
Average no. pages: 56
Libraries: BL=PP.6193.kdb; LIN=U.8/ULST; QUB=hAP4.U3.

A luxurious, if peripheral, publication (colour cover, high-quality woodcuts and photographic plates), contributors include Æ, plus almost the full roll-call of established literary talent in Northern Ireland at the time: Lynn Doyle, St. John Ervine, Forrest Reid, Richard Rowley, and illustrations from J. Humbert Craig, Paul Henry and William Conor.

THE ULSTER BOOK

Location:	Belfast (publisher Quota Press, 124 Donegall Street, printer F.J. Henry and Sons, Marquis Street)
Editor(s):	Ruddick Millar
Dates:	No.1 (1929)
No. of issues:	1?
Average periodicity:	Unknown
Average no. pages:	32
Libraries:	BL=PP.6180.ck; NLI=Ir 05 u 5.

The first issue has an article on 'The Drama in Ulster', a story by Thomas Carnduff, and poems by Carnduff and Millar himself. *The Ulster Book* is a little stuffy, but a decent effort; no more can be said on one issue.

THE CAPUCHIN ANNUAL

Location:	Dublin (publisher The Father Mathew Record Office, from 1940 publisher Capuchin Periodicals Office, from 1944 publisher's address changes to 2 Capel Street, from 1946 to Church Street; printer John English and Co., Wexford, from 1958, printer Dollard Printinghouse, Dublin)
Editor(s):	Fr Senan; from 1955, eds Fr Felix and Fr Henry; from 1956/57 ed. Fr Henry, 'Manager' Fr Virgilius; from 1971, Manager Fr Anthony; from 1974, Manager Fr Robert Noonan; from 1977, Manager Fr Anthony Boran
Dates:	1930–1977
No. of issues:	48
Average periodicity:	Annual
Average no. pages:	338; 522 (1953/1954–1969); 440 (1970–1977)
Libraries:	BL=PP.6193.kc; BCL=I/282.05 CAPU; LIN; NLI=Ir 2713 c 15; PSPL=052; QUB=hAP4.C2 (incomplete); RDS=NL53; RIA=RR Gall/37/G; TCD=58.tt.101; UCC (incomplete); UCD=J 941.5; UCG=255.36 (PS).

[The first issue claims a print run of 15,000; by 1940 the editorial is claiming that 25,000 copies were printed of that issue.]

With this publication the Catholic periodical in Ireland moves to a higher level. It is both less narrow and doctrinaire than, e.g., the *Catholic Book Bulletin*, and its production values are far higher (glossy, good-quality paper, lots of photographs, and regular colour prints). The bulk of the content is still devotional, but it is leavened with both fine art and literature, each issue usually including one literary article, one story and two or three poems.

These include: stories by Corkery, Kiely, McLaverty (a regular contributor) and Mervyn Wall; poems by de Blacam, Pearse Hutchinson, Benedict Kiely, Donagh MacDonagh, McGreevy, Pearse, Joseph Plunkett, Rowley, and Francis Stuart; and articles by Corkery, de Blacam, Gabriel Fallon (on the Abbey, 1937), Padraic Gregory ('Ulster's Contribution to Anglo-Irish Literature', 1940), Kiely, Compton MacKenzie, McGreevy and Cathal O'Byrne.

Despite this list, it is important to remember that literary material is very thin on the ground, and sprinkled throughout the long run, and after 1949 in particular, comes in short bursts, interspersed by periods of silence. For example: 1949–1952 includes a long article on Mangan (de Blacam), and two poems from Cathal O'Byrne; from 1953/54–1963, there is still some verse and prose, but it is entirely devotional and of poor quality, and by the end of this period the magazine is starting to look very old-fashioned indeed. During the years 1964–1966, there is an autobiographical piece by Brinsley MacNamara, a story by Mervyn Wall, and an article by Augustine Martin on James Stephens; from 1966–1970 there is very little literary material once again, and a substantial proportion of the magazine during 1966–1971 is given over to celebrating the anniversary of the Easter Rising; the 1970s see a number of poems and an obituary by Padraic Fiacc, a couple of poems from Conleth Ellis, an article on T.S. Eliot, and another on the state of the world by Arthur C. Clarke! After this flourish, the 1977 issue says that it will be the last published.

See Thomas Fox, 'Capuchin Annual, 1946–47', *Irish Bookman,* 1, 9 (April–May 1947), pp. 49–53.
See Rudi Holzapfel, 'A Survey of Irish Literary Magazines from 1900 to the Present Day', M Litt thesis (Trinity College Dublin, 1964), p. 91.
See Brian Fallon, *An Age of Innocence: Irish Culture 1930–1960* (Dublin, 1998), pp. 198, 235.

An author index (up to 1969) appears in Richard J. Hayes, *Sources for the History of Irish Civilisation: Articles in Irish Periodicals*, 5 vols (Boston, 1970).

INISFÁIL: A QUARTERLY MAGAZINE

Location:	Dublin (published 37 St Lawrence Road, Clontarf; printer Redmond Bros., The Printing House, Wafer Street, Enniscorthy)
Editor(s):	Margaret Spain ('Mary Kavanagh')
Dates:	Number 1 (December, January and February 1930/31)–volume 1, number 2 (March, April and May 1931)
No. of issues:	2
Average periodicity:	Quarterly (intended)
Average no. pages:	32
Libraries:	NLI=IR 05 i 24.

No connection with the *Inisfáil* which would be published three years later.

A highly eccentric production, including verses, one-act plays, stories, travel writing, translations from Heine, and two extended essays (one on Einstein, the other on Dante), every word of it by 'The Misses Spain', who heighten the sense of strangeness by using both their real and assumed names (varieties of Kavanagh), often on the same piece. A lightweight magazine, with an air of pious Catholicism.

THE ULSTER FREE LANCE, A PUBLICATION OF THE BELFAST WRITERS' CLUB

Location:	Belfast (printer Dorman and Co.)
Editor(s):	William Carter
Dates:	April 1932
No. of issues:	1?
Average periodicity:	Unknown
Average no. pages:	12
Libraries:	LIN.

An extremely slight production, in all senses, comprising one poem, one or two very short stories, and a couple of articles, the most substantial of which is May Morton's 'Literature – its place in life'.

The copy in the Linenhall Library includes a short, typed note by Carter, on the Belfast Writers' Club.

MOTLEY

Location:	Dublin (publisher Dublin Gate Theatre, Rotunda Buildings; printer Powell Press, 22 Parliament Street; also published in London by Beaumont, 75 Charing Cross Road)
Editor(s):	Mary Manning
Dates:	Volume 1, number 1 (March 1932)–volume 3, number 4 (May 1934)
No. of issues:	19
Average periodicity:	Monthly (with breaks during the summer months)
Average no. pages:	16
Libraries:	BL=PP.5196.i; NLI=Ir 391941 m 3 (January 1933–May 1934 only); TCD=79.a.121.

Mostly a theatre magazine, but makes room for the occasional poem by the likes of John Betjeman, Austin Clarke, Padraic Colum, Cyril Cusack, Bryan Guinness, Blanaid Salkeld, and Francis Stuart; a couple of articles by O'Faoláin (e.g. 'Provincialism and Literature', volume 1, number 3); and one interesting, if slightly chilling, longer piece. 'A Proposal for the Strengthening of the Censorship' (volume 2, number 5), by 'An Associate of the Irish Academy', condemns the loopholes in the censorship legislation and suggests a logical, final solution: the banning of all imported books and periodicals ('...our own thought is good enough, and we can well do without the productions of modern intellectuality so called...').

See Rudi Holzapfel, 'A Survey of Irish Literary Magazines from 1900 to the Present Day', M Litt thesis (Trinity College Dublin, 1964), p. 39.

See F.J. Hoffman, Charles Allen and C.F. Ulrich, *The Little Magazine: A History and a Bibliography* (Princeton, 1946); reprinted New York, 1967, p. 394.

An author index appears in Rudi Holzapfel, 'A Survey of Irish Literary Magazines from 1900 to the Present Day', M Litt thesis (Trinity College Dublin, 1964).

INISFÁIL, PUBLISHED TO MAINTAIN A SYMPATHETIC CONTACT BETWEEN IRISHMEN LIVING ABROAD

Location:	Dublin (publisher Hibernian Bank Chambers, St. Andrew Street, printer Parkgate Printing Works; also Lincoln's Inn Fields, London)
Editor(s):	Anon.
Dates:	March 1933
No. of issues:	1
Average periodicity:	Monthly (intended)
Average no. pages:	16
Libraries:	LIN.

Quite a glossy production, well illustrated, including some good plates. An anthology, this issue includes poems by Allingham, Emily Bronte, Ferguson, Thomas Moore and Rowley; stories by Shan Bullock and Francis Stuart; plates of illustrations by Paul Henry and John Lavery; and articles by Stephen Gwynn, Peadar O'Donnell, O'Faoláin and Brian Ua Nualláin.

No connection with Margaret Spain's *Inisfáil* of three years before.

See Rudi Holzapfel, 'A Survey of Irish Literary Magazines from 1900 to the Present Day', M Litt thesis (Trinity College Dublin, 1964), p. 40.

THE ULSTERMAN

Location:	Belfast (publisher The Ulster Publishing Co., 1a Hope Street, printer Dorman and Co., 1a Hope Street; with the third issue, the publisher moved to 5 Wellington Place)
Editor(s):	Anon.
Dates:	April 1933–July 1933
No. of issues:	4
Average periodicity:	Monthly
Average no. pages:	32
Libraries:	BL=PP.6193.kd; LIN; QUB=pqAP4.U5; RIA=Fr C/5/2/G Misc Box S–Z.

With its bold colour cover, this is a general magazine, with many articles on topics such as education, public finance and pig production, but it includes a sprinkling of literary material. As well as a regular drama column and some inferior poems and stories, there are articles by Denis Ireland and Helen Waddell, a reprint of a Thomas Davis poem, stories by Jack Loudan and Thomas Carnduff, and a number of short book reviews (including books by George Buchanan, Colum, Moira O'Neill and Waddell). The most interesting piece is a short interview with Bernard Shaw in the third issue.

THE IRISH STORYTELLER, 'THE MAGAZINE OF THE PEOPLE'

Location: Cork (publisher and printer The Lee Press, 21/22 South Terrace)
Editor(s):   Anon.
Dates: August 1935–November 1935
No. of issues: 3
Average periodicity: Monthly
Average no. pages: 24
Libraries: NLI=Ir 05 i 27.

An entertaining, popular paper, with some poems, anecdotes, and so on, as well as stories; none of them is any good.

See Rudi Holzapfel, 'A Survey of Irish Literary Magazines from 1900 to the Present Day', M Litt thesis (Trinity College Dublin, 1964), p. 42.

IRELAND TO-DAY, SOCIAL, ECONOMIC, NATIONAL, CULTURAL

Location: Dublin (publisher 'Editorial and Managerial Offices', 49 Stafford Street; printer Wood Printing Works)
Editor(s):   Michael O'Donovan (Frank O'Connor)
Dates: Volume 1, number 1 (June 1936)–volume 3, number 3 (March 1938)
No. of issues: 22
Average periodicity: Monthly
Average no. pages: 86
Libraries: BL=PP.6189.e; BCL=IR; LIN; NLI=Ir 05 i 25 (1971 reprint (Kraus Reprint Co., NY, 3 vols)); PSPL=052; QUB=hAP4.I71 (bound into 4 vols, first with short author index to vols 1 and 2); RDS=NL163; RIA=Fr C/2/1/D; TCD=92.p.7–74; UCC; UCD=J 050; UCG=052 (PS).

As the subtitle suggests, this was a general cultural and political review. If the *Irish Review* brought the concept of the Great Review into the twentieth century, transforming it into a new genre, a cross between the Great Review and the Little Magazine (the 'Little Review'?), then *Ireland To-Day* is the missing link between the *Irish Review* and *The Bell*.

The mix in a typical issue would include half a dozen essays (on literary topics, but also politics, economics, foreign affairs), plus a story and a couple of poems; each issue ended with the review section, which again covered art, music, cinema, as well as books (the books reviews were edited by O'Faoláin).

Again, like *The Bell*, the list of contributors is as varied as it is impressive: Erskine Childers, Brian Coffey, Colum, Corkery, Edmund Curtis, Denis Devlin, Ruth Dudley Edwards, Padraic Gregory, Bulmer Hobson, Patrick Kavanagh, Shane Leslie, Donagh MacDonagh, Eoin MacNeill, Michael McLaverty, Ewart Milne, T.W. Moody, Frank O'Connor, Peadar O'Donnell, O'Faoláin, Ernest O'Malley, Brian Ó Nualláin, Forrest Reid, Lennox Robinson, Owen Sheehy Skeffington and Mervyn Wall.

A feeling of the range may be given by listing the subjects of a few essays, which include archaeology, William Orpen, slum clearance, industrialisation, road safety and Lady Gregory. It is Nationalist, but far less hysterical than its 1920s precursors, and admits some complexities; socialist (or at least socially concerned); it has regular bulletins from the North; is extremely wide-ranging; and attracted the best of its generation. It was perhaps a little less radical, a little less literary, and the quality was perhaps slightly lower than that of *The Bell*, but it is most unfair that the later magazine has stolen most of its glory.

See Rudi Holzapfel, 'A Survey of Irish Literary Magazines from 1900 to the Present Day', M Litt thesis (Trinity College Dublin, 1964), p. 43.

See Roger McHugh and Maurice Harmon, *A Short History of Anglo-Irish Literature* (Dublin, 1982), p. 236.

See Terence Brown, *Ireland, A Social and Cultural History 1922–1985* (London, 1985), pp. 169–170.

See Peter Denman, 'Ireland's Little Magazines', Barbara Hayley and Enda McKay (eds), *300 Years of Irish Periodicals* (Mullingar, 1987), p. 132.

See Brian P. Kennedy, 'Ireland To-day, A brave Irish periodical', *Linenhall Review,* 5, 4 (Winter 1988), pp. 18–19.

A short author index to vols 1 and 2 is bound into the first of the four QUB volumes.

An author index appears in Rudi Holzapfel, 'A Survey of Irish Literary Magazines from 1900 to the Present Day', M Litt thesis (Trinity College Dublin, 1964).

An author index appears in Richard J. Hayes, *Sources for the History of Irish Civilisation: Articles in Irish Periodicals*, 5 vols (Boston, 1970).

A basic, online author index to *Ireland To-Day* by Mark McCloskey, can be found at www.may.ie/academic/english/itd.htm

LEAVES ('BILLEOGA'), POLITICAL-LITERARY-IRISH-IRELAND

Location: Dublin (publisher 5 Trinity Street, printer Cahill and Co., Ltd, Parkgate Printing Works)

Editor(s):   Anon.

Dates:	NLI has only volume 1, number 2 (February 1938)
No. of issues:	2?
Average periodicity:	Monthly
Average no. pages:	40
Libraries:	BL=PP.6189.f; NLI.

Highly political ('...forward the cause of the Sovereign Independence of Ireland, one, undivided and indivisible'), the single issue examined carries four essays, in both Irish and English; the quality is very poor.

See Rudi Holzapfel, 'A Survey of Irish Literary Magazines from 1900 to the Present Day', M Litt thesis (Trinity College Dublin, 1964), p. 44.

ON THE BOILER

Location:	Dublin (publisher Cuala Press, 133 Lower Baggot Street, printer Alex. Thom and Co., Ltd.)
Editor(s):	W.B. Yeats
Dates:	October 1938
No. of issues:	1
Average periodicity:	–
Average no. pages:	48
Libraries:	BL=Cup.407.a.4; NLI=LO; PSPL=828/YEA; QUB=hpPR5904/ON; TCD(Old Library)=Press A Cuala A.b.5; UCC (original; also 1971 reprint by Irish Universities Press).

From the 'Preface' – 'In this new publication I shall write whatever interests me at the moment...'. The remainder is a long, highly personal ramble covering art, censorship, 'Ireland after the Revolution', and much else besides. It includes a 'Crazy Jane' poem, and the text of *Purgatory*.

See Rudi Holzapfel, 'A Survey of Irish Literary Magazines from 1900 to the Present Day', M Litt thesis (Trinity College Dublin, 1964), p. 46.
See F.J. Hoffman, Charles Allen and C.F Ulrich, *The Little Magazine: A History and a Bibliography* (Princeton, 1946); reprinted New York, 1967, p. 347.
See John Kelly, *The Collected Letters of WB Yeats*, Volume 3: 1901–1904 (Oxford, 1994), p. 76n.

An author index appears in Rudi Holzapfel, 'A Survey of Irish Literary Magazines from 1900 to the Present Day', M Litt thesis (Trinity College Dublin, 1964).
Author and (limited) subject index appears in Stephen H. Goode, *Index to Commonwealth Little Magazines* (New York and London, 1966).
An author index appears in B.C. Bloomfield, *An author index to selected British 'little magazines', 1930–1939* (London, 1976).

THE BELL, A SURVEY OF IRISH LIFE

Location: Dublin (publisher Cahill and Co., 43 Parkgate Street, from volume 12, number 1 Cahill moves to 2 Lower O'Connell Street, from volume 16, number 2 publisher 14 Lower O'Connell Street; printer Cahill and Co., Ltd., Parkgate Printing Works, from volume 16, number 2, printer The Fleet Printing Co., Ltd, 6–7 Eccles Place, from volume 18, number 1 printer Cahill and Co., Ltd, Parkgate Street)

Editor(s):   Seán O'Faoláin; from volume 1, number 5 Poetry Editor: Frank O'Connor, Editorial Board: Maurice Walsh, Roisin Walsh, Eamonn Martin, Peadar O'Donnell; from volume 2, number 4 O'Connor joins Editorial Board, Geoffrey Taylor becomes Poetry Editor; from volume 12, number 1 O'Donnell takes over as editor, Louis MacNeice becomes Poetry Editor; from volume 17, number 2 Associate Editor: Anthony Cronin, Book Section: Hubert Butler, Music: John Beckett; from volume 18, number 1 Associate Editor: Anthony Cronin, Music Editor: John Beckett; from volume 19, number 8 shrunk back down to Associate Editor: Anthony Cronin

Dates: Volume 1, number 1 (October 1940)–volume 19, number 11 (December 1954) (publication suspended April 1948–November 1950)

No. of issues: 123

Average periodicity: Monthly (volume 1, number 1–volume 16, number 1); bi-monthly (volume 16, number 2–volume 19, number 11)

Average no. pages: 72; 64 (volume 18, number 1–volume 19, number 10)

Libraries: BL=PP.5938.bcq; LIN; NLI=Ir 05 (microfilm); PSPL=820.5; QUB=hAP4.B48 (incomplete); RDS=NL54; RIA=Fr C/Sect 1/1/F (v. incomplete); TCD=OLS L-2-50-69; UCC; UCD=J 820 (also on microfilm); UCG=800 (PS).

The mythical stature *The Bell* has acquired as the apotheosis of the Irish literary magazine is in large measure due to ignorance of the competition; however, no iconoclasm is called for, as it really is one of the finest literary magazines this country has produced. Its pluralist, liberal editorial stance is forty years ahead of its time; the range of topics covered, while vast, never becomes bewildering due to the anchor that stance provides; it has the vitality and direct connection to the cultural life of its time of the best Little Magazine, but the longevity and authority of a Review. No examination of the social and cultural history of Ireland during this period could be complete without an examination of its contents. Based at least partly on *Horizon*, the run commenced with a fitting editorial, discussing the choice of title: '...we could not have used any of the old symbolic words...'; 'All our symbols have to be created afresh... with all the vigour of the life we live in the Here and Now...'; '...if you look through this first number, you will see several things whose merit is not chiefly Art but Truth...'; '...Whoever you are, then, O reader, Gentile or Jew, Protestant or Catholic, priest or layman, Big House or Small House – THE BELL is yours.'

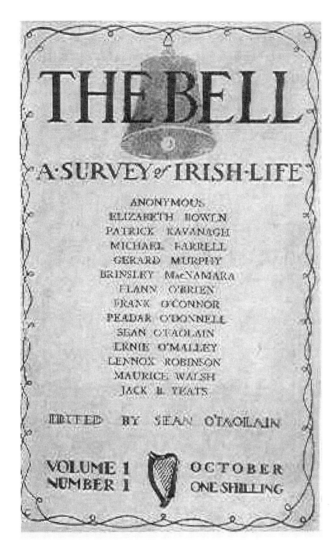

Any attempt to summarise the achievement of *The Bell* is immediately faced with an obvious problem: how to condense without reductionism, how to represent without endless lists? Firstly, every issue kicks off with an editorial, and O'Faoláin's editorials themselves would bear reproduction; their flavour and importance to the project rivalled those of Addison or Steele, and can be conveyed by noting that the most commonly repeated title for these discursions was 'One World'. Almost every issue has a column on drama; book reviews are never very long, nor are there very many of them. There is also a regular column, 'The Belfry', to introduce new writers, including at the start John MacDonagh, John Hewitt and Bryan MacMahon.

As for the rest, the eclecticism and quality are established in the first four issues, with stories by Lynn Doyle, Flann O'Brien, O'Connor, Peadar O'Donnell, O'Faoláin and Jack B. Yeats; poems by Kavanagh, C. Day Lewis and Donagh MacDonagh; short reviews by

Elizabeth Bowen, Denis Johnston, Mac Liammóir and O'Faoláin. Even at the start, one of the glories of *The Bell* is established, that is, the wide-ranging, polemical and just plain interesting general article: 'The Trade in Dublin', (O'Brien); articles on prisons, on teaching, slum life, theatre, furniture (O'Faoláin), juvenile crime, new plays, window displays, on Jack B. Yeats (O'Faoláin again), or standards in English. A variety of miscellaneous pieces completes the mix, including a fragment of autobiography from Robinson, short prose pieces by Bowen, Michael Farrell and Jack B. Yeats, 'Æ, A Portrait' (Frank O'Connor), translations from the Irish by Arland Ussher, and even a one-act play by Lennox Robinson.

With the fifth issue Frank O'Connor joins as Poetry Editor and, although poetry never was given the prominence in *The Bell* which most modern Irish literary magazines afford it, his choices were a little more contemporary; poems included came from Greacen, Kavanagh, Bryan MacMahon, Roibeard O'Farachain, and W.R. Rodgers. Another benefit from O'Connor's participation was the publication of part of his translation of 'The Midnight Court'. There were stories by O'Faoláin and Jack B. Yeats, a fragment of autobiography from Maura Laverty, and more of the general articles: on TB, dance halls (O'Brien), Belfast street songs, country bookshops, sea trout, St. Patrick's day (Doyle), 1916 ballads, fisheries, lino-cuts, Dublin street rhymes, O'Flaherty (O'Faoláin), unemployment and illegitimacy. The sense of *The Bell*'s being a harbinger of change was negatively reinforced by the inclusion in these issues of obituaries of Yeats (O'Connor), F.R. Higgins (O'Faoláin) and Joyce (Bowen).

With the start of the third volume, Geoffrey Taylor took over as Poetry Editor of a magazine which was established, confident – and successful (according to the editorial to volume 1, number 2 the first issue had sold out). *The Bell* now enters into its prime, an inspiring run which took it into its eleventh volume. The cream of the post-war generation are represented here, with poems from Maurice James Craig, Greacen, Gogarty, Sam Harrison, Hewitt, Hutchinson, Valentin Iremonger, Kavanagh, Donagh MacDonagh, MacNeice, McFadden, Colin Middleton, O'Connor and W.R. Rodgers; stories by Sam Hanna Bell, Patrick Campbell, MacMahon, O'Connor, O'Faoláin, James Plunkett and Terence de Vere White; and novel extracts from Gibbon, Kavanagh, Maura Laverty and O'Donnell. 'The Belfry' was replaced by 'The Bellman', in which we were invited to 'Meet' various writers, including Elizabeth Bowen. The team of reviewers was strengthened by the inclusion of Hubert Butler, John Hewitt, Valentin Iremonger, Vivian Mercier and Geoffrey Taylor, while more snippets of autobiography appeared, by Carnduff, Mac Liammóir and Robinson. The feast of general articles offered by *The Bell* in its prime is stunning, and can only be hinted at by listing the subjects: Dublin architecture, country doctors, the music hall, migration, 'Censorship, Law and Conscience', 'The Poetry of John Hewitt' (Taylor), 'Censorship: Principle and Practice', planning, theatre (Rutherford Mayne), novels (O'Faoláin), Allingham (Taylor), 'The Poetry of Austin Clarke' (Maurice James Craig), arts and crafts, 'Sex, Censorship and the Church', children's cinema, dancing classes (Bowen), Hugh O'Neill (O'Faoláin), 'Crime in Dublin', 'People and Pawnshops', 'Women in Public Life', Lennox Robinson, *War and Peace* (O'Faoláin), 'Crime in Dublin', anti-Semitism (O'Donnell), Joyce (O'Connor), literary activity in Belfast (Greacen), mathematics, 'Speaking as an Orangeman' (by 'One of Them'), hospitals, O'Casey (O'Faoláin), Irish cheese, nursing, new paintings, 'Other People's Incomes', 'Publishing in Ireland', 'Poetry in Ireland, A Discussion' (McFadden and Taylor), the Irish in Britain (O'Donnell), Lorca, India, boxing, 'Women in Politics' (Hanna Sheehy-Skeffington), history teaching, 'Our Canning Industry', 'The Craft of the Short Story' (O'Faoláin), music teaching, TB, 'Protestantism Since the Treaty', 'I Did Penal Servitude' (by 'D83222'), 'In Defence of Censorship' (Monk Gibbon), replies to Gibbon (from Shaw and O'Casey), theatre (O'Connor), cock-fighting, Thomas Davis, Jack B. Yeats, cinema, 'The Art of Mary Lavin', and James Joyce.

Another innovation of *The Bell* in this period, and one which was to be an example to future Irish literary magazines, was the 'themed' issue. These included: a 'Special Ulster Number' (volume 2, number 4 – poems by Hewitt and Rodgers; article on the Ulster Workhouse; stories by Doyle and McLaverty); 'The Five Strains' (volume 2, number 6 – on the influence of Gaelic, Latin, Norman French, Anglo-Irish and English on Irish writing); 'An Ulster Number' (volume 4, number 4 – more comprehensive and successful than the earlier attempt, with poems by Hewitt and Rodgers; a story by Sam Hanna Bell; 'Meet Rutherford Mayne' with the Bellman; a symposium, 'The Best Books on Ulster' (with contributions from Carnduff, Craig, Greacen, Doyle, Hewitt, Ireland, Mayne and Joseph Tomelty); translations from the Greek Anthology, by Forrest Reid; an article by Carnduff; and a one-act play from George Shiels); another issue devoted to Ulster (Volume 4, number 5), including 'Conversation Piece: An Ulster Protestant', by Rodgers; an article on Ulster writers, another on Colin Middleton (Hewitt); a stories by Rodgers and Doyle; and an Ulster folk tale. Volume 5, number 1 was a 'stories issue' (Bowen, Maura Laverty, O'Connor, O'Faoláin); volume 5, number 6 an 'International Number', containing Osbert Sitwell's autobiography, and articles on the Second World War (Alex Comfort), music (Arnold Bax) and P.G. Wodehouse. Two more issues with an international flavour were volume 8, number 6 (poems by Grigson, and article on Hardy (Day Lewis), and a poem in Irish), and volume 10, number 4. Finally, there was volume 8, number 5, a 'Summer Number' (unusually, this had twelve pages of photographs). One important aspect of *The Bell*'s commitment to openness and pluralism which is almost unique in this period is its open window to the North; three issues (volume 4, number 5, which is dominated by Ulster writers, and the two dedicated Ulster numbers) are given over almost entirely to strong voices from the fourth green field, while it is a rare number of the magazine which has no input from that quarter.

With volume 12, O'Donnell took over as editor, and the tenor of the magazine changed substantially, becoming less of a general review of Irish society, and more of a traditional literary magazine; the quality of the literary items is higher than for some time. O'Donnell's editorship is overshadowed by the brilliance of O'Faoláin's achievement, but it represents much more than a period of slow decline. In fact, although he soon ran into trouble (perhaps confirming that the Irish are not interested in great numbers in a purely literary magazine, and prefer their poetry leavened by more general pieces), for a while it looked like *The Bell* was entering on to a second high plateau. O'Donnell's *Bell* is slightly more prosy, and less interested in poetry, with more reviews; although it has to be acknowledged that the improvement in quality is partly because O'Faoláin is now free to contribute more. The next four volumes include: a novel extract from Kate O'Brien; stories by Hewitt, Kiely, Lavin, MacMahon, David Marcus, Michael J. Murphy, O'Faoláin and James Plunkett; and more serious reviews, by Louis le Brocquy, Butler, Clarke, Gibbon, Gogarty, Greacen, Hutchinson, Iremonger, Kavanagh, O'Casey, O'Donnell, O'Faoláin, Taylor and Mervyn Wall. The stable of poets is little changed: Day Lewis, Gibbon, Sam Harrison, Hewitt, Pearse Hutchinson, Iremonger, Kavanagh, MacNeice, McFadden, Milne, Rodgers and Taylor. The 'Bellman' column continues, allowing us to 'Meet Mr Patrick Kavanagh', and 'Meet Frank O'Connor', and there is another fragment of autobiography, this time from Denis Johnston. However, the general articles have lost some of their old sparkle, while becoming more literary (and taking themselves a little more seriously); we have: 'Aspects of Poetry Today' (Iremonger), 'The Satires of Eimar O'Duffy' (Mercier), Dunsany on Joseph Campbell, O'Faoláin on Shaw, 'The Poetry of F.R. Higgins' (Taylor), 'Poetry in Ireland Today' (Clarke), 'Tom Moore' (Taylor), 'Louis MacNeice: A First Study' (Iremonger), 'Songs of the Orangemen' (E.R.R. Green), 'Coloured Balloons, A Study of Frank O'Connor' (Kavanagh), 'Poetry in Ireland To-Day' (Kavanagh), and 'Some Aspects of Yeats and His Influence' (Cronin). In keeping with this trend, a couple of more substantial literary pieces are published, including an extract from *Tarry Flynn* (volume 14, numbers 2, 3, and 6), a verse drama by Iremonger (volume 14, number 4), and a long poem by Kavanagh (volume 15, number 2).

Volume 15, number 3 (April 1948) opens with an editorial address 'To Our Readers', revealing the magazine's growing financial problems, but vowing to carry on. Again, O'Donnell's more literary editorial line should not be entirely blamed for these; as he points out, the gap in the finances is at least partly due to the British Board of Trade restrictions on the import of Irish books (number 4 carries an article on this embargo). The editorial to volume 16, number 1 carries the sombre announcement: '*The Bell* Suspends Publication'; continuing problems caused by the British import restrictions, have led to a sober reflection: 'I have been of the opinion that the original impulse in *The Bell* has exhausted itself, and that if we are to serve any real purpose we must move closer to the problems of the moment – domestic and international.' It would be six months before *The Bell* was to reappear.

Volume 16, number 2 came out in November 1948, with a new subtitle ('A Magazine of Ireland To-Day'), reflecting O'Donnell's new focus. Anthony Cronin is now associate editor, and a new generation of Irish writers begins to appear alongside the survivors of the old regime: stories by the likes of Mary Beckett, Brian Friel and David Marcus; articles by Butler, Cronin and John Montague, (e.g. 'The Tyranny of Memory, A Study of George Moore'); and poems by Cronin and Richard Murphy. Perhaps as a result of Cronin's influence, the articles are in a narrower cultural/literary vein ('Belfast is an Irish City' (Carnduff), 'Tribute to William Carleton' (Montague), 'Letter from the North' (Buchanan), 'Some Notes on Writing in Ulster' (Hewitt), a piece on Eugene O'Neill, another on the Orange Order (O'Donnell), on Samuel Beckett and on Irish Protestants (Butler)); poetry is also afforded greater importance than for some time (alongside e.g. Hewitt, McFadden,

Montague and Milne, are introduced more new voices – Donald Davie, Padraic Fallon and Thomas Kinsella; Murphy's 'Voyage to an Island' is first published here).

However important the new literary material, and courageous the decision to plough more of a high cultural furrow, the last phase of *The Bell* was not a commercial success, and the signs of decline are all too apparent in its last years; from volume 18, number 1 even the physical dimensions of the magazine are smaller. The previous elaborate editorial structures, with various boards and specialist sub-editors, disappears, leaving just O'Donnell and Cronin. Even in its dotage, however, *The Bell* published material which would not have shamed its lesser rivals: poems by Cronin and Kavanagh; novel extracts from Kiely and O'Donnell; short stories by Mary Beckett and O'Flaherty; and stimulating reviews by Butler. In a bravura flourish, the penultimate issue (volume 19, number 9), takes the form of a collection of five short stories by James Plunkett, entitled *The Eagles and the Trumpets and other stories*.

See Richard Furze, '*The Bell, 1940–1954*', PhD thesis, UCD.

See Anon, *Irish poems of today: Chosen from the first seven volumes of the Bell* (Dublin, 1944).

See Vivian Mercier, 'The Fourth Estate, VI – Verdict on – The "Bell"', *The Bell*, 10, 2 (July 1945) pp. 156–164.

See 'Scrutator', 'Verdict on "The Bell"', *The Bell,* 10, 5 (October 1945) pp. 431–437.

See James Delahanty, 'The Bell: 1940–1954 [1]', *Kilkenny Magazine,* 1 (Summer 1960), pp. 32–37.

See James Delahanty, 'The Bell: 1940–54 (2)', *Kilkenny Magazine,* 2 (Autumn 1960), pp. 32–38.

See Richard J. Loftus, *Nationalism in Modern Anglo-Irish Poetry* (Wisconsin, 1964), pp. 19, 20, 193, 289n, 320–21.

See Paul Doyle, 'Seán O'Faoláin and *The Bell*', *Eire-Ireland,* 1 (Fall 1966), pp. 58–62.

See F.J. Hoffman, Charles Allen and C.F. Ulrich, *The Little Magazine: A History and a Bibliography* (Princeton, 1946); reprinted New York, 1967, p. 401.

See Rudi Holzapfel, 'A Survey of Irish Literary Magazines from 1900 to the Present Day', M Litt thesis (Trinity College Dublin, 1964), pp. 48–49.

See Dermot Foley, 'Monotonously Rings the Little Bell', *Irish University Review*, 6, 1 (Spring 1976), pp. 54–62.

See Hubert Butler, 'The Bell: an Anglo-Irish view', *Irish University Review*, 6, 1 (Spring 1976), pp. 66–72.

See Séan MacMahon, *The Best from 'The Bell'* (Dublin, 1978).

See Christopher Harries, 'The Hawk in its Flight', *Cork Review,* 2, 3 (June 1981), pp. 16–17.

See Roger McHugh, and Maurice Harmon, *A Short History of Anglo-Irish Literature* (Dublin, 1982), pp. 217, 234–235, 236, 249–250.

See Richard Kearney, 'Between Politics and Literature: The Irish Cultural Journal', *Crane Bag,* 7, 2 (Autumn 1983), pp. 160–171. Mentions *The Bell*.

See Hugh Bredin, 'Making War on the Thicks', *Fortnight,* 203 (April 1984), p. 20. Review of *The Best of the Bell*.

See Terence Brown, *Ireland, A Social and Cultural History 1922–1985* (London, 1985), pp. 176, 178, 196, 199–206; *passim* 208–215, 226–228, 257, 285, 296–298.
See Dillon Johnston, *Irish Poetry After Joyce* (Notre Dame, 1985), pp. 8–9, 41, 132.
See Seamus Deane, *Celtic Revivals* (London, 1985), p. 146.
See Peter Denman, 'Ireland's Little Magazines', Barbara Hayley and Enda McKay (eds), *300 Years of Irish Periodicals* (Mullingar, 1987), pp. 133–134.
See Norman Vance, *Irish Literature: A Social History – Tradition, Identity and Difference* (Oxford, 1990), p. 218.
See Roy Foster, *Paddy and Mr Punch* (London, 1993), pp. 111–112, 115, 117–118.
See Robert Greacen, 'An Irish Bennett', *Books Ireland,* 182 (December 1994), p. 318. Discusses O'Faoláin and *The Bell.*
See Declan Kiberd, *Inventing Ireland* (London, 1995), p. 366.
See John Goodby, 'New Wave I: 'A Rising Tide'; Irish Poetry in the 60s', in Theo Dorgan, *Irish Poetry Since Kavanagh* (Dublin, 1996), pp. 116–135, *passim.*
See Steven Curran, '"No, This is Not From *The Bell*": Brian O'Nolan's 1943 *Cruiskeen Lawn* Anthology', …*Éire-Ireland,* 32, 2 and 3 (Summer/Fall 1997), pp. 79–92. Commentary on O'Nolan's critique of *The Bell.*
See Brian Fallon, *An Age of Innocence: Irish Culture 1930–1960* (Dublin, 1998), pp. 13, 53, 70, 102, 127, 130, 176, 191, 232–234.
See Gerry Smyth, *Decolonisation and Criticism: The Construction of Irish Literature* (London, 1998), pp. 114–117.

An author index appears in Mary Grogan and E. Murray, *Index to the Bell*, for the Fellowship of the Library Association of Ireland, nd.
An author index appears in Rudi Holzapfel, 'A Survey of Irish Literary Magazines from 1900 to the Present Day', M Litt thesis (Trinity College Dublin, 1964).
An author index appears in Rudi Holzapfel, *An Index of Contributors to The Bell*, 1970.
An author index appears in Richard J. Hayes, *Sources for the History of Irish Civilisation: Articles in Irish Periodicals*, 5 vols (Boston, 1970).

"N"

Location: Dublin (first 7, editor's address c/o UCD; last issue 'Published by the Directors of "N", University College, Dublin, and printed by the Harcourt Press, 93, Harcourt Street, Dublin')
Editor(s):   Anon.
Dates: I.1 (nd)–II.2 (November 1941)
No. of issues: 8?
Average periodicity: Impossible to say; II.1 has poems dated 1939 and 1941, and II.2 is dated November 1941, so it is likely that all were produced during 1941
Average no. pages: 1; last issue 4
Libraries: UCD=SC 34.Va.1/1-7 (I.3 and I.4 missing).

The most extreme piece of ephemera I have yet come across – most of these issues are simply a single, roughly-typed A4 page, with as many poems on them as could be fitted in (usually three). At the bottom of one side a line is hand-drawn in ink, and below that a large letter "N". They mostly seem to have been mimeographed; only the last was printed, and it is no more than four sides of thin, green card, with a large "N" printed on the front, plus a number and date; three poems (typeset this time), and brief printing details at the end. One of the issues is not numbered (and so is likely the first?). None of the poets represented became well-known, and none of the poems is any good; the most frequent contributors are John V. Hoey, followed by Denise Murphy so, to judge by similar publications, it is at least likely that they were involved in an editorial capacity.

THE CIRCLE, ORGAN OF THE DUBLIN WRITERS' CIRCLE

Location:	Dublin (publisher Dublin Writers' Circle, 34 North Frederick Street, printer Frederick Press, South Frederick Lane)
Editor(s):	Liam Grant
Dates:	Volume 1, number 1 (December 1941)–volume 1, number 11 (Winter 1946)
No. of issues:	11
Average periodicity:	Quarterly
Average no. pages:	64
Libraries:	NLI=Ir 8205 c 6; TCD=31.nn.60, numbers 1–6 (first 6 issues only; 24 hours' notice).

Ostensibly to provide a platform for new writers, but the first issue rather gives the game away with its reference to 'the alien and Godless conception of life with which the great bulk of 'cross-Channel literature is informed'. The material is of very poor quality (the most significant contributions being one or two pieces each from Michael J. Murphy and Val Mulkerns), but it is interesting as an example of the kinds of attitude and self-imposed handicap which crippled many Irish outlets for writers in this period. The cover layout and subtitle change with every issue ('Organ of the Dublin Writers' Circle', 'Irish Magazine of New Writing', etc.).

An author index appears in Rudi Holzapfel, 'A Survey of Irish Literary Magazines from 1900 to the Present Day', M Litt thesis (Trinity College Dublin, 1964).
An author index appears in Rudi Holzapfel, *Author Index 3*, Carraig Books Ltd, (Blackrock, 1985), pp. 93–101.

ULSTER PARADE

Location:	Belfast (publisher The Quota Press, printer Belfast News-Letter, Donegall Street)

Editor(s):   Anon.
Dates: Numbers 1 (Summer 1942?)–12 (Winter 1946?) (calculated from hand-written dates on some issues in LIN)
No. of issues: 12
Average periodicity: Quarterly?
Average no. pages: 48 (first issue), 76 (2nd), then 112 (3–9); 68 (10–12)
Libraries: BL=X.989/26115IN; NLI=Ir 8208 u 4; PSPL=828; QUB=hPR8891.U4 (numbers 5 and 11 only); TCD=125.t.21–22.

First two numbers subtitled 'with humour to the fore'. A wartime morale-boosting exercise, with light verse, reminiscences, stories, belles lettres; the quality is fairly poor, and the most important author published is 'John o' the North'. One interesting aspect is how it embodies the unconscious side of the regionalism which wartime isolation developed in the six counties. Last issue has an insert saying that they are going to 'pause before promising further issues'.

See Rudi Holzapfel, 'A Survey of Irish Literary Magazines from 1900 to the Present Day', M Litt thesis (Trinity College Dublin, 1964), p. 52.

An author index appears in Richard J. Hayes, *Sources for the History of Irish Civilisation: Articles in Irish Periodicals*, 5 vols (Boston, 1970).

ULSTER VOICES

Location: Lisburn (publisher Ulster Voices Publications, 36 Magheralave Road, printer Thos. Johnstone, 75 Gt. Victoria St., Belfast)
Editor(s):   Roy McFadden and Robert Greacen
Dates: Number 1 (Spring 1943)–number 4 (December 1943)
No. of issues: 4
Average periodicity: Quarterly
Average no. pages: 6 (single folded sheet)
Libraries: LIN; NLI=Ir 82189 p 49; TCD=138.b.60, numbers 17–19.

A simple, small and stylish poetry broadsheet, folded into a more portable format, this is a most elegant response to wartime paper restrictions. Apart from short editorials, this title is entirely given over to poetry, and includes work by John Boyd, Alex Comfort, Robert Greacen, John Hewitt, Valentin Iremonger, Roy McFadden, Colin Middleton and Richard Rowley. With the last issue, the title changes to *Irish Voices*.

See F.J. Hoffman, Charles Allen and C.F. Ulrich, *The Little Magazine: A History and a Bibliography* (Princeton, 1946); reprinted New York, 1967, p. 367.

PUCK FARE

Location:	Dublin (published by the Writers' Guild of the WAAMA, 6 Merrion Sq.; printer Frederick Press)
Editor(s):	D.J. Giltinan, Associate Editor Desmond Ryan
Dates:	Christmas 1943
No. of issues:	1 issue only, not numbered
Average periodicity:	–
Average no. pages:	64
Libraries:	LIN (incomplete); NLI=Ir 3919 p 3; TCD=44.b.138.

An extremely lightweight but entertaining collection of stories, poems, and illustrations; Lennox Robinson contributes a memoir of Lady Gregory, Lynn Doyle a poem; there are also a couple of articles on the Irish theatre.

See Rudi Holzapfel, 'A Survey of Irish Literary Magazines from 1900 to the Present Day', M Litt thesis (Trinity College Dublin, 1964), p. 55.

LAGAN, A COLLECTION OF ULSTER WRITING

Location:	Lisburn (publisher Lagan Publications, Ballymacash, Lisburn; printer Lisburn Herald, from number 2 printer John Aitken and Son, Ltd; the third and fourth numbers are subtitled 'A Miscellany of Ulster Writing')
Editor(s):	John Boyd (numbers 3–4 = Associate Editors John Hewitt, Jack Loudan, David Kennedy and Roy McFadden)
Dates:	Number 1 (1944)–number 4 (1946; described on title page as 'Volume 2, No.1')
No. of issues:	4
Average periodicity:	Biannual (varies)
Average no. pages:	108; number 4 76
Libraries:	LIN (number 2 missing); NLI=numbers 1 (Ir 824 L 25), 2 (Ir 824 L 26) and 3 (Ir 824 L 27); PSPL=828; QUB=hAP4.L1 (number 1 (1944), 2 (1945) and 3 (1945) only; number 3 has had 11 pages ripped out); TCD=126.b.27, numbers 18–19.

This is a very good magazine, and despite its occasional lapse into *bell-lettrisme* it is unfortunate that it did not last longer; the quality is consistently high, and it also has an unusual degree of cohesion, around an implicit Ulster Regionalist agenda. Easily the best Ulster literary magazine since *Uladh*, forty years before, *Lagan* also kept one window open to internationalism (e.g. the handful of 'Poems from the Czech' in number 4), while providing serious treatment of the fine arts, including the new generation emerging, and is a league above its Northern contemporaries (*Ulster Parade*, *Ulster Quill*, etc.).

It has stories by Sam Hanna Bell, John Boyd, Gerard Keenan, Michael McLaverty and Joseph Tomelty; poems by M.J. Craig, Greacen, Sam Harrison, Hewitt, MacNeice, McFadden, May Morton, W.R. Rodgers and Rowley (as well as one by the painter, John Luke); substantial articles by J.C. Beckett ('The Anglo-Irish Tradition in Literature'), Buchanan, Hewitt (including the definitive credo, 'The Bitter Gourd, Some Problems of the Ulster Writer') and Denis Ireland; reviews, by Boyd, Hewitt and others; and a fragment of autobiography by Ireland. Issue 4 is a much diminished beast, although it has two substantial pieces; it opens with 'Armagh: The City Set on a Hill', the script of a radio broadcast by W.R. Rodgers, and also contains Hewitt's long poem 'Freehold'. Hewitt's main contributions ('The Bitter Gourd', and the poems 'Freehold' and 'Once Alien Here'), and Boyd's editorials (especially the last), form the core canon of Ulster Regionalism, supplemented by others (e.g. the pieces on the theatre in the province in the last issue), and come as close to a clear statement of principles as was perhaps possible.

See Roy McFadden, 'Reflections on Megarrity', *Threshold*, 5, 1 (Spring/ Summer 1961), pp. 28–29.

See Rudi Holzapfel, 'A Survey of Irish Literary Magazines from 1900 to the Present Day', M Litt thesis (Trinity College Dublin, 1964), p. 54.

See Peter K. McIvor, 'Regionalism in Ulster: An Historical Perspective', *Irish University Review*, 13, 2 (Autumn 1983), pp. 180–188, *passim*.

See Dillon Johnston, *Irish Poetry After Joyce* (Notre Dame, 1985), p. 41.

See Norman Vance, *Irish Literature: A Social History – Tradition, Identity and Difference* (Oxford, 1990), p. 218.

See Tom Clyde, 'Uladh, Lagan and Rann: The "Little Magazine" comes to Ulster', in Eve Patten, *Returning to Ourselves* (Belfast, 1995), pp. 145–153.

See Edna Longley, '"Between the Saxon Smile and Yankee Yawp": Problems and contexts of Literary Reviewing in Ireland', Jeremy Treglown and Bridget Bennett, *Grub Street and the Ivory Tower: Literary Journalism and Literary Scholarship from Fielding to the Internet* (Oxford, 1998), p. 209.

See Gillian McIntosh, *The Force of Culture* (Cork, 1999), pp. 268 and 292, also footnotes to pp. 215, 266, 293 and 301.

An author index appears in Richard J. Hayes, *Sources for the History of Irish Civilisation: Articles in Irish Periodicals*, 5 vols (Boston, 1970).

ULSTER QUILL, A MISCELLANY OF SHORT STORIES AND ARTICLES

Location:	Bangor (publisher S. Napier, 3 Alfred Street, printer John Aiken and Son, Ltd., 60 Great Victoria Street, Belfast)
Editor(s):	Samuel Napier
Dates:	Number 1 (March 1944)
No. of issues:	1?
Average periodicity:	Unknown

Average no. pages: 28
Libraries: BL=12359.f.20; LIN.

A selection of lightweight stories 'by Ulster journalists & short story writers', the only remotely significant piece to appear is an article on the future of Ulster theatre, by Joseph Tomelty.

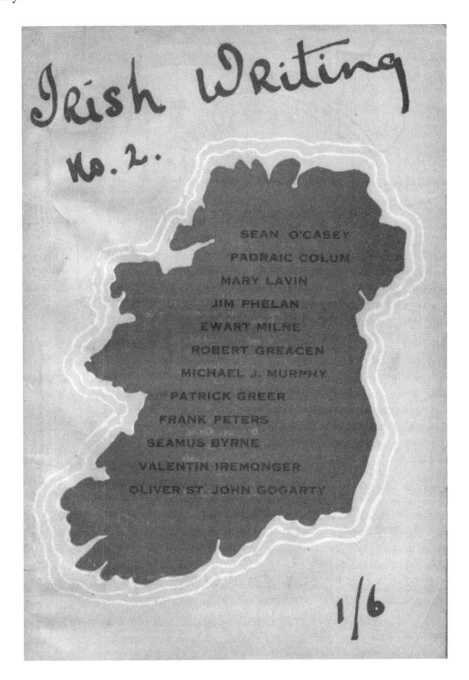

IRISH WRITING, THE MAGAZINE OF CONTEMPORARY IRISH LITERATURE

Location:	Cork (publisher Irish Writing, 15 Adelaide Street, from number 29 publisher Trumpet Books, 37 Leinster Road, Rathmines, Dublin; printer The Kerryman, Ltd, Russell Street, Tralee (1), Southern Star, Ltd., Skibbereen (2–8), D. and A. O'Leary Ltd., 25 Washington Street, Cork (9–28), from number 29 printer Nationalist Press) Clonmel
Editor(s):	David Marcus and Terence Smith; from number 29 S.J. White; number 33 Guest Editors Seamus O'Neill and Valentin Iremonger
Dates:	Number 1 (1946)–number 37 (Autumn 1957)
No. of issues:	37
Average periodicity:	Annual (1), biannual (2–3), then three or four per year
Average no. pages:	116 (1), then 96 (2–8), then 78 (9–24), then 64
Libraries:	BL=PP.6158.de; BCL (Kraus Reprint of issues 1–13; originals of numbers 11, 23, 29, 30, 34–36 and 37); LIN; NLI=Ir 82108 i 2; PSPL=820.91; QUB=hAP4.I9 (reprint of numbers 1–28 (Kraus Reprint, Nendeln, Lichenstein, 4 vols, 1970); then originals of 29–35 and 37); RIA=Fr C/1/6/A (incomplete); TCD=102.r.41, numbers.1–37; UCC; UCD=J 820; UCG=800 (PS, incomplete).

Despite the tweeness of the opening editorial ('[Irish writing is] half a gypsy as she goes her way, with a posy of wildness, to the world') and the garishness of the original cover, the contents of this magazine are often first-class, in particular the stories, by Mary Beckett, Joyce Cary, Myles na gCopaleen, Denis Ireland, Benedict Kiely, Mary Lavin, Sean Lucy, Donagh MacDonagh, Michael McLaverty, Michael J. Murphy, Kate O'Brien, Frank O'Connor, Sean O'Faoláin, Liam O'Flaherty, James Plunkett, Jean-Paul Sartre, Georges Simenon, Somerville and Ross, James Stephens and Mervyn Wall. All the most prominent poets of the day are also well-represented: Cronin, Day Lewis, Dunsany, Gogarty, Hewitt, Hutchinson, Iremonger, Joyce, Kavanagh, Richard Kell, MacNeice, McFadden, Milne, Strong and Stephens. Most these authors also contributed articles, usually on other writers (e.g. Vivian Mercier on Kate O'Brien or Greacen on Allingham) or related topics (Butler on censorship). There are a number of more substantial pieces, like the section of O'Casey's autobiography in number 12, the extracts from *Watt*, and from work in progress by Bowen or Francis Stuart. These are augmented by a steadily increasing number of short reviews.

From numbers 20–33 most issues include a small section at the back marked 'Supplement to "Irish Writing"', and edited by David Marcus; this is the 'undead' version of *Poetry Ireland*, an attempt to keep the name going after the magazine itself had folded (see entry on *Poetry Ireland* for details).

While many of the established favourites (Cary, Iremonger, Wall) continue to feature, under White's editorship new names begin to appear – Donald Davie, Dan Davin, Patrick Galvin, John Jordan, Thomas Kinsella – and he also experiments with themed issues (number 31 is a special Yeats number, with contributions from such academic critics as Peter Allt and Hugh Kenner, while number 33 focuses on writers in Gaelic, including Seán

Ó Riordáin and Maire Mac an tSaoi). He also publishes an extract from *Malone Dies*, some of Clarke's autobiography and the script of a radio play by Brendan Behan.

While it has no unifying agenda, and the quality of individual issues can vary dramatically, *Irish Writing* is a substantial achievement, gathering together the finest Irish writers from a variety of different camps into an eclectic mix.

See Anon., review of *Irish Writing* 21st birthday issue, *Quarryman*, December 1952, p. 43.

See Rudi Holzapfel, 'A Survey of Irish Literary Magazines from 1900 to the Present Day', M Litt thesis (Trinity College Dublin, 1964), p. 58.

See Roger McHugh and Maurice Harmon, *A Short History of Anglo-Irish Literature* (Dublin, 1982), pp. 236, 289.

See Terence Brown, *Ireland, A Social and Cultural History 1922–1985* (London, 1985), pp. 226–227.

See Peter Denman, 'Ireland's Little Magazines', Barbara Hayley and Enda McKay (eds), *300 Years of Irish Periodicals* (Mullingar, 1987), p. 135.

See Shirley Kelly, 'A Passionate Affair', *Books Ireland,* 179 (September 1994), pp. 193–195. Interview with Marcus, briefly covers *Irish Writing*.

See Brian Fallon, *An Age of Innocence: Irish Culture 1930–1960* (Dublin, 1998), pp. 13, 222, 235.

See Gerry Smyth, *Decolonisation and Criticism: The Construction of Irish Literature* (London, 1998), pp. 120–122.

An author index appears in Rudi Holzapfel, 'A Survey of Irish Literary Magazines from 1900 to the Present Day', M Litt thesis (Trinity College Dublin, 1964).

An author index appears in Richard J. Hayes, *Sources for the History of Irish Civilisation: Articles in Irish Periodicals*, 5 vols (Boston, 1970).

An author index appears in Rudi Holzapfel, *Author Index 3*, Carraig Books Ltd., (Blackrock, 1985), pp. 103–122.

Continued as:

NEW IRISH WRITING

Location:	Dublin (publisher and printer Burgh Quay, Dublin 2)
Editor(s):	David Marcus; from 1 January 1987, Anthony Glavin
Dates:	27 April 1968–8 April 1988
No. of issues:	900?
Average periodicity:	Weekly
Average no. pages:	1
Libraries:	BCL=IR; BL(Colin); NLI=2 anthologies ed. David Marcus – 1970–Ir 8208 m 10, 1976–Ir 82391 m 99; PSPL=079.415 (also the two anthologies=820.8); QUB=2 anthologies – 1970-hPR8844/5, 1976–hPR8844/6; RDS=NL51; TCD=Per Dept – 1931–77 in Newspaper Room, 1978 onwards in Microfilm Cabinet; UCD=STORE (also the two anthologies – Gen 820.8 IR MAR).

The first appearance of *NIW* in the *Irish Press* is accompanied by a short editorial, the only one to appear by Marcus – 'In the past thirty years or so Ireland has had a succession of literary magazines of which most enjoyed only a fleeting existence. Some, however, did achieve a decent life-span, together with a measure of distinction and a reputation far beyond this island – among these being, I believe, "Irish Writing", which I founded in 1946. Today, in an Ireland where accomplishment and promise have begun to create an atmosphere of real encouragement, there should be some publication whereby the greatest number of Irish writers can regularly have their work placed before the greatest possible number of Irish readers. The economics of magazine publishing being what they now are, the time is perhaps ripe to look to a national newspaper for the resources, the courage, and the breadth of vision to promote such a venture. That this weekly page of new Irish writing should find a willing sponsor in "The Irish Press", which in the past has numbered among its contributors many of Ireland's most famous authors, is, therefore, both fitting and proper. Together we aim not only to publish work by established Irish writers, but also to discover and foster the as yet unknown voices. The first issue of "Irish Writing", this page's spiritual predecessor, declared its concern to be with "what is vital in Irish letters" and this it pledged itself to present "in all its abounding variety." In "New Irish Writing" the pledge is undimmed; the pledge is renewed.'

Without giving too much credence to this slightly self-serving picture, it does capture nicely both Marcus's frustration, which is the frustration of every Little Magazine editor with the limitations of the medium, and his imaginative way out of the impasse. Indeed, I have not included any ordinary newspaper books pages in this study but, as a continuation of *Irish Writing*, this publication deserves to be made an exception. *NIW* appeared every Saturday in the *Irish Press*, and from the start had a strong emphasis on stories (see Marcus's introduction to the 1976 anthology, in which he worries about the survival of the short story), including samples by John Banville, Ita Daly, Aidan Higgins, Desmond Hogan, John B. Keane, Kiely, Lavin, Maurice Leitch, John McGahern, Janet McNeill, Brian Moore, Edna O'Brien, O'Faoláin, Julia O'Faoláin and William Trevor. There are also poems by Durcan, Hartnett, Heaney, Hewitt, Kell, Kennelly, Kinsella, C. Day Lewis, Lucy, Mahon, Montague, Muldoon, Simmons, Eithne Strong and Terence de Vere White.

After the first couple of years, signs of a slight reduction in commitment by the *Irish Press* begin to appear; first of all, *NIW* is generally reduced to half a page; by the 1980s, it is moved to Thursdays, and sometimes does not appear at all; within another year or two, it is moved about willy-nilly to suit the demands of the paper. Marcus finally ends his tenure on the issue for 25–27 December 1986, with a short editorial saying that Anthony Glavin will take over.

Whether it is a comment on Glavin's inferior taste and contacts, or on his commitment to new, unknown writers, the general standard of contributions under his regime is definitely inferior. In any event, this is not a happy period for *NIW*, even though on 11 April 1987 he announces the Hennessy Literary Awards for the best stories published in *NIW* in the previous year; their run in the *Irish Press* ends just a year later; on the following Monday the *Press* is relaunched as a downmarket tabloid. The authors featured in these last two years include: Mary Beckett, Dermot Bolger, Gerald Dawe, Greacen, Rita Ann Higgins, Bernard MacLaverty, Eithne Strong and Matthew Sweeney.

As with similar productions in the past (the *Nation*, the *Irish Homestead/Statesman*), the literary content of this incarnation of *NIW* looks like a small, unimportant section of the larger newspaper, but it must be remembered that, over the twenty years, it amounted to over 1,000 pages, which is equivalent to perhaps eight or ten issues of a standard literary magazine like *HU* or *Poetry Ireland Review*.

See David Marcus, *New Irish Writing 1, An Anthology from* The Irish Press series (Dublin, 1970).

See David Marcus, *New Irish Writing, from* The Irish Press *series* (London, 1976).

See Tony Farmer, '700 words by mid-October', *Books Ireland,* 47 (October 1980), p. 183. Interview with David Marcus, covering *New Irish Writing* and the *Irish Press*.

See Shirley Kelly, 'A Passionate Affair', *Books Ireland,* 179 (September 1994), pp. 193–195. Interview with Marcus, briefly covers *New Irish Writing*.

Continued as:

NEW IRISH WRITING

Location:	Dublin (publisher and printer 15 Lower Baggot Street, Dublin 2)
Editor(s):	Ciaran Carty, 'consultant editor' David Marcus
Dates:	6 November 1988–present
No. of issues:	200 (to date)
Average periodicity:	Weekly; from January 1991, Monthly
Average no. pages:	1
Libraries:	BCL=Newspaper Library; BL(Colin); NLI=Newspaper Floor; PSPL=Newspapers; TCD= Newspaper Room.

Seven months after it faded from the pages of the *Irish Press*, the seemingly irrepressible *NIW* appears again, this time in the *Sunday Tribune*; an announcement, including a potted history of *NIW* by Marcus, on 23 October 1988 says that it will start from the following week. The format is exactly the same: a single page, with the *NIW* logo at the top, and carrying usually a story and perhaps one or two poems. This time there are stories from: Dermot Bolger, Desmond Hogan, Frank McGuinness, Joseph O'Connor and Mary E. O'Donnell; and poems by: Eavan Boland, Sam Burnside, Dawe, Theo Dorgan, Paul Durcan, Seamus Heaney, Joan McBreen, John Montague and Matthew Sweeney.

From around Easter 1989, the ballast of contributions from famous names starts to run out, and more and more of the names are unknown (the most prominent now are Sara Berkeley, Clare Boylan, Evelyn Conlon and Janet Shepperson (stories), and Michael Foley, Greacen, Paula Meehan, Conor O'Callaghan and Woods (poems).

From August 1989, they are often reduced to three-quarters of a page or less, and in October the page is suspended, supposedly for the duration of the presidential campaign. In reality, it is three months before it reappears, this time restricted to the first Sunday of each month, and after this the heart seems to have gone out of the enterprise, and the quality of the material declines.

IRISH BOOKMAN

Location:	Dublin (publisher and printer 2–3 Yarnhall Street; from volume 1, number 12, printer Mahon's Printing Works)
Editor(s):	Seamus Campbell
Dates:	Volume 1, number 1 (August 1946)–volume 3, number 1 (December 1948)
No. of issues:	19
Average periodicity:	Monthly (until volume 2, number 1), then varies widely
Average no. pages:	96
Libraries:	BL=PP.6158.dd; LIN; NLI=Ir 8205 i 5; QUB=hPR8700.I5 (volume 1, number 12 (August 1947)–volume 2, number 1 (September 1947) only); TCD=I04.r.I.

A light magazine, but quite good (although it perhaps fades a little towards the end), mixing new material by young writers with general articles and reprints from other magazines. The *Bookman* was non-political and entertaining, and had a good mix of contents; the feel is of a mechanism for serious writers to reach a wider audience and make a bit of money, without going too far downmarket. The most frequent contributors are Benedict Kiely and Denis Ireland.

It includes stories by Alexander Irvine, Kiely, Donagh MacDonagh, Michael McLaverty, Michael J. Murphy, Joe O'Connor (i.e. Padraic Fiacc), James Plunkett and Joseph Tomelty; and poems by Padraic Fiacc, Padraic Gregory, Hewitt, Hutchinson, MacDonagh, David Marcus and McFadden. Also, amongst general articles on topics such as libraries, publishing, and so on, there are more literary efforts, such as pieces on Jane Barlow, Shan Bullock, Corkery, Joyce, Markievicz and James Stephens (all by Kiely); and on Austin Clarke, Padraic Colum and McLaverty (by Fiacc). Greacen also contributed a few pieces, e.g. 'Trends in Irish Poetry', or his article on early Dublin newspapers in the final issue. Each issue carried some short book reviews. The fourth issue had the entire first act of Tomelty's *All Soul's Night*.

See Rudi Holzapfel, 'A Survey of Irish Literary Magazines from 1900 to the Present Day', M Litt thesis (Trinity College Dublin, 1964), p. 57.

An author index appears in Richard J. Hayes, *Sources for the History of Irish Civilisation: Articles in Irish Periodicals*, 5 vols (Boston, 1970).

THE BLARNEY ANNUAL

Location:	Blarney (publisher Woodlands Press, St. Ann's Hill, printer Eagle Printing Works, Ltd, South Mall)
Editor(s):	Anon.
Dates:	Volume 1, number 1 (1948)–number 20 (Summer 1962)
No. of issues:	20
Average periodicity:	Annual (varies)

Average no. pages: 86 (1–9); 66 (10–20)
Libraries: BL=PP.6158.dea; LIN; NLI=Ir 914145 b 6 (5 and 6 missing);
                      PSPL=820.5; QUB=hDA900.B7; RIA=Fr Crypt/1/2/F Misc Box
                      A–C; TCD=144.s.45–46; UCD=STORE 820.

Amongst lots of articles on tourist sites, local history and characters, are to be found good stories, by Daniel Corkery, Lord Dunsany, Frank O'Connor, O'Faoláin, Robinson, L.A.G. Strong; poems by Greacen, Iremonger; and an article by Corkery.

Continued as:

THE BLARNEY ANNUAL OF FACT AND FANCY

Numbers 3–6, 1950–1953
Libraries, see above.

Introduces bright, colour covers, and little black and white photos of contributors, but not much else changes. Stories by Lavin, O'Flaherty, Michael J. Murphy and Bryan MacMahon; and poems and articles by Colum. QUB has volume 6 (Summer 1953), a special short stories issue, with twenty-two stories, and the authors include Bryan MacMahon, McLaverty, Michael J. Murphy and L.A.G. Strong. [The QUB copy of this issue was presented by McLaverty, and is inscribed by him.]

Continued as:

THE BLARNEY MAGAZINE, INCORPORATING THE BLARNEY ANNUAL OF FACT AND FANCY

Numbers 7–20, 1954–1962
Libraries: LIN (incomplete); QUB=hDA900.B7; RDS=NL57; UCD=STORE
                      820.

This incarnation is less literary, and more entertaining, though each issue usually starts off with a contribution from a famous name (these are often reprints from other sources). There are stories from Elizabeth Bowen, Colum and Lavin (as well as a 'Short Story Number', 11, with contributions from Joe O'Connor, L.A.G. Strong and Maurice Walsh); also poems by Séan O Ríordáin. Padraic Colum contributes a couple of articles, including one on 'Early Joyce' (number 11).

See Rudi Holzapfel, 'A Survey of Irish Literary Magazines from 1900 to the Present Day',
    M Litt thesis (Trinity College Dublin, 1964), p. 61.

POETRY IRELAND

Location: Cork (publisher Trumpet Books, 15 Adelaide Street, Cork, printer D.
                      and A. O'Leary Ltd., 25 Washington Street, Cork)

Editor(s):	David Marcus
Dates:	Number 1 (April 1948)–number 19 (October 1952)
No. of issues:	19
Average periodicity:	Quarterly
Average no. pages:	26
Libraries:	BL=PP.5126.ka; LIN; NLI=Ir 82108 p 3; PSPL=821.008; QUB=hPR8850.P7 (Kraus Reprint, Nendeln, Liechtenstein, 1970); RIA=Fr C/5/1/F Misc Box P–R (incomplete); TCD=131.r.20; UCD=J 820.

Although the agenda is now somewhat dated ('...Poetry cannot...flow from a people without the romantic temperament and poetic disposition...', 'Introduction', number 2), this is an excellent magazine, the first in Ireland devoted entirely to poetry. Within its apparently narrow remit, *Poetry Ireland* is often imaginative and flexible – issues are devoted to translations from the Irish lyrics (number 4), or a complete issue might be taken up with a translation of *The Midnight Court* (number 6, with an introduction by Colum; NB an Editor's Note points out that three short deletions have been made 'solely at the printer's request'!). One issue (number 7) carries only American poets, another writers from the North (number 8). Number 10 is really a full collection (*The Heavenly Foreigner and other poems*, by Denis Devlin) in disguise, with an introduction by Niall Sheridan, while number 13 is 'An Easter Rising Memorial Issue', selected and introduced by M.J. MacManus. It is surely a significant insight into the fiftieth anniversary commemoration that this is made up not of new poems, but rather of reprints of Æ, Dora Sigerson Shorter, Seamus O'Kelly, Oliver St. John Gogarty, Eva Gore-Booth, Joseph Campbell, James Stephens *et al*. In number 12 we find *The Poems of St. Columbanus*, translated and introduced by Perry F. Kendig.

Poems were published by: Beckett, Colum, Maurice James Craig, Anthony Cronin, ee cummings, Fiacc, Patrick Galvin, Greacen, Sam Harrison, Hewitt, Barbara Hunter, Pearse Hutchinson, Iremonger, Richard Kell, Kinsella, C. Day Lewis, Lord Longford, Sean Lucy, Donagh MacDonagh, Roy McFadden, Ewart Milne, May Morton, Val Mulkerns, Myles na nGopaleen, Arthur Power (his long poem 'The Portugese Bride'), Blanaid Salkeld, Bernard Share and William Carlos Williams.

A number of essays appeared: on Stephens's poetry by L.A.G. Strong, on Hewitt and Rodgers by Greacen, on Ulster poetry (Hewitt), and on MacNeice (Greacen), and on Thomas Moore, by J. Stephens. Marcus himself contributed short reviews to the first handful of issues, before being joined by others, including Hewitt.

A recurring theme in this series of *Poetry Ireland* is the ban on sales in Britain; the 'Introduction' to number 5 says that funds are short because of this, and calls for patrons to keep them going; number 8 again starts by bemoaning the British trade ban and appealing for funds. From number 14 a full page advertisement by Pye (Ireland) Ltd appears in every issue, presumably in response to this call for sponsors.

The standard of the contents is remarkably high throughout the run, and is further distinguished by being representative of the poetry being written in Ireland at that time, while not losing an international perspective. It perhaps starts to decline after the eighth issue, and this is increasingly noticeable from number 13. The final issue has an editorial, 'Farewell – (but not goodbye)': '...from 1953 onwards our larger and more widely read quarterly, *Irish Writing*, will contain in each issue a "A Poetry Ireland Supplement"'.

See Rudi Holzapfel, 'A Survey of Irish Literary Magazines from 1900 to the Present Day', M Litt thesis (Trinity College Dublin, 1964), p. 59.
See Gerry Smyth, *Decolonisation and Criticism: The Construction of Irish Literature* (London, 1998), pp. 120–122.

An author index appears in Rudi Holzapfel, 'A Survey of Irish Literary Magazines from 1900 to the Present Day', M Litt thesis (Trinity College Dublin, 1964).
An author index appears in Rudi Holzapfel, *Author Index 3*, Carraig Books Ltd, (Blackrock, 1985), pp. 123–135.
An author index appears in Richard J. Hayes, *Sources for the History of Irish Civilisation: Articles in Irish Periodicals*, 5 vols (Boston, 1970).

Continued as:

POETRY IRELAND

Location: Cork (publisher Irish Writing, 15 Adelaide Street, from number 29 publisher Trumpet Books, 37 Leinster Road, Rathmines, Dublin; printer The Kerryman, Ltd, Russell Street, Tralee (1), Southern Star, Ltd, Skibbereen (2–8), D. and A. O'Leary Ltd., 25 Washington Street, Cork (9–28), from number 29 printer Nationalist Press Clonmel)
Editor(s): David Marcus
Dates: Number 20 (March 1953)–number 28 (Winter 1955)
No. of issues: 9
Average periodicity: Three or four per year
Average no. pages: 6
Libraries: LIN; NLI=Ir 82108 i 2; PSPL=820.91; QUB=hAP4.I9 (reprint of numbers 1–28 (Kraus Reprint, Nendeln, Lichenstein, 4 vols, 1970); then originals of 29–35 and 37); RIA=Fr C/1/6/A (incomplete); TCD=102.r.41; UCD=J 820; UCG=800 (PS, incomplete).

This was a supplement to *Irish Writing*, comprising a distinct section of four to eight pages in length, with its own title block. It appeared in issues 22 (March 1953)–28 (September 1954), 30 (March 1955) and 33 (Winter 1955), and maintained its own, separate, numbering, running from number 20 (which appeared in *Irish Writing* 22) to number 28 (in *Irish Writing* 33). The editor was David Marcus; the editorial address remained at 15 Adelaide Street, Cork. Forty-four poems appeared in these nine 'issues', and contributors included Patrick Galvin, Robert Greacen, Richard Kell, Thomas Kinsella, Ewart Milne, Blanaid Salkeld and Bernard Share. The last 'issue', Guest Editor Valentin Iremonger, shared the theme of its *Irish Writing* host, that is contemporary writing in Gaelic, and it includes translations (by the authors, also by Valentin Iremonger, Marcus, and Donagh

MacDonagh) of poems by Brendan Behan, Máire Mac an tSaoi, and Séan Ó Riordáin. This last 'issue' was the only one of this series to have any sort of editorial feature, namely a short essay 'Gaelic Poetry Today', by Iremonger; it is also the only one to include book reviews (five pages of short reviews by Iremonger and Kinsella).

See Tony Farmer, '700 words by mid-October', *Books Ireland,* 47 (October 1980), p. 183. Interview with David Marcus, *Poetry Ireland* is discussed.
See Peter Denman, 'Ireland's Little Magazines', Barbara Hayley and Enda McKay (eds), *300 Years of Irish Periodicals* (Mullingar, 1987), p. 135.

Continued as:

POETRY IRELAND

Location: Dublin (publisher and printer Dolmen Press, 23 Upper Mount Street; from 1967 Dolmen moves to 8 Herbert Place, Dublin 2)
Editor(s):   John Jordan; Editorial Board James Liddy, James J. McAuley, Richard Weber; last issue actually assembled by John Montague
Dates: Number 1 (Autumn 1962)–number 7 and 8 (Spring 1968)
No. of issues: 7
Average periodicity: Annual
Average no. pages: 38
Libraries: BL=PP.8000.nd; NLI=Ir 82191 p 2; QUB=hPR8850.P7; TCD=Per 75–123; UCG=821.

Offered self-consciously as a new series of *Poetry Ireland* (and bearing the new 'Poetry Ireland Device', the drawing of the fabulous bird by Ruth Brandt which continued on into *Poetry Ireland Review*, and lasted until the 17th issue of that title, at the end of 1986), this incarnation is in many ways bigger and better than its predecessors. The quality of the contributions is at least as high; the 'look and feel' of the magazine is superior; and the presence of full-page advertisement for (amongst others) Pye, Massey-Ferguson, Guinness and Waterford Crystal even promises the kind of financial stability Marcus repeatedly begged for. The advertisement for the Dolmen Press which occasionally appeared on the back cover gives it the feel of a 'house magazine'; almost all the established poets appearing in this series of *Poetry Ireland* had collections published by Dolmen.

Poems were published by: Norman Dugdale, Austin Clarke (including a translation from Cervantes), Padraic Colum, Anthony Cronin, Leslie Daiken, Denis Devlin, Durcan, Fiacc, Monk Gibbon, Michael Harnett, Heaney, John Heath-Stubbs, John Hewitt, Pearse Hutchinson, Patrick Kavanagh, Richard Kell, Thomas Kinsella, Michael Longley, Donagh MacDonagh, Derek Mahon, Ewart Milne, John Montague, Rodgers, Jon Stallworthy and MacDara Woods. Although this series of *Poetry Ireland* did not publish book reviews, it did carry some important essays, including: a substantial piece on Synge's poetry, by Robin Skelton (number 1); an article on Devlin's poetry, by Coffey (number 2); and another on Hewitt, by Montague.

Despite at least matching the quality of the first series, not least in attracting the biggest established writers while at the same time spotting the best of the new talent, this version of *Poetry Ireland* was to be short-lived. Even the sponsors listed above could not support such a venture; by number 3 an editorial is already bemoaning the state of their finances. The last, double, issue (numbers 7 and 8 combined) includes a notice by Montague to say that this is the end of this series, and includes all the remaining material collected by Jordan.

See Lorna Reynolds, untitled review of first issue, *University Review*, 3, 4, pp. 61–64.

See Peter Denman, 'Ireland's Little Magazines', Barbara Hayley and Enda McKay (eds), *300 Years of Irish Periodicals* (Mullingar, 1987), p. 140.

An author and (limited) subject index appears in Stephen H. Goode, *Index to Commonwealth Little Magazines* (New York and London, 1966).

An author index appears in Richard J. Hayes, *Sources for the History of Irish Civilisation: Articles in Irish Periodicals*, 5 vols (Boston, 1970).

An author index appears in Rudi Holzapfel, *Author Index 3*, Carraig Books Ltd., (Blackrock, 1985), p. 79.

Continued as:

POETRY IRELAND

Location:	Dublin (typed and photocopied by the editor, 89 Carrick Road, Portmarnock)
Editor(s):	John F. Deane
Dates:	'First Newsletter' (September 1978)–'Sixteenth Newsletter' (March 1980)
No. of issues:	16
Average periodicity:	Quarterly
Average no. pages:	4
Libraries:	TCD=OLS X-1-361, number 1 (missing number 4).

Like the second series (1953–1955), a brave attempt to keep the name alive. This is a very fragile newsletter, comprising a couple of pages of news about poetry magazines and competitions, and so on, and usually a few poems. Contributors include: Rory Brennan, Michael Coady, Conleth Ellis, Anne Hartigan, James Liddy, Máire Mhac An tSaoi, Ewart Milne, Knute Skinner and Eithne Strong. From number 14, the address changes to 'The Nook', Mornington, Co. Meath; the last issue carries an essay on 'Austin Clarke, Theodore de Banville, and Yeats' by John Jordan. This incarnation of *Poetry Ireland* is a great tribute both to Deane's contacts and to his eye for talent; despite the ephemeral nature of the publication, the limited space available, and the inevitable difficulties of such a one-man-band operation, he managed to publish nearly four dozen poems, half of them by good but neglected established writers, the rest by unknowns who went on to have distinguished careers of one sort or another.

Continued as:

POETRY IRELAND REVIEW

Location:	Dublin (publisher Poetry Ireland, Mornington, Co Meath; from number 5 106 Tritonville Road, Sandymount; from number 9 35 Nth. Great George's Street, D1; from number 14 44 Upper Mount Street, Dublin 2; from number 41 Bermingham Tower, Upper Yard, Dublin Castle; number 9 printer Confidential Report Printing Ltd., Dublin, number 26 printer Sarsfield Press, Dublin, from number 29 Colour Books Ltd., Baldoyle Industrial Estate, Dublin 13)
Editor(s):	John Jordan (1–8), Thomas McCarthy (9–12), Conleth Ellis and Rita E Kelly (13), Terence Brown (14–17), Ciaran Cosgrove (18/19), Dennis O'Driscoll (20–21), John Ennis (22/23–25), Michael O'Siadhail (26–29), Máire Mhac an tSaoi (30–33), Peter Denman (34–37), Pat Boran (38), Seán Ó Cearnaigh (39), Pat Boran (40–42), Chris Agee (43/44), Moya Cannon (45–48), Liam O Muirthile (49), Michael Longley (50), Liam O Muirthile (51–52), Frank Ormsby (53–56), Catherine Phil McCarthy (57–)
Dates:	Number 1 (Spring 1981)–current
No. of issues:	58 issues (to Autumn 1998)
Average periodicity:	Three or four issues per year
Average no. pages:	54 (1–9); then 88 (10–23); 126 (24–44); 134 (45–58)
Libraries:	BL=ZC.9.a.3136; BCL=IR; LIN; NLI=Ir 82108 p 8; QUB=hPR8850.P75; TCD(Old Library)=OLS L-1-806, 807; then OLS L-3-29+30; then OLS L-5-241+885; then OLS L-6-371+855; UCD=J 820; UCG=821 (incomplete).

Poetry Ireland Review is not usually viewed as another series of the ongoing *Poetry Ireland* saga, but I think that there are enough links and continuities for it to be seen as such. Indeed, the first phase of *PIR*, under the stewardship of John Jordan, spends much of its editorial time stressing these links. First of all, there is the presence of Jordan himself, who edited all seven issues of the Third Series, in the 1960s. In his opening editorial and (more implicitly) in the issues which he produced, Jordan is at pains to emphasise the connections: with *Poetry Ireland* the organisation; via the continuity in contributors (half the poets in issue 1 of *PIR* also appeared in Series Three); through the re-use of Ruth Brandt's cover drawing; and so on.

   In fact, this fifth series could be seen as combining the pure poetry magazine of 1968 with the newsletter of 1978 and, while a reasonable enough strategy for getting the new series established, *PIR* under Jordan never really creates a clear identity of its own (beyond the occasionally eccentric typesetting – see the second number). The poetry is strong, and those represented include: Boland, Clarke, Cronin, Gerald Dawe, John F. Deane, Durcan, Conleth Ellis, Greacen, Heaney, Kennelly, Kinsella, Mahon, Medbh McGuckian, Milne, Montague, Murphy, Ní Chuilleanáin, Frank Ormsby, Peter Sirr, Eithne Strong, Francis

Stuart, Matthew Sweeney and Woods. As well as one or two short reviews in each issue, there is an essay on Scots Gaelic poetry in number 2; and a short play, by Padraic Colum, in number 3.

With issue 9 begins the tradition of changing editors after every three or four issues, an important reason why *PIR* has remained vital and been able to sustain itself over such a long run. However, the next nine issues represent a transitional period, during which the magazine attempts to free itself of the burden of its past and establish a clear identity. Gradually, during this time, the reviews get a little longer and more frequent, and some new names – including more women – begin to appear. As well as Dawe, Ellis, Galvin, Greacen, Heaney, Milne, Sirr, Sweeney and Woods, new poems are published by Sebastian Barry, Moya Cannon, Theo Dorgan, Michael Longley, Sean Lysaght, John Montague, Paul Muldoon, Julie O'Callaghan and James Simmons. And, although not heralded as such, number 11 includes a feature on women poets, with contributions from Eavan Boland, Ruth Hooley, Medbh McGuckian, Eiléan Ní Chuilleanáin, Nuala Ní Dhomhnaill, and Eithne Strong. Number 13 is a Special Eugene Watters Issue, containing a reprint of his long poem 'The Week-End of Dermot and Grace', plus essays by Conleth Ellis, Sean Lucy, etc. Number 14 has an interview with Derek Mahon, by Terence Brown.

With the double issue 18/19 (a special issue on Modern Latin American Poetry, an anthology of poems in translation (Neruda, Paz, Borges, etc.), framed by critical essays), the 'fabulous bird' disappears from the cover, and *PIR* begins to assume more or less the format which it has kept until the present day. The trend toward more prose continues, comprising about 40 per cent of issue 21. By now, the majority of the poetry is by a new generation of writers: Gavin Ewart, Peter Fallon, Rita Ann Higgins, Joan McBreen, Peter McDonald, Blake Morrison and Les Murray. Number 20 has an interview with Michael Hartnett; number 22 and 23 (two separate issues bound together) has examples and reviews of poetry in Irish and Scots Gaelic, while the second half is an 'Austin Clarke Supplement', with essays by Brown, Augustine Martin, Weber and Ellis. The broadening perspective opened in number 18/19 continues in number 24's articles on contemporary Spanish and Irish language poetry, with examples.

With number 25 *PIR* finishes its evolution and, with a new cover design (the stylised 'P'), for the first time since 1948 more than half the magazine is prose. Although more space is given to reviews, they tend to be portmanteaux, maybe reviewing nine collections at a time, and it is rare for an extended review to be given to one book. A little more space is given to Irish language material. Now *PIR* enters into stable, reliable (and perhaps slightly dull and worthy?) middle-age. With heavy symbolism, number 25 opens with an obituary of John Jordan. This phase (roughly number 25 to 38) features a series of important interviews, with Boland, Joseph Brodsky, John F. Deane, Peter Fallon, Miroslav Holub, Kinsella, Carol Rumens, Anne Stevenson, George Szirtes and Derek Walcott; these illustrate the new openness to international influences which characterised both *PIR* and Irish poetry itself during these years. The poets of this phase include: Sara Berkeley, Rory Brennan, Dorgan, Heaney, Fred Johnston, Longley, Tom MacIntyre, Frank McGuinness, Martin Mooney, Ní Dhomhnaill, Mary O'Donnell and Eithne Strong. Number 25 has a reprint of a lecture by Seamus Heaney on *Sweeney Astray*. There are articles on Padraic

Fallon and Patrick Kavanagh; a selection of poems by Italian women in number 32; and (number 39) a supplementary 'Scottish Issue', edited by William Neill, including poems by Douglas Dunn, Norman McCaig, Edwin Morgan, etc.

Numbers 39 to 49 mark the ascendancy of the Special Issue; whilst before *PIR* had the occasional feature or issue devoted to a single theme, now almost every number is given over to Contemporary Poetry in Irish (39), Politics (40), Sexuality (41), North America (43/44), The City and the Country (45), Migration and Emigration (46), The Sacred and the Secular (47), or Poetry and Survival (48). In many ways this is the golden age of *PIR*; it has the breadth of vision, the resources and the self-confidence to tackle this succession of Special Issues, and has attracted the talent (in both editors and contributors) to pull it off in style. A brief list of just the most important contributors to these issues will illustrate the point: Carol Ann Duffy, Laurence Ferlinghetti, Alan Ginsberg, Heaney, Michael Longley, Máire Mac an tSaoi, Medbh McGuckian, Montague, Nuala Ní Dhomhnaill, Greagóir Ó Dúill, Ruth Padel, Gabriel Rosenstock, Simmons, R.S. Thomas, Derek Walcott, C.K. Williams; these are the big guns of world poetry, not just of Ireland. In addition, with number 47, *PIR* moves to a beautiful new series of stylised photographic covers. Michael Longley's semi-anthology number 50, half new poems, half a selection from earlier issues, is the fitting climax to this period; poems are included by Sara Berkeley, Boland, Gerald Dawe, Kerry Hardie, Hartnett, Heaney, Kennelly, Mahon, Peter McDonald, McGuckian, Paula Meehan, Montague, Muldoon, Ní Dhomhniall, Peter Sirr, Sweeney and David Wheatley. No new direction has been embarked upon since this, and the issues after number 50 continue in the same (only slightly less high-quality) vein.

See Richard Hayes, '*Poetry Ireland Review*, Issues 1–21: A Review', *Poetry Ireland Review,* 36 (Autumn 1992), pp. 53–66.

See Anthony Roche, 'Platforms; the Journals, the Publishers', in Theo Dorgan, *Irish Poetry Since Kavanagh* (Dublin, 1996), pp. 71–81, *passim*.

See Ní Chuilleanáin, Eiléan, 'A Census of Places', *Cyphers,* 45 (Spring/Summer 1998), pp. 54–57. Short review of recent poetry journals.

See Edna Longley, '"Between the Saxon Smile and Yankee Yawp": Problems and contexts of Literary Reviewing in Ireland', Jeremy Treglown and Bridget Bennett, *Grub Street and the Ivory Tower: Literary Journalism and Literary Scholarship from Fielding to the Internet* (Oxford, 1998), p. 218.

Richard Hayes, *An index to Poetry Ireland Review Issues 1–21*, St Patrick's College (Maynooth, 1993), is a first-class author index to these issues, with a short introduction.

RANN, A QUARTERLY OF ULSTER POETRY

Location:	Lisburn (publisher Lisnagarvey Press; printer Victor McMurray, 12 Market Square; from number 13 H.R. Carter Publications Ltd, 2 Marcus Ward Street, Belfast, same printer)
Editor(s):	Barbara Hunter and Roy McFadden; number 11 edited John Hewitt;

	number 19 edited Raymond Hughes
Dates:	Number 1 (Summer 1948)–number 20 (June 1953)
No. of issues:	20
Average periodicity:	Quarterly until number 12, then triannual
Average no. pages:	12 (1–12); then 24 (13–19); final issue 72
Libraries:	BL=PP.5126.kaa; LIN (incomplete); NLI=Ir 82108 r 4; QUB=hPR8891.R1; TCD=136.b.126.

A slim but attractive publication, with cover illustrations by Catherine S. Wilson, H.E. Broderick, Anne Yeats, Paul Nietsche, William Conor and (most frequently) Rowel Friers. *Rann* by and large lets the poems speak for themselves, and includes a variety of material, but the tone and selection clearly reveal it as a (perhaps slightly semi-detached) wing of Ulster Regionalism. Its aims were limited, and it lacks the ambition of some of its contemporaries, but it has a satisfying seriousness and solidity.

Each issue carried a feature, 'Ancestral Voices', a selection from Ulster poets of the past, edited by John Hewitt. From number 7 there was usually one or two pages of short reviews, and from number 13 it was extended to cover drama and fine art. But the real business of *Rann* was poetry, and it published work by a wide range of writers, including Dannie Abse, Kingsley Amis, John Boyd, Buchanan, Joseph Campbell, Colum, Doyle, William Oxley, Greacen, Hewitt, Richard Kell, David Marcus, Roy McFadden, McLaverty, May Morton, W.R. Rodgers, Rowley and John Wain. The second issue contains the coup of a previously unpublished Yeats poem ('Reprisals'), while number 16 incorporated a selection of Belfast street songs.

There were a number of special issues, including number 6 ('John Lyle Donaghy, 1902–1949, Memorial Number', which includes a dozen unpublished poems), number 11, given over to a selection by Hewitt from James Orr, William Drennan, etc., and number 19, on contemporary Welsh writers, including R.S. Thomas and Henry Treece.

The final issue amounts to an anthology of contemporary Ulster writing, and is a summation of *Rann*'s aims and achievement, with poems by Colum, Greacen, Hewitt, Kell, McFadden, and Morton; essays (on Ulster poetry, novels and theatre) by Boyd, Hewitt, and others; and a nineteen-page bibliography of 'Ulster Books and Authors, 1900–1953'.

With the second issue, the subtitle changed to: *An Ulster Quarterly of Poetry*; and from number 13, to *An Ulster Quarterly, Poetry and Comment*.

See David Marcus, 'Reviews', *Poetry Ireland, 3* (October 1948), pp. 25–26. Short review of first issue.

See Roy McFadden, 'Reflections on Megarrity', *Threshold*, 5, 1 (Spring/ Summer 1961), pp. 30–31.

See Rudi Holzapfel, 'A Survey of Irish Literary Magazines from 1900 to the Present Day', M Litt thesis (Trinity College Dublin, 1964), p. 60.

See Dillon Johnston, *Irish Poetry After Joyce* (Notre Dame, 1985), p. 41.

See Peter Denman, 'Ireland's Little Magazines', Barbara Hayley and Enda McKay (eds), *300 Years of Irish Periodicals* (Mullingar, 1987), p. 135.

See Norman Vance, *Irish Literature: A Social History – Tradition, Identity and Difference* (Oxford, 1990), p. 218.

See Tom Clyde, 'Uladh, Lagan and Rann: The "Little Magazine" comes to Ulster', in Eve Patten, *Returning to Ourselves* (Belfast, 1995), pp. 145–153.

See Gerry Smyth, *Decolonisation and Criticism: The Construction of Irish Literature* (London, 1998), pp. 119–120.

An author index appears in Richard J. Hayes, *Sources for the History of Irish Civilisation: Articles in Irish Periodicals*, 5 vols (Boston, 1970).

Sheila Hamilton, 'Indexes to *Rann*', MA thesis (QUB, 1990).

ENVOY, A REVIEW OF LITERATURE AND ART

Location:	Dublin (publisher Envoy Publishing Co., 39 Grafton Street, printer Cahill and Co., Ltd, Parkgate Printing Works)
Editor(s):	John Ryan; Poetry Editor Valentin Iremonger; Associate Editor(s) J.K. Hillman (joined by Michael Heron, number 13; both joined by Owen Quinn, number 16; Hillman drops out, number 18)
Dates:	Volume 1, number 1 (December 1949)–volume 5, number 20 (July 1951)
No. of issues:	20
Average periodicity:	Monthly
Average no. pages:	96 (1–14); then 80
Libraries:	BL=PP.6189.eba; LIN; NLI=Ir 05 e 1; PSPL=820.5; QUB=hPR1.E7 (missing numbers 8 and 11), also Mif/AP4.E69; RDS=NL51; RIA=Fr C/1/4/E (incomplete); TCD=125.g.161–163; UCC (1950–1951 only); UCG=800 (Off Site).

The title is explained in the opening editorial, where it is hoped that would stand 'abroad as envoy of Irish writing and at home as envoy of the best in international writing'. Bright, commercial (lots of advertisements), but not afraid of ambitious material (e.g. the extract from *Watt*, in number 2), *Envoy* is a very good magazine which somehow never quite manages to become a great one. It would have had much greater impact had it been a quarterly and so needed less 'padding'; the economics would also have been much easier, as is acknowledged in the closing editorial.

The basic format was obviously taken from *The Bell*, although *Envoy* was always less politically interventionist; the editorial 'Foreword' to volume 3, number 9 famously says that: 'The younger poets . . . take their nationality more for granted . . . [and are] rather more concerned with the craftsmanship involved in trying to write good poetry', while in volume 4, number 13 they stated that they would not publish articles on any of these topics 'unless it has literary value: 1. The Turf Development Board. 2. How to live on £400 a year. 3. Borstal and gaols. 4. Holidays in Ireland . . .'. One can imagine all of these appearing in *The Bell*. Each issue carries at least one story (from a distinguished roster which included Brendan Behan, Colum, Robert Farren, Brian Inglis, Gerard Keenan, Kiely, Lavin, Brian

Nolan, Séan O'Faoláin, Francis Stuart, and also a prose piece by Gertrude Stein); poems by Behan, Cronin, Hewitt, Hutchinson, Kavanagh, Kell, McFadden, Milne, Montague, Murphy and Cecil Salkeld; and general articles on a wide range of topics (stage Irishry, Croce, Nijinsky or Mac Liammóir on acting). One characteristic of *Envoy* was the seriousness with which it addressed, examined and promoted Irish painters and sculptors as well as writers (Ryan was himself both a writer and a painter), and each issue had an illustrated article on a contemporary artist (e.g. Le Brocquy, George Campbell, Middleton, Dan O'Neill). Each issue also benefited from Kavanagh's typically astringent and personal 'Diary' (indeed, the final editorial claimed this as one of the journal's real achievements, despite the fact that Kavanagh often took directly opposing positions to the editorials), a clear model for his own later *Kavanagh's Weekly*; and there were articles on a range of writers, including Auden, Joyce, Pearse, Stuart, and Yeats.

Number 17 was a special on James Joyce, and included articles by Brian Nolan, Denis Johnston, etc., and also some unpublished Joyce letters; this was an important piece of flag-flying for *Envoy*, aligning it with the banned Modernist, and also furthering its pro-European credentials. Finally, there were a few interesting one-offs: the long review of Louis MacNeice's *Collected Poems*, the autobiographical fragment by Francis Stuart, or the translation from Chekov by Hubert Butler.

See Rudi Holzapfel, 'A Survey of Irish Literary Magazines from 1900 to the Present Day', M Litt thesis (Trinity College Dublin, 1964), p. 62.

See John Ryan, *Remembering how We Stood* (Dublin, 1975), *passim*. Autobiography.

See Roger McHugh and Maurice Harmon, *A Short History of Anglo-Irish Literature* (Dublin, 1982), p. 236.

See Terence Brown, *Ireland, A Social and Cultural History 1922–1985* (London, 1985), pp. 226–227; 233–234; 298; and 321.

See Dillon Johnston, *Irish Poetry After Joyce* (Notre Dame, 1985), pp. 41, 133.

See Peter Denman, 'Ireland's Little Magazines', Barbara Hayley and Enda McKay (eds), *300 Years of Irish Periodicals* (Mullingar, 1987), pp. 136–137.

See Hubert Butler, 'Envoy and Mr Kavanagh', *The Sub-Prefect Should Have Held His Tongue* (Harmondsworth, 1990), pp. 83–91.

See John Goodby, 'New Wave I: "A Rising Tide"; Irish Poetry in the 60s', in Theo Dorgan, *Irish Poetry Since Kavanagh* (Dublin, 1996), pp. 116–135, *passim*.

See Anthony Roche, 'Platforms; the Journals, the Publishers', in Theo Dorgan, *Irish Poetry Since Kavanagh* (Dublin, 1996), pp. 71–81, *passim*.

See Brian Fallon, *An Age of Innocence: Irish Culture 1930–1960* (Dublin, 1998), pp. 13, 68, 100, 151, 232, 234.

See Gerry Smyth, *Decolonisation and Criticism: The Construction of Irish Literature* (London, 1998), pp. 118–119.

See Edna Longley, '"Between the Saxon Smile and Yankee Yawp": Problems and contexts of Literary Reviewing in Ireland', Jeremy Treglown and Bridget Bennett, *Grub Street and the Ivory Tower: Literary Journalism and Literary Scholarship from Fielding to the Internet* (Oxford, 1998), p. 208.

An author index appears in Rudi Holzapfel, 'A Survey of Irish Literary Magazines from 1900 to the Present Day', M Litt thesis (Trinity College Dublin, 1964).

An author index appears in Richard J. Hayes, *Sources for the History of Irish Civilisation: Articles in Irish Periodicals,* 5 vols (Boston, 1970).

Michael O'Neill, 'Indexes to Envoy', MA thesis (QUB, 1987).

An author index appears in Rudi Holzapfel, *Author Index 3*, Carraig Books (1992) pp. 137–147.

ICARUS, UNIVERSITY OF DUBLIN

Location:	Dublin (publisher Trinity College, printer Turner's Printing Works, Longford, number 49 printer Clearprint)
Editor(s):	As with many university publications, an editorial committee, which changed with practically every issue; members included Rivers Carew, Donald Davie, Richard Kell, Derek Mahon, Douglas Sealy and Bernard Share; from number 27 the editor is Anon., although the editorial to number 41 laments the loss of Alec Reid (implying that he has been editor for these issues), and welcomes Dr O'Connor.
Dates:	Number 1 (May 1950)–number 49 (1966)
No. of issues:	47
Average periodicity:	Triannual (varies)
Average no. pages:	32; 42 (21–33); 56 (34–47); 64 (49)
Libraries:	BL=PP.4970.eca; NLI=IR 8205 i 6 (first 19 only); PSPL=820.5; QUB=hLF909.I2 (numbers 2 (October 1950), 16 (May 1955), 43 (May 1964), 46 (1965) and 49 (1966) only); RDS=NL53 (incomplete); TCD=IN.C.TRI; UCC; UCG=820 (PS).

This is a classic example of a modern student literary magazine, whose general style, production quality and cover layout changes with practically every issue. In the first nineteen issues, the poetry is dominated by Donald Davie, Richard Kell, Alec Reid, Douglas Sealy, Bernard Share and Richard Weber; there are also stories by Bryan MacMahon, Derek Mahon and Share, an article on Kavanagh, a radio play (by Conor Farrington), and a reprint of Yeats's 'Reprisals'. From numbers 20–27, the main poets are Bruce Arnold, Rivers Carew, Anne Cluysenaar, R.W. Ewart, Rudi Holzapfel, Thomas Kinsella, Sean Lucy and Arland Ussher.

From 27 onwards, the magazine enters its most consistent and rewarding period, during which practically every issue carries poems by Brendan Kennelly, Michael Longley and Derek Mahon, joined towards the end by Eavan Boland (and with occasional contributions from Jeni Couzyn, Holzapfel, Montague, Joan Newmann and MacDara Woods). Holzapfel and Kennelly contribute stories, and Edna Broderick book reviews. In addition, number 38 reprints some poems by W.R. Rodgers, and 49 has a prose piece by William Burroughs. During this period *Icarus* feels like the product of a cohesive and energetic group of young writers, and far surpasses its student peers. An editorial in number 47 says that 'the last issue of Icarus had its fingers very badly scorched', which generated a large debt, but that they were determined to press on; the last issue I have seen came out just a few months later.

[The following advertisement appears in *Icarus* 37 in 1961: 'Mrs Hedli MacNeice (Tel. Kinsale 155), The Spinnaker, Scilly, Kinsale, County Cork – Plain & Continental Food, Wines.']

See Alec Reid, 'One Man's Icarus', in *Icarus,* 30 (March 1960) pp. 10–13.

See Rudi Holzapfel, 'A Survey of Irish Literary Magazines from 1900 to the Present Day', M Litt thesis (Trinity College Dublin, 1964), pp. 68–69.

An author index appears in Rudi Holzapfel, 'A Survey of Irish Literary Magazines from 1900 to the Present Day', M Litt thesis (Trinity College Dublin, 1964).

An author and (limited) subject index appears in Stephen H. Goode, *Index to Commonwealth Little Magazines* (New York and London, 1966).

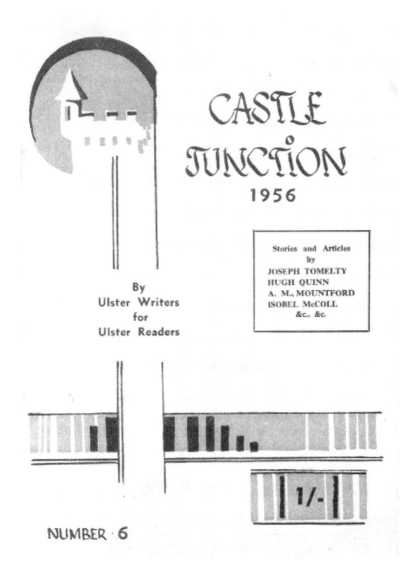

CASTLE JUNCTION

Location:	Belfast (publisher Belfast Writer's Group; printer Spectator, Bangor)
Editor(s):	George A. Osborough (number 5), Elizabeth C. May (number 6)
Dates:	Number 1 (1951)–number 6 (1956)
No. of issues:	6
Average periodicity:	Annual
Average no. pages:	24 (number 4), then 34 (numbers 5 and 6)
Libraries:	LIN; QUB=hpPR8844/CAST (number 6 only).

A lightweight selection of stories, anecdotes and poems, each issue graced by a story from a major author: Michael McLaverty or Joseph Tomelty, in these issues.

See Anon., editorial, *Q*, 14 (Hilary 1957).

Q, A PUBLICATION OF THE STUDENTS' REPRESENTATIVE COUNCIL OF THE QUEEN'S UNIVERSITY OF BELFAST

Location:	Belfast (publisher QUB SRC, printer Tradepress, 19 Adelaide Street)
Editor(s):	Varies; number 12, Sheela O'Hara; number 14, Don Carleton and committee; number 15, George McConnell; number 16, Denis Tuohy; number 17, David Jenkins; number 18, Margaret Ogle
Dates:	1951–1960?
No. of issues:	19?
Average periodicity:	Biannual
Average no. pages:	Varies widely, but average 42
Libraries:	BL=PP.6180.cgc (incomplete); LIN; QUB(Arc)=876 (incomplete).

The Editorial to number 14 (Hilary 1957) spends most of its time condemning Ulster writing: 'Our poets and literary magazines are saddest of all.' Number 12 has a short review of *The Less Deceived*, by John Betjeman. After this only student writing appears; the only items of interest in numbers 14–18 are poems by Denis Tuohy and Wesley Burrowes, and a story by Stewart Parker.

Continued as:

THE Q REVIEW

Location:	Belfast (printers Ulster Productions Co., Ltd, The Nendrum Press, 13 High Street, Comber; from number 22, Nelson and Knox, Ltd, Townhall Street)
Editor(s):	Varies; numbers 20 and 21, Ian J. Hill; number 22, David Graham.
Dates:	1960–1961?
No. of issues:	3?

Average periodicity: Biannual
Average no. pages: Varies widely, but average 42
Libraries: LIN; QUB(Arc)=876 (incomplete).

[Named as *Q Review* on cover, though inside still described and numbered as *Q*.]

This series has a wacky new 1960s format, with cut and paste graphics, different colours and textures of paper, etc. (most of issue 20 is bound upside down, presumably deliberately?). These three issues contain (amongst lesser material) three poems by Stewart Parker, and two by Michael Longley.

See Anon., 'Battle Hymn of the Q Review', *Interest*, 3, 4, p. 7 ('I have seen Him in the pages of the Sinful Q Review/They have published awful writers where we once read Bill and Steve').

KAVANAGH'S WEEKLY, A JOURNAL OF LITERATURE AND POLITICS

Location: Dublin (publisher Peter Kavanagh, 62 Pembroke Road, printer Fleet Printing Co., Ltd, 6 Eccles Place)
Editor(s):   Patrick Kavanagh
Dates: Volume 1, number 1 (12 April 1952)–volume 1, number 13 (5 July 1952)
No. of issues: 13
Average periodicity: Weekly
Average no. pages: 8
Libraries: BL=PP.6193.kdd; LIN (incomplete); NLI=LO (1981 reprint); QUB=hqPR8700.K2; RIA=Fr C/1/6/C Misc Box I–K (incomplete); TCD=Gall.BB.11b.40; UCC (Goldsmith Press Reprint, 1981); UCD=J 050.

Even by the standards of Irish literary magazines, this is a supreme folly – an independently published, literary/political magazine, with no staff, and little capital, to be published weekly! In actual fact, much of the content is not literary, but rather consists of the Kavanagh brothers' rants on any subject which came to mind – the Budget, tourism, alcohol – and which together form a perfect distillation of the inertia in the Ireland of that time, and of the creative mind's need to rebel against it. A favourite target is self-consciously stereotypical 'Irish' behaviour by public figures, or 'buckleppin'', as it is known on these pages. There are a couple of irregular columns, 'Literature', which gives Patrick Kavanagh a platform from which to take pugnacious swipes at his peers in the Dublin literary scene, and another untitled one which gives Gerard Keenan space to do the same for Belfast. Amongst all this, there are also a couple of poems from Kavanagh, a fragment of *Tarry Flynn*, and a couple of articles by Myles Na nGopaleen.

The twelfth number carries an announcement that the next issue will be the last – unless the editors 'receive in the meantime a sum of £1,000 or upwards'! The final issue is just four pages long, and entirely given over to a fierce polemic, 'The Story of An Editor Who Was Corrupted by Love', which encapsulates both *Kavanagh's Weekly* at its finest, and the editor's rage against the entropy and small-minded provincialism he saw around him: 'The first thing that we must emphasise is that we are not closing down primarily for lack of money or because our circulation was too small... last week we sold out... First, there is the absence of writers and, secondly, the absence of an audience. Like the chicken and the egg, it is hard to say which of these comes first... cowardice... so-called Gaelic poets weren't worthy of the name, they were nothing but drunken clowning entertainers... a sort of cynical disbelief in life... Did the Cultural Relations Council give us any support? They were one of our nastiest opponents... the Arts Council, worse if such were possible...'. This issue was limited to a hundred copies, twenty of which were signed by Kavanagh (the copy in TCD is one of these).

See Rudi Holzapfel, 'A Survey of Irish Literary Magazines from 1900 to the Present Day', M Litt thesis (Trinity College Dublin, 1964), p. 65.
See James McKenna, 'Kavanagh's Weekly, Thirty Years Later', *Era,* 6 (1982), pp. 27–28.
See Dillon Johnston, *Irish Poetry After Joyce* (Notre Dame, 1985), pp. 41, 122, 133.
See Antoinette Quinn, *Patrick Kavanagh: Born-Again Romantic* (Dublin, 1991), pp. 279–284.
See Anthony Roche, 'Platforms; the Journals, the Publishers', in Theo Dorgan, *Irish Poetry Since Kavanagh* (Dublin, 1996), pp. 71–81, *passim.*
See Brian Fallon, *An Age of Innocence: Irish Culture 1930–1960* (Dublin, 1998), pp. 261, 263.
See Gerry Smyth, *Decolonisation and Criticism: The Construction of Irish Literature* (London, 1998), pp. 103–112.
See Edna Longley,'"Between the Saxon Smile and Yankee Yawp": Problems and contexts of Literary Reviewing in Ireland', Jeremy Treglown, and Bridget Bennett, *Grub Street and the Ivory Tower: Literary Journalism and Literary Scholarship from Fielding to the Internet* (Oxford, 1998), p. 206.

An author index appears in Rudi Holzapfel, 'A Survey of Irish Literary Magazines from 1900 to the Present Day', M Litt thesis (Trinity College Dublin, 1964).

THE CRITERION

Location:	Galway (publisher Arts Society, UCG, printer Connacht Tribune, Market Street; from 1978, printer Standard Printed Products)
Editor(s):	from 1969, Brian O'Rourke, Assistant Editor Anne-Marie O'Healy; from 1971, Luke Gibbons, Assistant Tom Duddy; from 1972, Tom Duddy, Assistant Joe Ducke; from 1974, Edmund Lenihan and Michael Gorman; from 1975, Ollie Jennings; from 1978, John Maguire; from 1979, Ann O'Leary; from 1980, Peter Conry; from

	1981, Grainne McMorrow; from 1982, Nora Walls; from 1983, Charlie McBride; from 1984, Dervla Brown and James Harrold.
Dates:	1953–1984?
No. of issues:	32?
Average periodicity:	Annual
Average no. pages:	54; from 1979, 48
Libraries:	NLI=Ir 8205 c 18; TCD=Per 90–464 (from 1973 only); UCG=378 (PS).

Originally an informal, nicely produced magazine, quite old-fashioned for its time, and including very little literary material, from the late 1960s *Criterion* began to change, and include an increasing number of poems and stories in each issue; although the typography and layout were not that different, it did also begin to sport more trendy covers, from 1978 in a nice, brown card. As with all student publications, the quality could vary widely, but it included poems from Eva Bourke, Gerald Dawe, Seamus Heaney, Fred Johnston, Richard Murphy, Kathleen Raine and Lorna Reynolds; and stories by Benedict Kiely and John McGahern. Each issue was titled with its year (*Criterion 1971*, *Criterion '82*, etc.), and the 1983 issue was an anthology to mark its thirtieth birthday. A solid, rather than terribly exciting, journal.

See Rudi Holzapfel, 'A Survey of Irish Literary Magazines from 1900 to the Present Day', M Litt thesis (Trinity College Dublin, 1964), p. 66.
See Gerald Dawe, *Criterion 1953–1983, An Anthology* (1983).

UNIVERSITY REVIEW, OFFICIAL ORGAN OF THE GRADUATES' ASSOCIATION OF THE NATIONAL UNIVERSITY OF IRELAND

Location:	Dublin (publisher GANUI, Newman House, 86 St. Stephen's Green, from volume 3, number 8, publisher moves to 76 Fitzwilliam Lane, Dublin 2, printer Fleet Printing Co., 6/7 Eccles Place, from volume 1, number 6, printer Mount Solus Press, Blackrock, from volume 1, number 9 printer Monument Press, Dublin and Bray, from volume 1, number 10 printer Mount Solus Press, from volume 2, number 11, printer Monument Press, from volume 3, number 9, printer Leinster Leader Ltd, Naas)
Editor(s):	An eight to twelve member board, including at various times James Hogan, Roger McHugh and, most consistently, Lorna Reynolds; from volume 5, number 1 the board remains in place, but Maurice Harmon is named as Editor, with Donal McCartney as his Assistant and Michael P. Gallagher as Book Reviews editor.
Dates:	Volume 1, number 1 (Summer 1954)–volume 5, number 2 (Summer 1968)
No. of issues:	39

Average periodicity: Triannual
Average no. pages: 84 (volume 1); then 74 (volumes 2 and 3); then 100 (volume 4); then
                      136 (volume 5)
Libraries: NLI=Ir 37841 u 7; QUB=hAP4.U6; RIA=Fr C/3/1/B; TCD=Per 891.6
                      (incomplete); UCD=J 800; UCG=378.155.

According to the 'Foreword' to the first issue, the *University Review* was founded 'to
promote the aims of the Graduates' Association', would be 'conducted independently of
the University and College authorities', and would 'strive to reflect the intellectual life of
the National University'; it was to receive some funding from the NUI, and would make
up the rest from advertising. During its first phase (up to around volume 2, number 9) it
stuck fairly closely to those stated aims, and so is of less importance as a literary magazine.
The vast bulk of its content during these years is decidedly non-literary, although it did
carry a translation into Irish of four cantos from Dante's *Inferno*; translations into English
of a selection of contemporary Italian verse (by Lorna Reynolds); some previously
unpublished notes by Wilde for one of his American lectures; a short story by Mary Lavin;
a reminiscence of her college days from Kate O'Brien; and a number of articles, including
John Jordan on O'Casey, Denis O'Donoghue on *Riders to the Sea*, Vivian Mercier on Irish
Comedy, and Kate O'Brien on Turgenev. In addition, they published the occasional
original poem, and obituaries of Seumas O'Sullivan and Lennox Robinson.

A second phase, more literary and less concerned with reporting college news, begins
with the appearance of important new names, primarily that of Brian Coffey, who kicks off
his involvement with a sequence of nine poems in volume 2, number 10. Poems also
appear by Pearse Hutchinson, Kinsella, James Liddy and Thomas MacGreevy, as well as
older writers such as Colum and Clarke. The undoubted climax of poetic input into *UR* is
volume 3, number 5, which is twice the usual size and completely given over to
reproducing 'The Complete Poems of Denis Devlin'. A short autobiographical extract
appears (in volume 3, number 2) by Kate O'Brien; Kiely and Tom MacIntyre contribute
stories, and serious articles are published, on Denis Devlin, James Joyce, James Stephens
(Augustine Martin), William Carlos Williams and W.B. Yeats (Kinsella). Volume 3,
number 8 is a 'Special Yeats Edition', with poems by James Liddy and Lorna Reynolds
and half a dozen articles by such commentators as Coffey, Donoghue, Thomas McGreevy
and John O'Meara.

University Review's third, and last, phase comprises its final two volumes, and ran from
Spring 1967 to Summer 1968; this began with a 'Jonathan Swift Tercentenary Issue' and
ended with Eilís Dillon's translation of the 'Lament for Art O'Leary', but also included
articles, including Thomas Flanagan on Yeats, and a more impressive series of poems, by
Clarke, Heaney and Kinsella, and a short prose extract from Mervyn Wall.

See Rudi Holzapfel, 'A Survey of Irish Literary Magazines from 1900 to the Present Day',
    M Litt thesis (Trinity College Dublin, 1964), p. 67.

An author index appears in Richard J. Hayes, *Sources for the History of Irish Civilisation:
    Articles in Irish Periodicals*, 5 vols (Boston, 1970).

Continued as:

IRISH UNIVERSITY REVIEW, A JOURNAL OF IRISH STUDIES

Location:	Shannon (publisher Irish University Press, Shannon, printer Robert Hogg; from Spring 1972, printer Dorset Press, Dublin; from Autumn 1972, publisher moves to 81 Merrion Square, Dublin, printer Elo Press Ltd., Dublin 8; from Spring 1974 publisher Room J210, Arts Building, University College, Dublin 4, printer Task Print and Packaging Ltd, Naas; from Spring 1976, printer Task Print (Dublin) Ltd, Rialto; from Autumn 1977 printer Folens and Co. Ltd., Airton Road, Tallaght; from Spring 1978 publisher Wolfhound Press, 98 Ardilaun, Portmarnock, Co. Dublin; from Spring 1984, publisher Wolfhound Press, 68 Mountjoy Square, Dublin 1; from Spring 1987, publisher Brophy Books, 108 Sundrive Road, Dublin 4, printer Kilkenny People Printing Ltd.; from Spring 1991, printer Colour Books Ltd., Dublin 13)
Editor(s):	Maurice Harmon (with a prestigious Advisory Board (including originally Richard Ellmann and T.R. Henn), and Editorial Board (including John O'Meara and Roger McHugh), and an Executive Board (with O'Meara, McHugh and Harmon); from Spring 1987, Ed. Christopher Murray (with same Board structure); from Spring 1998, Ed. Anthony Roche; volume 10, number 1 Ed. Christopher Murray; volume 21, number 1 Ed. Peter Denman; volume 23, number 1 Ed. Anthony Roche; volume 24, number 1 Ed. Brian Donnelly; volume 26, number 2 Ed. Anne Fogarty)
Dates:	Volume 1, number 1 (Autumn 1970)–present
No. of issues:	55 (to Spring 1998)
Average periodicity:	Biannual
Average no. pages:	156
Libraries:	BL=P.521/966; BCL=IR; LIN; PSPL=052 (1974–1976); QUB=hAP4.I8; RDS=NL153; RIA=RR Gall/37/F; TCD=Per 891.6; UCC; UCG=378.155.

The second series of the *University Review* (from the title page of the first issue: 'The *Irish University Review* is a continuation of the *University Review* which was the organ of the Graduates' Association of the National University of Ireland.'); like many long-running Irish literary magazines, the *IUR* established a clear formula from its first issue, and has rarely deviated from it over a thirty-year period. A refinement, rather than a radical departure from the *University Review*, *IUR* sticks to the same layout, tone and contents, it just does everything more professionally and consistently (that superstructure of Advisory, Editorial and Executive Boards is a clear statement of seriousness). After only three years, Harmon established the comforting rhythm of having a special issue every Spring, followed by a more general issue in the Autumn; in fact, *IUR*'s attachment to its formula is such that on the rare occasions when they deviate it from it (e.g. volume 26, number 2), they feel the need to explain and apologise in a special editorial.

Their special issues are comprehensive and authoritative (if, in choice of subject, a little unadventurous compared with, say, *Poetry Ireland Review*), corralling articles by most of the academic big guns and contemporary artists, along with autobiographical, biographical and bibliographical features and interviews, and they have addressed (in order of publication): Austin Clarke, Séan O'Faoláin, Brian Coffey, Mary Lavin, Sean O'Casey, John Banville, James Joyce, 'The Long Poem', Samuel Beckett, Tom Murphy, Brian Moore, John Montague, 'Contexts of Irish Writing', Maurice Harmon, Eavan Boland, Richard Murphy, Derek Mahon, Irish Women Playwrights, Spenser in Ireland and 'Literature, Criticism & Theory'. Contributors to these *tours d'horizon* include: (in the early years) Cyril Cusack, Eil's Dillon, Maurice Harmon, Rüdiger Imhof, John Jordan, Kennelly, Kinsella, F.S.L. Lyons, Mercier and Robert Welch; then John Banville, Terence Brown, Coffey, Neil Corcoran, John Cronin, Dawe, Seamus Deane, Barbara Hayley, Aidan Higgins, Desmond Hogan, Mahon, Augustine Martin, Montague, Brian Moore, Stewart Parker and Francis Stuart; and in more recent years, as well as Peter Denman, Dillon Johnston, Sean Lysaght and Frank McGuinness, a more female line-up, including Boland, Biddy Jenkinson, Medbh McGuckian, Ní Chuilleanáin, Mary O'Donnell and Ann Saddlemeyer. Atypical are the issues devoted to John Banville (which was largely given over to 'The Newton Letter' and an interview with Banville), and to Brian Coffey (containing one long poem, thirteen translations, and a sequence of short poems by Coffey).

The alternating, more general, issues also carry many heavyweight articles on a range of subjects; in the early years these could as often be about historical or geographical topics as literature, but very quickly the focus moved more towards the latter. A wide range of Irish writers have received a single article in *IUR*, including Æ, Carleton, Corkery, Ferguson, Aidan Higgins, Hyde, Denis Johnston, Kennelly, Kinsella, Le Fanu, Merriman, John Mitchell, Montague, Muldoon, O'Connor, O'Flaherty, Ormsby, Forrest Reid, Shaw, Stephens, Stuart and Wilde. More favoured are those who are granted two or three mentions, e.g. Banville, Denis Devlin, Gregory, Lavin, MacNeice, Mangan, McGuckian, McGuinness, George Moore, Murphy, Swift and Synge. Then come the élite, who have had around half a dozen articles devoted to them: Beckett, Heaney, Flann O'Brien, O'Casey and Friel. Finally, we reach the summit, where we meet Joyce (eleven articles) and, of course, Yeats (seventeen articles). Whether this is a comment on the conservatism of the various editors and Board members of *IUR*, or on the preoccupations of Irish academe generally, is impossible to say.

New, creative writing has never played a major role in *IUR*, although every issue has contained some; the editors have tended to play safe with their choices, and predominantly the authors featured have already established reputations. In nearly thirty years there have been nearly sixty appearances by poets in these pages, the majority of them a single exposure (this includes names such as Boland, Kennelly, Kinsella, Ní Chuilleanáin and Tom Paulin). A few have been more favoured, including Deane (four), Fallon (two), Heaney (two), Milne (three), Montague (two) and Simmons (two), while the clear favourites are Tom MacIntyre (five) and Dawe (six). (One glaring omission is Michael Longley, who has also never been granted a special issue.) The rest is a more lightweight selection, of stories (O'Faoláin, Stuart), short plays (Boucicault, Clarke, Colum, Teresa Deevy, O'Connor), translations (of the 'Lament for Art O'Leary' (Eil's Dillon), or Neruda (Coffey)), and autobiography (Montague, O'Faoláin).

Irish University Review is associated with the International Association for the Study of Anglo-Irish Literature, and is provided to the members of that organisation. For them, each second issue also carries a 'Bibliography Bulletin', listing Irish books published in the previous year. Every issue carries a section of reviews, often quite substantial, and provided by all the writers mentioned above.

See Anon., 'Special issues', *Books Ireland,* 25 (July 1978), pp. 119-120. Short review of *Irish University Review,* 8, 1.

See Bernard Share, 'Current Periodicals', *Books Ireland,* 36 (September 1979), p. 144. Short review of *IUR,* 9, 1.

See Kane Archer, 'Sifting the evidence', *Books Ireland,* 44 (June 1980) p. 112. Short review of *IUR,* 10, 1.

See Bernard Share, 'Taking up the slack', *Books Ireland,* 86 (September 1984) pp. 157–158. Short review of *IUR,* 14, 1.

An author 'Index to Volumes 1–15, 1970–1985' appears in volume 15, number 2 (Autumn 1995), pp. 263–300.

THE GOWN, A STUDENT PUBLICATION OF QUEEN'S UNIVERSITY

Location:	Belfast (publisher QUB Students' Representative Council, printer Duffy Bros., 47 Divis Street)
Editor(s):	Various anonymous committees
Dates:	Number 1 (26 April 1955)–volume 43, number 1 (September 1997)
No. of issues:	500?
Average periodicity:	Monthly
Average no. pages:	8–12
Libraries:	BL(Colin) (volume 3, number 1 (12 October 1956)–volume 6, Number 12 (6 May 1960), and volume 8, number 1 (6 October 1961)–volume 8, number 10 (11 May 1962) only); QUB(Arc)=876 (number 1 (26 April 1955), 2 (12 May 1955) and 2 'Free Issue' (26 May 1955); then volume 2, number 1 (19 October 1955)–volume 5, number 13 (9 October 1959); volume 6, number 2–volume 9, number 3; volume 9, number 6–volume 10, number 7; volume 11, number 2–volume 25, number 5 (15 March 1979) with only a few omissions; then volume 30, number 4 (February 1984)–volume 43, number 1 (September 1997), with lots of gaps.

A student newspaper, preoccupied with issues such as grants, entertainment and accommodation (apart from a period in the late 1960s and early 1970s when the political events outside intrude), the *Gown* has very little literary material. Volume 7, number 5 (9

December 1960) has a positive review of *Gorgon* by Stewart Parker on page 10; a 'Profile' feature started in volume 6, and in volume 8, number 1 (6 October 1961) this deals with Parker himself (p. 8); finally, volume 15, number 9 (4 March 1969) carries a short interview with Michael MacLiammoir, by Simon Callow.

See John Goodby, 'New Wave I: "A Rising Tide"; Irish Poetry in the 60s', in Theo Dorgan, *Irish Poetry Since Kavanagh* (Dublin, 1996), pp. 116–135, *passim*.

Continued as:

GOWN LITERARY SUPPLEMENT

Location:	Belfast (1972, publisher QUB Students' Representative Council, 1985–January 1989, Gown Publications, Students Union; 1972, printer Duffy Bros., 47 Divis Street, 1978–unknown, 1984-Spring/Summer 1990 – Ronan Press Limited, Annesborough Industrial Area, Lurgan)
Editor(s):	1972 – Peter Tonkin and Tony Dumphy; 1978 – Gerry Carleton; 1985–1987 – Martin Hill and Kevin Smith; 1989–1990 – John Brown and Martin Crawford
Dates:	1972-Spring/ Summer 1990? (Unnumbered)
No. of issues:	9?
Average periodicity:	Highly irregular
Average no. pages:	12 (1972–1985); 36 (1986–1989); 48 (January 1989–1990)
Libraries:	QUB(Arc)=876.

The first of these was an extra eight pages inserted into the middle of volume 19, number 3 of the 'parent' publication, *The Gown* (7 November 1972), and included a poem by Paul Muldoon, two by Seamus Heaney, and a story by Bernard MacLaverty.

Literary Supplement 1978 was the first independent publication, and had a story by Michael Foley, and poems by Paul Durcan, Tom Paulin, William Peskett, Meta Mayne Reid and James Simmons.

Literary Supplement '84, has an autobiographical article on his time at Queen's by Philip Larkin; an interview with Paul Muldoon; and poems from John Hughes, Peter McDonald, Roy McFadden, Martin Mooney and Matthew Sweeney.

Gown Literary Supplement's most productive phase begins in 1985, with an issue marked volume 31, number 4. Now reduced to A4 size, it begins to appear more regularly, and acquires both a cohesive look, and a distinct editorial personality, for the first time. Over the next six issues they have a series of high-profile interviews, with Boland, Durcan, Alisdair Gray, Heaney, Medbh McGuckian, Bernard MacLaverty and Craig Raine. There are short book reviews; there is an extract from a play by Paulin; an autobiographical piece by McFadden; and stories by John Banville, John Kelly and Martin Mooney. Above all there are dozens of poems, poems by Norman Dugdale, Sam Burnside, Ciarán Carson, Gerald Dawe, Ian Duhig, Paul Durcan, Gavin Ewart, Michael Foley, Roy Fuller, Allen Ginsberg, Alisdair Gray, Robert Greacen, Seamus Heaney, John Hewitt, Rita Ann Higgins, Selima Hill, Ruth Hooley, John

Frank Ormsby

Tom Paulin

Hughes, Fred Johnston, Robert Johnstone, Brendan Kennelly, Tom Leonard, Denise Levertov, Michael Longley, Joan McBreen, Peter McDonald, Roy McFadden, Medbh McGuckian, Martin Mooney, Paul Muldoon, Ní Chuilleanáin, Nuala Ní Dhomhnaill, Frank Ormsby, Tom Paulin, Carol Rumens, Janet Shepperson, Simmons, Ian Crichton Smith, Ken Smith, Matthew Sweeney, C.K. Williams and Hugo Williams. In these pages, the regionalist urge which always seems to be at least latent in literary magazines from Ulster is clearly in evidence, and (when we exclude the imported foreign stars) the editors seem to be keen to build up a representative mix of writers who first appeared in the 1940s and 1950s (Greacen, Hewitt, McFadden); in the 1960s (Heaney, Longley, etc.); and new writers from the North.

See Martin Crawford, 'The Gown Literary Supplement', in Daniel Smyth and Paul O'Kane (eds), *The Gown: 35 Years* (Belfast, 1990), p. 29.

Continued as:

GLS, MAGAZINE OF NEW WRITING AND THE ARTS

Location:	Belfast (printer Priory Press, Holywood)
Editor(s):	Martin Crawford and Martin Mooney
Dates:	'New Series', number 1 (February 1993)–number 3 (Winter 1993)
No. of issues:	3
Average periodicity:	Triannual
Average no. pages:	36
Libraries:	none

Visually attractive, in this incarnation greater attention is paid to non-verbal arts, and space is also given to broader reflections on such subjects as the romance of steam trains and football. The focus, although inevitably diluted, remains literary, with book reviews, a couple of short stories and, as ever, lots of poetry. The main poets featured are: Janice Fitzpatrick-Simmons, Fred Johnston, Martin Mooney, Julie O'Callaghan, Janet Shepperson and James Simmons.

THE SHANNONSIDE ANNUAL

Location:	Tralee (Printer The Kerryman, Ltd, Tralee)
Editor(s):	Asdee Tostal Committee
Dates:	Volume 1, number 1 (1956)–volume 1, number 4 (1959)
No. of issues:	4
Average periodicity:	Annual
Average no. pages:	90
Libraries:	BL=PP.6158.deb; BCL=I/914.17605 SHAN (incomplete); NLI=Ir 94146 s 2; PSPL=914.196 (incomplete).

Edited 'in co-operation with the people of North Kerry and its exiles'; a sentimental magazine aimed at the overseas (particularly the American) market, most of its contents are instantly forgettable (reprinting of 'The Cliffs of Duneen', etc.), but it does have a few contributions from famous names. These include autobiographical snippets from Bryan MacMahon and Brendan Kennelly; poems by John B. Keane and MacMahon; an article by MacMahon; a short play by MacMahon; and a story by Kennelly.

See Rudi Holzapfel, 'A Survey of Irish Literary Magazines from 1900 to the Present Day', M Litt thesis (Trinity College Dublin, 1964), p. 68.

THRESHOLD

Location: Belfast (publisher Lyric Players Theatre, 11 Derryvolgie Avenue, Belfast, printer Doric Printing. From Summer 1967 Lyric moves to 23 Grosvenor Road, Belfast 12; from Summer 1969 printer Guilfoyle Printing Co., 78a Peters Hill. From Summer 1970 Lyric moves to 55 Ridgeway Street, Belfast 9. From Spring 1976 printer Elo Press Ltd, Dublin 8; from Autumn 1980 printer Belfast Litho Printers Ltd; from Winter 1983 printers Graphic 3; from Winter 1985 printers The Universities Press (Belfast) Ltd.

Editor(s): Mary O'Malley, Poetry Editor John Hewitt; from Spring 1960 joined by 'Contributing Editors' John Montague, Roger McHugh, Benedict Kiely and Desmond Fennell; from Autumn 1960 John Boyle joins 'Contributing Editors'; from Autumn 1961 Editor Boyle, Poetry Editor Hewitt, with no others; number 17 Editor McHugh; number 18 Editor Roy McFadden; number 19 Editor McHugh; number 20 Editor Brian Friel; number 21 Editors Sam Hanna Bell and John Boyd; number 22 Editor Seamus Heaney; number 23 Editor John Montague; number 24 Editor Boyd and James O'Malley; from number 25 Editors Boyd and Patrick Galvin; number 27 no editor given; number 28 Editors Boyd and Stephen Gilbert; number 29 Editor Boyd; number 30 Editor McHugh; number 31 Editor Hewitt; number 32 Editor Seamus Deane; number 33 Editors Boyd and Gerald Dawe; number 34 Editors Boyd and Daniel J. Casey; number 35 Editors Boyd and Hewitt; number 36 Editor Boyd; from number 37 Editors Boyd and Desmond Maxwell.

Dates: Volume 1, number 1 (February 1957)–volume 5, number 2 (Autumn/Winter 1961/62); number 17 (no date)–number 39 (Autumn 1990)

No. of issues: 39

Average periodicity: Quarterly; from 1960, biannual; from number 17, annual

Average no. pages: 90

Libraries: BL=PP.5196.hb; BCL=IR; LIN; NLI=Ir 8205 t 3; PSPL=820.5; QUB=hAP4.T5 (volume 1, number 1–number 31 only); RDS=NL54; RIA=Fr C/5/2/A (incomplete); TCD (Old Library)=OLS L-2-189-192; UCD=J 820; UCG=052 (PS).

Threshold

Contributors :

MARY BECKETT

R. D. C. BLACK

T. P. FLANAGAN

JOHN HEWITT

PEARSE HUTCHINSON

JOHN JORDAN

RUDOLF KLEIN

ROGER McHUGH

EILIS McCARTHY

ANDRE ROUYER

Editor : MARY O'MALLEY

VOL. 1   FEBRUARY 1957   No. 1

TWO SHILLINGS and SIXPENCE

Started as the organ of the Lyric Players (later the Lyric Theatre), and so from first to last a stream of articles on the theatre and playwrights runs through almost all issues, covering Beckett (by Alec Reid), Behan (Augustine Martin), O'Casey (Simmons), Shaw (John Jordan, also by Vivian Mercier), Synge (Seamus Deane) and Yeats (Donoghue). A number of plays, or extracts from them, are also published, including Hewitt's *The Bloody Brae*, and an untitled extract by Mahon, while the whole of number 27 (Spring 1976) is devoted to three plays by Patrick Galvin. In addition, volume 3, number 2 (Summer 1959) hosted a debate on the controversy stirred up by Sam Thompson's *Over the Bridge*, with contributions from O'Malley, McFadden and Janet McNeill. Otherwise, *Threshold*'s career divides neatly into two phases, 1957–1967 and 1969–1990 (or before and after the move to Ridgeway Street).

Unlike earlier magazines, e.g. *Samhain*, intended as the voice of a theatre company, *Threshold* also succeeds as a broader literary magazine, with good quality reviews, articles and original writing. In the first phase, there were: stories by Mary Beckett, John Boyd, Friel, Tom MacIntyre, Montague, Michael J. Murphy, Kate O'Brien and James Plunkett; extracts from novels by Sam Hanna Bell, Kiely, Thomas Kilroy, Maurice Leitch and John McGahern; autobiography by Denis Ireland; and poems by Colum, Padraic Fiacc, Galvin, Hutchinson, Kell, Kinsella, McFadden, Milne, Montague, Frank O'Connor and Ezra Pound. The articles range widely, covering young Irish painters, visits to the North by the likes of Pearse or Kavanagh, traditional music, the New Right in America, or contemporary life in the Eastern bloc, but the majority are devoted to Irish writers and writing: a piece on the process of writing, by McNeill; Hewitt's 'Irish Poets, Learn your Trade'; Hewitt on Kavanagh, or MacDonagh; McFadden on Ulster writers of the 1940s and early 1950s; or Coffey on Beckett. Finally, each issue usually finished with a substantial review, usually by Hewitt, occasionally by W.R. Rodgers or Montague. Volume 4, number 1 (Spring/Summer 1960) has a piece on the winners of their 'May Morton Memorial Poetry Competition', in which McFadden came second and the winner was Montague (with 'Like Dolmens Round My Childhood'). Number 19 (Autumn 1965) celebrated the centenary of Yeats's birth with articles by Clarke, McHugh and O'Malley, while this phase closed with a bumper twenty-first birthday issue, designated an 'anthology of Ulster writing', and with contributions (some previously published) from Joyce Cary, Greacen, Hewitt, MacNeice, McFadden, McLaverty, Montague, Michael J. Murphy, Brian O'Nolan, Rodgers, Joseph Tumelty [*sic*] but also from a younger generation like Seamus Deane, Friel, Heaney, Michael Longley, Mahon, Brian Moore, Stewart Parker and Simmons. The combination of theatre house journal and wide-ranging articles at times makes *Threshold* look like it was striving to be a provincial cross between *Samhain* and the *Bell*: smacking of the Left Book Club and the age of verse drama, by the mid-1960s it was starting to look as anachronistic and out of touch as the *Dublin Magazine* of the 1950s. This is only emphasised by the presence of Longley, Mahon, Parker and so on in the anthology.

Despite the fact that it was largely edited by a stalwart of the old brigade, John Boyd, phase two begins confidently in number 22 (Summer 1969) with a strong issue dominated by the new generation: a Heaney article on Hewitt's poetry, and poems by Kinsella, Longley,

John Boyd

Mahon, Montague, Muldoon and Simmons. For the next decade, this second wind is maintained: stories by Anne Devlin, Aidan Higgins, Maurice Leitch and John McGahern; autobiography from Seamus Deane, Brian Moore and James Simmons; and poems by Dawe, Durcan, Foley, Friel, Heaney, Ormsby, Paulin and Matthew Sweeney. The articles, now more narrowly focused, are also by the likes of Deane and Simmons. Number 28 (Spring 1977) is dedicated to Forrest Reid (including contributions from John Boyd, George Buchanan, E.M. Forster, McGahern and Simmons), and number 34 is a (slightly lacklustre) 'Irish-American Issue'. Indeed, the weaknesses of this last issue highlight an increasing loss of momentum in *Threshold*, which began to run out of steam at the start of the 1980s. Quite rightly, among all these bright new things they maintained regular contact with all their regulars, and Norman Dugdale, Greacen, Hewitt, McFadden, Montague and the rest continued to contribute poems and articles; but throughout the 1980s there is a growing sense of there being more old hands around, and more old, reprinted material, more obituaries and a general sense of looking back, not forward. This is exemplified by number 37 (Winter 1986/87) which, while fine in itself, contains an obituary of McHugh, some unpublished autobiography from O'Faoláin, poems by Dugdale, Hewitt and Rodgers, and an article on Colum. In this light, it is no surprise that the enterprise ground to a halt within two years.

One last word should be said about the covers of this periodical which, until terminal decline started with number 34, were always striking; artists included Louis le Brocquy, Gerard Dillon, Rowel Friers, Colin Middleton, Neil Shawcross and Anne Yeats.

See John Jordan, 'Two Literary Reviews', *Hibernia*, 25, 4 (April 1961), p. 21.

See Rudi Holzapfel, 'A Survey of Irish Literary Magazines from 1900 to the Present Day', M Litt thesis (Trinity College Dublin, 1964), p. 69.

See Kevin Boyle, 'Threshold: the Northern Crisis', *Fortnight,* 2 (9 October 1970), p. 22. A review of this issue, ed. Montague.

See Derek Simpson, untitled review of *Threshold* 27, *Fortnight*, 133 (24 September 1976), p. 14.

See J.B. Kilfeather, untitled review of *Threshold* 28, *Fortnight,* 149 (10 June 1977), p. 16.

See Dillon Johnston, *Irish Poetry After Joyce* (Notre Dame, 1985), p. 42.

See Peter Denman, 'Ireland's Little Magazines', Barbara Hayley and Enda McKay (eds), *300 Years of Irish Periodicals* (Mullingar, 1987), p. 136.

See Norman Vance, *Irish Literature: A Social History – Tradition, Identity and Difference* (Oxford, 1990), p. 218.

An author index (up to 1969) appears in Richard J. Hayes, *Sources for the History of Irish Civilisation: Articles in Irish Periodicals*, 5 vols (Boston, 1970).

FOCUS, A MONTHLY REVIEW

Location:	Dublin (publisher 18 Ely Place, Dublin, printer Publicity and Art Printing Co., Ltd, 26 Pearse Street, Dublin; from volume 2 printer Turner's Printing Co. Ltd, Earl Street, Longford; from volume 3, number 7 publisher 4 Herbert Street, Dublin)
Editor(s):	Risteárd Ó Glaisne; volume 8–9, 'Acting Editor' W.R. Grey
Dates:	Volume 1, number 1 (January 1958)–volume 9, number 12 (December 1966)
No. of issues:	108
Average periodicity:	Monthly
Average no. pages:	48 (volume 1); 32 (volume 2–volume 5); 24 (volume 6–volume 9)
Libraries:	LIN; NLI=IR 05 f 10; QUB=hAP4.F65; RDS=NL53; TCD=Per 76–298; UCG=052 (PS).

'An independent, interdenominational, Irish Protestant journal, it essays a constructive, Christian analysis of Irish and world trends, sociological, cultural, political, economic, ecclesiastical and theological...[and will] encourage among our people a greater appreciation of their role in contemporary society.' (volume 1, number 1, p. 1).

Carries a wide range of articles – 'On Being a TD', citizenship, Penal Times, Albert Camus – fulfilling the above aim; the tone is a little earnest and stilted, something like an Anglican vicar's 'nice' response to *The Bell* (the 'Editorial Council' includes three Reverends, a Councillor and a TD). Fascinating for the social historian for its insight into how the post-Yeats generation of Irish Protestants adjusted to finding a new role in the Republic, less so for its contribution to literature. This comprises an occasional poem or story; some literary articles – on the Irish identity (Bernard Share); on Joyce Cary; on Lennox Robinson (Rutherford Mayne); on Samuel Beckett, or James Joyce, or Patrick Kavanagh; on T.S. Eliot, Æ, C.S. Lewis and F.R. Higgins; and an obituary of Sam Thompson. Each issue ends with a couple of pages of short book notices, including a handful through 1962–1963 by Michael Longley.

UNIVERSITY GAZETTE

Location:	Dublin (address Nullamore University Residence, Milltown, published by Dublin Post, printer Monument Press, Dublin and Bray; from number 10 printer Mount Solus Press Ltd, Tritonville Road, Sandymount; from number 33 publisher 9 Hume Street, Dublin 2; from number 34 publisher 86 St. Stephen's Green, Dublin 2)
Editor(s):	Anon. (numbers 8 and 9 Ed. Leo Hickey, Board inc. MacDara Woods; numbers 11–13 Ed. Denys Turner, Board including Ní Chuilleanáin; numbers 19–25 Ed. Peter Bristow; from number 27 Ed. Brendan Dowling; from number 33 Ed. Brian O'Rourke; from number 34 Ed. Fergus Killoran)
Dates:	1959–1968?
No. of issues:	35?
Average periodicity:	Triannual
Average no. pages:	10 (6–13); 16 (14–35)
Libraries:	BL=PP.7611.it (incomplete); NLI=Ir 3784105 u 7 (incomplete); TCD=Per 75–334.

[From number 19, subtitle 'An Irish Inter-University Magazine'.]

A magazine trying to bring together students in UCC, UCG, UCD and QUB, with a handful of short stories, some general pieces and a back page of poems in each issue. Interesting because of a number of famous names who were students at the time; there were poems from Seamus Deane, Rudi Holzapfel, Derek Mahon, MacDara Woods (non-students, e.g. Brendan Kennelly and Montague, also contributed occasionally). They also boasted an interview with Cyril Cusack, and an article by Kate O'Brien.

See Rudi Holzapfel, 'A Survey of Irish Literary Magazines from 1900 to the Present Day', M Litt thesis (Trinity College Dublin, 1964), p. 75.

GORGON, A PUBLICATION OF THE ENGLISH SOCIETY

Location: Belfast (badly typed and mimeographed)
Editor(s):   Committee
Dates: Number 1 (1959?)–5? (Hilary 1961)
No. of issues: 5
Average periodicity: Annual?
Average no. pages: 26
Libraries: LIN (Hilary 1961 only); QUB(Arc)=876 (numbers 3–5 only)

It may be a coincidence, but QUB has copies of only the three issues of *Gorgon* (3, 4 and 5) which feature work by Heaney (both under his own name, and the pen-name 'Incertus'); there also appears a poem by Stewart Parker (number 3), and another two by Seamus Deane (4 and 5). Heaney is also thanked for his help in an editorial role, and he wrote the editorial for the third issue.

See Stewart Parker, untitled review of *Gorgon*, *The Gown*, 7, 5 (9 December 1960), p. 10.

WRITERS' DIGEST

Location: Dublin (publisher 64 Tritonville Road, Ballsbridge, printer the Anglo-Celt, Ltd, Cavan)
Editor(s):   Nicholas O'Hare, Poetry Editor Kevin Faller
Dates: Number 1 (Autumn 1959)–number 4 (Autumn 1960)
No. of issues: 4
Average periodicity: Quarterly
Average no. pages: 68
Libraries: NLI=Ir 8205 w 2; TCD=Per 75–480.

As proclaimed in the first editorial, the purpose of *Writers' Digest* was to help new writers make their first appearance in print; the magazine itself is attractively enough presented, although the quality of the material is poor, and none of the contributors went on to greater achievements.

See Rudi Holzapfel, 'A Survey of Irish Literary Magazines from 1900 to the Present Day', M Litt thesis (Trinity College Dublin), 1964, p. 72.

NONPLUS

Location: Dublin (publisher Nonplus, 1 Wilton Place, Dublin (although '© 1959, by Irish Channels Limited'?), printer Dolmen Press, Dublin)
Editor(s):   Patricia Murphy
Dates: Number 1 (October 1959)–number 4 (Winter 1960)

No. of issues: 4
Average periodicity: Quarterly
Average no. pages: 102
Libraries: BL=PP.4881.sdu; LIN; NLI=Ir 05 n 13; PSPL=805; QUB=hAP4.N7;
                     RIA=Fr C/5/1/D Misc Box N-O; TCD(Old Library)=Press A Dol
                     1959 NON 14; UCD=J 050.

The usual very attractive, quality Liam Miller production, albeit one which is quite interesting, without really taking on a life of its own. Each issue opens with a major political article – on the Cold War, on foreign policy, on being a 'West Briton' (Brian Inglis), and on Sarajevo (Hubert Butler) – and further in, another, equally heavyweight piece is to be found (subjects include the history of the French Revolution, Max Jacob, the GAA (Kavanagh), Camus, Heidegger, and philosophy. Each issue also contains a reprinted selection from 'Cruiskeen Lawn', and a rather lacklustre selection of poems and prose (the best of these is in issue 1, with new work from Patrick Kavanagh). In the final analysis, the contents do not ever really gel.

See Rudi Holzapfel, 'A Survey of Irish Literary Magazines from 1900 to the Present Day', M Litt thesis (Trinity College Dublin, 1964), p. 71.

An author index appears in Rudi Holzapfel, 'A Survey of Irish Literary Magazines from 1900 to the Present Day', M Litt thesis (Trinity College Dublin, 1964).

THE KILKENNY MAGAZINE, AN ALL-IRELAND LITERARY REVIEW

Location: Kilkenny (publisher Kilkenny Literary Society, 35 High Street
                     Kilkenny, printer The Kilkenny Journal)
Editor(s):   James Delahanty, Assistant Editor, Frank McEvoy
Dates: Number 1 (Summer 1960)–number 18 (Autumn/Winter 1970)
No. of issues: 18
Average periodicity: Quarterly (1-7); then biannual, but varies
Average no. pages: 64 (1–5); 80 (6–9); 150 (10–18)
Libraries: LIN; NLI=Ir 8205 k 3; PSPL=820.5; QUB=hPR8700.K4 (missing
                     first issue); RIA=Fr C/1/6/C; TCD=OLS L-3-731; UCC; UCD=J 820
                     (incomplete); UCG=941.89 (PS).

The *Kilkenny Magazine* opens with an extended article by James Delahanty, 'The Bell: 1940-54 [1]', in which he explicitly identifies with the earlier magazine. One of the prime strengths of the *Kilkenny Magazine* was its stories, and they printed contributions by John Banville, Brian Friel, John Jordan, Mary Lavin, Tom MacIntyre, Bryan MacMahon, McGahern, McLaverty, John Montague and Frank O'Connor. There was also much strong poetry, by Rivers Carew, Clarke, Colum, Conleth Ellis, Fiacc, Harnett, Heaney, Hewitt, Jordan, John B. Keane, Kennelly, Kinsella, Liddy, Milne, Montague, Newmann and O'Connor. Book reviewers included Delahanty himself, and Kate O'Brien; Butler contributes a couple of interesting articles, alongside one on Yeats (by Kavanagh), and another on Kavanagh himself (Colum).

However, while some of the contributors (e.g. Butler) appeared in *The Bell*, *Kilkenny Magazine* remained a more narrowly literary publication, and Delahanty never came close to the range of interests, the quality of writing, nor indeed the popular appeal of his model.

An editorial to the third issue announces that An Chomhairle Ealaion is giving them a little money.

See John Jordan, 'Two Literary Reviews', *Hibernia*, 25, 4 (April 1961), p. 21.
See Rudi Holzapfel, 'A Survey of Irish Literary Magazines from 1900 to the Present Day', M Litt thesis (Trinity College Dublin, 1964), p. 74.
See Peter Denman, 'Ireland's Little Magazines', Barbara Hayley and Enda McKay (eds), *300 Years of Irish Periodicals* (Mullingar, 1987), p. 139.

An author index appears in Rudi Holzapfel, 'A Survey of Irish Literary Magazines from 1900 to the Present Day', M Litt thesis (Trinity College Dublin, 1964).
An author index (up to 1969) appears in Richard J. Hayes, *Sources for the History of Irish Civilisation: Articles in Irish Periodicals*, 5 vols (Boston, 1970).

INTEREST, AN INDEPENDENT UNIVERSITY MAGAZINE

Location:	Belfast (publisher Interest Publications, 22 University Square, Belfast 7, printer Ulster Productions Co. Ltd. at the Nendrum Press Comber; from volume 3, number 2 printer Enterprise Printing Service, Up. Library St., Belfast; May 1969 printer Botanic House Printers, Botanic Avenue, Belfast 7)
Editor(s):	Stewart Parker (and sub-editors for literary, political, features and reviews); from volume 2, number 2 Nan Shearan (with Parker on an editorial Board); from volume 3, number 4 Alan Gabbey (Parker drops out); from volume 5, number 1 Angela McCourt and Maurice Gallagher; volume 6, number 1 Maurice Gallagher; May 1969 Ed. Martyn Turner.
Dates:	Volume 1, number 1 (November 1960)–volume 6, number 1 (May 1966) and unnumbered issue May 1969
No. of issues:	22?
Average periodicity:	Triannual
Average no. pages:	14 (volumes 1 and 2); 34 (volumes 3–6); 30 (May 1969)
Libraries:	LIN (incomplete); QUB(Arc)=876 (incomplete).

A student magazine, with the individual personality of Stewart Parker stamped heavily upon it (he contributes some half dozen poems, two or three articles and a couple of stories; in addition, some unsigned pieces in the first issues read very much like Parker's work). Aside from him, there are one or two interesting articles and reviews, including pieces by Philip Hobsbaum and Eamonn McCann, and a review of Hobsbaum's *Group Anthology* by Heaney. There are two stories from Bernard MacLaverty, and quite a few poems, by (amongst others) Seamus Heaney, Ian Hill, Hobsbaum, Laurence Lerner, Parker, Simmons and Joan Watton (later Newmann).

The issue from May 1969 has a better card cover, and lots of little illustrations and cartoons; there are two poems by Michael Stephens, and a feature on Carolyn Mulholland.

ACORN, A LITERARY MAGAZINE PUBLISHED BY THE ENGLISH DEPARTMENT AT MAGEE UNIVERSITY COLLEGE, LONDONDERRY

Location:	Derry (publisher Magee University College, printer The Derry Standard, Ltd.)
Editor(s):	Alan Warner
Dates:	Volume 1, number 1 (Winter 1961)–number 13 (Spring 1968)
No. of issues:	13
Average periodicity:	Biannual
Average no. pages:	28 (1–4); 14 (5–7); 40 (8–11); 28 (12–13)
Libraries:	BCL=PyF BST; LIN; NLI=Ir 8205 a 3; TCD=IN.C.MAG.

Starts off as an A5 little magazine, in look and feel very like *Rann*. Despite disclaiming any Regionalist agenda, it does have a strong local flavour. Articles by Barbara Hunter, O'Faoláin, W.R. Rodgers (on Ulster), Warner (on Kavanagh); poems by T.R. Henn, Hewitt, Hunter, Kennelly, Liddy; interviews with Friel and Hobsbaum.

See Rudi Holzapfel, M Litt thesis, 'A Survey of Irish Literary Magazines from 1900 to the Present Day', M Litt thesis (Trinity College Dublin, 1964), p. 77.

An author index appears in Richard J. Hayes, *Sources for the History of Irish Civilisation: Articles in Irish Periodicals*, 5 vols (Boston, 1970).

THE DOLMEN MISCELLANY OF IRISH WRITING

Location:	Dublin (publisher and printer Dolmen Press, 23 Upper Mount Street, Dublin)
Editor(s):	John Montague (poetry editor Thomas Kinsella)
Dates:	Number 1 (1962)
No. of issues:	1
Average periodicity:	–
Average no. pages:	120
Libraries:	BL=PP.8000.dk; NLI=LO; PSPL=820.5; QUB=hPR8844.D6; TCD (Old Library)=Press A, Dol 1962 12; UCC; UCD=820.8 IR.

Although only one issue actually appeared, others were intended – the introduction says:

'Future issues will, of course, depend upon your support', and refers to itself as a magazine (rather than an anthology, or other one-off publication).

This is a 'showcase' magazine, in this case intended both to illustrate the strength of the Dolmen Press roster, and to advertise to the world (particularly the New World) that Yeats and Joyce were dead and that a new generation of Irish writers was clamouring for their attention. It had a huge impact (not least because of a publishing tie-in with OUP); e.g. it includes extracts from what would become *Langrishe Go Down* and *The Barracks* within a few pages of one another. There is prose by Aidan Higgins, John Jordan, John McGahern, Brian Moore and James Plunkett; an article on Goldsmith, by John Montague; reviews by Montague and John Jordan; and poetry by Pearse Hutchinson, Valentin Iremonger, Thomas Kinsella, James Liddy, and Richards Murphy and Richard Weber.

See Rudi Holzapfel, 'A Survey of Irish Literary Magazines from 1900 to the Present Day', M Litt thesis (Trinity College Dublin, 1964), p. 80.
See John Goodby, 'New Wave I: 'A Rising Tide'; Irish Poetry in the 60s', in Theo Dorgan, *Irish Poetry Since Kavanagh* (Dublin, 1996), pp. 116-135, *passim*.
See James Liddy, 'How We Stood with Liam Miller: *The Dolmen Miscellany*, 1962', *New Hibernia Review,* 2, 3 (Autumn 1998), pp. 9–15.

An author index appears in Rudi Holzapfel, 'A Survey of Irish Literary Magazines from 1900 to the Present Day', M Litt thesis (Trinity College Dublin, 1964).

ARENA

Location:	Coolgreaney (publisher Coolgreany, Inch, Co. Wexford, printer Leinster Leader, Naas)
Editor(s):	James Liddy and Liam O'Connor; from number 2, also Michael Harnett
Dates:	Number 1 (Spring 1963)–number 4 (Spring 1965)
No. of issues:	4
Average periodicity:	Irregular
Average no. pages:	26
Libraries:	BL=PP.8001.gk; BCL=I/821 AREN (1982 reprint); LIN; NLI=Ir 8205 a 4; PSPL=820.5; QUB=hfPR8700.A7 (1982 reprint); TCD=Per 80–35.

Designed by Liam Miller, *Arena* is not typical of his work, being in a *Kavanagh's Weekly*-type newspaper format. There are poems by Leland Bardwell, Christy Brown, Clarke, Cronin, Paul Durcan, Robert Graves, Harnett, Hutchinson, Kavanagh, Kinsella, James Liddy, Mahon, Montague, Lorna Reynolds, Knute Skinner, Weber and Woods; stories by Jordan, Lavin, Tom MacIntyre and Montague; and an extract from a James Plunkett novel. The editorial to number 4 announces the title's closure with this longer issue. Despite its deliberately downmarket appearance, the level of the contributions (the poetry in particular) is pretty good.

See Rudi Holzapfel, 'A Survey of Irish Literary Magazines from 1900 to the Present Day', M Litt thesis (Trinity College Dublin, 1964), p. 82.

See James Liddy, *This Was Arena* (Naas, 1982). Reprint of all four issues, plus introductory essay.

See Peter Denman, 'Ireland's Little Magazines', Barbara Hayley and Enda McKay (eds), *300 Years of Irish Periodicals* (Mullingar, 1987), p. 140.

An author index appears in Rudi Holzapfel, 'A Survey of Irish Literary Magazines from 1900 to the Present Day', M Litt thesis (Trinity College Dublin, 1964).

An author and (limited) subject index appears in Stephen H. Goode, *Index to Commonwealth Little Magazines* (New York and London, 1966).

An author index appears in Richard J. Hayes, *Sources for the History of Irish Civilisation: Articles in Irish Periodicals*, 5 vols (Boston, 1970).

MAÑANA

Location:	Dublin (published by 'the Phrynge', 9 Lower Baggot Street, printer Brunswick Press, 179 Pearse Street)
Editor(s):	Peter Ryan and Eli Renn
Dates:	No.1 (May 1963) only?
No. of issues:	1?
Average periodicity:	Unknown
Average no. pages:	8
Libraries:	BL=PP.8001.cf; NLI=Ir 05 p 32.

Poems and essays, including some by Rudi Holzapfel and Brendan Kennelly.

See Rudi Holzapfel, 'A Survey of Irish Literary Magazines from 1900 to the Present Day', M Litt thesis (Trinity College Dublin, 1964), p. 81.

An author index appears in Rudi Holzapfel, 'A Survey of Irish Literary Magazines from 1900 to the Present Day', M Litt thesis (Trinity College Dublin, 1964).

THE NORTHERN REVIEW A QUARTERLY MAGAZINE OF THE ARTS

Location:	Comber (publisher Eusemere, Comber, Co. Down, from number 2, publisher Northern Review, 33 Howard Street, Belfast; from number 3 publisher Flat 4, Hope House, College Park, Belfast; printer Thos. Brough, Cox and Dunn, Ltd., Stanhope House, Belfast 13, from number 3 printer Ulster Productions Co. Ltd., The Nendrum Press, Comber)
Editor(s):	Patrick Lynch and Michael Mitchell (and Board, including Philip Hobsbaum); from number 2 Ed. Mitchell, and Heaney and Michael

	Longley have joined the Board
Dates:	Volume 1, number 1 (Spring 1965)–volume 1, number 3 (1967)
No. of issues:	3
Average periodicity:	Annual
Average no. pages:	88
Libraries:	LIN; NLI=Ir 805 n 4; QUB=hAP4.N8; RIA=Fr C/5/1/D Misc Box N-O.

A very handsome production, with good colour covers, reproductions of photographs and paintings, all well produced. As *Lagan* was the product of the Regionalist group around Hewitt, so *Northern Review* is the product of Hobsbaum's Belfast Group. Although tempered by contributions from famous contacts of Hobsbaum, a regionalist agenda is strongly implicit, including material by, and about, such alumni of an earlier generation as Boyd, Rodgers and MacNeice. It was all very classy, but had no hope of lasting (it cost ten times as much as the recently deceased *Arena*).

Northern Review published poems by Norman Dugdale, Heaney, Hobsbaum, Ted Hughes, Michael Longley, Mahon, Joan Newmann, Stewart Parker, Peter Redgrove and Arthur Terry; and stories by John Banville, John Boyd, Tom MacIntyre and Stewart Parker. There are also a number of good articles, for example Anthony Burgess on Aldous Huxley, Hobsbaum on Joyce Cary, Denis Ireland on Yeats, George MacCann on MacNeice, and Eamonn McCann on Sam Thompson; and reviews by a number of hands, including Michael Allen, Seamus Heaney, Edna Longley and Frank O'Connor. In addition, W.R. Rodgers contributed an editorial to number 2, and John Boyd an obituary of Frank O'Connor (number 3).

THE HOLY DOOR

Location:	Dublin (publisher 156 Botanic Road, Glasnevin, Dublin 9)
Editor(s):	Brian Lynch
Dates:	Number 1 (Summer 1965)–number 3 (Spring 1966)
No. of issues:	3
Average periodicity:	'Published occasionally'
Average no. pages:	34
Libraries:	BL=PP.8007.eg; LIN; NLI=IR 8205 h 2.

Declared in the opening editorial to be '…devoted to the new mind and the new eye-glimpses of which were to be found in ARENA'; rough and ready production, but the quality of the contents is high. There are poems by Auden, Bardwell, Christy Brown, Cronin, Paul Durcan, Michael Harnett, Hutchinson, Kavanagh, Kinsella, Liddy, Milne, Montague, Neruda (trans. Robert Bly); stories by Aidan Higgins and MacIntyre; an article by Cronin; a novel extract by Harnett; and some reviews. A bitter little footnote in the second issue declares: 'no thanks are due to the Arts Council'.

Author and (limited) subject index appears in Stephen H. Goode, *Index to Commonwealth Little Magazines* (New York and London, 1966.)

An author index appears in Richard J. Hayes, *Sources for the History of Irish Civilisation: Articles in Irish Periodicals*, 5 vols (Boston, 1970).

PHOENIX, A REVIEW OF POETRY, CRITICISM AND THE ARTS (NEW QUARTERLY SERIES)

Location:	Belfast (publisher Phoenix, 74 Fitzroy Avenue, Belfast, printer Botanic House Printers Ltd., 48 Botanic Avenue, Belfast)
Editor(s):	Harry Chambers
Dates:	Number 1 (March 1967)–number 3 (Spring 1968)
No. of issues:	3
Average periodicity:	Irregular
Average no. pages:	58
Libraries:	BCL=IR; LIN; NLI=Ir 8205 p 8; QUB=hAP4.P5; TCD=Per 80–607.

Phoenix was produced wherever Chambers happened to be living, and was only published from Belfast for this short series. I have decided to include it, even though the third number was printed in Manchester, as all three were substantially filled with Irish material, and even the third was simply a continuation of the Belfast period.

Opens with a 'Special Arts in Ulster Issue'; this has poetry by Heaney, Mahon, and Longley (who also contributes a sequence); photographs of sculpture by Carolyn Mulholland; an article on Brian Moore (Chambers); a review of first 12 Festival Poetry Pamphlets; and a book review by Edna Longley. The second issue is more of the same, with poems by Heaney, Longley and Montague; photographs of paintings by John Pakenham; poems in translation by Mahon; and reviews of the next three Festival Poetry Pamphlets, and of Lowell (Mahon). Finally, the last issue has a review of a James Simmons's first collection, as well as poems by Dugdale, Heaney, Longley, Patric Stevenson and Simmons.

See Peter Denman, 'Ireland's Little Magazines', Barbara Hayley and Enda McKay (eds), *300 Years of Irish Periodicals* (Mullingar, 1987), p. 142.

AGORA, UNIVERSITY-SEMINARY MAGAZINE

Location:	Maynooth (publisher St. Patrick's College, printer Leinster Leader Ltd., Naas)
Editor(s):	Michael Ledwith; from volume 2, number 1 Sean Larkin; from volume 3, number 1 Dermot O'Neill; plus 21 Regional Editors in colleges and seminaries across Ireland (plus London and Rome)
Dates:	Volume 1, number 1 (Spring 1967)–volume 3, number 1 (Spring 1969)
No. of issues:	4

Average periodicity: Biannual
Average no. pages: 56
Libraries: NLI=IR 3784105 a 3; TCD=Per 80-808 (incomplete).

Overwhelmingly theological, with articles on the role of the nun in a university, or on the church in the Third World, but does carry some half-dozen poems in each issue, along with the occasional short story, and an article on Graham Greene (volume 3, number 2). None of the contributors went on to greater things.

SGANARELLE, A DUBLIN UNIVERSITY MODERN LANGUAGES LITERARY MISCELLANY

Location: Dublin (publisher TCD)
Editor(s):   Ronald Wilson, Bill Valk (1), Editorial Staff Geraldine Mitchell, Kevin Doyle, Chris Dove; Ed. Mike Hoey (3)
Dates: Unnumbered issue (17 April 1967–TCD OPAC); number 3 (December 1968–TCD OPAC) [these datings match internal evidence]
No. of issues: 3?
Average periodicity: Irregular
Average no. pages: 32 and 54
Libraries: TCD=Per 91-704.

[Sganarelle is a character from a Molière play.]

The first issue is a classic example of the 1960s student reaction to the linotype machine – different coloured papers, different coloured text, arbitrary font changes and lots of photos and drawings. It carries enthusiastic articles on surrealism, Yevtushenko and Grass, and a couple of (very) free-verse poems. The only memorable contribution is an interview with Tyrone Guthrie. Issue 3 is a much plainer and cheaper production, and has articles on contemporary Czech writing and Malraux, and a couple of poems.

WORDS

Location: Belfast (publishers Words Magazine, 2 Glanworth Drive, Belfast 15, printers William Sweeney Ltd., 153 North Street, Belfast 1).
Editor(s):   Dermot Marshall, Michael Boyle, Oliver Kennedy.
Dates: Number 1, December 1967
No. of issues: 1?
Average periodicity: Unknown
Average no. pages: 20
Libraries: None (copy in author's possession).

WORDS

No. 1   2/6

DECEMBER   1967

Words by:

Dermot Marshall, Peter Gerrard,
John Morrow, Oliver Kennedy,
Ralph Bossence.

Words with:

Mike Emmerson.
Festival '67.

Words on:

The Freedom of the Press.
An Island Paradise.

Poetry by:

Seamus Heaney, Padriac Fiacc,
Conleth Ellis, Michael Boyle,
Terry Fleming.

Emerged from a creative writing class attended by the editors, includes a story by John Morrow; an article by Ralph Bossence; and poems by Conleth Ellis, Padraic Fiacc and Seamus Heaney.

BROADSHEET

Location:	Dublin (publisher Hall Flat, 4 Upper Mount Street, Dublin 2; from number 5, Flat 2, 15 Herbert Place, Dublin 2; from number 7, 10 Herbert Lane, Dublin 2. Printer Louis Clear; from number 3, printer Clearprint; from number 23, printer Reprographics Ltd.)
Editor(s):	Hayden Murphy, Benedict Ryan; from number 2, Murphy is sole editor
Dates:	Number 1 (February 1968)–number 26–30 (June 1978)
No. of issues:	26
Average periodicity:	Irregular
Average no. pages:	1
Libraries:	BL=P.2000/654 (incomplete); LIN (last issue only); NLI=ILB 821 (incomplete); TCD=Old Library, Papyrus Case 2, number 1 (incomplete).

For most of its run a true Broadsheet, ranging from a single, large sheet up to six sheets; most have cut-and-paste type graphics, or drawings, nearly always in black-and-white (the only exception is the most spectacular number, 10, for which two of the six sheets were printed in full colour). From the bibliographer's viewpoint, *Broadsheet* is highly frustrating; none of the sheets carries an issue number, a date, or even (apart from number 21) a page number, so it is extremely difficult to work out the original order of some of this material. A couple of the issues in TCD (numbers 4 and 10) are associated with a fairly large, brown paper envelope, covered in designs and contributors' names, in which the sheets presumably came. From the seventh issue to the eleventh, the sheets shrank slightly, to well below Broadsheet size; they were then restored.

Traditionally, this type of publication has been seen as belonging to the guerrilla tradition, a quick and cheap method of breaking into publication which will be short-lived and of limited impact. *Broadsheet* is rather different. Not only were some of the issues (number 10 in particular) much more technically ambitious, but the quality of the contributors sets this magazine in the front rank of its contemporaries – Leland Bardwell, Boland, Eamonn Carr, Cronin, Seamus Deane, Durcan, Peter Fallon, Hartnett, Heaney, Rudi Holzapfel, Hutchinson, Jordan, Brendan Kennelly, Kinsella, Liddy, Longley, MacIntyre, Mahon, Gerald Mangan, Montague, Richard Murphy, Ní Chuilleanáin, Porter, Simmons, Knute Skinner, Strong, Stuart, Colm Tóibín and Woods are among the names which appear; and, although some of these are clearly guest appearances by star names, even the core group of writers who appear regularly, five, seven, even ten times, is still impressive – Bardwell, Hartnett, Heaney, Hutchinson, Jordan, Kennelly, Ní Chuilleanáin and Woods. In his 1983 booklet, Murphy says that 1,000 copies were printed of each issue.

Given the lack of detail referred to in the opening paragraph, the following summary is recorded:

Table 1

Issue	Number of sheets	Date
1	1	February 1967
2	1	May 1967
3	5	December 1967
4	5	May 1968
5	1	June 1969
6	1	September 1969
7	1	March 1970
8	2	June 1970
9	1	August 1970
10	6	March 1971
11	1	April 1971
12	1	August 1971
13	1	December 1971
14	1	May 1972
15	1	September 1972
16	1	December 1972
17	1	March 1973
81	1	June 1973
19	1	October 1973
20	1	March 1974
21	6	June 1974
22	1	December 1974
23	1	March 1975
24	1	July 1975
25	1	March 1976
26-30	6	June 1978

See Hayden Murphy, *Broadsheet 1967–1978: Poetry, Prose and Graphics* (Edinburgh, 1983). Short introductory essay, issue by issue commentary (date, number printed, etc.) and author index.

See Hayden Murphy, *Broadsheet retrospective: making an exhibition for myself* (Edinburgh, 1985).

EVERYMAN, AN ANNUAL RELIGIO-CULTURAL REVIEW

Location:	Benburb (publisher Servite Priory, Benburb, Co. Tyrone; printer Cityview Press Ltd., Dublin 1)
Editor(s):	Cyril Farrell, Edmund Haughey, Gerard McCreesh, Denis Haughey, Seamus Heaney
Dates:	Number 1 (1968)–number 3 (1970)
No. of issues:	3
Average periodicity:	Annual
Average no. pages:	156
Libraries:	BL=P.801/1245; LIN; NLI=Ir 05 e 5; PSPL=820.5; QUB=hAP4.E9; RIA=Fr C/1/1/B; TCD=Per 80–206; UCD=J 050.

Reminiscent of an attempt to update for a new era the old, Catholic annual of the more broad-minded, even liberal type. Each one carries photo-features, articles on religious and philosophical questions, and short prose pieces on a range of topics; it represents a vital expression of contemporary attempts to conjure an alternative to division and strife, but is not of great importance as a literary magazine. It published poems by Peter Fallon, Heaney, Kennelly, Michael Longley, Mahon, Montague and others, as well as a verse-play by Heaney; a couple of stories by Joseph Tomelty; an interview with Mac Liammóir (by Heaney); and a couple of articles, including John Cronin on Beckett, and Brian Friel on theatre. Number 3 focuses on the North.

An author index (up to 1969) appears in Richard J. Hayes, *Sources for the History of Irish Civilisation: Articles in Irish Periodicals*, 5 vols (Boston, 1970).

Continued as:
AQUARIUS (FORMERLY EVERYMAN), AN ANNUAL RELIGIO-CULTURAL REVIEW

Location:	Benburb (publisher Servite Priory, Benburb, Co. Tyrone; printer Cityview Press Ltd., Dublin 1)
Editor(s):	Cyril Farrell
Dates:	Number 4 (1971)–number 7 (1974)
No. of issues:	4
Average periodicity:	Annual
Average no. pages:	144
Libraries:	LIN; NLI=Ir 05 e 5; PSPL=820.5; QUB=hAP4.E9; RIA=Fr C/1/1/B; TCD=Per 80–206; UCD=J 050 (incomplete).

The look and feel of this series is exactly the same as that of *Everyman*. However, it published a wider range of literary material, including more than sixty poems, by Eamon Carr, Harry Clifton, John Cronin, John F. Deane, Seamus Heaney, John Montague, James Simmons and Eithne Strong. There were also stories (by Desmond Hogan, Benedict Kiely,

Mary Lavin, and Michael McLaverty); autobiographical fragments by Friel and Kiely; an extract from a Thomas Murphy play; and a number of articles, including Joan Baez on non-violence, Estyn Evans on Ulster, and John Hewitt on Protestant identity.

See Tom Hadden, review of issue 1 of *Aquarius, Fortnight,* 22 (6 August 1971), p. 24.

THE HONEST ULSTERMAN, MONTHLY HANDBOOK FOR A REVOLUTION

Location: Castlerock (publishers The Honest Ulsterman, Main St., printers Regency Press, 76–80 Union Street, Belfast; from August 1968, publishers 15 Kerr Street, Portrush; from December 1969, publishers 56 University Street, Belfast BT7 1HB; from September 1973, publishers 26 Eglantine Avenue; from March 1974, 50 Eglantine Avenue; from Winter 1975, publishers 70 Eglantine Avenue, Belfast BT9 6DY; from Summer 1989, publishers 159 Lower Braniel Road, Belfast BT5 7NN; from February 1993, publishers 14 Shaw Street, Belfast BT4 1PT. From Autumn 1990, printers Noel Murphy Printing Ltd., 7 Lower Crescent, Belfast; from November 1995, publishers 103 Strandburn Drive, Belfast BT4 1NB; from June 1996, publishers 49 Main Street, Greyabbey BT22 2NF)

Editor(s): James Simmons; number 12 (April 1969) Guest Editor Michael Stephens; number 13 (May 1969) Guest Editor Michael Foley; from December 1969, Editors Michael Foley and Frank Ormsby; from September 1972, Editor Frank Ormsby; from May 1984, Editors Frank Ormsby and Robert Johnstone; from Summer 1989, Editors Ruth Hooley and Robert Johnstone; from February 1993, Editors Tom Clyde and Robert Johnstone; from November 1993, Editor Tom Clyde; from June 1994, Editor Tom Clyde, Associate Editor Ruth Hooley; from September 1994, Frank Sewell joins as another Associate Editor.

Dates: Number 1 (May 1968)–number 107 (April 1999)

No. of issues: 107 to date

Average periodicity: Monthly; from January 1970, bimonthly; from March 1972, quarterly; from September 1972, bimonthly; from March 1973, irregular; from Autumn 1984, biannual

Average no. pages: 40; from July 1969, 30; from January 1970, 44; from March 1974, 96; from Winter 1986, 108

Libraries: BCL=IR; BL=P.810/433; LIN; NLI=Ir 8205 h 4; PSPL=820.5; QUB=hAP4.H7; TCD=Per 73–479; UCD=J 800.

[From number 21 (January/February 1970), drops 'handbook for a revolution'.]

Ulster's most successful literary magazine has, through three decades and many personnel changes, managed to maintain high standards and introduce many important new writers.

THE
HONEST ULSTERMAN

a magazine of revolution

LOVE

EXILE

HUMANISM

HASHISH

Courage

History

LOUIS McNIECE

Education

NEW SONG

Mary O'Malley

Drawing by
COLIN MIDDLETON

ROGER McGOUGH

STEVIE SMITH

JOHN HEWITT
BRENDAN KENNELLY

MICHAEL STEPHENS

W. PRICE TURNER

DEREK MAHON

JOHN D. STEWART

PETER LEWIS

JOHN HEARSUM

GAVIN EWART

3/- MAY 1968

Edited by
JAMES SIMMONS

The title's first phase was inaugurated by James Simmons in 1968 with an inheritance from his father; for the next year and a half, the *Honest Ulsterman* would be another of those delightful personal vehicles, the embodiment in print of one man's restless personality (a letter from Simmons to the present writer, dated 7 May 1990, claims that 'The first issue was mostly written by me, and thereafter I sometimes used pseudonyms like Stanley Middleton or Derek Montgomery'). A manifesto was sent to the press in April 1968: 'an opportunity for the best Ulster writers to be read regularly in their own country...The *Honest Ulsterman* will be a regional magazine in the same sense as *Huckleberry Finn* is a regional novel...Properly understood, Literature is a key to Religion, Politics and Philosophy...' Not the least valuable aspect of the first nineteen issues is that they capture so perfectly the Zeitgeist of the times; from the first editorial: 'This is a watershed in history...Ghandi...is the man of the moment, and Churchill seems to have been dead a hundred years...yet, however ridiculous and old-fashioned it seems, violence still haunts us...'. Another way in which it captured that moment is when, in October 1968, its printers were visited by the RUC, after pressure from Stormont to investigate this new revolutionary movement; this, despite the fact that Simmons had placed on record in his second editorial the kind of revolution he was talking about: 'The revolutionary process inside a man sometimes produced by literature, making him see the world fresh'.

As for the literature published, it too was exciting and important. There were articles on Joyce Cary, drugs, Billie Holiday (by Michael Longley), Flann O'Brien, theatre and MacNeice; some autobiographical pieces by Hewitt; an interview with Roger McGough; stories by Michael Foley, John McGahern, John Morrow and Stewart Parker; an extract from a novel by Anthony C. West; and, above all, poetry, by Dugdale, Gavin Ewart, Fiacc, Tony Harrison, Heaney, Hewitt, Hobsbaum, Kennelly, Michael Longley, Mahon, Roger McGough, Kate Middleton, Montague, Muldoon (some of his earliest work), Frank Ormsby, Simmons, Stevie Smith and Michael Stephens. The first handful of issues had one token book review each but, as the initial impetus began to flag, they became more important. While confined to a few pages at the back, the reviewers included Simmons himself, and Edna Longley, Mahon and Ormsby. Along the way, there was the occasional eccentricity, for example the spoof pamphlet included with number 9, 'The Speeches of John McQuade, Esq., (compiled by an earnest admirer)' [McQuade was a real, ex-docker, ex-boxer, extreme unionist Northern Ireland MP, whose words needed little satirising]. The issue edited by Foley is indistinguishable from the rest, while that supervised by Stephens is an appalling mess of concrete poetry and self-indulgence, whose announcement that four poems and a quote from William Burroughs had to be cut due to 'intimidation on our printers by the police (just doing our job)' serves only to increase one's estimation of the force.

In his letter (see above), Simmons also claimed that 'These first issues are absolutely different from what followed in that the magazine was always being pushed by the editor into confronting society and trying to find a way that literature could act dynamically on other people', and this does capture the change which occurred after the magazine changed hands. Whatever heights it might scale in the future, from this point the *Honest Ulsterman* would be 'only' a literary magazine. Whether this was due to the personalities of the new editors, or to a more general change in attitudes from the idealistic 1960s to the despairing early 1970s, can only be speculated upon; but what is certain is that Foley and Ormsby inherited the title in difficult circumstances. They had to convince the Arts Council to replace the private funding which Simmons had provided, and continue to bring out a regular magazine while their city centre printers were suffering, directly or indirectly, from an intense bombing campaign. Still, their *Honest Ulsterman* continued to capture the literary and cultural atmosphere of the North, this time the surge of talented writers and interest in them which emerged in the 1970s. There are more articles, and they tend to concentrate more on living writers, on Friel, James Plunkett, W.R. Rodgers (by Ormsby), or Brian Moore (Simmons); most importantly, with number 29, Gerard Keenan starts his column, 'The Business Section', which was to appear in almost every subsequent issue, and which would cover everything from comic strips, French Impressionism and Rabelais, to jazz, Proust and New Wave cinema. There are stories, mostly by John Morrow, but also Joseph Biggar, Greacen, Desmond Hogan, Bernard MacLaverty and Simmons; extracts from novels by Biggar and Parker; fragments of autobiography from Sam Thompson; and many more reviews, by Foley, Morrow, Paul Muldoon, Ormsby, Parker and Simmons. Once again, the core of the magazine's achievement lies in its poetry: Eamon Carr, Ciarán Carson, Tony Curtis, Dugdale, Ewart, Foley, Greacen, Harrison, Heaney, Hewitt, Kennelly, Michael Longley, Mahon, W.F. Marshall, Montague, Muldoon, Joan Newmann, Ormsby, Stewart Parker, Simmons, Ken Smith and Eithne Strong.

In the Autumn of 1972, Foley resigned as editor and Ormsby more than rose to this new challenge; indeed, under his individual guidance the *Honest Ulsterman* was about to enter its golden age, a sustained period when it was regularly producing cohesive issues in which covers, layout, reviews, articles, graphics and in-jokes combined with the best new writing of the time to produce some of the best examples of this or any other contemporary Little Magazine. He built on the basic strengths established with Foley, maintaining the same core group of writers, but extending it in interesting ways. Hogan and Morrow continue to provide a stream of stories, with Foley and MacLaverty, but there are also one-offs from Fred Johnston and Francis Stuart. The reviewing is taken much more seriously, with more space devoted to it, and a strong team of regular reviewers: Carson, Foley, Ormsby and Simmons as before, but also Michael Allen, Brian Andrews, Buchanan, Gerald Dawe, Seamus Deane, Hewitt, Robert Johnstone, Edna Longley, David Montrose and Tom Paulin. And the poetry continued to dominate: Carr, Carson, Tony Curtis, Dugdale, Ewart, Foley, Greacen, Harrison, Heaney, Hewitt, Kennelly, Michael Longley, Mahon, W.F. Marshall, Montague, Muldoon, Joan Newmann, Ormsby, Parker, Simmons, Smith and Strong, but also Fleur Adcock, Kate Allen, Buchanan, Harry Clifton, Dawe, Deane, Durcan, Tess Gallagher, Patrick Galvin, Ruth Hooley, Johnstone, Edna Longley, Tom MacIntyre, Peter McDonald, McFadden, Maeve (later Medbh) McGuckian, Ewart Milne, Andrew Motion, Sean O'Brien, Julie O'Callaghan, Paulin, Peter Porter, Meta Mayne Reid, Carol Rumens, William Scammell, Matthew Sweeney and R.S. Thomas.

All the longer-lived titles eventually enter into settled middle-age, when their format is established, they have a regular stable of writers, and the issues seem to roll off the production line; for *HU* this happens around 1978, and for the next few years the only interruption to the schedule is the occasional special issue (an extended 50th number, with a long radio play by Stewart Parker; a George Buchanan Supplement in number 59, with a number of articles and an interview; 'The War Years in Ulster' (number 64), with contributions from Sam Hanna Bell, Buchanan, Greacen, Hewitt, Montague, Morrow, McFadden and Simmons; and number 73, dedicated to MacNeice). By the early 1980s, there is a creeping feeling that they have got into a rut, that the routine is a little too easy and there are few surprises. In 1984 Robert Johnstone joined Ormsby as co-editor and an unsettled period of change begins. New poets join the squad of regulars – Fleur Adcock, Ian Duhig, Alasdair Gray, Selima Hill, Judith Kazantzis, Craig Raine, John Whitworth, and there are more translations, from Russian or Romanian writers; the team of regular reviewers is similarly augmented, by Tom Clyde, Martin Mooney and Michael Parker. There is an attempt to approach the issue of criticism more seriously, with 'The *HU* Critical Forum', an occasional feature edited by John Wilson Foster, and addressing the big issues with pieces by luminaries such as Richard Kearney. Johnstone also brought a new level of professionalism to the production of the magazine, and the virtual disappearance of the previously regular apologies for misprinting or mangling work. However, in retrospect it is hard to avoid feeling that this experiment was less than successful. While much good work continued, most of the new talent was not Irish, and the magazine began to lose its identity and its connections with its roots; in addition, for the first time, the reviews and articles eclipsed the poetry, making it into a very different kind of publication. In 1989, Ormsby retired after twenty years service, to be replaced by Ruth Hooley, and the process began of steering *HU* back to the mixture and focus it had previously had. The core of loyal writers remained (Hill, McBreen, McDonald, Mooney, with reviewers Clyde, Dawe and Simmons), but new talent emerged – Olivia Byard, Clyde Holmes, Adrian Rice – and a couple of special issues emphasised the change (number 91, on Irish women writers, with contributions from Linda Anderson, Jennifer Fitzgerald, Tess Gallagher, McBreen, Janet Shepperson; and a W.R. Rodgers supplement in number 92, edited by Clyde, and featuring articles by Douglas Carson, Clyde and Dawe, and some of Rodgers's own poems). This period of flux ended when Hooley left, to be replaced as co-editor for two issues by Tom Clyde; Johnstone then left in turn, bowing out with a highly impressive 25th anniversary issue (contributions from Fleur Adcock, Ciarán Carson, Dawe, Gavin Ewart, Foley, Selima Hill, Hooley, Johnstone, Edna Longley, Michael Longley, McFadden, McGuckian, Muldoon, Ormsby, Tom Paulin and Simmons).

Clyde took over as sole editor in 1993 (with Hooley rejoining as Associate soon after, joined by Frank Sewell in 1995), and in the intervening years has completed the process of moving *HU* firmly back to its Ulster and Irish roots. His period in office has been marked, so far, by a vastly increased role for writing in the Irish language (original texts appearing with translations, either by the author or by Sewell), and by a much heavier reliance on special issues, for example number 97 on the Belfast Group (with input from Dawe, Dugdale, Heaney, Hobsbaum, Edna Longley, Michael Longley, Newmann and Parker) or 101 on prose (with a critical overview of Glenn Patterson's career, and stories from Linda Anderson, Kate Newmann and Bridget O'Toole). Most of the special features have had guest editors for that section, with expertise in particular areas (Sam Burnside produced a feature on writers from Derry and the North-West (number 99), and Gerry Hull another on writing from the southern Border counties (102)). Reviewers in this era have included Clyde, Patricia Craig, Gerald Dawe, Martin Mooney and David Wheatley, while poetry has once more increased in importance, with contributions from Olivia Byard, Dawe, Kerry Hardie, Michael Longley, MacIntyre, Derek Mahon, Joan McBreen, McGuckian, Mooney, Newmann, Ní Dhomhnaill, Greagóir Ó Dúill, Cathal O Searcaigh, Janet Shepperson and David Wheatley. While still not clear of the shadow of either Simmons's founding efforts or of Ormsby's massive contribution, it is clear that a new phase in the life of HU has begun, and that it will continue as the North of Ireland's pre-eminent literary magazine.

Cathal O Searcaigh

See Marshall Douglas, 'Fifty Honest Ulstermen', *Fortnight,* 121 (20 February 1976), p. 13. Review of *HU*50.

See Robert Johnstone, 'The Honest Ulsterman, Summary of contents, numbers 1–78' (Belfast, 1985).

See Dillon Johnston, *Irish Poetry After Joyce* (Notre Dame, 1985), pp. 44, 128, 257.

See Peter Denman, 'Ireland's Little Magazines', Barbara Hayley and Enda McKay (eds), *300 Years of Irish Periodicals* (Mullingar, 1987), p. 142.

See Sydney Bernard-Smith, 'Outing for feminism' *Books Ireland,* 118 (November 1987) p. 235. Short review includes *HU*83.

See Robert Johnstone, 'Handbook for a (peaceful) cultural revolution', *Fortnight,* 263 (June 1988), p. 29. Article on *HU*.

See Norman Vance, *Irish Literature: A Social History – Tradition, Identity and Difference* (Oxford, 1990), p. 218.

See James Simmons, 'Some Notes on the Origins of The Honest Ulsterman', *Honest Ulsterman,* 95 (May 1993), pp. 3–11.

See Carol Rumens, 'Memories of the HU', *Honest Ulsterman,* 95 (May 1993), pp. 107–108.

See Dennis O'Driscoll, untitled review of *Honest Ulsterman,* 95 (25th Anniversary Issue), *Fortnight*, 320 (September 1993), p. 49.

See Seamus Deane, *Celtic Revivals* (London, 1985), p. 160.

See Gerard Keenan, *The Professional, The Amateur and the Other Thing* (Belfast, 1995). Selection from the 'Jude the Obscure' column.

See Anthony Roche, 'Platforms; the Journals, the Publishers', in Theo Dorgan, *Irish Poetry Since Kavanagh* (Dublin, 1996), pp. 71–81, *passim*.

See John Goodby, 'New Wave I: "A Rising Tide"; Irish Poetry in the 60s', in Theo Dorgan, *Irish Poetry Since Kavanagh* (Dublin, 1996), pp. 116–135, *passim*.

See Edna Longley, '"Between the Saxon Smile and Yankee Yawp": Problems and contexts of Literary Reviewing in Ireland', Jeremy Treglown and Bridget Bennett, *Grub Street and the Ivory Tower: Literary Journalism and Literary Scholarship from Fielding to the Internet* (Oxford, 1998), p. 215.

Tom Clyde, *HU: An Author Index to Issues 1–99* (Belfast, 1995).

Tom Clyde and Andreas Schachermayr, *HU: An Author Index to Issues 100–107* (Greyabbey, 1999).

MOTUS, PERIODICAL OF THE ARTS

Location:	Cork (publisher Arts Society, UCC
Editor(s):	Roderic Campbell; from number 2 Associate Editor Gabriel Rosenstock; from number 4 Assistant Editors Nuala Ní Dhomhnaill and Peter Denman.
Dates:	Issue 1 (Summer 1968)–issue 4 (Spring 1970)
No. of issues:	4
Average periodicity:	Irregular
Average no. pages:	48
Libraries:	NLI=Ir 82191 p 50; PSPL=821 (incomplete); QUB=hAP4.M9.

A standard 1960s 'street'-style magazine: badly typed copy, cheap graphics, and stapled together (number 2 is printed on yellow paper); in this case there is also some portentous editorialising about artistic integrity and dialectics. Its main interest is the involvement in the editorial team of writers who would go on to much greater things. The issues carry a mix of translations, drawings and poems, including some by Peter Denman, Gabriel Rosenstock and Richard Murphy. The final issue includes a folded A4 sheet of poems (marked 'Motus Supplement 1'), with poems, including a few by Denman and Rosenstock.

An editorial in the final issue claims a circulation of over 1,000, but says they are facing a financial crisis, and have had to increase the cover price by 50 per cent; this was evidently not enough to ward off disaster.

CAPELLA

Location:	Dublin ('published by the Tara Telephone', 30 Thorncliffe Park, Rathgar, Dublin 14; printer Print-PR Ltd.)
Editor(s):	Eamon Carr, Peter Fallon
Dates:	QUB has numbers 3 (December 1969), 4 (April 1970) and 5/6 (April 1971)
No. of issues:	5?
Average periodicity:	Annual?
Average no. pages:	32?
Libraries:	QUB=hPR8850.C2.

An all-poetry magazine, with typical cover art by Jim Fitzpatrick. Poets published included Leland Bardwell, Eamon Carr, Peter Fallon, Alan Ginsberg, Heaney, Adrian Henri, Hutchinson, Kennelly, Michael Longley, Roger McGough, Ní Chuilleanáin, Brian Patten, and Simmons. Number 3 opens with a line drawing by John Lennon. The material is generally good, the typography (apart from the last issue) always poor .

THE BOOK OF INVASIONS

Location:	Dublin (publisher Tara Telephone Publications, 30 Thorncliffe Park, Rathgar, Dublin 14, printer Ben-Day Press Ltd., Dublin 2)
Editor(s):	Eamon Carr and Peter Fallon
Dates:	'Chapter' 1 (1969)–'chapter' 4 (1970)
No. of issues:	4
Average periodicity:	Bimonthly?
Average no. pages:	1 (broadsheet)
Libraries:	BL=P.901/713 ('Chapter 2' only); NLI=LO LB 99 (missing number 1); QUB=hPR8850.B7 (no.1 only); TCD=194.p.10.

Another 1960s broadsheet, with illustrations by Jim Fitzpatrick, the *Book* is all poetry, and includes contributions from Leland Bardwell, Carr, Peter Fallon, Adrian Henri, Brendan Kennelly and Roger McGough.

THE LACE CURTAIN, A MAGAZINE OF POETRY AND CRITICISM

Location: Dublin (publisher New Writers Press, 19 Warrenmout Place, Dublin 8, from number 6 61 Clarence Mangan Road; printer Dorset Press Ltd., Hill Street, from number 6 Elo Press Ltd., Dublin 8)

Editor(s):   Michael Smith and Trevor Joyce; from number 4, Smith alone

Dates: Number 1 (1969)–number 6 (Autumn 1978)

No. of issues: 6

Average periodicity: Irregular

Average no. pages: 72

Libraries: BL=YA.1989.b.1905; LIN; NLI=Ir 8205 l 5; PSPL=820.5 (incomplete); QUB=hPR8700.L1; RDS=NL52; TCD=Press A New W 1970 LAC 1–6; UCC.

Exactly as described in the subtitle, *Lace Curtain* has poems by Bardwell, Brian Coffey, Cronin, Durcan, Patrick Galvin, Hartnett, Hutchinson, Jordan, Kinsella, Liddy, Thomas MacGreevy, Mahon, Montague, Ní Chuilleanáin, Lorna Reynolds, Gabriel Rosenstock, Skinner and Woods. Articles, sometimes quite substantial, are contributed by (amongst others) Galvin and Liddy. Although not billed as such, number 4 is a special issue, with the focus on Irish writers of the 1930s; this has poems by Beckett, Coffey, Kavanagh, Leventhal, MacGreevy, na gCopaleen and Reynolds; an interview with Mervyn Wall; and a piece of autobiography by Clarke. The appearance of *Lace Curtain* improves steadily with each issue, from plain A5 through decorated A5, to decorated and larger, to highly glossy and noticeably larger.

See Peter Denman, 'Ireland's Little Magazines', Barbara Hayley and Enda McKay (eds), *300 Years of Irish Periodicals* (Mullingar, 1987), p. 140.

See John Goodby, 'New Wave I: 'A Rising Tide'; Irish Poetry in the 60s', in Theo Dorgan, *Irish Poetry Since Kavanagh* (Dublin, 1996), pp. 116–135, *passim*.

A basic, online author index to *Lace Curtain* by Eoin Meegan, can be found at www.may.ie/academic/english/laceinto.htm

ATLANTIS

Location: Dublin (publisher 2 Belvedere Place, Dublin 1; printer Dolmen Press)

Editor(s):   Seamus Deane, Derek Mahon, Hugh Maxton, Augustine Martin, Michael Gill

Dates: Number 1 (March 1970)–number 6 (Winter 1973/74)

No. of issues: 6

Average periodicity: Irregular

Average no. pages: 86

Libraries: BL=P.701/390; LIN; NLI=Ir 05 d 5; PSPL=052; QUB=hAP4.A8;

RDS=NL54; RIA=Fr Crypt/Sect 1/1/C; TCD=Per 81–195; UCC; UCD=J 800; UCG=052 (offsite, incomplete).

The opening editorial states: 'In any culture, discussion, informed commentary, a climate of literate interest, are a necessary hypothesis. It is one to which Ireland pays lip service... We propose... to provide a focus for all that buzz...'; this is a little pompous, but justified in the case of this polished 'showcase' magazine. Each issue carries a letter from abroad – London, San Francisco, proclaiming clearly the editors' internationalist credentials. There are also heavyweight articles aplenty: Conor Cruise O'Brien on Burke, Denis Donoghue on Lawrence, Seamus Deane on the situation in Northern Ireland, Liam de Paor on political developments in the Republic, as well as pieces on everything from Sean O Riada, Solzhenitsyn, Pirandello and MacNeice, to politics, film, Structuralism, Foucault, and all points east. One distinguishing characteristic of *Atlantis* is the prominence given to prose work by most of the leading authors of the day, including novel extracts from John Banville, Brian Moore and Francis Stuart and stories by Isaac Babel, George Mackay Brown, J.G. Farrell, Desmond Hogan, Francis Stuart and William Trevor. There is also poetry by Gerald Dawe, Tony Harrison, Hartnett, Heaney, Kinsella, Tom MacIntyre, Mahon, Hugh Maxton, Montague, Ní Chuilleanáin, Richard Ryan, Simmons and Knute Skinner. Although not formally designated as special issues, number 5 is devoted to debating the concept of a 'New Ireland', with articles on political structures, trade unions, education, theatre, etc. by various authors, while the last issue is dominated by translations of stories from eastern Europe. 'Impressive' in its way, rather than engaging, as is often the case with these 'showcase' magazines, and a little full of its own importance. Nevertheless, *Atlantis* contains much worthy material.

See W.J. McCormack, 'Remembering Atlantis (1970–1974)', W.J. McCormack, *The Battle of the Books* (Mullingar, 1986), pp. 9–12.
See Peter Denman, 'Ireland's Little Magazines', Barbara Hayley and Enda McKay (eds), *300 Years of Irish Periodicals* (Mullingar, 1987), pp. 143–145.
See John Goodby, 'New Wave I: 'A Rising Tide'; Irish Poetry in the 60s', in Theo Dorgan, *Irish Poetry Since Kavanagh* (Dublin, 1996), pp. 116–135, *passim*.

A short, anonymous author index to *Atlantis* 1–4 appears in *Atlantis,* 6 (Winter 1973/4), pp. 71–72.
A basic, online author index to *Atlantis* by Enda P. Guinan, can be found at www.may.ie/academic/english/atlantis.htm

ID

Location:	Belfast (publisher Eye Publications, 2 Ulsterville Gardens, Belfast 9; number 5, publisher 5 Camden Street, Belfast 9)
Editor(s):	Terri Hooley
Dates:	Number 1 (1970)–number 5 (1971?)

No. of issues: 5?
Average periodicity: Unknown
Average no. pages: Varies widely
Libraries: TCD=OLS X-1-612, number 1.

Whether of experiment or of self-indulgence, this magazine nears the outer limits of Irish literary magazines; packed with the cut-and-paste, freeform extravagances of its era, produced as cheaply as possible, *ID* demands a reaction from the reader. Fold-out pages, different colours of paper, every possible visual gimmick is used. There are poems by Denis Greig and Brian Keenan. The third issue, rather implausibly, claims a circulation of 2,000; number 5 carries no date, but discusses Bloody Sunday as a recent event.

See Paula Howard, *Irish Sectarian Periodicals* (Belfast, 1973).

EGO

Location: Belfast (ID Magazine, c/o Botanic House Printers, 48 Botanic Avenue, Belfast BT7 1JR)
Editor(s):   Terri Hooley
Dates: Number 1 (September 1970?)–number 6 (1971?)
No. of issues: 6?
Average periodicity: Unknown
Average no. pages: Varies widely
Libraries: TCD=OLS X-1-612, number 2 (missing first issue).

Proclaims itself 'free to all subscribers of ID'; like *ID*, terms like 'Love and Peace', and even 'groovy' are used liberally, and the faces of Angela Davis and George Jackson appear regularly (there is very little mention of the Troubles, however). If anything, an even more extravagant bag of visual gimmicks than its parent: free stickers, inserts, posters are all included. There are poems from Dennis Greig, Peter Fallon and William Oxley, but the most interesting piece is an interview with Rory Gallagher in number 6.

See Paula Howard, *Irish Sectarian Periodicals* (Belfast, 1973).

FORTNIGHT, AN INDEPENDENT REVIEW FOR NORTHERN IRELAND

Location: Belfast (publisher Fortnight Publications Ltd., 61 Great Victoria Street, Belfast, printer Morton Newspaper Group, Windsor Avenue, Lurgan; from 1972, publisher 15 James Street South BT2 7GA; from January 1976 publisher moves to 7 Lower Crescent, Belfast BT7 1NR, printer Noel Murphy (same address); from January 1989 publisher moves to 113 University Street, Belfast, printer Regency

Press, Belfast; from December 1989 publisher moves back to Lower Crescent, and Noel Murphy resumes as printer)

Editor(s): Tom Hadden, Deputy Editor Martyn Turner; from January 1976 Robert Johnstone and Phil Nichols become Assistant Editors (Johnstone in charge of reviews); from October 1976 Editor Ciaran McKeown, Deputy Editor Robert Johnstone; February 1977 McKeown resigns, replaced by Committee of Johnstone, Sarah Nelson, and Douglas Marshall, with Advisor Tom Hadden; from September 1977 Committee changes to Michael McKeown, Johnstone and Marshall; December 1977 Hadden retires as Advisor; from October 1979 Committee changes to Tom Hadden, Johnstone, Chris Moffat, Martyn Turner; from December 1981 Andy Pollak joins Committee; from January 1983 Pollak becomes editor, Committee otherwise unchanged; from July/August 1983 Noel Russell joins as 'Books/Arts Editor'; from 21 January 1985 Martin O'Hagan is Assistant Editor; from 4 February 1985 Noel Murphy joins the Committee; from 16 December 1985 Editor Leslie Van Slyke, Committee Hadden, Johnstone, Moffat, Murphy, Turner, Pollak; from 27 January 1986 Moyra Henry joins Committee; from September 1986 Editor Robin Wilson, Bob Purdie joins Committee; from October 1986 Edna Longley joins Committee; from November 1986 Literary Editor James Simmons; from February 1988 Johnstone, Henry and Purdie leave committee; from January 1989 Sheila Hamilton, Paul Nolan, James Odling-Smee and Jonathan Stephenson join Committee; from April 1989 Literary Editor Medbh McGuckian; from December 1990 Tess Hurson joins Committee; from January 1991 Damian Smyth joins Committee; from July/ August 1992 Pollak leaves Committee; from September 1992 Arts Editor Damian Smyth, Committee Suzanne Breen, Gordon Guthrie, Hadden, Hurson, Edna Longley, Moffat, Nolan, Stephenson, Colm Tóibín, Martyn Turner; from December 1992 Philip Orr and Fintan O'Toole join Committee; from June 1993 Orr replaced on Committee by Pol Ó Muir' and Emily O'Reilly; from July/August 1993 Assistant Editor Damian Smyth; from September 1993 Deputy Editor Damian Smyth, Nuala Haughey joins Committee; from February 1994 Fergal Cochrane joins Committee; from April 1995 Editor John O'Farrell; from May 1995 Production Editor Smyth, Committee renamed Editorial Board and joined by Wilson; from July 1995 Smyth resigns as Production Editor; from September 1995 Production Editor Martin Crawford; from November 1996 Board Breen, Cochrane, Liz Fawcett, Adrian Guelke, Hadden, Hurson, Longley, Fiona McMillen, Moffat, Nolan, O'Reilly, O'Toole, Pollak, Tóibín, Turner, Wilson, John Woods; from July/August 1997 Michelle McAuley joins Board.

Dates: Issue 1 (25 September 1970)–ongoing; from October 1976 title changes to *The Northern Irish Fortnight*, an independent review; from February 1977 title changes to *Fortnight, an independent review*; from January 1978 title changes back to *Fortnight, An Independent Review for Northern Ireland*

No. of issues: 374 (to November 1998); ongoing

Average periodicity: Fortnightly (one issue each in July and August); from October 1979 monthly

Average no. pages: 24; from January 1976, 20; from October 1979, 24; from December 1981, 32; from December 1983, 42; from December 1984, 28; from October 1986, 32; from September 1992, 48; from April 1995, 42

Libraries: BCL=IR; BL(Colin); LIN (microfiche); NLI=Ir 3305 f 2; QUB=hqAP4.F7; RIA=Fr C/Sect 1/4/F; TCD=Per 72–467; UCC; UCD=J 320 (incomplete).

The editorial twists and turns of *Fortnight* on first sight seem an exemplar of polymorphic perversity, characterised by endless changes of Editor, Deputy Editor, Assistant Editor and Editorial Committee, compounded by several switches from fortnightly publication to monthly, and back again; however, since most of the scene changes leave the core cast unchanged, the identity and quality of the magazine itself have been relatively unaffected. There are three clear changes of direction, roughly a decade apart: when Robert Johnstone first takes up (in 1977) the key role he was to maintain for a decade and rule by Committee was established a few months later; when Robin Wilson takes over as Editor at the end of 1986 and Edna Longley and James Simmons join the team; and when John O'Farrell takes charge in April 1995.

From the start, half a dozen pages were given over to reviews of books, films, and so on, and in this first phase the literary reviews were dominated by a group of writers who were, or would shortly become, associated with the *Honest Ulsterman*: Michael Foley, Robert Johnstone, Frank Ormsby and James Simmons, alongside Maurice Leitch, Edna Longley and Gerald Dawe. A handful of poems were also published, by Foley, Heaney and Simmons, but the most interesting literary items to be published were the sequence 'Butcher's Dozen' (Kinsella), an interview with Edna O'Brien, and an article on Ulster poets by Harry Chambers.

The pace begins to quicken with the admission of Johnstone to the editorial team (in early 1976). The core reviewing group now comprises Dawe, Foley, Grace Ingoldby and Edna Longley, led by Johnstone himself and supplemented by the occasional 'name' contribution, from John Banville or John Montague. A sporadic 'Literary Supplement', or 'Literary Section' appears, usually four pages, and given over to creative writing, featuring Dawe, Foley, Hewitt, Ruth Hooley, Johnstone, Michael Longley, McFadden, MacLaverty, Muldoon, Paulin and Simmons, and many short stories by John Morrow. There are also a number of important individual pieces: an extract from a play by Muldoon; the serialised novel by Foley, *The Passion of Jamsie Coyle*; Heaney's article, 'Among Schoolchildren'; an autobiographical reminiscence on Derry by Seamus Deane; short autobiographical pieces from Dawe, Foley, Heaney, Mahon, Muldoon, Michael Longley and Simmons; and an interview with John Hewitt.

The 'golden age' of *Fortnight* (so far) begins in late 1986, with the succession of Robin Wilson to the Editor's post; like many other magazines, this is the period when the authoritative political coverage, the wide-ranging and incisive cultural content, even the quality of the covers, all come together with blithe confidence. The reviewers are now led by Dawe, and regulars such as Edna Longley and Simmons (and the 'specials' from John Boyd, Kennelly, Martin McGuinness and Eiléan Ní Chuilleanáin), are joined by a group of younger contributors: Tom Clyde, Martin Mooney, Eve Patten, Janet Shepperson and Damian Smyth.

The main innovation during these years, *Fortnight*'s equivalent of more conventional literary magazines' 'Special Issues', is the production of more than a dozen supplements, separate publications supplied free with the magazine. Some of these had no literary relevance at all, but many of them were either purely literary (devoted to Samuel Beckett, George Birmingham, Shan Bullock, Sam Hanna Bell, Lynn Doyle, John Hewitt, Michael MacLaverty, Janet McNeill, Stewart Parker, Forrest Reid, Joseph Tomelty and W.B. Yeats) or, where they dealt with broader cultural phenomena, brought writing into the debate (*Sexual Subjects* is on the position of women in Ireland, but includes poems by Hooley; *Religion in Ireland* includes Tess Hurson's article on religion in Ulster novels; *Free Thought in Ireland* has a Hewitt poem, an Edna Longley article on Hubert Butler, and Sam Burnside on Sam Thompson).

Simmons embarks on a regular column, 'The foreman's estimates', in which he ruminates on anything that takes his fancy; there are first-class poems by Dugdale, Boland, Dawe, Durcan, Greacen, Tony Harrison, Heaney, Hewitt, Selima Hill, Michael Longley, Joan McBreen, McFadden, Montague and Simmons, and work from younger poets such as Ian Duhig, Fred Johnston, Martin Mooney, Cathal O Searcaigh, Adrian Rice, David Wheatley and Howard Wright. Outstanding moments include: an article on poetry by Heaney, and his obituary of McLaverty; interviews with Dermot Bolger, Roddy Doyle, Heaney, Michael Longley, Muldoon and Cathal O Searcaigh; and a touching piece by Michael Longley on Brian Keenan.

John O'Farrell's tenure (starting in April 1995) has paid less attention to literature, and has largely abandoned some of the innovations of the previous regime, such as the supplements. Nevertheless, this period has still seen long-time reviewers Dawe and Edna Longley (and 'specials' Carlo Gebler and Roy McFadden) joined by Martin Mooney, Pat Ramsey and Carol Rumens; the publication of poems by Chris Agee, Norman Dugdale, Joan McBreen, McFadden and David Wheatley; and one or two interesting interviews, such as Rumens's encounter with Seamus Deane.

See Martyn Turner, 'The Early Struggles of a Mad Little Magazine'. *Fortnight*, 200 (December 1983–January 1984), p. 16. On starting *Fortnight*.
See Roy Foster, *Paddy and Mr Punch* (London, 1993), p. 37.
See Edna Longley, ' "Between the Saxon Smile and Yankee Yawp": Problems and contexts of Literary Reviewing in Ireland', Jeremy Treglown and Bridget Bennett, *Grub Street and the Ivory Tower: Literary Journalism and Literary Scholarship from Fielding to the Internet* (Oxford, 1998), p. 214.

Bill Rolston, *The Index 1970–1987, Nos 1–250*, Fortnight Publications (Belfast, 1987). This is incomplete. For example, book reviews are excluded, as are serialised stories and regular columns; there is a serious need to extend the scope of this index and bring it up to date.

P

Location:	Coleraine (publisher New University of Ulster, hand-printed)
Editor(s):	mostly Anon., although one issue was 'compiled' by Kevin Durham
Dates:	1970–1972
No. of issues:	24
Average periodicity:	Monthly?
Average no. pages:	16 (though varies widely)
Libraries:	UU=PN 1010 P2.

Another extraordinary product of the late 1960s and early 1970s – two dozen little magazines, very crudely typed and copied, but with very bright covers (all hand designs, all different, from completely black to Day-Glo orange); three of them are devoted to single authors ('knuckles', Phil Kelly and Pete Newmann), and are marked 'a P pamphlet'; there are no editorials, and none are numbered or dated (although going by the library catalogue, and by internal evidence, they must all have been produced during the period 1970–1972). In size, they vary from A5 to A4 to foolscap, with one or two in unusual formats (e.g. 10in x 4in), and from eight pages to twenty-eight.

Although only one issue credits an editor (Kevin Durham), the hand of James Simmons (then teaching at NUU) is strongly in evidence (some seven poems and four stories are credited to Simmons, and some of the anonymous and pseudonymous material may be his also) and there seems to be a connection with the 'Resistance Cabaret' poetry and musical events he ran at that time.

Most of the contributions are undistinguished student juvenilia – revolution/anarchy, nihilism and first sexual encounters predominate. The only substantial names to appear (apart from Simmons himself) are Sam Burnside, Michael Stephens and Arthur Watson.

NEW YEATS PAPERS

Location:	Dublin (publisher and printer Dolmen Press, 8 Herbert Place, Dublin 2; from number VIII (1974) Dolmen moves to North Richmond Industrial Estate, North Richmond Street, Dublin 1; from number XVIII (1980) moves to The Lodge, Mountrath, Portlaoise)
Editor(s):	Liam Miller
Dates:	I (1971)–XX (1981)
No. of issues:	20

Average periodicity: Irregular; 1971–1978 usually triannual, then roughly annually
Average no. pages: 88 (but varies widely)
Libraries: BL=X.0900/318; NLI= Different card for each issue: 1- Ir 92 y 55; 2-
                    Ir 82189 y 58; 3- Ir 737 y 1; 5- Ir 750 y 4; 7- Ir 655 p 13; 8- Ir 82189
                    y 76; 9- Ir 82189 y 74; 10- r 82189 y 74; 11- Ir 82189 y 74; 12-Ir
                    82189 y 74; 14- Ir 700 p 37; 15- Ir 82189 y 35; 16- Ir 800 p 43; 18-
                    Ir 82189 y 117; 19-Ir 824 y 20; 20-Ir 82289 p 47;
                    QUB=hPR5907.N5; UCC; UCD=Gen 821 IR.

Sometimes not counted as an Irish literary magazine but, given the many weird and
wonderful forms these have taken, *New Yeats Papers* seems a fairly conventional
candidate: a consecutively numbered series, issued by the same publisher under the same
editor, and often produced more than once per year. *New Yeats Papers* was a platform for
the further development of papers given at the Yeats Summer School, and was produced
and designed by Liam Miller – that is, it is easy to read, satisfying to hold, and beautiful
to look at. Issues are often illustrated, with photographs, reproductions of manuscripts, and
illustrations (often by Jack B. Yeats). Every aspect of Yeatsiana is given authoritative
coverage – family history, magic, literary friends, the plays, and so on; the authors are
often major players, such as Kathleen Raine.

YEATS STUDIES, AN INTERNATIONAL JOURNAL

Location: Galway (publisher University College Galway, printer Robert Hogg,
                    Irish University Press, Shannon)
Editor(s):   Robert O'Driscoll and Lorna Reynolds, also an Advisory Board
                    including Russell Alspach, Richard Ellmann, A. Norman Jeffares,
                    and Brendan Kennelly.
Dates: Number 1 (Beltaine 1971)–number 2 (Beltaine 1972)
No. of issues: 2
Average periodicity: Annual
Average no. pages: 175
Libraries: BL=P.901/735; LIN; NLI=Ir 82189 y 43; QUB= hPR5907.Y4;
                    RDS=LR; TCD=HIB 828.912 YEAg L16; UCD=J 820;
                    UCG=828.991.

A mixture of substantial essays on aspects of Yeats and his work (some from young
researchers, but also pieces from big fish like Anne Saddlemeyer), previously unpublished
Yeats material (e.g. letters), with reproductions of book covers and illustrations.

CRAB GRASS: POETICAL SONATAS

Location:	Belfast (publishers 7 Rugby Road, Belfast 7, printers Botanic House Printers Ltd., 48 Botanic Avenue, Belfast BT7 1JR)
Editor(s):	John Gilbert
Dates:	1972?
No. of issues:	4?
Average periodicity:	Unknown
Average no. pages:	30
Libraries:	BL=P.901/587; LIN; QUB=hAP4.C9.

Physically, one of the most extreme of the experimental publications of the early 1970s (predictably enough, it seems to be linked with Terri Hooley – see *Id* and *Ego* above). While number 1 is relatively restrained, with just a couple of fold-out pages and lots of Python-esque graphics, number 2 has a supplement, 'The Crabgrass Music Dropout', with sheet music for a radical performance piece, and a transparent envelope stuck to a page, with five small pieces of paper inside, with the words 'Do', 'Not', 'Love', 'Make' and 'Beds' printed on them; the cover of number 3 is silvered, every page has an illustration, there are two fold-out pages, and a small plastic bag (2in x 1in) containing equally small sheets of paper with drug-influenced 'messages' on them; number 4 is similar, and includes 'The Crabgrass Graffiti Kit', some stickers with equally random sayings. The only writer of any stature to appear is Peter Fallon.

MINERVA, A MAGAZINE OF MODERN POETRY

Location:	Dublin (editors' home addresses 49 Sycamore Road, Mt Merrion and 38 Leopardstown Ave., Blackrock, first three issues typed and mimeo-graphed; number 4, printer Pronto Print, 10 Camden Street Upper, D2)
Editor(s):	Patrick Murray and Colm Holmes (1–2), Patrick Murray and David Kane (3–4)
Dates:	Number 1–number 3 (no date; 1973- TCD OPAC)
No. of issues:	4
Average periodicity:	Irregular
Average no. pages:	12 (1–3), 18 (4)
Libraries:	TCD=Per 81-789 (incomplete; offsite, 24 hours' notice).

The first three numbers seem to have been completely home-produced, with typing rather than typesetting the order of the day (and poor typing at that). They have poems by both editors, plus Kennelly, Bernard O'Donohoe and 'Pete Fallon'. Number 4, though properly printed, is still pretty messy; poems by both editors, plus Fallon.

CRAB GRASS

·POETICAL· SONATAS·

CARET, A POETRY MAGAZINE

Location: Belfast (publisher 31 Marlborough Park Central, printer Swiftprint
                     Limited, 10 Brand's Arcade, Belfast 1; last issue published England)
Editor(s):   Robert Johnstone, Trevor McMahon and William Peskett; from
                     number 4, Edited McMahon and Peskett; from number 8/9 Edited
                     McMahon
Dates: Number 1 (Autumn 1972)–number 8/9 (Spring/Summer 1975)
No. of issues: 7
Average periodicity: Triannual
Average no. pages: 40
Libraries: LIN; NLI=Ir 82191 c 17; QUB=hPR1225.C2; TCD=Per 81–766.

A classic, A5 Little Magazine, with basic typesetting, but put together with great
enthusiasm and care; each issue has pen-and-ink illustrations, and often one artist supplies
these for an entire issue, giving it a visual cohesion (for example, Carolyn Mulholland's
drawings in the first issue, or Brian Ballard's in number 3). The quality of the literary
material is very high (despite the subtitle, issues usually have a story), but after three years
it seems to have run out of steam.

   Poets featured include Ciarán Carson, Tony Curtis, Dugdale, Douglas Dunn, Gavin
Ewart, Foley, Hobsbaum, Robert Johnstone, Michael Longley, Maeve McCaughan,
Muldoon, Ormsby, Paulin, Peter Porter, Meta Mayne Reid and Simmons, while there are
short stories from Bernard MacLaverty, Paulin, and Anne Tannahill.

IRISH WRITINGS FROM THE AGE OF SWIFT

Location: Dublin (publisher Cadenus Press, 6 Richmond Hill, Monkstown,
                     printer (1) Cuala Press, (2 and 3) Andrew Carpenter, (4–10) Dolmen
                     Press)
Editor(s):   Andrew Carpenter; volume 5 Edited J.G. Simms and Denis
                     Donoghue; volume 6 Edited Alan Bliss; volume 7 Edited Carpenter;
                     volume 8 Edited Robert Mahony; volume 9 Edited Alan Bliss; and
                     volume 10 Edited Christopher Murray
Dates: Volume 1 (1972)–volume 10 (1979)
No. of issues: 10
Average periodicity: Annual
Average no. pages: Varies widely, from 64 to 384
Libraries: BL=Cup.405.k.1; NLI=each volume catalogued separately (Ir 828 c
                     4, Ir 8211 c 1, Ir 826 c 4, Ir 252 k 5, Ir 32341 m 63, Ir 827s 42, Ir 824
                     f 6, Ir 8211 r 2, Ir 400 s 6); QUB=hPR8833.I6; UCC.

Very similar to *New Yeats Papers*, but if anything an even more lavish Liam Miller production (he designed the series – volumes include coloured type, or fold-out maps, and are hand-printed in quarter-calf; they are also in a limited, numbered edition). The titles of the individual volumes are: *Miscellanies in Prose; Miscellanies in Verse; Letters to and from Persons of Quality; Archbishop King's Sermon on Predestination; The Case of Ireland Stated by William Molyneux; A Dialogue in Hybernian Stile Between A & B; Adventure at Sienna; Different Styles of Poetry; Spoken English in Ireland 1600–1740; and St. Stephen's Green, or The Generous Lovers.*

NEPTUNE'S KINGDOM, POETRY BROADSHEET

Location: Kilkee (publisher 5 Victoria Terrace, Kilkee, Co Clare, home printed)
Editor(s): Martin Gleeson
Dates: Number 1 (1972)–number 3 (1974)
No. of issues: 3
Average periodicity: Annual
Average no. pages: 10 (1), 32 (2 and 3)
Libraries: NLI=Ir 05 p 42; TCD=194.u.15, number 15 (1), OLS L-4-203, number 16 (2), and 178.n.13, number 10 (3); UCG=821 (PS).

The first number is very roughly typed and mimeographed and, despite the subtitle, not a broadsheet. It has poems by the editor, Anthony Cronin, James Liddy and Knute Skinner. Number 2, though still calling itself a Broadsheet, is actually A5, but at least is better produced; it has poems by the editor, J.F. Deane and Liddy. The quality is better still for issue 3 (now subtitled 'Poetry Review'), and the poems are by Peter Fallon, Liddy and Skinner.

SOUNDINGS '72, AN ANNUAL ANTHOLOGY OF NEW IRISH POETRY

Location: Belfast (publisher Blackstaff Press, 84 Wandsworth Road, Belfast 4, printer Belfast Litho Printers Limited)
Editor(s): Seamus Heaney ('72 and 2); James Simmons (3)
Dates: Number 1 (1972)–number 3 (1976)
No. of issues: 3
Average periodicity: Annual (intended, though actually appeared biennially)
Average no. pages: 76
Libraries: LIN; NLI=Ir 82191 s 12; PSPL=821.008; QUB=hPR8850.S7; TCD=OLS 186.p.37, number 10; UCD=Gen 821.08.

[The second number was entitled *Soundings 2, An anthology of new Irish poetry*; the third *Soundings 3, An annual anthology of new Irish writing*.]

A showcase production, and a curious hybrid, as revealed in the first sentence of the first editorial: 'This book could be regarded as an anthology, but its function is closer to that of a poetry magazine...'. In any event, it published the cream of contemporary Irish writing: poems by Eavan Boland, Carson, Dawe, Seamus Deane, Fallon, Foley, Heaney, Hewitt, Kennelly, Kinsella, Michael Longley, Mahon, McFadden, Milne, Montague, Muldoon, Richard Murphy, Ní Chuilleanáin, Frank Ormsby, Stewart Parker and Simmons, and prose by Foley, MacLaverty, Morrow and Jude the Obscure.

ERA

Location:	Dublin (publisher and printer The Goldsmith Press, 60 Woodpark, Castleknock; from number 2 publisher at 19c Garville Road, Rathgar; from number 4 publisher at The Curragh, Co. Kildare)
Editor(s):	Desmond Egan
Dates:	Number 1 (Spring 1974)–number 6 (1982)
No. of issues:	6
Average periodicity:	Irregular
Average no. pages:	54 (1–3); 44 (4–6)
Libraries:	BCL=IR (incomplete); LIN; NLI=Ir 8205 e 2; QUB=hqPR8700.E8; TCD(Old Library)=OLS L–2–71, number 2.

First three issues roughly A5, last three A4 (and more social/political comment); number 5 is subtitled 'Ireland's liveliest review of the Arts', number 6 'irelands [*sic*] liveliest review'. It is liberally sprinkled with drawings. There is poetry by Durcan, Desmond Egan, Fallon, Fiacc, Hartnett, Kavanagh, Kinsella, Ormsby and Skinner; an article on 'The Great Hunger'; and an extract from *By Night Unstarred* (Kavanagh).

WORDSNARE, A MAGAZINE OF NENAGH VERSE

Location:	Nenagh (printer The Nenagh Guardian Ltd.)
Editor(s):	Donal A. Murphy, Mary O'Donoghue, Noel Ryan
Dates:	Number 1 (Summer 1974)–number 3 (Summer 1977)
No. of issues:	3
Average periodicity:	Irregular
Average no. pages:	36
Libraries:	NLI=Ir 82191 w 8; PSPL=821.008; QUB= hPR8850.W8; RIA=Fr C/5/2/G Misc Box S-Z; TCD=Per 81–126; UCD=J 820.

The stated purpose of this magazine is twofold, to preserve 'enduring verse from and about Nenagh', and to publish new work; most of the latter is by schoolchildren, and the only significant examples of the former are reprints of poems by Thomas MacDonagh.

BROADSHEET

Location:	Dublin ('published for The Poetry Workshop, UCD', 54 Foster Avenue, Mt Merrion)
Editor(s):	Gerard Fanning
Dates:	NLI has number 5 (1975) only
No. of issues:	5?
Average periodicity:	Unknown
Average no. pages:	1 (broadsheet)
Libraries:	NLI=LO LB 99.

'This edition dedicated to the late Austin Clarke'. A poetry-only publication, including poems by Carson, Harry Clifton, Dawe, Seamus Deane, Michael Foley, John Hewitt, Tom MacIntyre, John Montague, Ormsby, Simmons and Colm Tóibín.

See Gerald Dawe, untitled review of *UCD Poetry Broadsheet* 5, *Fortnight,* 113 (24 October 1975), p. 13.

CYPHERS

Location:	Dublin (publisher 3 Selskar Terrace, Ranelagh, Dublin 6, printer Elo Press Ltd., Dublin 8)
Editor(s):	Leland Bardwell, Eiléan Ní Chuilleanáin, Pearse Hutchinson, MacDara Woods, Associate Editor Peter Fallon (1–5)
Dates:	Number 1 (June 1975)–number 46 (Winter 1998)
No. of issues:	46 (to date)
Average periodicity:	Biannual
Average no. pages:	58
Libraries:	LIN; NLI=Ir 82189 c 139; QUB=hPR1225.C9; RIA=RR Gall/40/B; TCD(Old Library)=OLS L-4-10, 412, 421; UCC; UCD=J 820; UCG=800 (PS, 1975–1984).

Amazingly consistent Little Magazine, maintaining the same editors, the same printers, the same format and tone for twenty-five years; even the cover design has changed only once during that period. Mostly poetry (including one or two per issue in Irish), with just the occasional short story, there are usually two or three short reviews at the back, and the odd drawing. *Cyphers* has never had any manifestoes or editorials, it just gets on with business. The four editors themselves, along with Galvin and John F. Deane, provide a backbone of their own contributions, right through the run; in fact, they provide nearly a quarter of all work published.

Then there are two distinct groups of regular contributors; for the first half of *Cyphers'* life, Sebastian Barry, Paul Durcan, John Jordan, Matthew Sweeney and Ewart Milne, and for the second, Rita Ann Higgins, Joan McBreen and Janet Shepperson. Beyond these stalwarts, who give the magazine a consistency of quality and tone, are the vast bulk of contributors who provide only one or two pieces each; most of these are unknowns, but there is a surprisingly high number from established writers, or those who went on to become established. The old favourites include: John Hewitt, James Liddy, Robert Greacen, John Montague, James Simmons, Derek Mahon, Aidan Higgins, John Banville, Eithne Strong and Tom MacIntyre. The succeeding waves of new stars include: Ciarán Carson, Seamus Heaney, Dermot Healy, Michael Stephens, Michael Foley, Nuala Ní Dhomhnaill, Medbh McGuckian, Cathal Ó Searcaigh, Knute Skinner, Sara Berkeley, Peter Sirr, Clairr O'Connor, Theo Dorgan, Moya Cannon, Sam Burnside, Paula Meehan, Eva Bourke, Celia de Friene, Martin Mooney, David Wheatley, Frank Sewell, Joan Newmann and Howard Wright.

One of the most consistently satisfying of little poetry magazines, one which knows its strengths and sticks to them.

See Dillon Johnston, *Irish Poetry After Joyce* (Notre Dame, 1985), p. 44.
See Anthony Roche, 'Platforms; the Journals, the Publishers', in Theo, Dorgan, *Irish Poetry Since Kavanagh* (Dublin, 1996), pp. 71–81, *passim*.
See John Goodby, 'New Wave I: 'A Rising Tide'; Irish Poetry in the 60s', in Theo Dorgan, *Irish Poetry Since Kavanagh* (Dublin, 1996), pp. 116–135, *passim*.

THE MAYNOOTH REVIEW (REVIEÚ MHÁ NUAD), A JOURNAL OF THE ARTS

Location: Maynooth (publisher St. Patrick's College)
Editor(s):   Cathal Ó Háinle
Dates: Volume 1, number 1 (June 1975)–volume 6, number 2 (May 1982)
No. of issues: 12
Average periodicity: Biannual
Average no. pages: 84
Libraries: BL=P.901/3001; LIN; NLI=Ir 05 m 19; QUB=AP4.M4; RIA=Fr C/5/1/A; TCD=Per 91-384; UCC; UCD=J 050; UCG=052.

Each issue carries a handful of academic articles, mostly on matters of faith and academic organisation, but sometimes literary, including George Watson on Beckett, and on W.B. Yeats, Declan Kiberd on Synge, and Patricia Coughlan on Beckett.

QUARTO, THE MAGAZINE OF THE LITERARY SOCIETY

Location: Coleraine (publisher the Literary Society of the New University of Ulster, printer the NUU; from November 1975 printer display aids [*sic*], Coleraine; from January 1977 printer Robert Swindells, Cambridge; from 1983 printer New University of Ulster; from 1987 printer Noel Murphy)

Editor(s):   Anon. (volume 1, number 1); Paul Wilkins (volume 1, number 2); from volume 7 Editorial Board Jonathan Brooks, Daniel J. Casey, John Dorins, Lesley Watts, James Simmons; from volume 9 Board Bridget O'Toole, Zebedee Alby, Kevin McKay, Alastair Chatwin, Tanya Greenfield, Mark Stevens, Jim Neeson and Frank Hagan; from volume 10 Board Chatwin, Neeson, Liam Black, Stevens, William Emslie, McKay, O'Toole; an un-numbered issue, Winter 1987/88, was guest edited by Martin Lynch; volume 11 Editorial Committee Judith Heraghty, Frank Galligan, Geraldine Grey

Dates: November 1975–1992

No. of issues: 17

Average periodicity: Biannual (1975-1978); then annual

Average no. pages: 48

Libraries: BCL=IR (Winter 1987/88 only); LIN (numbers 7, 8, 9 and 11 only); QUB=hqAP4.Q2 (volume 8 (1981–1982) only); TCD=Per 91-646; UCD=J 820; UU=4 PR1.Q2 (1975–1992) (full run).

Starting out roughly A4 in size, *Quarto* was a very basic production, typed and stapled, and with a plain cover (from November 1975, it became *Quarto, Magazine of The Literary Society of The New University of Ulster*); from 1977 until 1980 it became a standard A5 Little Magazine, with a stylishly illustrated cover; it then reverted to A4 (while keeping up the higher production values), and became simply *Quarto, Literary Magazine*. The editorial to the last issue (Summer 1991) says it is a 'revival' of *Quarto*.

The quality of the contents varied widely from issue to issue, some were dull and unremarkable, others sparkled, for example the Special Seamus Heaney Number (volume 2, number 1), which had poems by Seamus Heaney (including early worksheets of four published poems), as well as Moyra Donaldson and Simmons, and reviews and articles on Heaney. They had a substantial number of 'gift' poems from famous names to leaven the student contributions, including Heaney again, also Norman Dugdale, Paul Durcan, Tess Gallagher, Hewitt, Michael Longley, Ormsby, Tom Paulin and Jon Silkin; Gerald Dawe, Derek Mahon and Muldoon were a little more generous; while the biggest such coup was a short prose piece from William Burroughs (February 1979). The regulars included Frank McGuinness and Bridget O'Toole (both offering poetry, as well as prose), and the biggest contributors by some way were Michael Stephens and Simmons. Stories were supplied by John Hewitt, John Morrow, Frank McGuinness, Michael J Murphy and Bob Welch. Apart from a few short reviews in each issue, the other important items are: short interviews with John McGahern (March 1976), Hewitt (1980/81) and McGuinness (Winter 1987/88); and an article on Mahon (1983/84). A good, but rarely remarkable, student literary magazine.

THE STONY THURSDAY BOOK

Location: Limerick (publisher 128 Sycamore Avenue, Rathbane, Limerick, printer Limerick Offset Printers, 93 O'Connell Street; from number 4, publisher calling themselves The Treaty Press; from number 8 printer Limerick Leader Ltd.)

Editor(s):   John O'Dell Liddy, Jim Burke; from number 7, Ed. John Liddy, Guest Ed. John Jordan; from number 8, Ed. John Liddy, Assistant Liam Liddy.

Dates: Number 1 (1975)–number 8 (1982?)

No. of issues: 8? (all QUB has, missing number 6)

Average periodicity: Biannual (intended, actually more erratic)

Average no. pages: 44

Libraries: BL=P.901/3084; LIN; NLI=Ir 8205 s 11; PSPL=823.91 (incomplete); QUB=hPR8700.S8; TCD=OLS L-4-474.

Starts very amateurishly, with most of the contents of the first few issues by the editors (with a few contributions from Sean Lysaght and Knute Skinner). By number 4, it has become slightly more professional, and the poets represented include Durcan, Greacen, McFadden, Aidan Murphy and Sweeney. Number 5 has poems by Leland Bardwell, Hartnett, Sean Lysaght, Hayden Murphy, Skinner and Eithne Strong, and some short book notices, and discusses the concept of 'the new Munster poetry'. The avatar of this journal is Kate O'Brien; in early issues they reprint a handful of her letters, and number 3 has an article on her by John Jordan, while number 7 is basically a special O'Brien issue (including one of her stories, articles by Boland, Benedict Kiely, Lorna Reynolds, etc.), as well as poems by Eithne Strong and a story by Greacen. Number 8 is given over to articles on, and a selection of, contemporary US poetry, including an interview with Ginsberg, and one of his poems.

AUSTIN CLARKE BROADSHEET

Location: Dublin (publisher 2 Upper Hatch Street, Dublin 2)

Editor(s):   Patrick King

Dates: 1976

No. of issues: 2?

Average periodicity: Unknown

Average no. pages: 1 (broadsheet)

Libraries: NLI=LO LB 99; QUB=hpPR8851.A9; TCD=OLS Papyrus Case 2, number 20.

Containing only poetry, printed on heavy brown paper, includes contributions from Ciarán Carson, Seamus Deane, Thom Gunn, Brendan Kennelly, Thomas Kinsella, Philip Larkin, Michael Longley, Frank McGuinness, Murphy, Ormsby and Simmons. The name is presumably explained by Clarke's death, which had occurred recently.

BOOKS IRELAND, A MONTHLY REVIEW

Location:	Dublin (publisher Kingston House, Ballinteer, Dublin 14, from number 35 (August 1979) publisher moves to Goslingstown, Kilkenny, from number 117 publisher moves to 11 Newgrove Avenue, Dublin 4; printer Alfa Print Ltd., Deerpark Road, Athlone, Co Westmeath)
Editor(s):	Bernard Share, Eagarthóir Gaeilge Séamus Ó Saothra'; from number 40 (January/February 1980) Eagarthóir Gaeilge Douglas Sealy; from number 119 announces that they 'can no longer support an independent editor', and none is listed; issue 125 (special issue 'John Bull's Biggest Minority') Guest Ed. Jonathan Moore; from issue 146 Eagarthóir Gaeilge Alan Titley; from issue 176 (April 1994) Features Editor Shirley Kelly)
Dates:	Number 1 (March 1976)–ongoing (number 221, April 1999 last issue examined)
No. of issues:	221 issues (to date)
Average periodicity:	10 issues per year
Average no. pages:	24; from issue 111, 32
Libraries:	BCL=IR; BL=P.901/3011; LIN; NLI=Ir 018 b 4; QUB=hqZ2034.B7 (issue 151 missing); RIA=Fr C/2/5/G; TCD=Per 76–896; UCC; UCD=GR 015.415; UCG=070.5 (PS).

A unique institution, a combination of trade paper (with lots of puffs for forthcoming titles from Irish publishers, and technical articles on libraries, reading trends, sales figures, and so on) and literary review. Like all the longest running titles, *Books Ireland* hits on its successful formula at an early date, and there are no radical transformations throughout the run; rather, any changes are slow and organic. It starts off as a physically modest enterprise, a little under A5 in size, the covers in two spot colour; within half a dozen issues, the first full-colour cover appears, and by issue 20 it has established itself, moving up to full A4 size, with better paper, more illustrations, and slightly longer reviews. With issue 20, the subtitle becomes 'the month's review'; from issue 30, 'News and Reviews'; and from issue 100 'News – Views – Review'. The layout of the cover changes after 90 or so issues; a dozen or so numbers later and reviews begin to appear on the cover, but after another half dozen, they go back to colour illustrations, although now with photographs; after issue 150 they switch to the full-colour drawings which they have retained until the present. The last number in each year is issued with a loose page containing a brief index of titles reviewed that year.

From the start, *Books Ireland*'s main contribution to Irish writing has been the provision, month after month, of a clutch of short reviews of new titles which are (at the very least) solid, informative and accessible; often they are much more than that. In the early issues, about a dozen titles were reviewed in each issue (often grouped together in portmanteau reviews). Once they got into their stride, however, they found a more successful formula for dealing with book reviews than any of their contemporaries; *Books Ireland* has been remarkably successful in attracting and developing good quality reviewers, and in keeping them on for sometimes extraordinary stretches (Leo Daly, for instance, contributed his first review to issue 5, and his last (to date) to issue 204). Reviewers tend to join in bunches, then a hard core emerges which carries on reviewing, sometimes with gaps, often for years; this gives the reader an ongoing relationship with the reviewer, we get to know their strengths, weaknesses and hobby-horses, and this informs our reading of the review. *Books Ireland* has been more successful at cultivating this relationship between reviewer and reader than any other periodical since the Victorian period. The various batches of reviewers include: Addis, Paul Bew, Bill Bolger, Tom MacIntyre, Matson, Alec Reid, Share and Simmons; Kane Archer, Bruce Arnold, Leo Daly, Charles Davidson, Ida Grehan, Roy Johnston, Marian Keaney, Séamus Ó Saothra', Sydney Bernard Smith and Rosita Sweetman; Ted Bonner, Aubrey Dillon-Malone, Robin Dudley Edwards, Grattan Freyer, Robert Greacen, Ann Quinn, Douglas Sealy, Janet Madden Simpson and Henry Wheeler; H.M. Buckley, Maurice Craig, John F. Deane, John Dunne, Emelie FitzGibbon, John Kirkaldy, Bill Maxwell, W.J. McCormack, Kevin O'Higgins, Gary Redmond and Joy Rudd; Chris Agee, Maeve Binchy, Rachel Campbell, Tom Clyde, Conleth Ellis, Matthew Feheney, John Hanratty, Desmond MacAvock, Deirdre Madden, Hugh Maxton, Anne O'Connor, Bill Rolston and Matthew Sweeney; Rory Brennan, Treasa Brogan, Celia de Fréine, Fred Johnston, Anthony J. Jordan, Carla King, Mairín Martin, J. Ardle McArdle, J.J. O'Dowd, Hugh Oram, Bruce Stewart, Alan Titley and Oonagh Warke; and, most recently, Tony Canavan, Teresa Doran, Jack Hanna, Maurice Harmon, Brian Power, Carole Redford, Lucille Redmond, David Wheatley and G.V. Whelan. Their names are worth listing both to indicate the range of talent, but also because they provide the core of the magazine. The outstanding performer is John Dunne, who has contributed some ninety reviews so far. Finally, there are also a number of 'star' reviewers, who perhaps contribute only one or two pieces each, usually on their own 'specialist subject'; this list includes: D. George Boyce, Desmond Fennell, Benedict Kiely, Jessie Lendennie, Donal Lunny, Patrick MacCabe, Bernadette McAliskey, Ciaran O'Driscoll and Bridget O'Toole.

Occasionally, space is found for other items – profiles of Samuel Beckett, Patrick MacGill, Ewart Milne, Brian Moore, Dervla Murphy and Michael J. Murphy by a variety of hands, and (from Greacen) articles on Æ, Shan F. Bullock, Joyce Cary, St. John Ervine and Forrest Reid. There are short articles on publishing in Ulster (Michael Longley), on writing poetry (Kennelly), or on publishers like the Dolmen Press (issue 6). Scattered through the run are brief interviews, with Dermot Bolger, Evelyn Conlon, Roddy Doyle, John B. Keane, Thomas Kinsella, Michael Longley, Deirdre Madden, David Marcus, Patrick MacCabe, Colm Tóibín, William Trevor and Martin Waddell.

Throughout the 1970s, *Books Ireland* does not print any original material; then, in its late 70s, there starts a 'Preview' section, with short extracts from selected forthcoming books, and from the early 100s they will occasionally reprint a poem from a collection which is being reviewed. The big breakthrough comes in the Summer of 1996, when a new section appears at the rear of the magazine, 'New Writing', in which they publish poems and short stories. To date over 200 poems and 40 stories have been published, by writers including: Sam Burnside, Anthony Cronin, Celia de Fréine, Greacen, Kerry Hardie, Maurice Harmon, Peter Hollywood, Fred Johnston, Tom MacIntyre, Niall McGrath, Noel Monahan, Martin Mooney, William Oxley, Frank Sewell, Knute Skinner, Eithne Strong, Francis Stuart, Robert Welch, David Wheatley and MacDara Woods. While this list contains many strong writers, it does not take many risks, and in fact the criticism that (so far) 'New Writing' has been dominated by older, established writers and by *Books Ireland* reviewers is hard to refute.

ROSCREA WRITING, POETRY AND VERSE OF ROSCREA PEOPLE

Location:	Roscrea (publisher Roscrea People Co-operative Society Ltd., printer J.F. Walsh, Main Street, Roscrea)
Editor(s):	George Cunningham
Dates:	Number 1 (March 1976)
No. of issues:	1?
Average periodicity:	Quarterly (intended)
Average no. pages:	36
Libraries:	NLI=Ir 82191 r 5; QUB=hpPR8844.R7; RIA=AP 1976; TCD=OLS L-4-331, no.2; UCC.

A very old-fashioned feel to this local publication, which was limited to 200 copies and numbered and signed by the editor. Full of poems by local people, none of which is any good.

THE MONGREL FOX, A QUARTERLY PUBLISHED BY THE IRISH WRITERS' CO-OPERATIVE

Location:	Dublin (publisher 82 Upper Rathmines Road, Dublin 6, printer The Anglo-Celt; from 2, publishers 34 Leeson Park, Dublin 6)
Editor(s):	John Feeney, Co-editors Ronan Sheehan, Lucile Redmond (1) Ed. Sheehan, Co-ed Feeney and Redmond (2)
Dates:	Number 1 (December 1976)–number 2 (April 1977)
No. of issues:	2?
Average periodicity:	Quarterly?
Average no. pages:	20
Libraries:	BL=P.901/3074; NLI=Ir 8205 m 11; PSPL=828 (incomplete); QUB=hPR8700.M8; RIA=AP 1976 (incomplete); TCD=Per 90–376; UCD=J 820.

Very ephemeral, with poems and stories; the only significant pieces are an article on Séan O'Faoláin by Sheehan, and another by Richard Kearney on film.

CASTLE POETS

Location:	Limerick (publisher Limerick Poetry Circle, printer McKerns Printing Works Ltd., Glentworth Street, Limerick)
Editor(s):	Anon.
Dates:	1966, 1970, 1977
No. of issues:	3
Average periodicity:	Irregular
Average no. pages:	32
Libraries:	BL=P.909/42089 (1977 only); NLI=Ir 82191 c 22 (1977 only); QUB=hpPR8858/DOYL (1970, 1977); TCD=194.u.15, no.3; 178.p.17, no.2; OLS L-4-413, no.15.

A collection of local verses and illustrations, the only recognisable contributor being James Liddy.

BEGGAR'S BRIDGE

Location:	Galway
Editor(s):	Michael Gorman
Dates:	1977–1978
No. of issues:	2?
Average periodicity:	Annual?
Average no. pages:	16
Libraries:	UCG=820 (PS).

The second issue is subtitled: 'A Magazine of Short Stories and Poems'. The voice of the Galway Writers' Workshop, it is a flimsy A4 student magazine, typewritten rather than typeset and liberally illustrated with doodles and drawings. Contributors include Joyce McGreevy and Fred Johnston as well as the editor, but the contents are generally adolescent and immature.

THE CRANE BAG

Location:	Dublin (publisher The Crane Bag, Balnagowan, Palmerstown Park, Dublin 6, printer Folens and Co. Ltd., Airton Road, Tallaght)
Editor(s):	Mark Patrick Hederman, Richard Kearney, plus an Editorial Board of around a dozen, including Seamus Deane; a number of Guest Editors were used, including Seamus Deane (volume 3, number 2), Christina Nulty (volume 4, number 1), Barre Fitzpatrick (volume 4, number 2), Timothy Kearney (volume 5, number 1), Declan Kiberd (volume 5, number 2), Ronan Sheehan (volume 6, number 2)

Dates: Volume 1, number 1 (Spring 1977)–volume 9, number 2 (Autumn
                          1985)
No. of issues: 17
Average periodicity: Biannual
Average no. pages: 130 (though varies widely)
Libraries: BCL=IR; BL=P.971/405; LIN; NLI=Ir 8205 c 11; PSPL=941.5;
                          QUB=hAP4.C95 (volume 3, number 1 missing); RIA=Fr C/2/2/B;
                          TCD=OLS L-5-93-96; UCC; UCD=J 050; UCG=700.

Another milestone in Irish publishing, in many ways a self-conscious successor to *Atlantis*
(see above), the *Crane Bag* ostentatiously screams quality (and money!), with its tasteful
colour covers (designed by Louis le Brocquy), its illustrations, and its carefully 'designed'
typography and layout. From the first issue, it demands to be taken seriously, and the
breadth and quality of the contents often justify this demand; however, the tendency
toward preciousness and even pomposity to which *Crane Bag* was on occasions
susceptible is also evident from the start (see the framing editorials which begin and end
the first issue, respectively entitled 'Endodermis' and 'Epidermis').

    Although not primarily a literary magazine (investigating, rather, culture and society
in the widest sense), it does carry a good deal of literary material (although no new,
creative writing). All issues are 'Special', that is, they focus on a particular topic, and a list
of these may give some idea of the scope of the *Crane Bag*: 'Anglo-Irish Literature:
Perspectives', 'Images of the Irish Woman', 'Minorities in Ireland', 'Socialism and
Culture' and 'Media and Popular Culture' are among the topics tackled; sales fluctuated
widely, depending on the topic chosen, and the combination of disparate issues and lack of
a fixed editorial voice meant that *Crane Bag* failed to establish a reader base (see
Denman). These issues gave the (usually well-chosen) contributors plenty of space to
develop their arguments; most issues also carried a 'Response' section, where writers of
differing views were invited to respond to articles in that issue or the previous one. No
creative writing was featured at all, but there is a series of important articles on literary
topics, including: Hederman on Synge, Francis Stuart on literature and politics, Ní
Chuilleanáin on 'Woman as Writer', Montague, Vivian Mercier and Hederman on Joyce,
Edna Longley on 'Poetry and Politics in Northern Ireland', and perhaps two dozen more,
many of which are devoted to the further dissection of Shaw, Wilde, Yeats, Joyce and
Beckett. A couple of issues are dominated by literary debate, including volume 3, number
2 ('Anglo-Irish Literature: Perspectives', which covers the comic tradition in Irish drama,
Yeats's plays, and Northern poetry), and volume 6, number 1 ('James Joyce & The Arts in
Ireland' – five articles on Joyce, by Hederman, Kearney and others). There are also some
important interviews: Heaney (interviewed by Deane), a joint interview with Hewitt and
Montague, and an interview with Borges (by Heaney and Kearney). The *Crane Bag* marks
an important turning-point in the cultural debate in Ireland, and is written out of a period
of outstanding insecurity and questioning in the Southern state; it set an example for later
journals, for example the *Irish Review*, even if its eclecticism now seems rather frenetic,
and its attempt to locate the imaginary 'fifth province' smacks of unnecessary pessimism.

See B.S., 'Departure Platform' *Books Ireland,* 14 (June 1977), pp. 121–122. Short review of *Crane Bag,* 1.

See Anon., 'Three bags full', *Books Ireland,* 28 (November 1978), pp. 181–182. Short review of *Crane Bag,* 2, 1 and 2

See Bernard Share, 'Current Periodicals', *Books Ireland,* 36 (September 1979), p. 144. Short review of *Crane Bag,* 3, 1.

See Janet Madden Simpson, 'Joining the ladies', *Books Ireland,* 50 (February 1981), pp. 12–13. Short review of *Crane Bag,* 4, 1.

See Mark Patrick Hederman and Richard Kearney (eds), *The Crane Bag Book of Irish Studies (1977–1981)* (Dublin, 1983). The first five volumes reproduced.

See Richard Kearney, 'Between Politics and Literature: The Irish Cultural Journal', *Crane Bag,* 7, 2 (Autumn 1983), pp. 160–171. Mentions *Crane Bag.*

See Gene Kerrigan, 'Idle ill-informed Intellectuals', *Fortnight,* 211 (17 December 1984–20 January 1985), p. 22. Review of *Crane Bag*, 8, 1.

See Dillon Johnston, *Irish Poetry After Joyce* (Notre Dame, 1985), p. 139.

See W.J. McCormack, '*The Crane Bag* (1977–1985)', W.J. McCormack, *The Battle of the Books* (Mullingar, 1986), pp. 48–52.

See Peter Denman, 'Ireland's Little Magazines', Barbara Hayley and Enda McKay (eds), *300 Years of Irish Periodicals* (Mullingar, 1987), p. 145.

See Roy Foster, *Paddy and Mr Punch* (London, 1993), p. 37.

THE BELLE, A QUARTERLY JOURNAL OF BELLES-LETTRES

Location: Dublin (publishers 68 Foxrock Park, Dublin 18 and 255 Navan Road, Dublin 6, printer Reprint Ltd.)
Editor(s):   Kevin Kiely
Dates: Number 1 (Autumn 1978)–number 2 (1979)
No. of issues: 2
Average periodicity: Annual
Average no. pages: 78
Libraries: BL=P.901/3199; NLI=Ir 8205 b 10; PSPL=820.5; QUB=hPN2.B33 (number 2 only); TCD(Old Library)=OLS 192.n.43; UCD=J 820.

Basic covers and typesetting, includes reviews, poems and prose (a lot of it by Kevin Kiely); the interesting contributions are an article by Anthony Cronin, a short satirical play by Francis Stuart, and poems by Cronin and William Oxley.

THE DRUMLIN, A JOURNAL OF CAVAN LEITRIM AND MONAGHAN

Location: Cootehill (publisher Rakane, Kill, Cootehill, printer Abbey Printers (Cavan) Ltd.; from 2 publisher 27 Main Street, Cavan)

Editor(s):   Dermot Healy
Dates: Number 1 (Autumn 1978)–number 2 (Winter 1979)
No. of issues: 2
Average periodicity: Annual
Average no. pages: 86
Libraries: BL=P.803/998; NLI=Ir 05 d 34; QUB=hPR8700.D7; RIA=Fr
                        C/1/3/D; TCD=Per 91.792; UCC.

One of the most successful (if short-lived) attempts in recent years to merge the local-
interest magazine with literary material, *Drumlin* combines local history and children's
stories with good-quality poems and stories. Contains a John McGahern story, an article
on Wilde, an extract from a Tom MacIntyre play, and poems by Eavan Boland and Leland
Bardwell.

See Leland Bardwell, untitled review of first issue of *The Drumlin, Cyphers,* 10 (Spring
    1979), pp. 51–52.

NORTHERN LIGHTS

Location: Belfast (publisher and printer 7 Lower Crescent, BT7)
Editor(s):   Anon.
Dates: Number 1 (October 1978)–number 8 (May 1979)
No. of issues: 8
Average periodicity: Monthly
Average no. pages: 32
Libraries: LIN.

A brightly presented, A5 listings and events guide, interesting mainly as another product of the
Lower Crescent gang who produced *Fortnight* and contributed to *HU*, and illustrating the
activity on the Belfast scene at the time. It has the occasional review and one or two poems per
issue, but the contributors include some established names: Michael Brophy, Robert
Johnstone, Douglas Marshall, Medbh McGuckian and Damian Smyth; McGuckian also
contributes one of the reviews (of John Hewitt's *Rain Dance* and a collection by Wes Magee).

THE CORK REVIEW

Location: Cork (publisher Triskel Arts Centre, 4 Beasly Street, South Mall,
                        printer Lee Press, South Terrace; from number 5, Triskel moves to 8
                        Bridge Street, printer changes to Forrest Print and Stationery Ltd.,
                        Great William O'Brien Street)
Editor(s):   Paul Durcan; Assistant Editor Patrick McQuoid; from number 5,
                        Editor Tina Neylon

Dates:	Number 1 (November/December 1979)–volume 2, number 3 (June 1981)
No. of issues:	6
Average periodicity:	Biannual
Average no. pages:	48
Libraries:	BCL=IR; LIN; NLI=Ir 705 c 10; RIA=Fr C/1/2/E; QUB=hqPR8700.C7; TCD(Old Library)=OLS X-1-435; UCC (1980–1981 only); UCD=J 820.

A4 in size, and populist in design, the *Cork Review* did not fulfil its original promise. This is unfortunate, because under Durcan its unfussy style combined with top-drawer talent to great effect. There were interviews with Richard Kearney, Derek Mahon, Francis Stuart and Freddie White (usually carried out by Durcan himself); articles by Seamus Heaney, Benedict Kiely, John Montague and Francis Stuart; stories by Nell McCafferty and Stuart; an extract from John Banville's *Kepler*; poems by Durcan himself, and by Theo Dorgan, Heaney, Sean Lucy, Mahon and Eiléan Ní Chuilleanáin; and some brief reviews, usually of films or theatre productions. After Durcan left, the quality of the material declined, and it gradually became more of a listings magazine.

POETRY GALWAY

Location:	Galway
Editor(s):	Patrick F. Sherran
Dates:	1981
No. of issues:	2
Average periodicity:	Quarterly
Average no. pages:	16
Libraries:	None.

Poetry Galway, although described on the cover as a 'broadsheet', was A4 in size, typed and folded to make A5. It was either photocopied or else printed very poorly. It quickly metamorphosed into:

Continued as:

THE SALMON

Location:	Galway (publisher The Salmon, Baranna, Annaghdown, Co. Galway, printer Clódóir' Lurgan, Inverin, Co. Galway; from number 9 publisher 46a Forster Street, Galway; from number 10, publisher 10 Glen View, Riverside, Galway; from number 13, publisher Auburn House, Upper Fairhill Road, Claddagh, Galway, printer TipSet, Galway; from number 21, printer Berry's, Westport; from number 23, printer Colour Books, Dublin)

Editor(s):   M.G. Allen (Chairman), Micheál Ó Riada (Irish Ed.), Jessie
                    Lendennie, Luke Geoghegan, Mary Dempsey; from number 6,
                    Geoghegan drops out; from number 10, Dempsey drops out; from
                    number 17, Ó Riada drops out; from number 18, Séamus McAndrew
                    takes over as Irish Editor; from number 19, Lendennie and
                    McAndrew sole editors; from number 20, Máire Holmes takes over
                    as Irish Editor
Dates: number 3 (1982)–number 24/25 (Winter 1990)
No. of issues: 24
Average periodicity: Triannual
Average no. pages: 32 (5–6); 44 (7–15); 64 (16–18); 120 (19–24/25)
Libraries: BL=P.901/3704; BCL=IR; LIN; NLI=Ir 82191 s 39 (incomplete);
                    QUB=hPR8858.S2; TCD=Per 91-659; UCG=800.

[The cover of number 6 has both *The Salmon* and *Poetry Galway No.6* on it.]

The Salmon often gives the impression that it is primarily by and for writers, rather than general readers; e.g. number 7 has a 'workshop', in which Fred Johnston is quizzed in detail about the production of one of his poems. It seems to have seen its mission as being a platform for new work, and sometimes this led to issues which were stuffed with new poems, but whose quality was dubious. There were usually one or two prose pieces per issue, but poetry is *Salmon*'s main concern; no reviews nor articles were published. The most regular contributors are Rita Ann Higgins, Fred Johnston and Knute Skinner; close behind are Eva Bourke, Moya Cannon, Dawe, James Liddy and Ciaran O'Driscoll. Then come the masses, with one or two poems each: Chris Agee, Sara Berkeley, Boland, Sam Burnside, Michael Coady, John F. Deane, Michael Egan, Conleth Ellis, Gavin Ewart, Ruth Hooley, Lendennie, Joan McBreen, Nuala Ní Dhomhnaill, Gabriel Rosenstock, Carol Rumens and Eithne Strong.

   There was a steady improvement, issue on issue, in the physical quality of the *Salmon*, with more illustrations and better paper being used; it also expanded in size every few issues but, by the end, there was a feeling that their good quality writing was stretched rather thinly over the expanses of paper, and that the idea had really been taken as far as it could go.

See Anthony Roche, 'Platforms; the Journals, the Publishers', in Theo Dorgan, *Irish Poetry Since Kavanagh* (Dublin, 1996), pp. 71–81, *passim*.

THE BEAU, AN ANNUAL PUBLICATION OF AND ABOUT LITERATURE

Location: Dublin (publisher 255 Navan Road, Dublin 7)
Editor(s):   Maurice Scully
Dates: Number 1 (1981)–number 3 (1983/1984)
No. of issues: 3

Average periodicity: Annual
Average no. pages: 90
Libraries: BCL=IR; PSPL=820.8; QUB=hPN2.B3; RIA=Fr Crypt/Sect 1/1/F
                          Misc Box A-C; TCD=Per 90-173; UCD=J 820.

[Number 2 is subtitled 'an annual publication of literature and art'; number 3 'an annual publication of art and enquiry'.]

Presented in two sections, the first of creative writing, the second given over to essays on writing. Number 2 is on better paper, and has a colour cover and half a dozen black and white illustrations. There are poems by Bolger, Coffey, Cronin, Durcan, Enright, Ewart, Jordan, Milne and Oxley; and essays on the Irish short story, Goldsmith, etc.

The editorial to issue 3 says that Scully is retiring and handing over editorship to others, although this does not seem to have happened. Also, one of the essays in this issue says that the *Beau* is the successor to the *Belle* (they share an editorial address).

TRACKS

Location: County Meath/Dublin (editorial addresses 'The Nook', Mornington/
                       19 Monastery Crescent, Clondalkin; from number 3, publisher
                       Aquila: Ireland, PO Box 1, Drogheda, Co Louth; from number 5,
                       publisher Mornington, Co Meath; from number 6, publisher Dedalus
                       Press, 46 Seabury, Sydney Parade Avenue, Dublin 4)
Editor(s):   John F. Deane (poetry) Jack Harte (fiction); from number 6, Deane
                       edits alone
Dates: Number 1 (1982)–number 10 (1994)
No. of issues: 10
Average periodicity: Annual
Average no. pages: 62
Libraries: BL=ZC.9.a.1109; BCL=IR; NLI=Ir 8088 t 7; QUB=hAP4.T65;
                       TCD=Per 90-420; UCD=J 820.

A mixture of poems and stories, with no editorial, *Tracks* has a striking cover design and a strong visual identity; there is a heavy emphasis on translated work from eastern Europe and Scandinavia. There are stories by Borges and Pat McCabe; poems by Rory Brennan, Seamus Deane, Selima Hill, Kinsella, James Liddy, Mary O'Donnell, Maxton, William Oxley, Carol Rumens and R.S. Thomas; a prose piece from Sebastian Barry; and an extract from a novel by John Banville. Number 4 is a special issue, presented as a pamphlet of poems by Tomas Tranströmer, translated by Deane (also, Heaney contributes an introduction to Tranströmer's work, in issue 6); number 7 is a special 'Thomas Kinsella issue', with articles by Dennis O'Driscoll, Douglas Dunn, McCormack, Eavan Boland, Gerald Dawe and Conleth Ellis (the last three also contribute an accompanying poem), and an interview with Thomas Kinsella (by Deane). Number 10 has a feature on Richard Murphy, including a number of explicatory prose pieces and poems by Murphy himself.

THE BELFAST REVIEW

Location:	Belfast (Publisher PO Box 71, Belfast 7; printer Regency Press; from number 17 publishers Hype Publishing, 117 Fitzroy Avenue, BT7)
Editor(s):	Damian Gorman, Production Editor Kerry Campbell, Literary Editor Patrick Williams; from number 14 Ed. Liam Logan, Production Ed. Joe Murphy; from issue 16 'Poetry', Ed. Kevin Smith; from number 17, Ed. Anna Mooney, Deputy Ed. Grainne O'Kane, Poetry and Literature Ed. Smith.
Dates:	Number 1 (Autumn/Winter 1982)–number 17 (Autumn 1987)
No. of issues:	17
Average periodicity:	Quarterly
Average no. pages:	36 (1–4); 32 (5–15); 48 (16–17)
Libraries:	BCL=IR; BL=ZC.9.b.1202; LIN; NLI=Ir 805 b 9; QUB=hqDA996. B7 (numbers 11, 12, and 15 missing); UCC.

A bright and breezy A4 review, a mixture of events listings, articles, personal comment and poetry, which looks and feels very much like *Fortnight*'s leisure-hours counterpart. It has lots of general interest articles, on Van Morrison, Belfast's best pubs, poverty, and so on; Ciarán Carson contributes a column on Irish traditional music, which continues through the series. The literary material is mainly concentrated in short book reviews (mostly by Williams and Gorman, although number 16 features John Hewitt on Roy McFadden), and the 'Poetry Supplement', which includes strong work, from Fleur Adcock, Dawe, D.J. Enright, Damian Gorman, Alisdair Gray, Heaney, Ruth Hooley, Robert Johnstone, Levertov, Peter McDonald, McGuckian, Montague, Martin Mooney, Muldoon, Oxley, Paulin, Shepperson, Simmons and Williams. There are a number of interviews: Hewitt (by John Midgley, issue 2), Oxley (Williams, issue 3), Edna Longley (issue 12), Durcan (Gorman, issue 13), and Derek Bell (issue 15); issue 11 has a Brian Moore short story, issue 5 carries a short autobiographical piece by Hewitt, and issue 10 a Heaney article on Ted Hughes.

From the fourteenth issue, the quality declines, and less space is set aside for reviews and poems, although numbers 16 and 17 are better, with glossy paper and lots of photographs.

WATERMARK, ULSTER POLYTECHNIC REVIEW

Location:	Jordanstown (publisher Watermark, 12 G 09, Ulster Polytechnic, Jordanstown, Co. Antrim, printer Design Incorporated, 101 University Street, Belfast)

Editor(s):   Brian McCalden, Editorial Advisors Lynda Henderson, Bill Roches
Dates: Number 1 (1982)–number 3 (no date – 1984?)
No. of issues: 3
Average periodicity: Annual
Average no. pages: 28
Libraries: BL=P.861/473; LIN; QUB=hAP4.W3; TCD=Per 74-407.

[Number 2 subtitled 'Ulster Polytechnic Students' Review'; number 3 subtitled 'The Ulster University Review'.]

An amateurish production, mostly given over to articles on student issues and wider politics, it does carry some poems (Robert Johnstone the only important contributor) and a handful of book reviews in each issue.

THE MARTELLO MAGAZINE

Location: Blackrock (publisher 38 Main Street; printer Reprint Limited; from number 3 publisher moves to Newtown Lodge, Blackrock)
Editor(s):   Maureen Charlton and John Stafford
Dates: Number 1 (Winter 1982)–number 6 (Spring 1990)
No. of issues: 6
Average periodicity: Annual (1–4); biennial (5–6)
Average no. pages: 48; then 72
Libraries: QUB=hNX1.M2; TCD=OLS L-1-751 (3 issues only, another at PER 91– 87); UCD J 700.

A curious little magazine – a rather austere card cover, and very poor typesetting, hide a secret: *Martello* covers fine art as well as literature, and includes beautiful, full-colour, photographic-quality reproductions of contemporary works of art, glued on to the pages. There are also poems, from Anthony Cronin, John Jordan, John Montague and W.R. Rodgers; an interview with Patrick Kavanagh; and articles (amongst many on fine art), on Nora Barnacle, James Joyce, Patrick Kavanagh and Samuel Beckett. (Much of the literary material is, obviously, posthumous.)

NORTH

Location: Belfast (publisher 10 Stranmillis Park, Belfast BT9 5AU), from number 4 printer Noel Murphy Printing, 7 Lower Crescent, Belfast 7; from number 7 publisher c/o Crescent Arts Centre, 2/4 University Road, Belfast 7
Editor(s):   John Hughes; from number 3 Editor Hughes, plus Editorial Committee of Andrew Elliott, Adrian Maddox, Kevin Smith, Pat Ramsay; from number 5/6 Hughes edits alone

Dates: Number 1 (Winter 1983/84)–number 7 (Winter/ Spring 1987)
No. of issues: 7
Average periodicity: Triannual
Average no. pages: 54 (numbers 1 and 2); 34 (numbers 3–7)
Libraries: BCL=IR; LIN; QUB=hPR8700.N8; UCC.

Always striking, with black and white cover art, after an initial two issues in A5, *North* quickly mutated into another of those 1980s 'style'-type magazines, trying to be more populist and approachable in look and feel. Most new literary magazines start out with a portion of 'goodwill' poems from established names, then establish their identity and get into their stride; *North* never really developed beyond the first stage, and deteriorates noticeably in its last two issues.

There were poems from: Gerald Dawe, John F. Deane, Seamus Deane, Foley, Greacen, Ruth Hooley, John Hughes, Robert Johnstone, Peter McDonald, Medbh McGuckian, Muldoon, Sean O'Brien, Clairr O'Connor, Ormsby, Paulin, Simmons, Peter Sirr, Matthew Sweeney and C.K. Williams. There was a substantial book review section, and the reviewers included: Tom Clyde, Aidan Higgins, Peter McDonald, Sean O'Brien and Matthew Sweeney. In addition, they ran the occasional novel extract (from Dermot Bolger, John Banville and Dermot Healy); the double issue 5/6 had a story by Patrick McCabe; and number 4 an interview with John Hewitt.

See John Hewitt, review of *North* issues 1 and 2, *Linenhall Review*, 1, 2 (Summer 1984),
 p. 27.

THE LINENHALL REVIEW

Location: Belfast (publisher Linen Hall Library, 17 Donegall Square North,
       Belfast 1, printer Ronan Press, Lurgan)
Editor(s):   John Gray and Paul Campbell
Dates: Volume 1, number 1 (Spring 1984)–volume 12, number 2 (Winter
       1995/96)
No. of issues: 24
Average periodicity: 4 per year (volumes 1–5); triannual (volume 6); biannual (volume 7);
       triannual (volume 8–volume 11)
Average no. pages: 32 (volume 1); 36 (volume 2); 40 (volume 3); 36 (volumes 4– 12)
Libraries: BL=P.803/1502; BCL=IR; LIN; NLI=Ir 8205 1 94; QUB=hqAP4.L7
       (volume 11, number 2 missing); RIA=Fr C/1/6/F; TCD(Old
       Library)=OL 010.5 BEL; UCD=GR 015.415; UCG=941.67.

Another of the attempts in the mid-1980s to make literary/cultural magazines more appealing to the public, by a combination of switching up to A4 in size, adopting eye-catching cover art and glossy paper, and including a certain proportion of less intimidating, lower-brow content (see *North*, the *Belfast Review*, etc.; although the *Linenhall Review* is easily the most successful of the genre, indeed, in its prime, it was a worthy peer of *Books Ireland*). There are also Linen Hall Library news and pieces on old printers and book collecting (from volume 3, number 1 incorporates *Irish Booklore*). At the end of each year they included a good index to the volume.

Book reviews are its main strength, and reviewers include: J.R.R. Adams, Chris Agee, Jonathan Bardon, Derek Bell, Paul Bew, C.E.B. Brett, Terence Brown, Tom Clyde, Gerald Dawe, John F. Deane, John Grey, John Hewitt, Frank Ormsby, Eve Patton, Tom Paulin, Bob Purdie and James Simmons. The reviews are generally a little longer and more in-depth than *Books Ireland*, and over the decade-long run nearly six hundred pages of reviews were published.

There are articles on a wide variety of topics, including: Irish women's fiction (Susan McKay), Field Day, Sam Thompson (Paddy Devlin), Thomas Kinsella (Dawe), Michael Longley, the Belfast Group, Medbh McGuckian, Wilde's visit to Belfast, Meta Mayne Reid and on Ulster Regionalism. The *Linenhall Review* also carried an important series of good interviews; subjects included Sam Hanna Bell, Ciarán Carson, Seamus Heaney, Bernard MacLaverty, Brian Moore, Graham Reid, Joseph Tomelty and William Trevor.

In the mid-1990s the Linen Hall Library embarked on an ambitious programme of rebuilding and expansion, and the *Linenhall Review* was an unfortunate casualty of the increased demands on staff time; it was suspended, and to date has not reappeared.

See John Goodby, 'New Wave I: 'A Rising Tide'; Irish Poetry in the 60s', in Theo Dorgan, *Irish Poetry Since Kavanagh* (Dublin, 1996), pp. 116–135, *passim*.

THE PORTLIGHT, A WORKERS/WRITERS ANTHOLOGY

Location:	Belfast
Editor(s):	Anon.
Dates:	Number 1 (Winter 1985/86)–3 (Spring 1987)
No. of issues:	3
Average periodicity:	Annual
Average no. pages:	20
Libraries:	LIN; QUB=hqDA900.P8 (Spring 1986 only).

A workers' solidarity publication with copious thanks given to the staff of the Linenhall Library, and carrying a mixture of pure political articles, personal reminiscences, stories and poems. There appear to be two issues numbered '1', the first with a red ink cover (and carrying a profile of the 'Docker Poet', John Campbell), the second (Spring 1986) in black; from a purely literary standpoint, none of it is significant.

Bibliography

ABBREVIATIONS

The following abbreviations have been used in this book:

BCL   Belfast Central Library
BL   British Library
BL(Colin)   British Newspaper Library, Colindale
LIN   Linenhall Library Belfast
MAR   Marsh's Library, Dublin
NLI   National Library of Ireland
PSPL   Pearse Street Public Library, Dublin
QUB   Queen's University Belfast
QUB(Arc)   Queen's University Belfast, Archive
RDS   Royal Dublin Society
RIA   Royal Irish Academy
TCD   Trinity College Dublin
UCC   University College Cork
UCD   University College Dublin
UCG   University College Galway
UU   University of Ulster

BOOKS

Adams, J.R.R., *The Printed Word and the Common Man: Popular Culture in Ulster 1700–1900* (Belfast, 1987).

Anderson, Benedict, *Imagined Communities, Reflections on the Origin and Spread of Nationalism* (London, 1983).

Anon., *Irish Pleasantry and Fun: A selection* (Dublin, 1892).

Anon., *Irish poems of today: Chosen from the first seven volumes of the Bell* (Dublin, 1944).

Beetham, Margaret, *A Magazine of her Own?: Domesticity and desire in the woman's magazine 1800–1914* (London, 1996).

Bloomfield, B.C., *Beltaine* (London, 1970).

Bloomfield, B.C., *Samhain* (London, 1970).

Bradbury, Malcolm and McFarlane, James (eds), *Modernism 1890–1930* (Harmondsworth, 1976).

Brown, Stephen J., *The Press in Ireland* (Dublin, 1937).

Brown, Terence, *Ireland, A Social and Cultural History 1922–1985* (London, 1985).

Clifford, Brendan, *The Origins of Catholic Nationalism, Selections from Walter Cox's 'Irish Magazine'* (Belfast, 1992).

Coakley, Davis and Horgan, Mary (eds), *Through the Eyes of Quarryman* (Cork, 1972).

Cole, Richard Cargill, *Irish Booksellers and English Writers 1740–1800* (London, 1986).

Davis, Herbert, *The Examiner* (Oxford, 1940; second edition 1957).

Dawe, Gerald, *Criterion 1953–1983, An Anthology* (1983).

Deane, Seamus, *Celtic Revivals* (London, 1985).

Dessain, Revd C. Stephen, *The Letters and Diaries of John Henry Newman* (Oxford, 1961–1977), vols: XVII, XVIII and XIX, *passim*.

Ehrenpreis, Irvin, *Swift the Man, His Works and the Age*, 3 volumes (London, 1962).

Ellis, Frank H., *Swift vs. Mainwaring, The Examiner and The Medley* (Oxford, 1985).

Fallon, Brian, *An Age of Innocence: Irish Culture 1930–1960* (Dublin, 1998).

Feather, John, *A History of British Publishing* (London, 1988).

Foster, R.F., *Modern Ireland 1600–1972* (London, 1988).

Foster, Roy, *Paddy and Mr Punch* (London, 1993).

Görtschacher, Wolfgang, *Little Magazine Profiles: The Little Magazines in Great Britain* (Salzburg, 1993).

Hardy, Philip Dixon, *Pic Nics from the Dublin Penny Journal, being a Selection from the Legends, Tales and Stories of Ireland* (Dublin, 1836).

Harmon, Maurice, *Select Bibliography for the Study of Anglo-Irish Literature and Its Backgrounds* (Dublin, 1977).

Hederman, Mark Patrick and Kearney, Richard (eds), *The Crane Bag Book of Irish Studies (1977–1981)* (Dublin, 1983).

Hoffman, F.J., Allen, Charles and Ulrich, C.F., *The Little Magazine: A History and a Bibliography* (Princeton, 1946).

Howard, Paula, *Irish Sectarian Periodicals* (Belfast, 1973).

Inglis, Brian, *The Freedom of the Press in Ireland 1784–1841* (London, 1954).

Johnston, Dillon, *Irish Poetry After Joyce* (Notre Dame, 1985).

Keenan, Gerard, *The Professional, The Amateur and the Other Thing* (Belfast, 1995).

Kelly, John, *The Collected Letters of WB Yeats*, Volume 1: 1865–1895 (Oxford, 1986).

Kelly, John, *The Collected Letters of WB Yeats*, Volume 2: 1896–1900 (Oxford, 1997).

Kelly, John, *The Collected Letters of WB Yeats*, Volume 3: 1901–1904 (Oxford, 1994).

Kiberd, Declan, *Inventing Ireland* (London, 1995).

Liddy, James, *This Was Arena* (Naas, 1982).

Loftus, Richard J., *Nationalism in Modern Anglo-Irish Poetry* (Wisconsin, 1964).

Double issue of the *Long Room*, numbers 14 and 15, 1976, devoted to *DUM*.

Madden, R. Robert, *The History of Irish Periodical Literature* (London, 1869).

Marcus, David, *New Irish Writing 1, An Anthology from* The Irish Press *series* (Dublin, 1970).

Marcus, David, *New Irish Writing, from* The Irish Press *series* (London, 1976).

McCormack, W.J., *The Battle of the Books* (Mullingar, 1986).

McCormack, W.J., *Dissolute Characters, Irish literary history through Balzac, Sheridan*

Le Fanu, Yeats and Bowen (Manchester, 1993).

McCormack, W.J., *From Burke to Beckett: Ascendancy, Tradition and Betrayal in Literary History* (Cork, 1994).

McHugh, Roger and Harmon, Maurice, *A Short History of Anglo-Irish Literature* (Dublin, 1982).

McIntosh, Gillian, *The Force of Culture: Unionist Identities in Twentieth-century Ireland* (Cork, 1999).

McKenna, Brian, *Irish Literature 1800–1875* (Detroit, 1978).

MacMahon, Séan, *The Best from 'The Bell'* (Dublin, 1978).

Moody, T.W., Martin, F.X. and Byrne, F.J. (eds), *A New History of Ireland, Volume IX: Maps, Genealogies, Lists* (Oxford, 1984).

Munter, Robert, *The History of the Irish Newspaper 1685–1760* (Cambridge, 1967).

Murphy, Daniel J., *Lady Gregory, The Journals Volume I* (Gerrards Cross, 1978).

Murphy, Hayden, *Broadsheet 1967–1978: Poetry, Prose and Graphics* (Edinburgh, 1983).

Murphy, Hayden, *Broadsheet Retrospective: Making an Exhibition for Myself* (Edinburgh, 1985).

Partridge, A.C., *Language and Society in Anglo-Irish Literature* (Dublin, 1984).

Phillips, James W., *Printing and Bookselling in Dublin, 1670–1800* (Dublin, 1998).

Pollard, M., *Dublin's Trade in Books, 1550–1800* (Oxford, 1989).

Power, John, *List of Irish Periodical Publications (chiefly literary) from 1729 to the Present Time* (London, 1866).

Report of the NEWSPLAN project in Ireland (London/Dublin, 1992).

Ryan, John, *Remembering how we Stood* (Dublin, 1975).

Smyth, Daniel and O'Kane, Paul (eds), *The Gown: 35 Years* (Belfast, 1990).

Smyth, Gerry, *Decolonisation and Criticism: The Construction of Irish Literature* (London, 1998).

Sullivan, Alvin (ed.), *British Literary Magazines: The Augustan Age and the Age of Johnson, 1698–1788* (Westport, 1983).

Sullivan, Alvin, *British Literary Magazines: The Romantic Age, 1789–1836* (Westport, 1984).

Sullivan, Alvin, *British Literary Magazines: The Victorian and Edwardian Age, 1837–1913* (Westport, 1985).

Sullivan, Alvin, *British Literary Magazines: The Modern Age, 1914–1984* (Westport, 1986).

Summerfield, Henry, *Æ – Selections from the Contributions to 'The Irish Homestead'* (Gerrard's Cross, 1978).

Thuente, Mary Helen, *The Harp Re-strung, The United Irishmen and the Rise of Irish Literary Nationalism* (New York, 1994).

Tyrrell, R.Y., *Echoes from Kottabos* (London, 1906).

Vance, Norman, *Irish Literature: A Social History – Tradition, Identity and Difference* (Oxford, 1990).

Welch, Robert (ed.), *Oxford Companion to Irish Literature* (Oxford, 1996).

Woolley, James, *The Intelligencer* (Oxford, 1992).

Yeats, Jack B., *Broadside Characters: Drawings* (Dublin, 1971).

INDEXES

Anon., *Index to the first twenty-five volumes of the Irish Monthly, from July, 1873, to December, 1897* (London, 1899).

Anon., *Index of Contributors to Hermathena, 1873–1943* (London, 1944).

Anon., *The Dublin Magazine Index, vol.I to vol. XV* (covers 1926–1940) (nd).

Anon., *Dublin Magazine Index* (1926–52) (nd).

Bloomfield, B.C., *An author index to selected British 'little magazines', 1930–1939* (London, 1976).

Burke, M., Clossick, E., Hanlon, P. and McKenna, J., *Index to Walker's Hibernian Magazine* (for Fellowship of the Library Association of Ireland) (nd).

Clyde, Tom, *HU: An Author Index to Issues 1–99* (Belfast, 1995).

Clyde, Tom and Schachermayr, Andreas, *HU: An Author Index to Issues 100–107* (Greyabbey, 1999).

Elyan, David and Holzapfel, Rudi (eds), *The Dubliner, Vol.1, No.1–Vol.3, No.4, An Index to Contributors* (New Square Publications, 1965).

Furlong, E.J.J., *Index to 'Hermathena', 1944–1964* (Dublin, 1965).

Goode, Stephen H., *Index to Commonwealth Little Magazines, 1964–1965* (New York and London, 1966).

Griffin, M., *Index to The Irish Review* (for the Fellowship of the Library Association of Ireland) (nd).

Grogan, Mary and Murray, E, *Index to the Bell* (Library Association of Ireland) (nd).

Hayes, Richard J. (ed.), *Sources for the History of Irish Civilisation: Articles in Irish Periodicals*, 5 vols (Boston, 1970).

Holzapfel, Rudi *Author Index 3* (Carraig Books Ltd., Blackrock, 1985).

Houghton, Walter (ed.), *The Wellesley Index to Victorian Periodicals 1824–1900*, 5 volumes (Toronto, 1966–1989).

Hyland, C.P., *A Topographical Index to Five Nineteenth Century Literary Periodicals* ('printed by the author', 1979).

Johnstone, Robert, 'The Honest Ulsterman, Summary of contents, numbers 1–78' (Belfast, 1985).

Kerrigan, E.M., *Index to Studies vols. 1–20* (UCD?, nd).

Killen, John, *An Index to The Microscope (1799) and to the Belfast Literary Journal (1816)* (Belfast, 1994).

McKenna, L., *Irish Poems Appearing in 'The Irish Monthly'* (1930).

O'Rahilly, Aloysius, *Studies: General index of Volumes 1–50, 1912–1961* (Ros Cré, 1966).

Poole, William Frederick, *Poole's Index to Periodical Literature*, revised edition (Gloucester, Mass., 1963).

Rolston, Bill, *The Index 1970–1987, Nos. 1–250* (Fortnight Publications, Belfast, 1987).

Sader, M. (ed.), *Comprehensive Index to English-Language Little Magazines 1890–1970* (Millwood, 1976).

ARTICLES

Anon., untitled letter to editor, *Anthologia Hibernica* (October 1793).

Anon., 'A Note on the *DUM*', *Dublin Penny Journal,* 2 (1834).

Anon. (Isaac Butt), 'The Close of the Year', *Dublin University Magazine,* 6 (1835).

Anon., 'The Dublin Penny Journal', *Dublin University Magazine,* 15 (1840).

Anon., 'A Literary Causerie', *Dana,* 1, 12 (April 1905).

Anon., untitled article in *Irish Book Lover,* 10 (1913).

Anon., review of *Irish Writing* 21st birthday issue, *Quarryman* (December 1952).

Anon., editorial, *Q,* 14 (Hilary 1957).

Anon., untitled article in *The Irish Book,* 1, 2 (1959).

Anon., 'Battle Hymn of the Q Review', *Interest,* 3, 4 (1960?).

Anon., 'Special issues', *Books Ireland,* 25 (July 1978).

Anon., 'Three bags full', *Books Ireland,* 28 (November 1978).

Archer, Kane, 'Sifting the evidence', *Books Ireland,* 44 (June 1980).

Atkinson, F.M., 'A Literary Causerie', *Dana,* 1, 8 (December 1904).

Bardwell, Leland, untitled review of first issue of *The Drumlin, Cyphers,* 10 (Spring, 1979).

Beckett, J.C., 'Literature in English, 1691–1800', in Moody, T.W. and Vaughan, W.E. (eds), *Oxford New History of Ireland*, volume IV, *Eighteenth Century* (Oxford, 1986).

Bernard-Smith, Sydney, 'Outing for feminism', *Books Ireland,* 118 (November 1987).

Bigger, F.J., 'The Rushlight and the Irish Rushlight', *Irish Book Lover,* 3 (1912).

Boyle, Kevin, 'Threshold: the Northern Crisis', *Fortnight,* 2, (9 October 1970).

Bredin, Hugh, 'Making War on the Thicks', *Fortnight,* 203 (April 1984).

B.S., 'Departure Platform', *Books Ireland,* 14 (June 1977).

Butler, Hubert, 'The Bell: an Anglo-Irish view', *Irish University Review*, 6, 1 (Spring 1976).

Butler, Hubert, '*Envoy* and Mr Kavanagh', *The Sub-Prefect Should Have Held His Tongue* (Harmondsworth, 1990).

Carleton, William, 'The Dublin University Magazine and Mr Lever', *The Nation* (7 October 1843).

Chuto, Jacques, 'Mangan, Petrie, O'Donovan, and a Few Others: The Poet and the Scholars', *Irish University Review*, 2, 2 (Autumn 1976).

Clyde, Tom, 'Uladh, Lagan and Rann: The "Little Magazine' comes to Ulster", in Eve Patten, *Returning to Ourselves* (Belfast, 1995).

Crone, John S., 'The Monthly Museum', *Irish Book Lover,* 6 (1914).

Curran, Steven, '"No, This is Not From *The Bell*": Brian O'Nolan's 1943 *Cruiskeen Lawn* Anthology', *Éire-Ireland,* 32, 2 and 3 (Summer/Fall 1997).

Dawe, Gerald, untitled review of *UCD Poetry Broadsheet* 5, *Fortnight,* 113 (24 October 1975).

Dawe, Gerald, untitled review of *St. Stephen's, Fortnight,* 130 (July 1976).

Delahanty, James, 'The Bell: 1940–1954 [1]', *Kilkenny Magazine,* 1 (Summer 1960).

Delahanty, James, 'The Bell: 1940–54 (2)', *Kilkenny Magazine,* 2 (Autumn 1960).

Denman, Peter, 'Ireland's Little Magazines', Barbara Hayley and Enda McKay (eds), *300 Years of Irish Periodicals* (Mullingar, 1987).

Donaldson, A.G., 'Editorial', *Northman*, 15, 1.

Doyle, Paul, 'Seán O'Faoláin and *The Bell*', *Eire-Ireland*, 1 (Fall 1966).

Eglinton, John, 'The Beginnings of Joyce', *Irish Literary Portraits* (London, 1935).

Eisenstein, Elizabeth L., 'Some Conjectures about the Impact of Printing on Western Society and Thought', *Journal of Modern History*, 40, 1 (March 1968).

Farmer, Tony, '700 words by mid-October', *Books Ireland*, 47 (October 1980).

Foley, Dermot, 'Monotonously Rings the Little Bell', *Irish University Review*, 6, 1 (Spring 1976).

Fox, Thomas, 'Capuchin Annual, 1946–47', *Irish Bookman*, 1, 9 (April–May 1947).

Goodby, John, 'New Wave I: 'A Rising Tide'; Irish Poetry in the 60s', in Theo Dorgan, *Irish Poetry Since Kavanagh* (Dublin, 1996).

Greacen, Robert, untitled article in *The Bell*, 5, 5 (February 1943).

Greacen, Robert, 'An Irish Bennett', *Books Ireland*, 182 (December 1994).

Hadden, Tom, review of issue 1 of *Aquarius*, *Fortnight*, 22 (6 August 1971).

Harries, Christopher, 'The Hawk in its Flight', *Cork Review*, 2, 3 (June 1981).

Hayes, James, 'Old Popular Pennyworths', *Irish Book Lover*, 2 (1911).

Hayes, Richard, 'Poetry Ireland Review, Issues 1–21: A Review', *Poetry Ireland Review*, 36 (Autumn 1992).

Hayley, Barbara, 'Irish Periodicals from the Union to the Nation', in P.J. Drudy (ed.), *Anglo-Irish Studies II* (Bucks, 1976).

Hayley, Barbara, 'A Reading and Thinking Nation: Periodicals as the Voice of Nineteenth-Century Ireland', in Barbara Hayley and Enda McKay (eds), *300 Years of Irish Periodicals* (Mullingar, 1987).

Hewitt, John, review of North issues 1 and 2, *Linenhall Review*, 1, 2 (Summer 1984).

Hogan, James, untitled article in the *Lace Curtain*, 1 (1969).

Holland, M, 'The Cork Magazine and its Writers', *Journal of the Ivernian Society*, 7 (1915).

Holzapfel, Rudi, 'A Note on the Dublin Magazine', *Dublin Magazine*, 4, 1 (Spring 1965).

Inglis, Brian, 'The Press', in McDowell, R.B. (ed.), *Social Life in Ireland 1800–45* (Dublin, 1957).

Innes, C.L., '"A voice in directing the affairs of Ireland": *L'Irlande libre, The Shan Van Vocht and bean na h-Eireann*', in Paul Hyland and Neil Sammells (eds), *Irish Writing, Exile and Subversion* (London, 1991).

Jack, J.H., 'The Periodical Essayists' in Boris Ford (ed.), *Pelican Guide to English Literature Volume Four* (Harmondsworth, 1957).

Johnstone, Robert, 'Handbook for a (peaceful) cultural revolution', *Fortnight*, 263 (June 1988).

Jordan, John, 'Two Literary Reviews', *Hibernia*, 25, 4 (April 1961).

Kearney, Richard, 'Between Politics and Literature: The Irish Cultural Journal', *Crane Bag*, 7, 2 (Autumn 1983).

Kelly, Shirley, 'A Passionate Affair', *Books Ireland*, 179 (September 1994).

Kennedy, Brian P., 'Ireland To-day, A brave Irish periodical', *Linenhall Review*, 5, 4 (Winter 1988).

Kerrigan, Gene, 'Idle ill-informed Intellectuals', *Fortnight*, 211 (17 December 1984–20 January 1985).

Kilfeather, J.B., untitled review of *Threshold* 28, *Fortnight*, 149 (10 June 1977).

Liddy, James, 'How We Stood with Liam Miller: *The Dolmen Miscellany*, 1962', *New*

Hibernia Review, 2, 3 (Autumn 1998).

Longley, Edna, '"It is time that I wrote my will": Anxieties of Influence and Succession', in Warwick Gould and Edna Longley (eds), *Yeats Annual No. 12* (London, 1996).

Longley, Edna, '"Between the Saxon Smile and Yankee Yawp': Problems and contexts of Literary Reviewing in Ireland', Jeremy Treglown and Bridget Bennett, *Grub Street and the Ivory Tower: Literary Journalism and Literary Scholarship from Fielding to the Internet* (Oxford, 1998).

Marcus, David, 'Reviews', *Poetry Ireland,* 3 (October 1948).

Marshall, Douglas, 'Fifty Honest Ulstermen', *Fortnight,* 121 (20 February 1976).

May, Robert, 'Rare Sligo Magazine', *Irish Book Lover,* 6 (1914).

McFadden, Roy, 'Reflections on Megarrity', *Threshold,* 5, 1 (Spring/Summer 1961).

McGrath, Kevin, 'Writers in The Nation 1842–45', *Irish Historical Studies,* 6 (1949).

McIvor, Peter K., 'Regionalism in Ulster: An Historical Perspective', *Irish University Review,* 13, 2 (Autumn 1983).

McKenna, James, 'Kavanagh's Weekly, Thirty Years Later', *Era,* 6 (1982).

McKenna, Wayne, 'W.B. Yeats, W.J. Turner and Edmund Dulac: The *Broadsides* and Poetry Broadcasts', Warwick Gould, *Yeats Annual* No.8 (1991).

Meehan, Helen, 'Shan Van Vocht' in *Ulster Local Studies,* 19, 1 (Summer 1997).

Mercier, Vivian, 'The Fourth Estate, VI – Verdict on 'The Bell'', *The Bell,* 10, 2 (July 1945).

M.H., 'Brief – but not very passionate', *Awake,* 6, 8 (29 February 1964).

Miller, Liam, 'The Dun Emer Press', *Irish Book,* 2, 3/4 (Autumn 1963).

Montag, Tom, 'The Little Magazine/Small Press Connection: Some Conjectures', *TriQuarterly,* 43 (1978).

Ní Chuilleanáin, Eiléan, 'A Census of Places', *Cyphers,* 45 (Spring/Summer 1998).

O Casaide, Séamus, 'Watty Cox and His Publications', *Bibliographical Society of Ireland Publications,* 5 (1935).

O'Donnell, Donat, 'The Catholic Press, A Study in Theopolitics', *The Bell,* 10, 1 (June 1945).

O'Donoghue, D.J., 'The Cork Magazine', *Irish Book Lover,* 6 (1915).

O'Donoghue, D.J., 'Duffy's Fireside Magazine', *Irish Book Lover,* 7 (1915).

O'Donoghue, D.J., untitled piece in *Irish Book Lover,* 8 (1915).

O'Driscoll, Dennis, untitled review of *Honest Ulsterman* 95 (25th Anniversary Issue), *Fortnight,* 320 (September 1993).

O'Faoláin, Sean, '1916–1941: Tradition and Caution', *The Bell,* 2, 1 (1941).

O'Hegarty, PS, article in *Irish Book Lover,* 25 (1937).

O'Mahony, D.D., 'Samhain – 1904', *Blarney Magazine,* 14 (Summer 1958).

Parker, Stewart, untitled review of *Gorgon, The Gown,* 7, 5 (9 December 1960).

Pittion, J.-P., '"A Literary Journal" (Dublin, 1744–9): Reflections on the Role of French Culture in Eighteenth-century Ireland', *Hermathena,* 121 (1976).

Power, Patrick, article in *Cork Historical and Archaeological Society Journal,* 14 (1939).

Quinn, Antoinette, *Patrick Kavanagh: Born-Again Romantic* (Dublin, 1991).

Reid, Alec 'One Man's Icarus', in *Icarus,* 30 (March 1960).

Reynolds, Lorna, untitled review, *University Review,* 3, 4.

Roche, Anthony, 'Platforms; the Journals, the Publishers', in Theo Dorgan, *Irish Poetry Since Kavanagh* (Dublin, 1996).

Rolleston, T.W., 'Kottabos and Some of Its Poets', *Irish Fireside,* 1 (1887).

Rumens, Carol, 'Memories of the HU', *Honest Ulsterman,* 95 (May 1993).

Russell, Matthew, 'Signatures in the Old Nation Newspaper', *Irish Monthly,* 17 (1889).

Russell, Matthew, 'Signatures in the Nation and the Celt', *Irish Monthly,* 17 (1889).

Russell, Matthew, 'Anonymities Unveiled: Contributors to Duffy's Fireside Magazine', *Irish Monthly,* 20 (1892).

Sadleir, Michael, 'The Dublin University Magazine: the History, Contents and Bibliography', *Bibliography Society of Ireland Journal,* 5, 4 (1938).

'Scrutator', 'Verdict on "The Bell"', *The Bell,* 10, 5 (October 1945).

Share, Bernard, 'Current Periodicals', *Books Ireland,* 36 (September 1979).

Share, Bernard, 'Taking up the slack', *Books Ireland,* 86 (September 1984).

Simmons, James, 'Some Notes on the Origins of The Honest Ulsterman', *Honest Ulsterman,* 95 (May 1993).

Simpson, Derek, untitled review of *Threshold 27, Fortnight,* 133 (24 September 1976).

Simpson, Janet Madden, 'Joining the ladies'. *Books Ireland,* 50 (February 1981).

'T.C.D.' [pseudonym], 'Kottabos', *Irish Book Lover* 6, 5 (December 1914.

Turner, Martyn, 'The Early Struggles of a Mad Little Magazine' *Fortnight,* 200 (December 1983–January 1984).

Wall, Thomas, 'Catholic Periodicals of the Past', *Irish Ecclesiastical Record,* 102 (1964).

UNPUBLISHED DISSERTATIONS

Bradley, William, 'The Poetry of the Nation, 1842–1848', PhD thesis (University of London, 1977).

Burnham, Richard, 'Seumas O'Sullivan and The Dublin Magazine', PhD thesis (UCD, 1977).

Furze, Richard, 'The Bell, 1940–1954', PhD thesis (UCD).

Hagan, Edward A., 'Standish James O'Grady and the All-Ireland Review', PhD thesis (State University of New York, 1977).

Hamilton, Sheila, 'Indexes to Rann', MA thesis (QUB, 1990).

Holzapfel, Rudi, 'A Survey of Irish Literary Magazines from 1900 to the Present Day', M Litt thesis (Trinity College Dublin, 1964).

McBride, John P., 'The Dublin University Magazine: Cultural Nationality and Tory Ideology in an Irish Literary and Political Journal, 1833–1852', PhD thesis (TCD, 1987).

O'Neill, Michael, 'Indexes to Envoy', MA thesis (QUB, 1987).

Smith, Edward Doyle, 'A Survey and Index of the Irish Statesman (1923–1930)', dissertation (University of Washington, 1966).

INTERNET RESOURCES

Guinan, Enda P, author index to *Atlantis*: www.may.ie/academic/english/atlantis.htm

Meegan, Eoin, author index to *Lace Curtain*: www.may.ie/academic/english/laceinto.htm

Mark McCloskey, author index to *Ireland To-Day*: www.may.ie/academic/english/itd.htm

Part 3
Appendices

Appendix 1: Alphabetical Index

Appendix 2: Distribution Maps

Figure 1 Locations and starting dates, 1700–1749

Figure 2 Locations and starting dates, 1750–1789

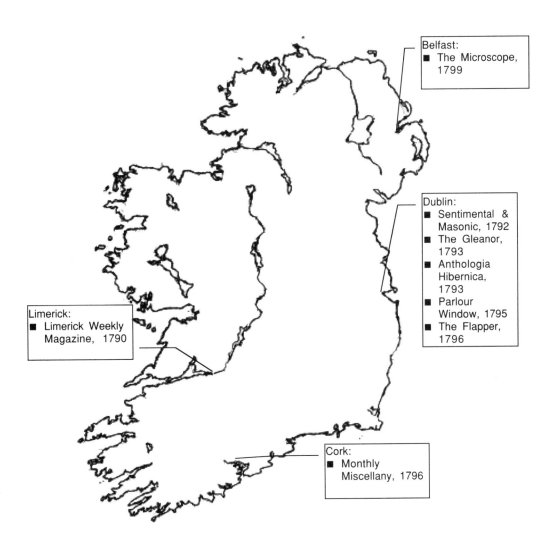

Figure 3 Locations and starting dates, 1790–1799

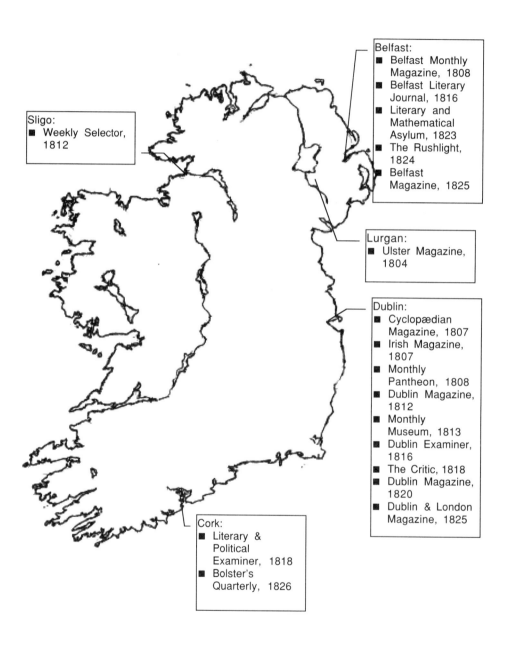

Figure 4 Locations and starting dates, 1800–1829

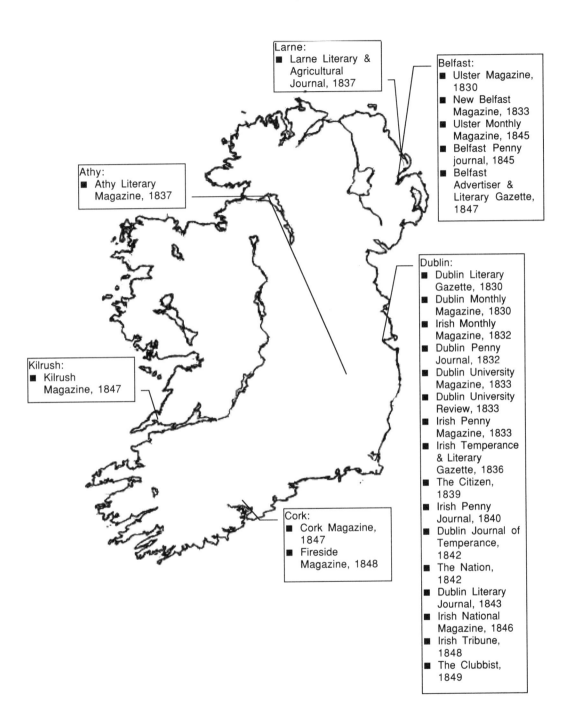

Figure 5 Locations and starting dates, 1830–1849

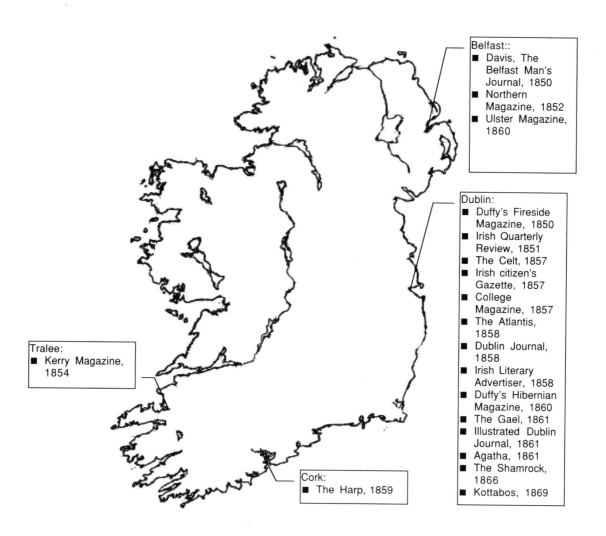

Figure 6 Locations and starting dates, 1850–1869

Figure 7 Locations and starting dates, 1870–1891

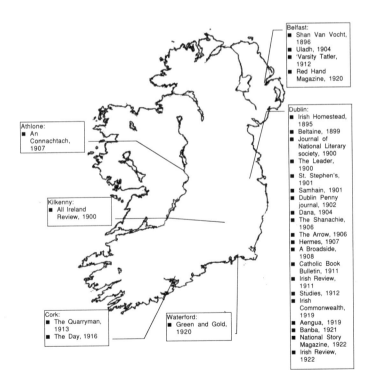

Figure 8 Locations and starting dates, 1892–1922

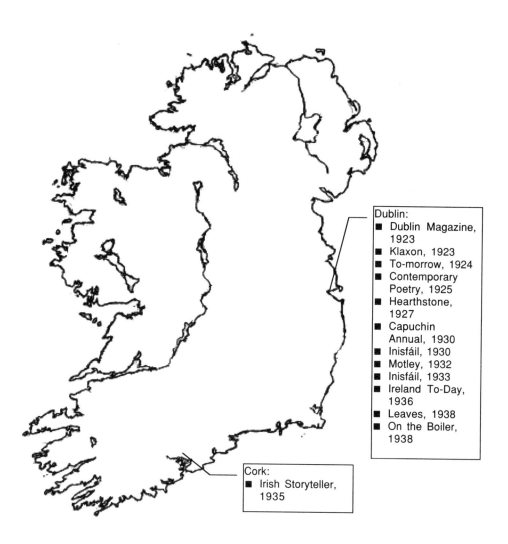

Figure 9 Locations and starting dates, 1923–1939

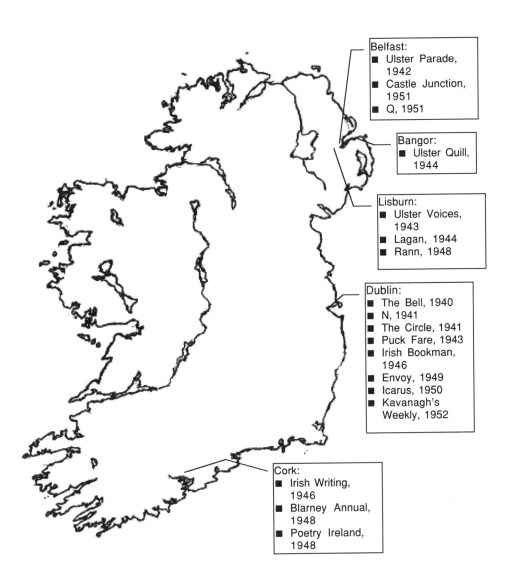

Figure 10 Locations and starting dates, 1940–1952

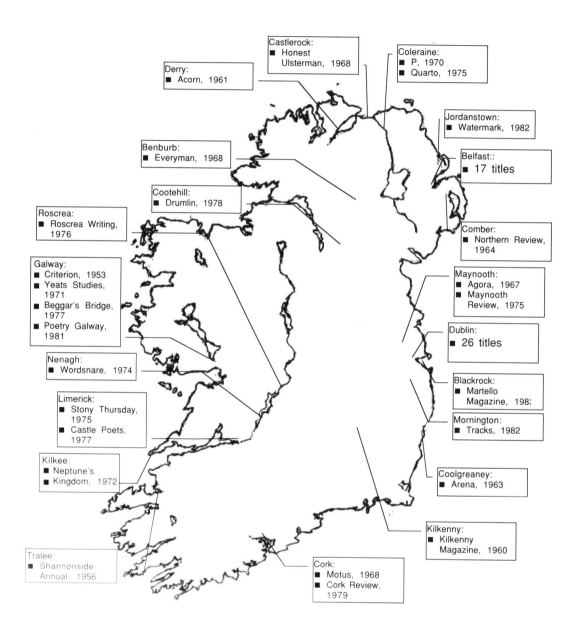

Castlerock:
■ Honest
   Ulsterman, 1968

Coleraine:
■ P, 1970
■ Quarto, 1975

Derry:
■ Acorn, 1961

Jordanstown:
■ Watermark, 1982

Belfast::
■ 17 titles

Benburb:
■ Everyman, 1968

Cootehill:
■ Drumlin, 1978

Comber:
■ Northern Review,
   1964

Roscrea:
■ Roscrea Writing,
   1976

Maynooth:
■ Agora, 1967
■ Maynooth
   Review, 1975

Galway:
■ Criterion, 1953
■ Yeats Studies,
   1971
■ Beggar's Bridge,
   1977
■ Poetry Galway,
   1981

Dublin:
■ 26 titles

Nenagh:
■ Wordsnare, 1974

Blackrock:
■ Martello
   Magazine, 198:

Limerick:
■ Stony Thursday,
   1975
■ Castle Poets,
   1977

Mornington:
■ Tracks, 1982

Kilkee:
■ Neptune's
■ Kingdom, 1972

Coolgreaney:
■ Arena, 1963

Kilkenny:
■ Kilkenny
   Magazine, 1960

Tralee:
■ Shannonside
   Annual, 1956

Cork:
■ Motus, 1968
■ Cork Review,
   1979

Figure 11 Locations and starting dates, 1953–1985

Appendix 3: Chronological Charts

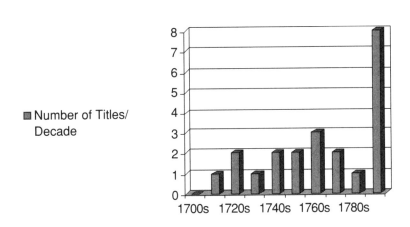

Chart 1 Number of new titles starting in each decade of the eighteenth century

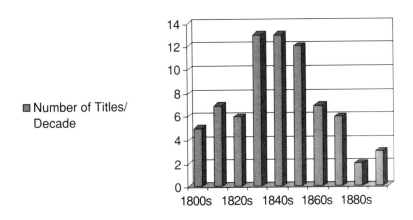

Chart 2 Number of new titles starting in each decade of the nineteenth century

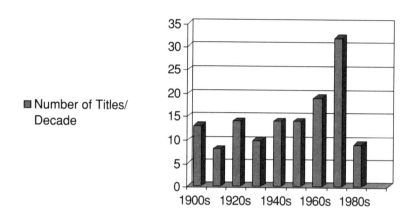

Chart 3 Number of new titles starting in each decade of the twentieth century